image COMICS PRESENTS

The LAST CHRISTMAS™

FOR IMAGE COMICS

Robert Kirkman - chief operating officer
Erik Larsen - chief financial officer
Todd McFarlane - president
Marc Silvestri - chief executive officer
Jim Valentino - vice-president

Eric Stephenson - publisher
Ron Richards - director of business development
Jennifer de Guzman - pr & marketing director
Branwyn Bigglestone - accounts manager
Emily Miller - accounting assistant
Jamie Parreno - marketing assistant
Emilio Bautista - sales assistant
Jaemie Dudas - administrative assistant
Jeremy Sullivan - digital rights coordinator
Tyler Shainline - events coordinator
David Brothers - content manager
Jonathan Chan - production manager
Drew Gill - art director
Monica Garcia - senior production artist
Vincent Kukua - production artist
Jenna Savage - production artist
Addison Duke - production artist

www.imagecomics.com

THE LAST CHRISTMAS Hard Cover. November 2013. Published by Image Comics, Inc., 2001 Center Street, 6th Floor, Berkeley, California 94704. Originally published in single magazine form as THE LAST CHRISTMAS #1-5. PRINTED IN CANADA.

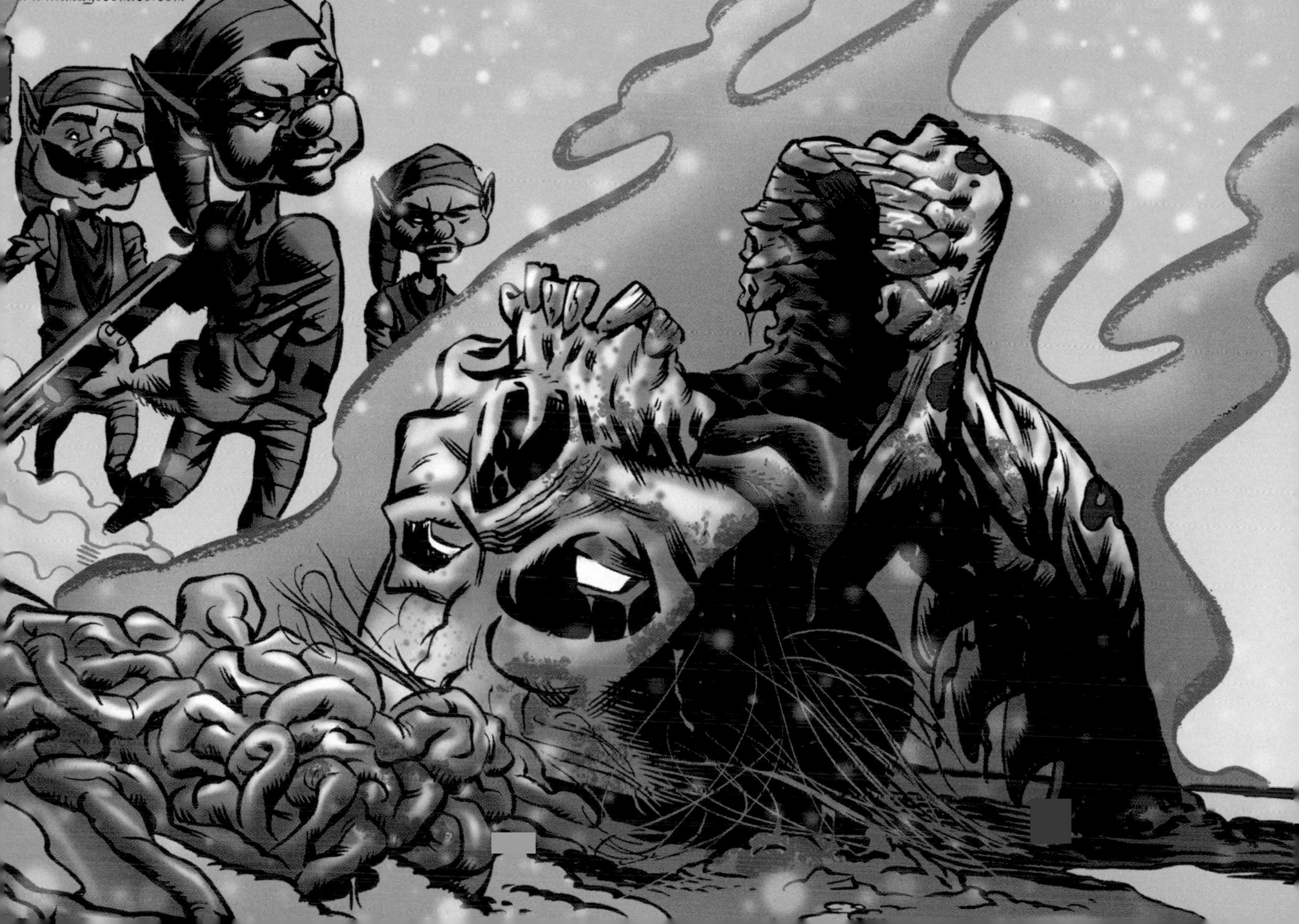

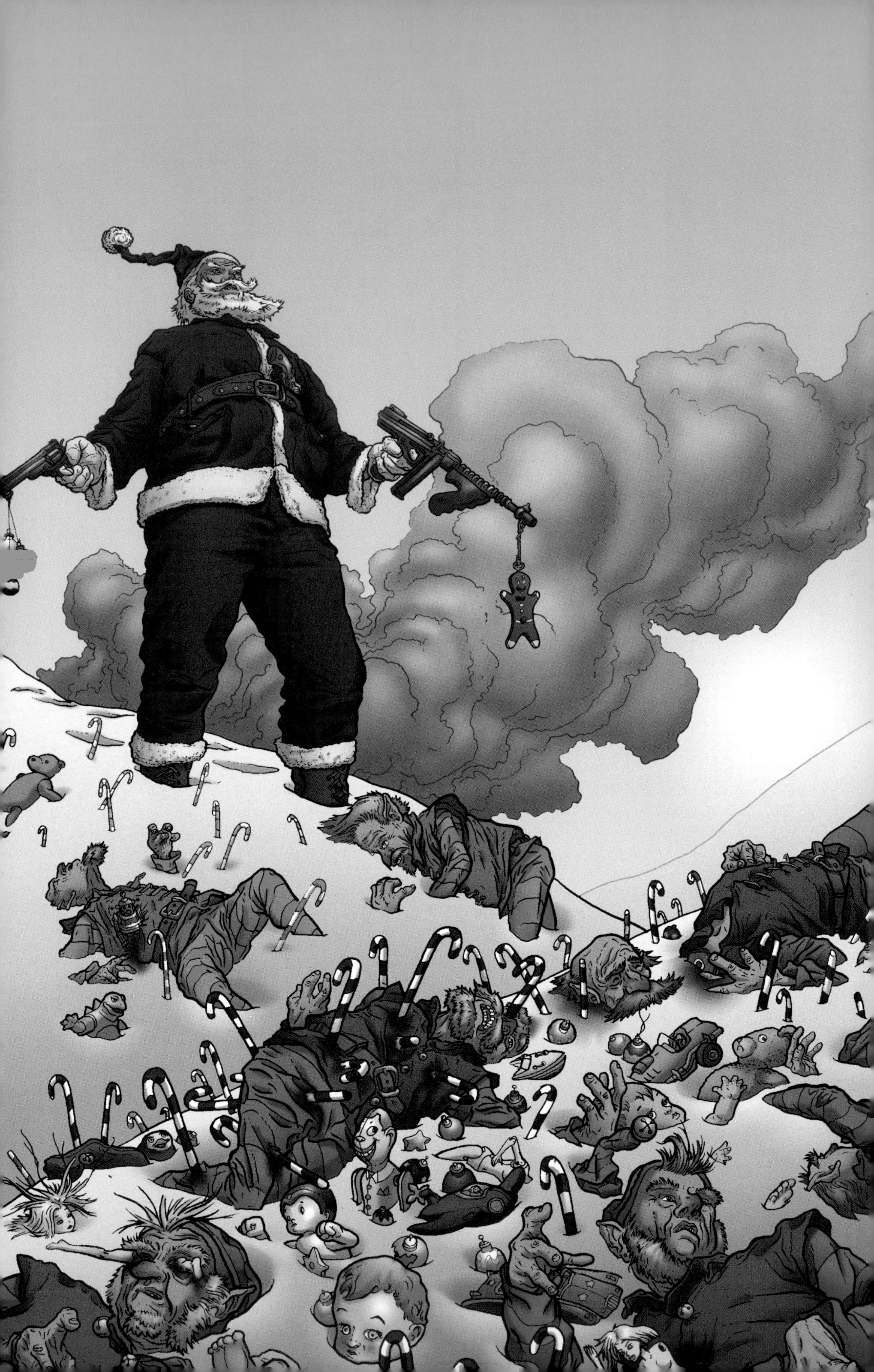

The LAST CHRISTMAS™

Created and written by
Gerry Duggan & Brian Posehn

penciled by Rick Remender

inked by Hilary Barta

colored by Michelle Madsen

covers by
Geof Darrow
issue 1
Kieron Dwyer & Hilary Barta
issue 2
Rick Remender
issues 3 & 4
Tony Moore
issue 5

lettered by Ed Dukeshire

background assist by Chris Carman

logo design by Todd Klein

hard cover
penciled by Rick Remender
inked by Hilary Barta
colored by Michelle Madsen

back cover art by
Geof Darrow

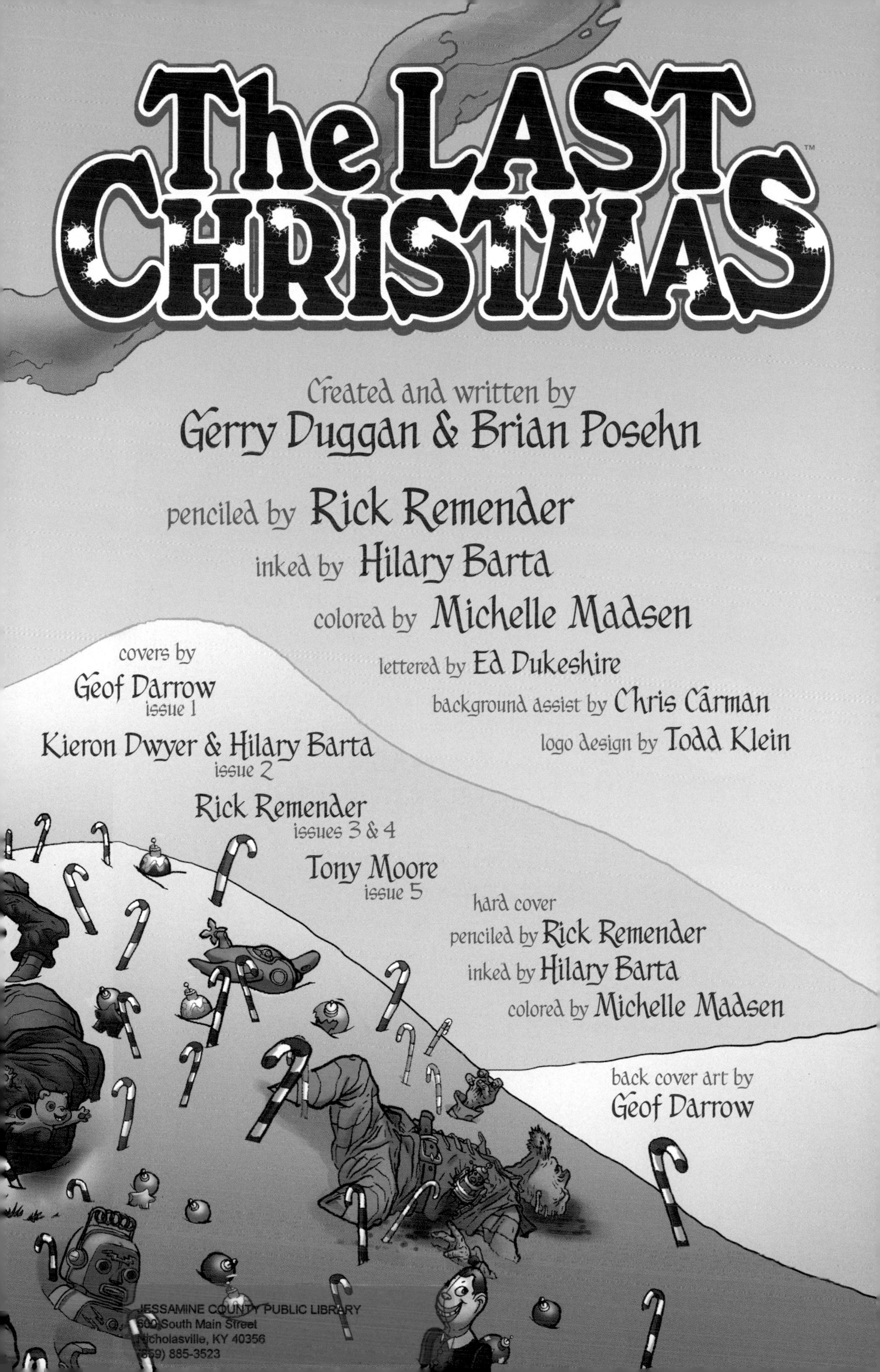

T'was the night before --

-- fuck it, I just can't believe
I'm doing a lame "Night Before" parody
Instead of an intro that screams to the sun
'Bout the brilliance of what these three wise men have done
First Gerry and Brian, inspired and true
And Remender - inking their Horror-tide brew

Herein you will find:
Mutants, sleighbells and gore
Blood and elves, knives and reindeer
And maybe a whore

(Wait, was there a whore?
It all gets so muddled
"Apocalypse Claus" -
'Tis so strange I'm befuddled?)

The plot is so simple
The Earth's near-expired
And Santa, bereft
Sets his old bones a-fire

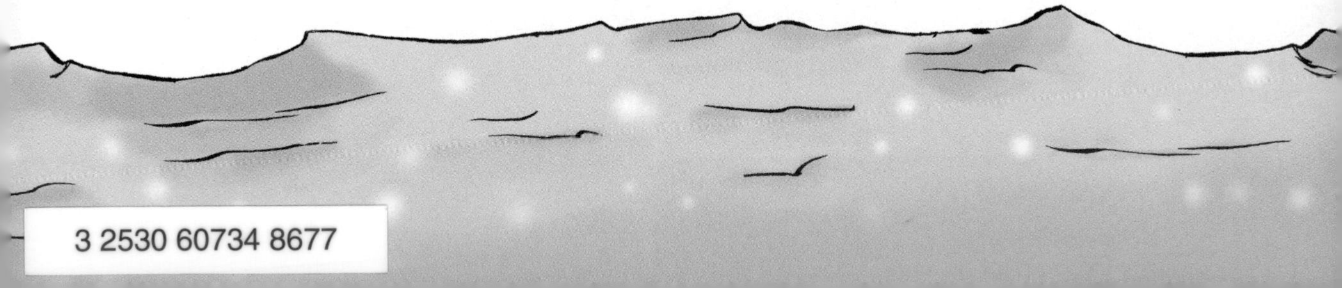

No, literally, he burns
The old coot wants to die
But he can't - he's been cursed
With immoral-i-t-y

So he must find the last child
Who thinks Santa is real
And like Wayne in the Searchers
His fate's seemingly sealed

And that's just the beginning
There's hilarity and fright
So I bid you farewell
And to all a good --

-- Fuck it, again, with the
"Night Before" shit
This intro is over
Last Christmas - read it!

-Patton Oswalt
The Comedians of Comedy
King of Queens

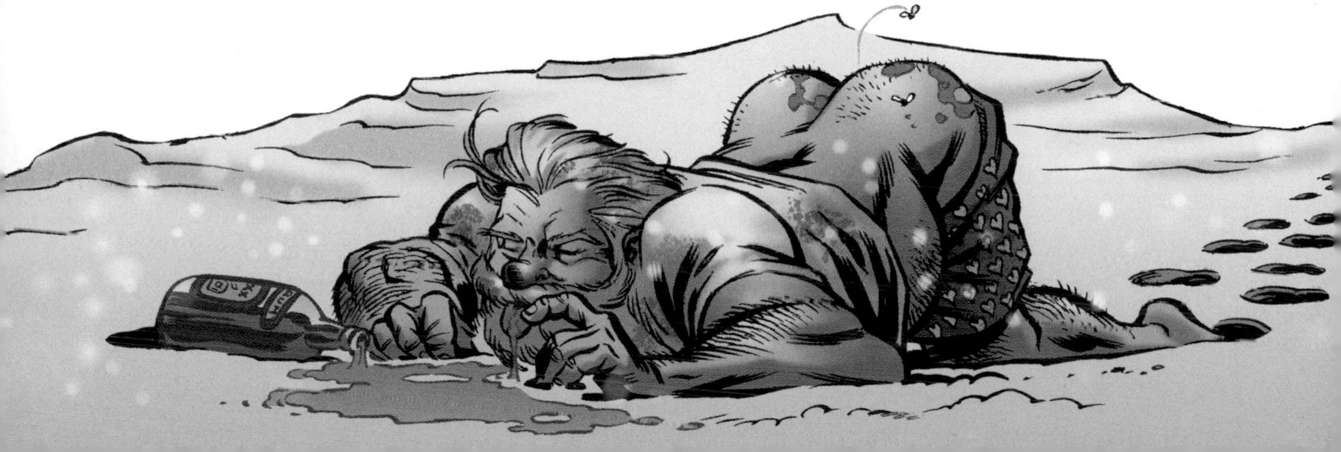

To the good little boy or girl that's reading this:

Hopefully you just flipped to the back of this piece of fucking ape-shit book, and you didn't attempt to read it, or worse -- succeed in finishing it.

If you want to read a humorous comic book drop this and try Archie. To the naughty folks that paid money for this book I have two questions:

First, what are you going to do with the coal you're getting for the next 10 years, and second: can you believe the assholes that crapped this out? If you're looking for a slightly more festive holiday book why don't you go read the Koran?

It's with a heavy heart that I tell you that everyone that worked on this book is being DISAVOWED by the North Pole. Current and past employees at Image Comics are going right on Santa's no-fly list. Except for Hilary Barta, but only because we don't even have that gal in our files. It's probably the pen name of some degenerate tracer. What a shame, because she put down some of most lovely blacks I've ever seen.

At least the other "creators" had the decency to sign their names to this roiling diaper-load.

I don't like saying that something is completely awful, even this trash so I'll just say the covers were certainly very interesting and the colors were so pretty -- very Christmasy! Poor Michelle Madsen. To be stuck in cahoots with these insensitive rubes...

Where to start with little Rick Remender? Our sweet little elves worked through their anger by making a life-size Rick doll, sucking on candy canes until they were a wicked sharp point, and then shoving candy canes into the Remendoll's butt. (The elves have no word for sodomy, so please don't judge them.) Rick has said he "needed the money" when he agreed to pencil the comic, but I've never understood why he didn't just go back to the truck stops. There's a certain dignity in that kind of prostitution, Rick. And I know you're reading this to see what I say about you, you narcissist.

Which brings us to Brian Posehn and Gerry Duggan...they're both terribly fat and I am sure they will die soon. Brian's dad went to heaven when Brian was very young, so he didn't have his heart broken by his son. (I have it on good authority that Jesus hypnotized Brian's dad into thinking that his son was a hilarious comedian and talented actor and author, Patton Oswalt.) Brian's mom weeps every night into a pillow she's made from the hair of nice boys. She meets these boys at the mall and when she tells them who her son is, they pull out their own hair and give it to her. Brian's wife and kid changed their names and moved to a small town on the coast of Oregon to get away from the myriad of terrible smells that fall out of Brian's stupid, un-fuckable body all day. Brian has a comedy career where he makes fun of himself. God beat you to it, you fucking hairy mongoloid.

You know how you get a Gerry? Suck out what little talent Kevin Smith has, replace it with custard and now you're close to Gerry. Look into Gerry's eyes and you see a nightmarish dollhouse where every doll is missing its' head and has their broken limbs crammed up their plastic shitting holes. The man is an abortion of sadness and mania. His repugnant figure is clearly due to him eating his feelings. And everyone else's feelings. Everyone reading this; stop feeling things now so that fucking fat-tard will die of starvation.

They wrote a screenplay for this tale not long after 9/11, when it surely felt that the world was ending. How Hollywood managed to say no to such an obvious franchise is beyond me, but they did, and if those two balding chimpanzees would have left The Last Christmas on Hollywood's dustbin, well I think I could have forgiven them...but they couldn't let go of it. They embarked on their labor of twisted love, and you're holding the result.

You have to give them credit for nailing the character of Gary. Snowmen are gayer than Freddie Mercury on Christmas, and that's just a fact. I suppose you might be thinking "Wow, Mrs. C comes across as a little miffed." You bet your Christmas balls I am!

They kill me -- off panel! I don't get to do anything cool, except stick my dead fucking feet out. I guess nobody ever saw THE ROAD WARRIOR? Really? No clever take on the damsel in distress -- I just get to die?

What cunts. (I mean this in the very British sense of the word) Don't worry, I'll feed the swear jar later.

There are a few other jerks to call out -- like Ed Dukeshire, Todd Klein, Hilary Barta, Tony Moore, Jonathan Chan, Tyler Shainline, Branwyn Bigglestone (an elf name!) Eric Stephenson, Erik Larsen, Robert Kirkman, Drew Gill, Ron Richards, Addison Duke, Dave Rath, Harris Miller II (La Di Da, fancy-pants!) and Geof Darrow... they all thought it would be so funny to help ruin Christmas. Congrats, assholes. Hope you're happy. It's all your fault that this is being reprinted into a hardcover.

I should go now. I don't want to dwell on this awful book for another moment. Santa is almost done with his nap, so I have to put in another tray of cinnamon ginger bread cookies before he wakes.

Stay Nice!

MRS. CLAUSE

Chapter 1

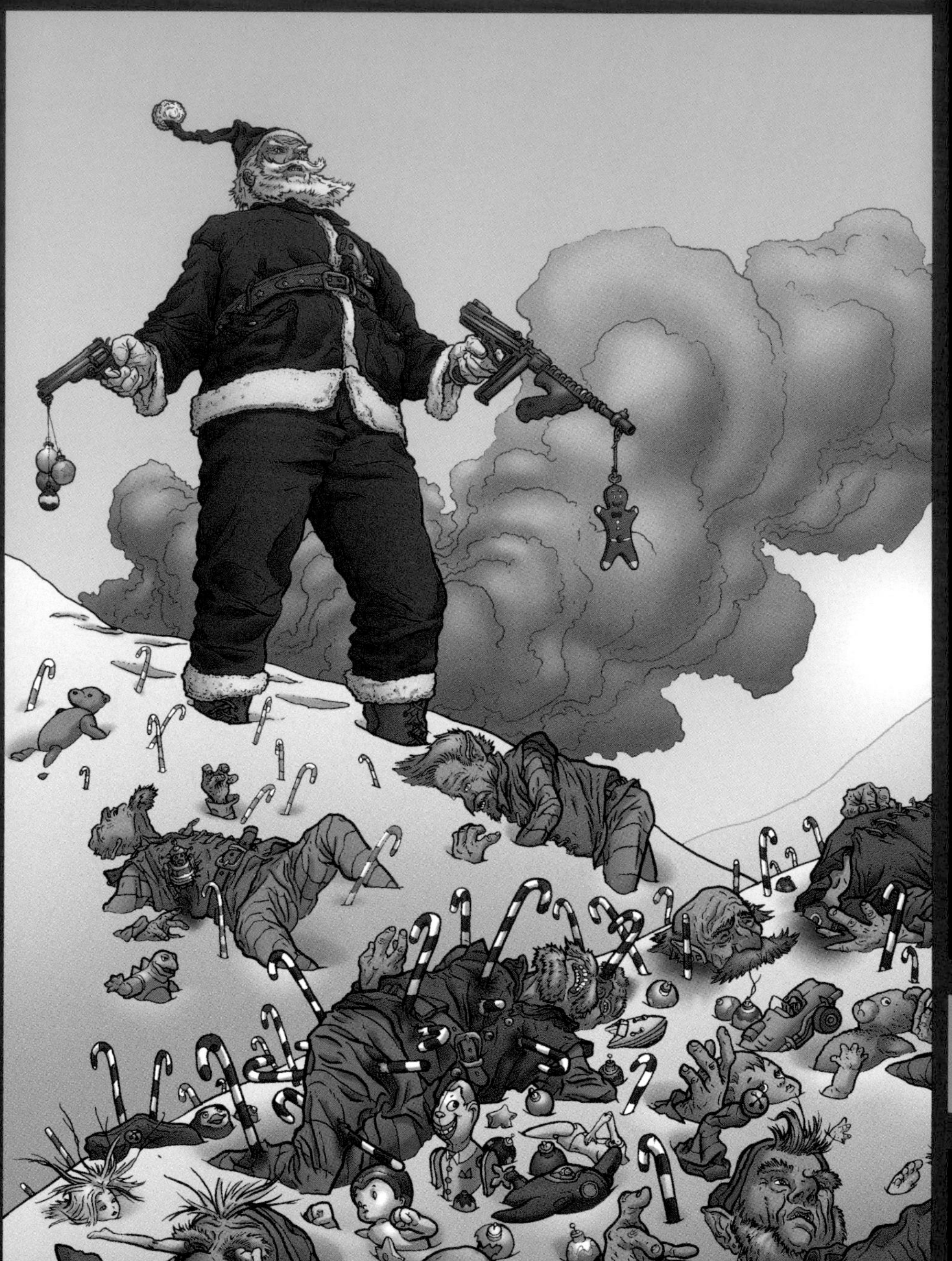

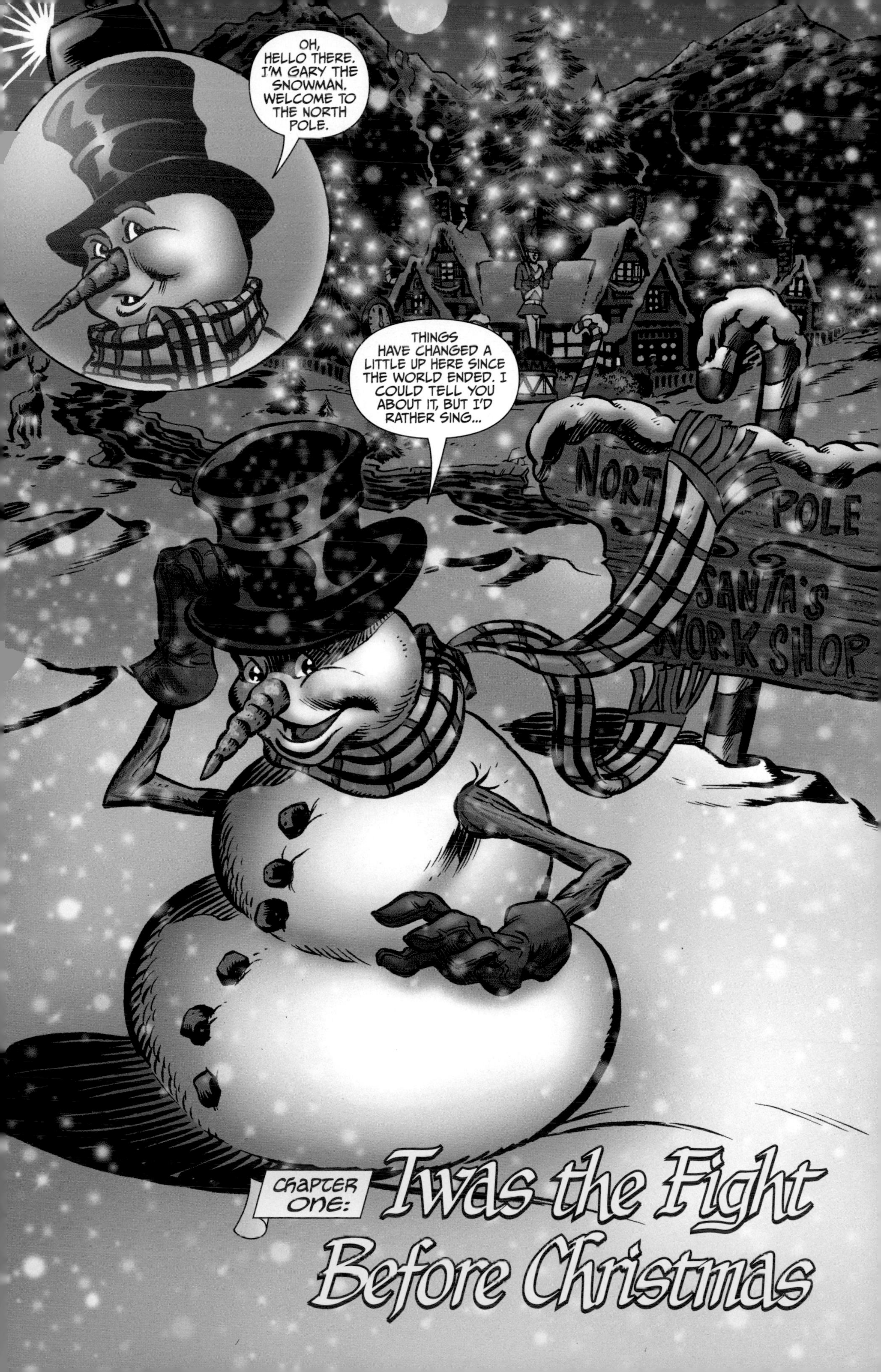
OH, HELLO THERE. I'M GARY THE SNOWMAN. WELCOME TO THE NORTH POLE.
THINGS HAVE CHANGED A LITTLE UP HERE SINCE THE WORLD ENDED. I COULD TELL YOU ABOUT IT, BUT I'D RATHER SING...
NORT POLE
SANTA'S WORK SHOP
CHAPTER ONE: Twas the Fight Before Christmas

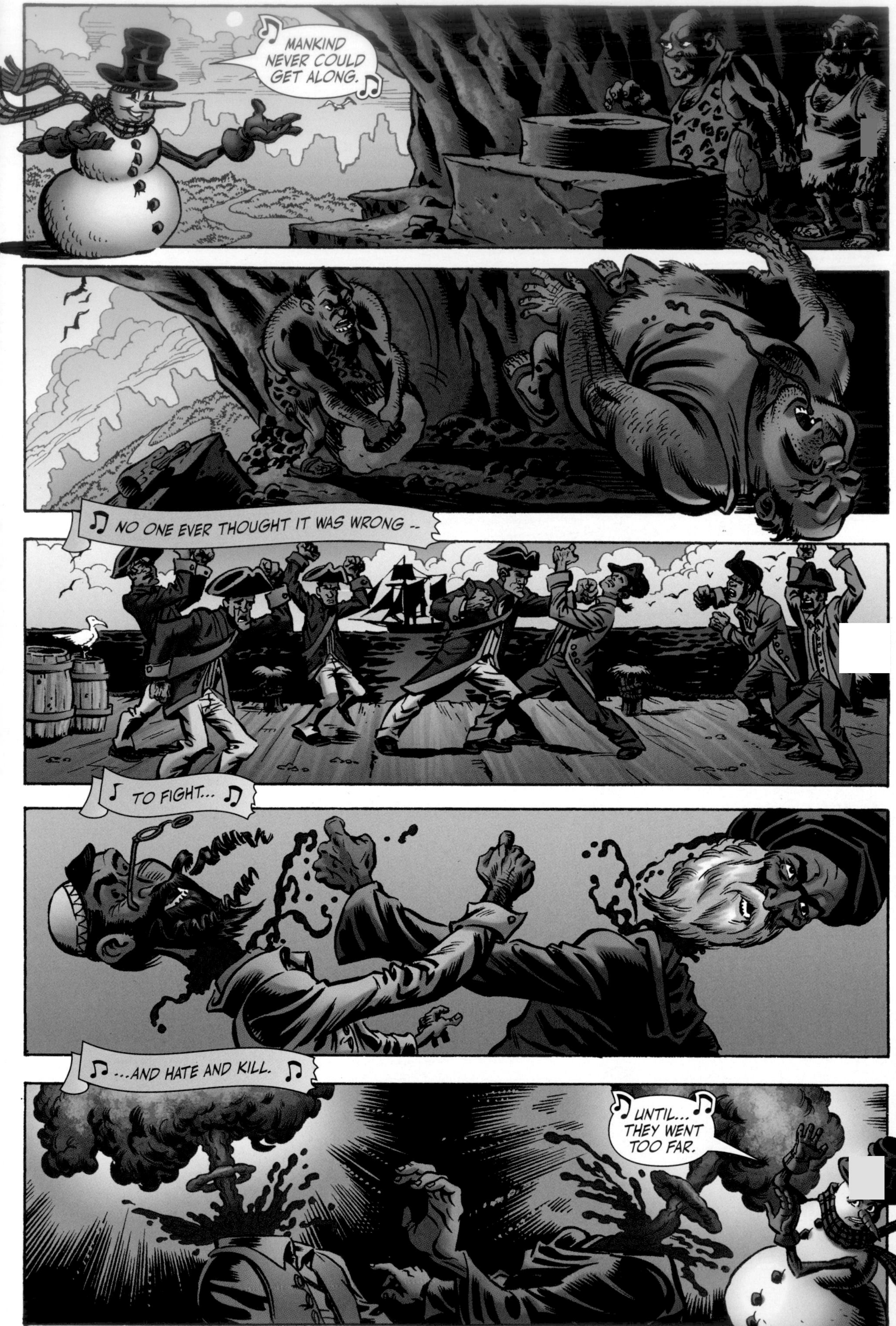
MANKIND NEVER COULD GET ALONG.
NO ONE EVER THOUGHT IT WAS WRONG --
TO FIGHT...
...AND HATE AND KILL.
UNTIL... THEY WENT TOO FAR.

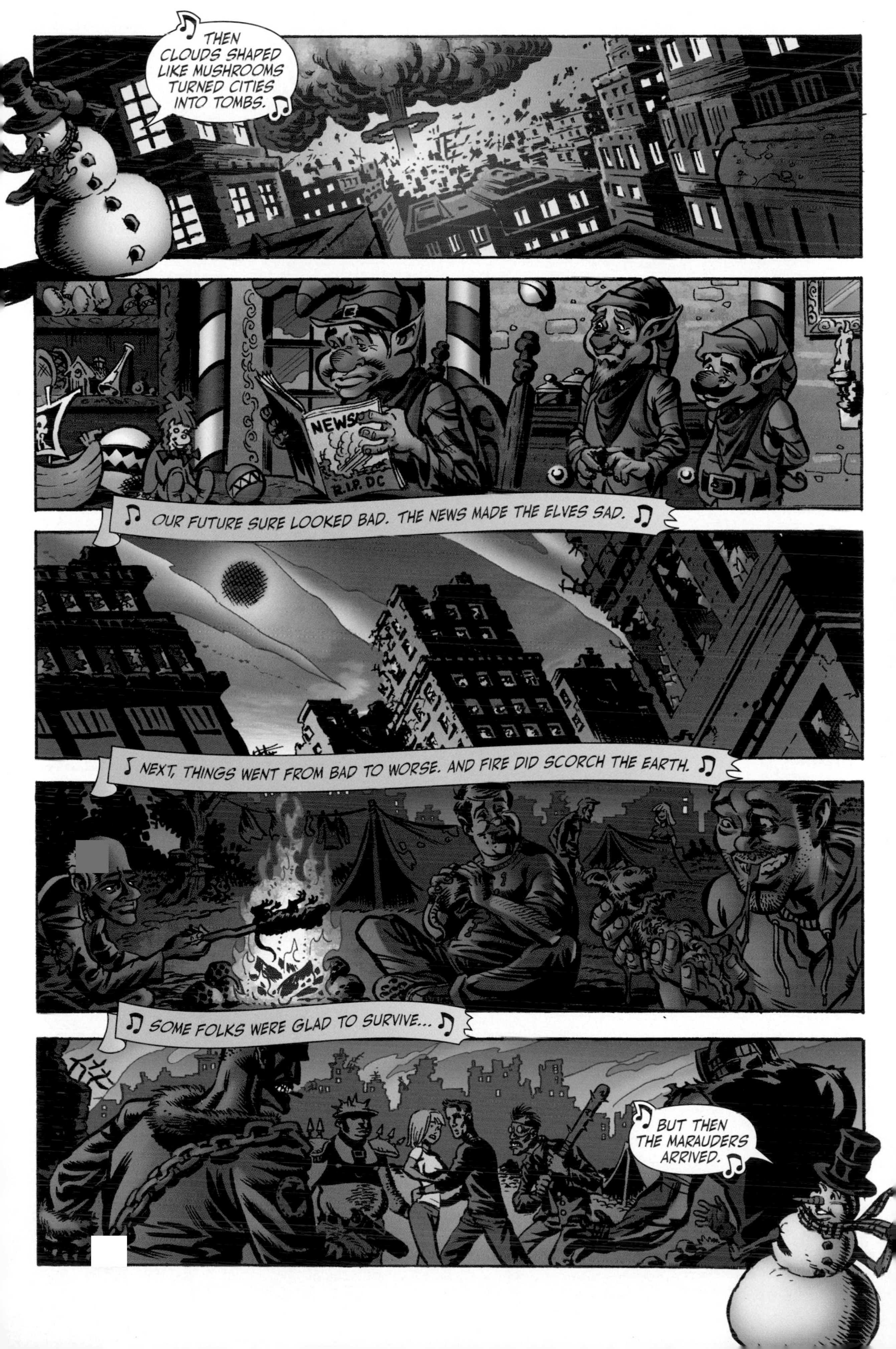
THEN CLOUDS SHAPED LIKE MUSHROOMS TURNED CITIES INTO TOMBS.
NEWS
R.I.P. DC
OUR FUTURE SURE LOOKED BAD. THE NEWS MADE THE ELVES SAD.
NEXT, THINGS WENT FROM BAD TO WORSE. AND FIRE DID SCORCH THE EARTH.
SOME FOLKS WERE GLAD TO SURVIVE...
BUT THEN THE MARAUDERS ARRIVED.

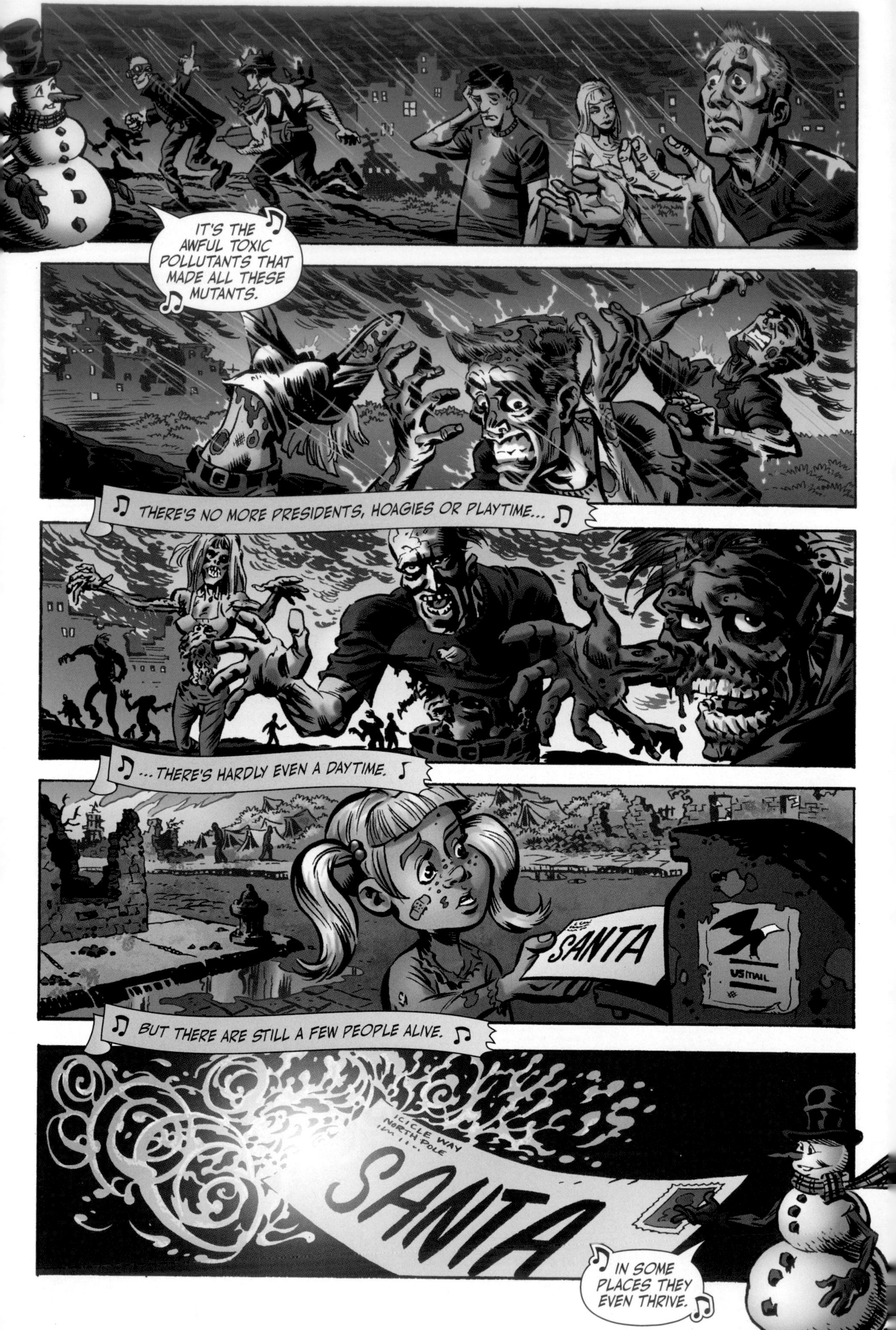
IT'S THE AWFUL TOXIC POLLUTANTS THAT MADE ALL THESE MUTANTS.
THERE'S NO MORE PRESIDENTS, HOAGIES OR PLAYTIME...
...THERE'S HARDLY EVEN A DAYTIME.
SANTA
US MAIL
BUT THERE ARE STILL A FEW PEOPLE ALIVE.
ICICLE WAY
NORTH POLE
SANTA
IN SOME PLACES THEY EVEN THRIVE.

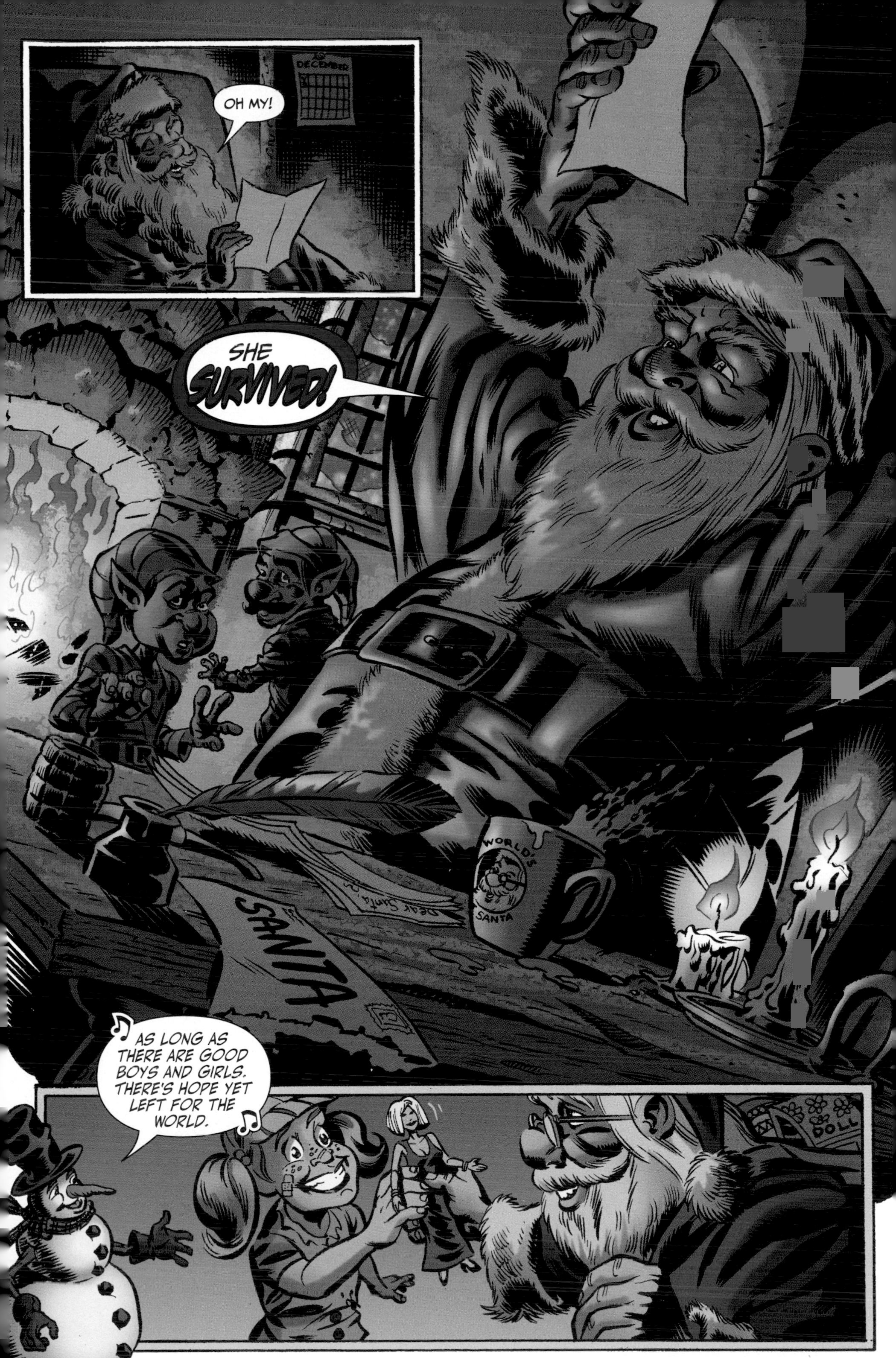
DECEMBER
OH MY!
SHE SURVIVED!
WORLD'S SANTA
Dear Santa
SANTA
AS LONG AS THERE ARE GOOD BOYS AND GIRLS. THERE'S HOPE YET LEFT FOR THE WORLD.
DOLL

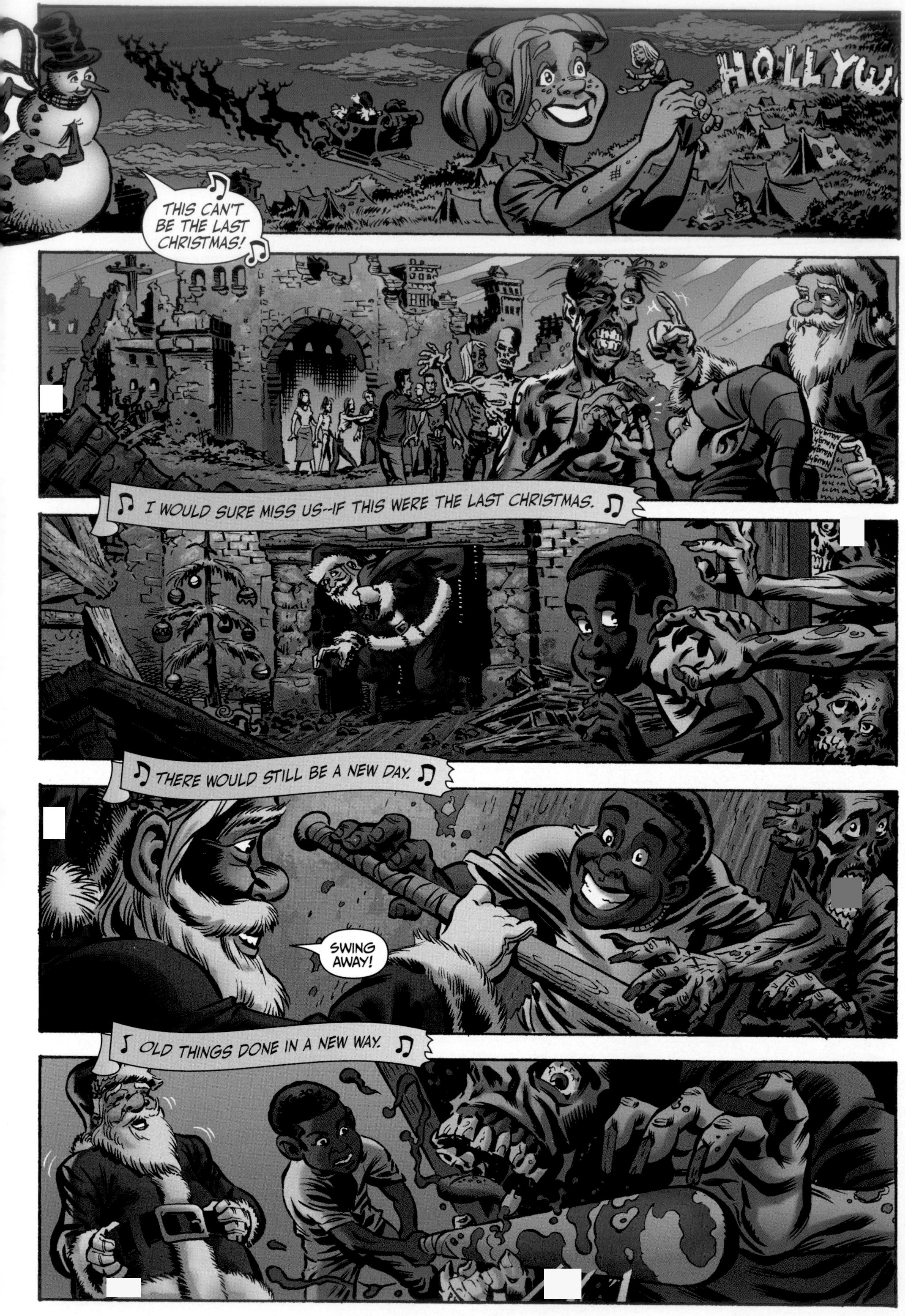
THIS CAN'T BE THE LAST CHRISTMAS!
I WOULD SURE MISS US--IF THIS WERE THE LAST CHRISTMAS.
THERE WOULD STILL BE A NEW DAY.
SWING AWAY!
OLD THINGS DONE IN A NEW WAY.

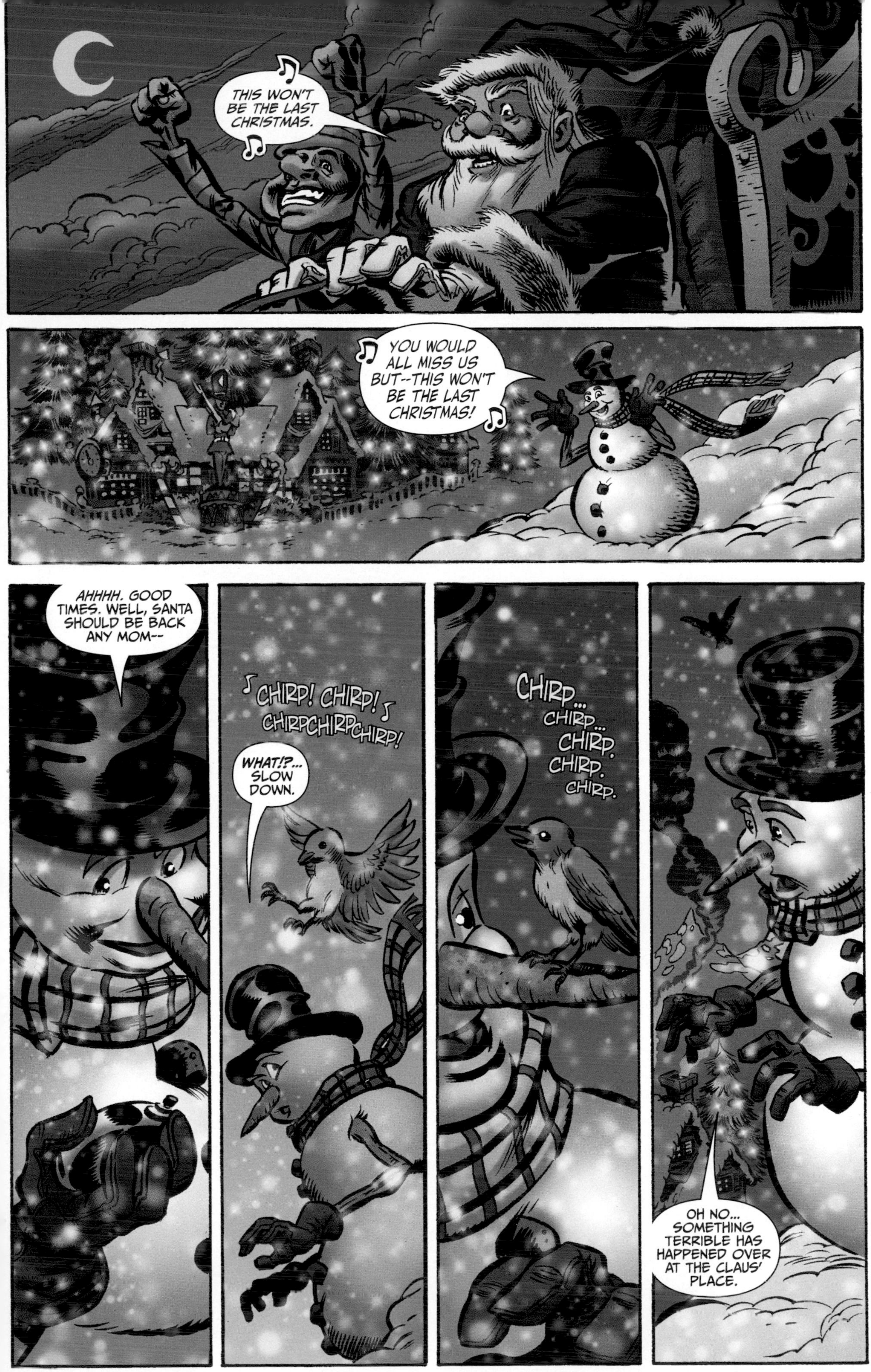

THIS WON'T BE THE LAST CHRISTMAS.
YOU WOULD ALL MISS US BUT--THIS WON'T BE THE LAST CHRISTMAS!
AHHHH. GOOD TIMES. WELL, SANTA SHOULD BE BACK ANY MOM--
CHIRP! CHIRP! CHIRPCHIRPCHIRP!
WHAT!?... SLOW DOWN.
CHIRP... CHIRP... CHIRP. CHIRP. CHIRP.
OH NO... SOMETHING TERRIBLE HAS HAPPENED OVER AT THE CLAUS' PLACE.

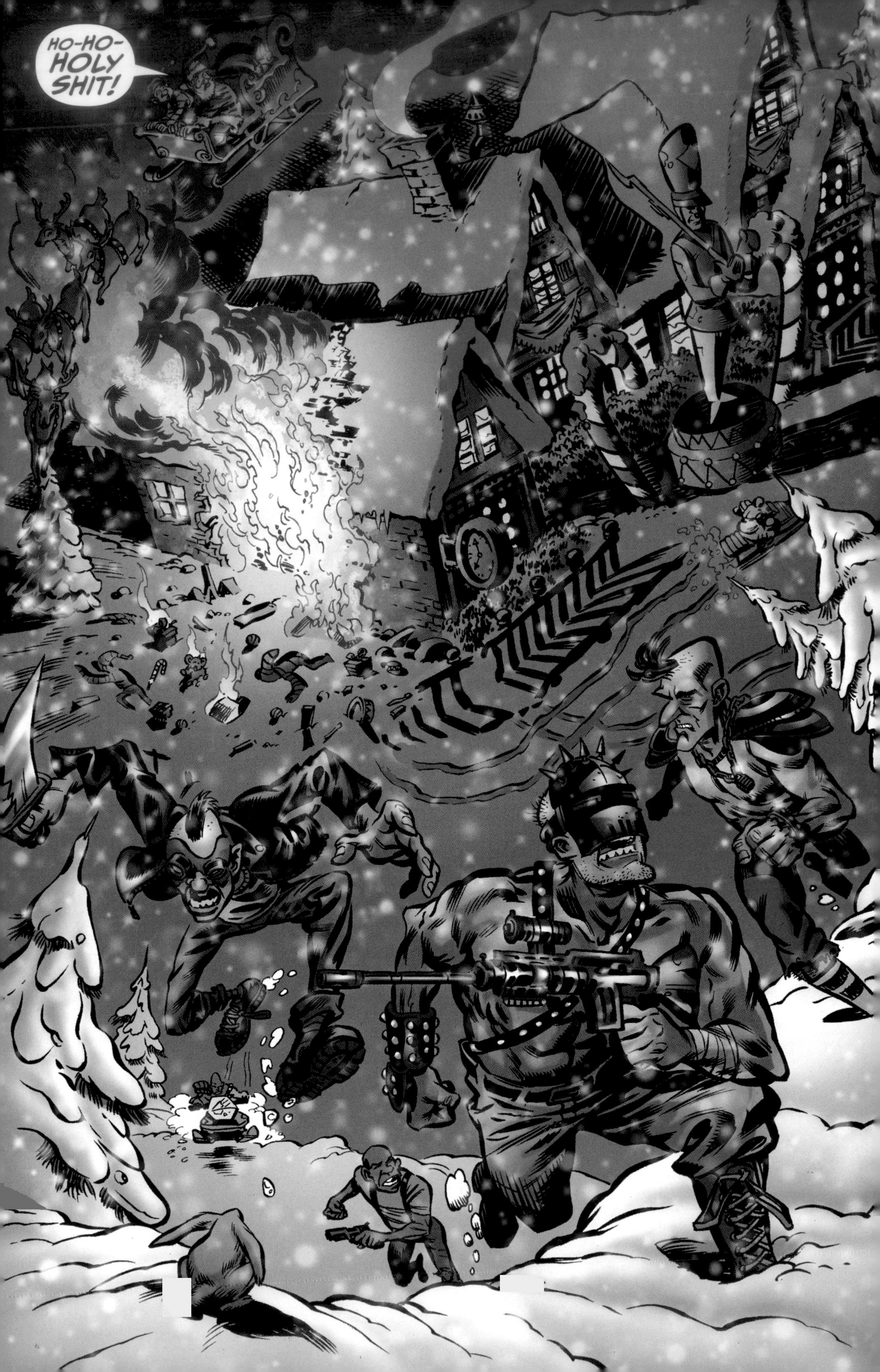
HO-HO-HOLY SHIT!

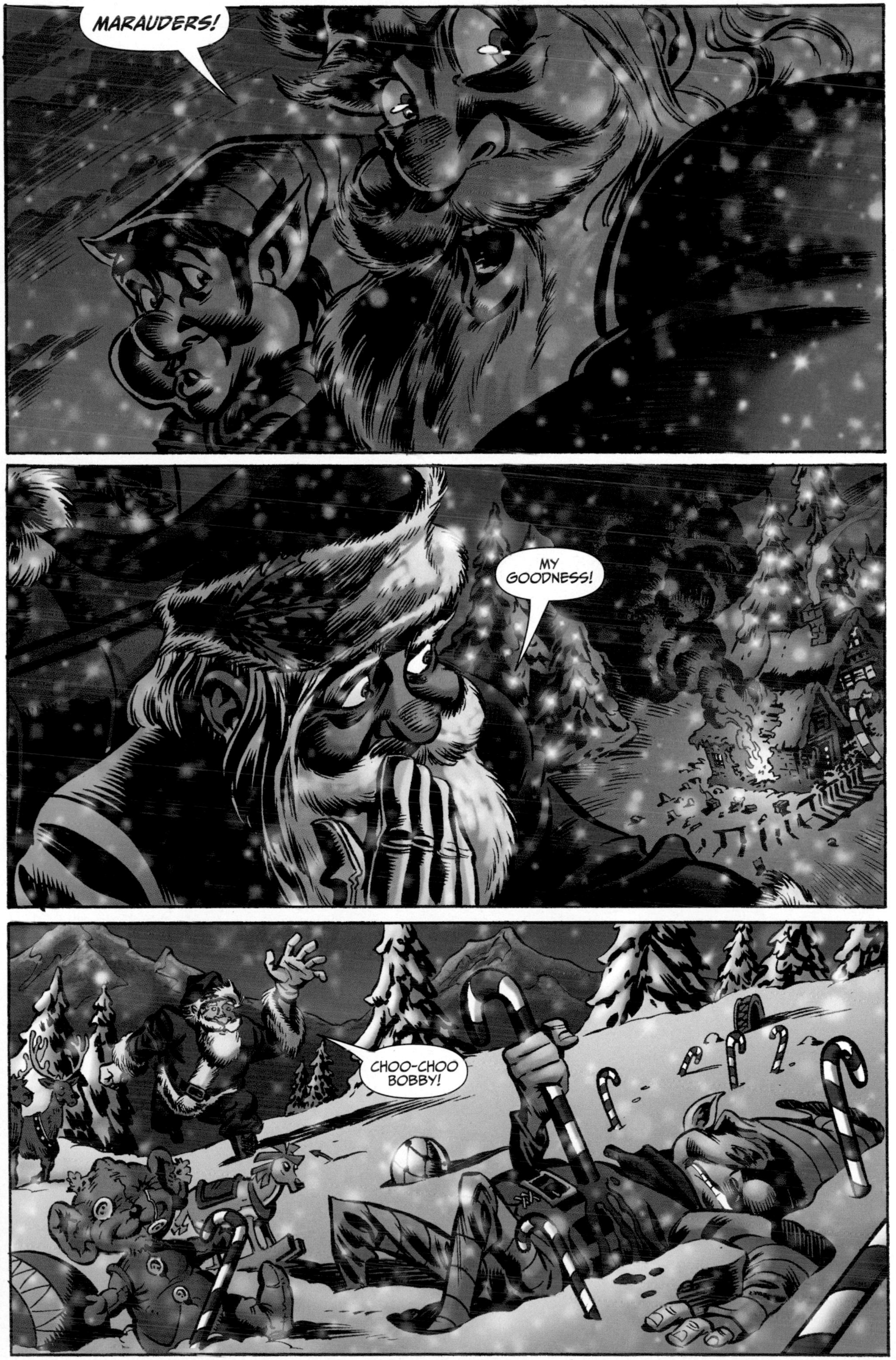
MARAUDERS!
MY GOODNESS!
CHOO-CHOO BOBBY!

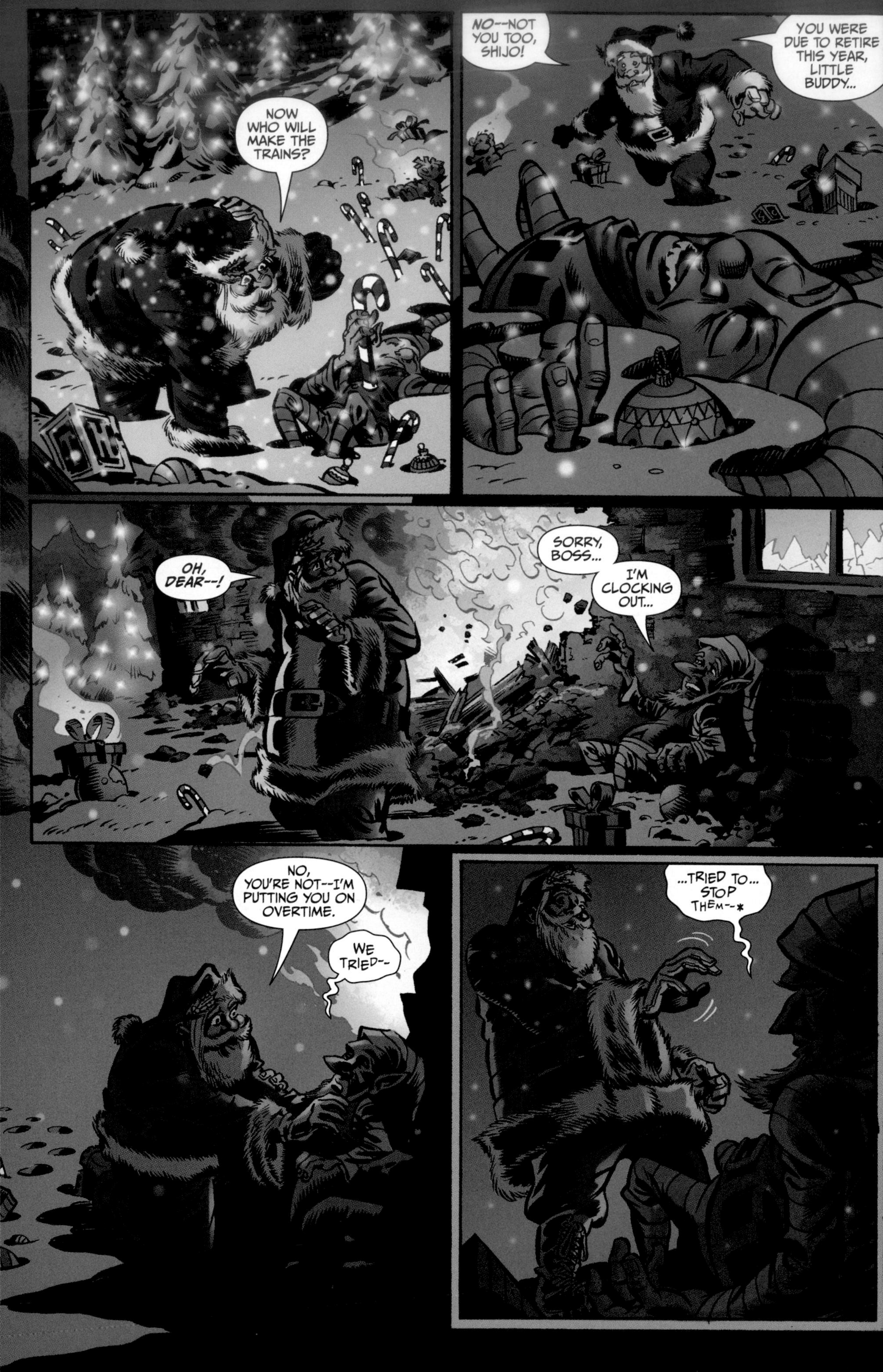
NOW WHO WILL MAKE THE TRAINS?
NO--NOT YOU TOO, SHIJO!
YOU WERE DUE TO RETIRE THIS YEAR, LITTLE BUDDY...
OH, DEAR--!
SORRY, BOSS...
I'M CLOCKING OUT...
NO, YOU'RE NOT--I'M PUTTING YOU ON OVERTIME.
WE TRIED--
...TRIED TO... STOP THEM--*

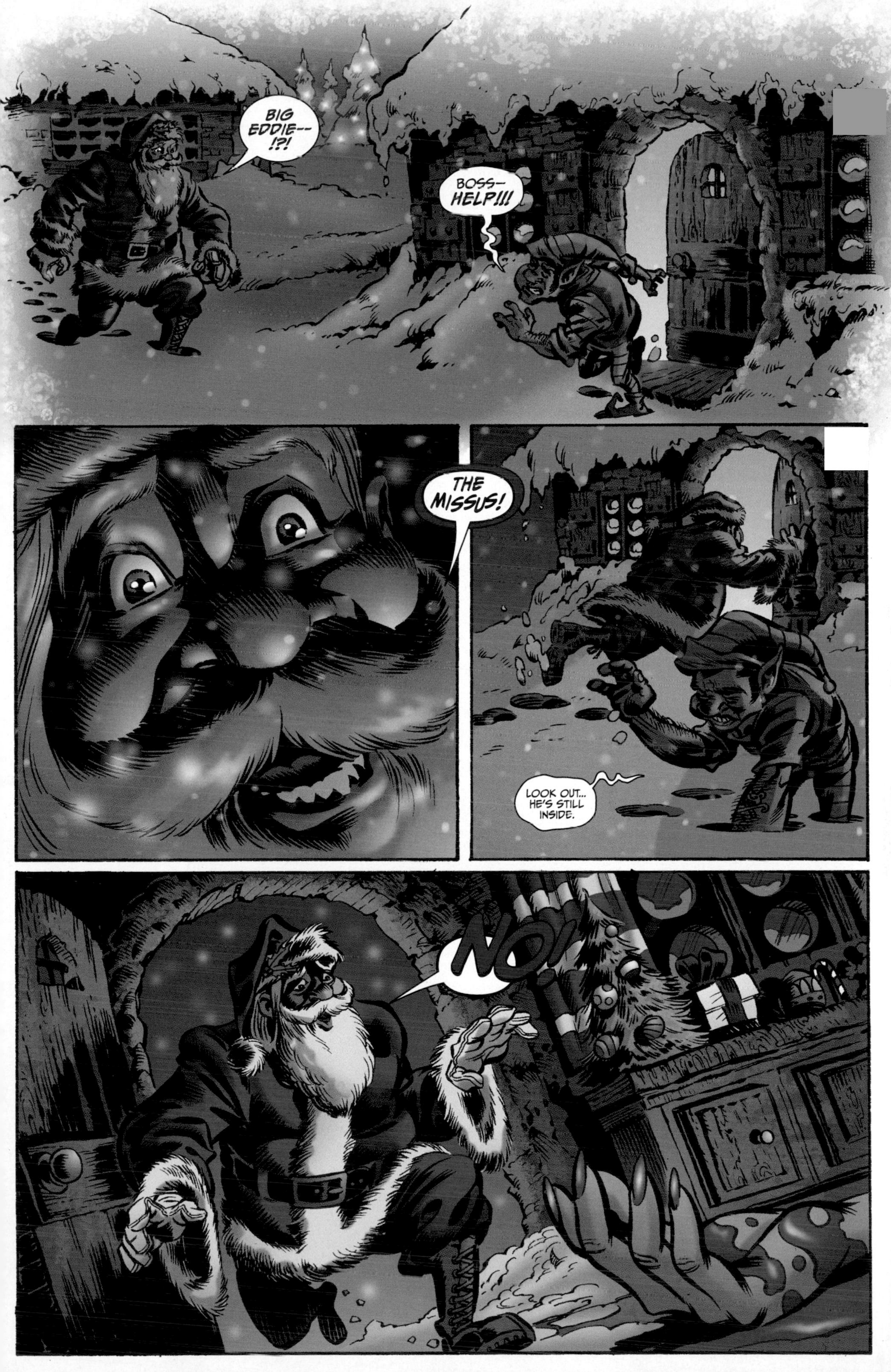
BIG EDDIE-- !?!
BOSS-- HELP!!!
THE MISSUS!
LOOK OUT... HE'S STILL INSIDE.
NO!

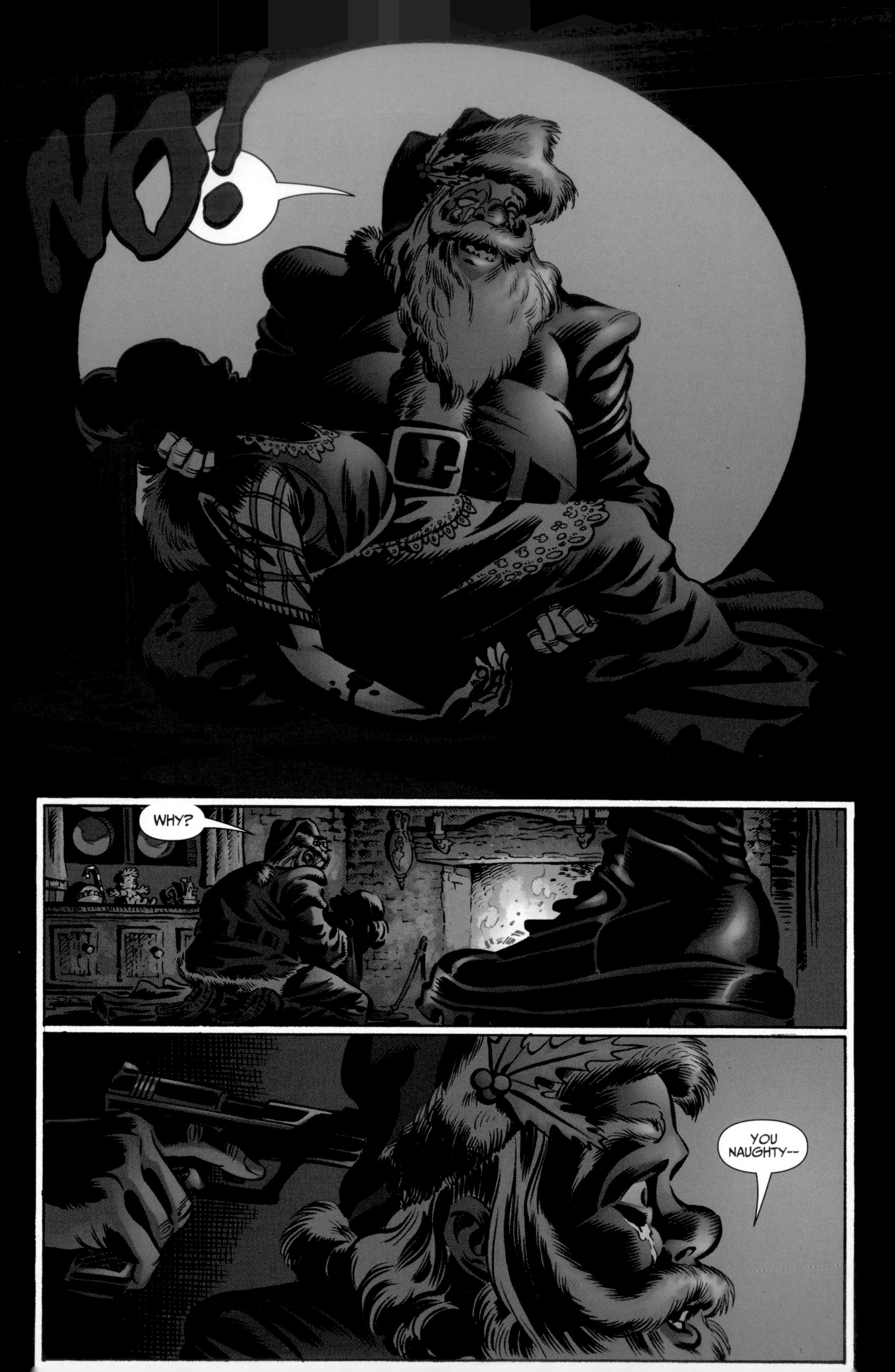
NO!
WHY?
YOU NAUGHTY--

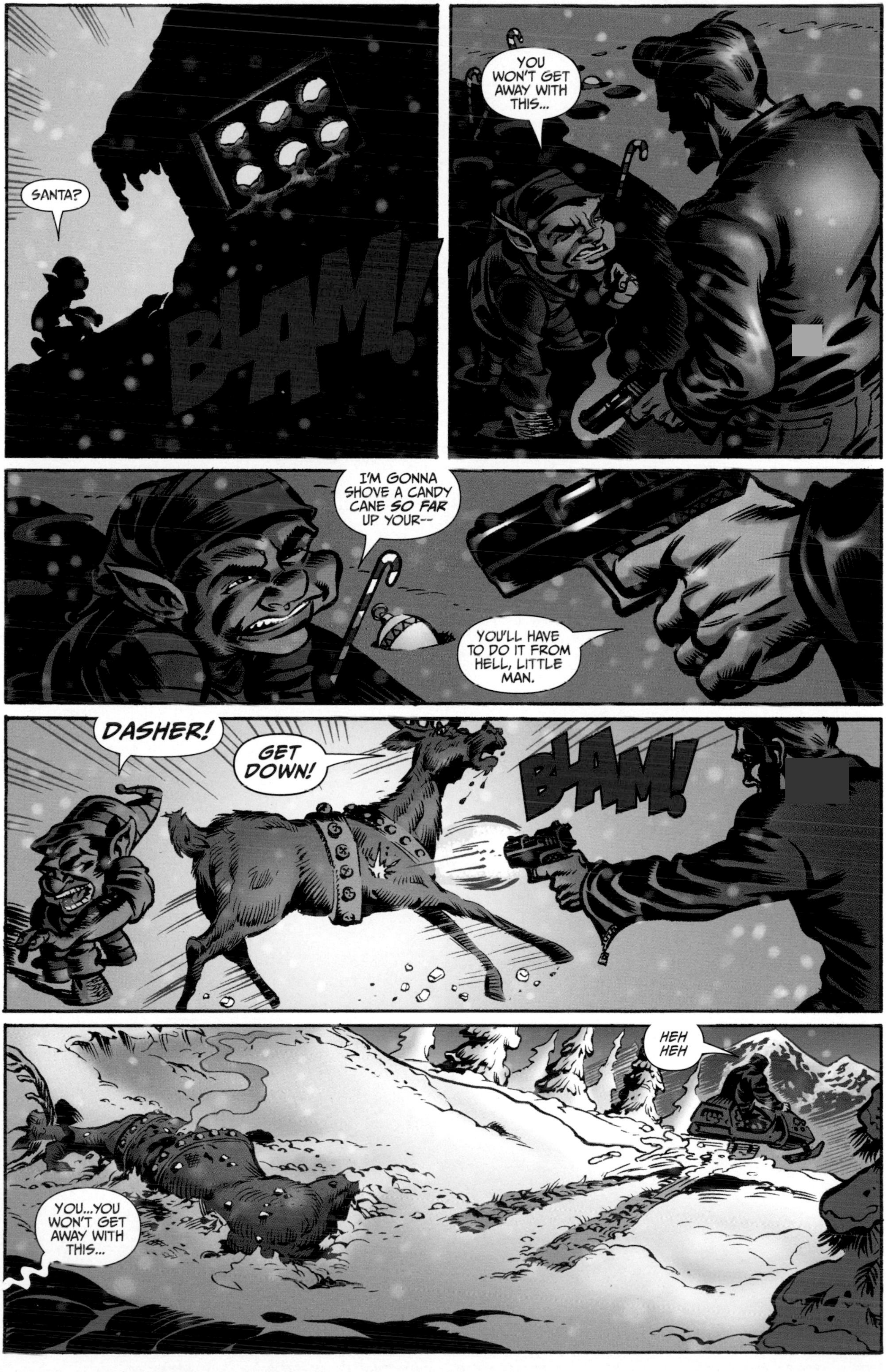
SANTA?
BLAM!
YOU WON'T GET AWAY WITH THIS...
I'M GONNA SHOVE A CANDY CANE SO FAR UP YOUR--
YOU'LL HAVE TO DO IT FROM HELL, LITTLE MAN.
DASHER!
GET DOWN!
BLAM!
HEH HEH
YOU...YOU WON'T GET AWAY WITH THIS...

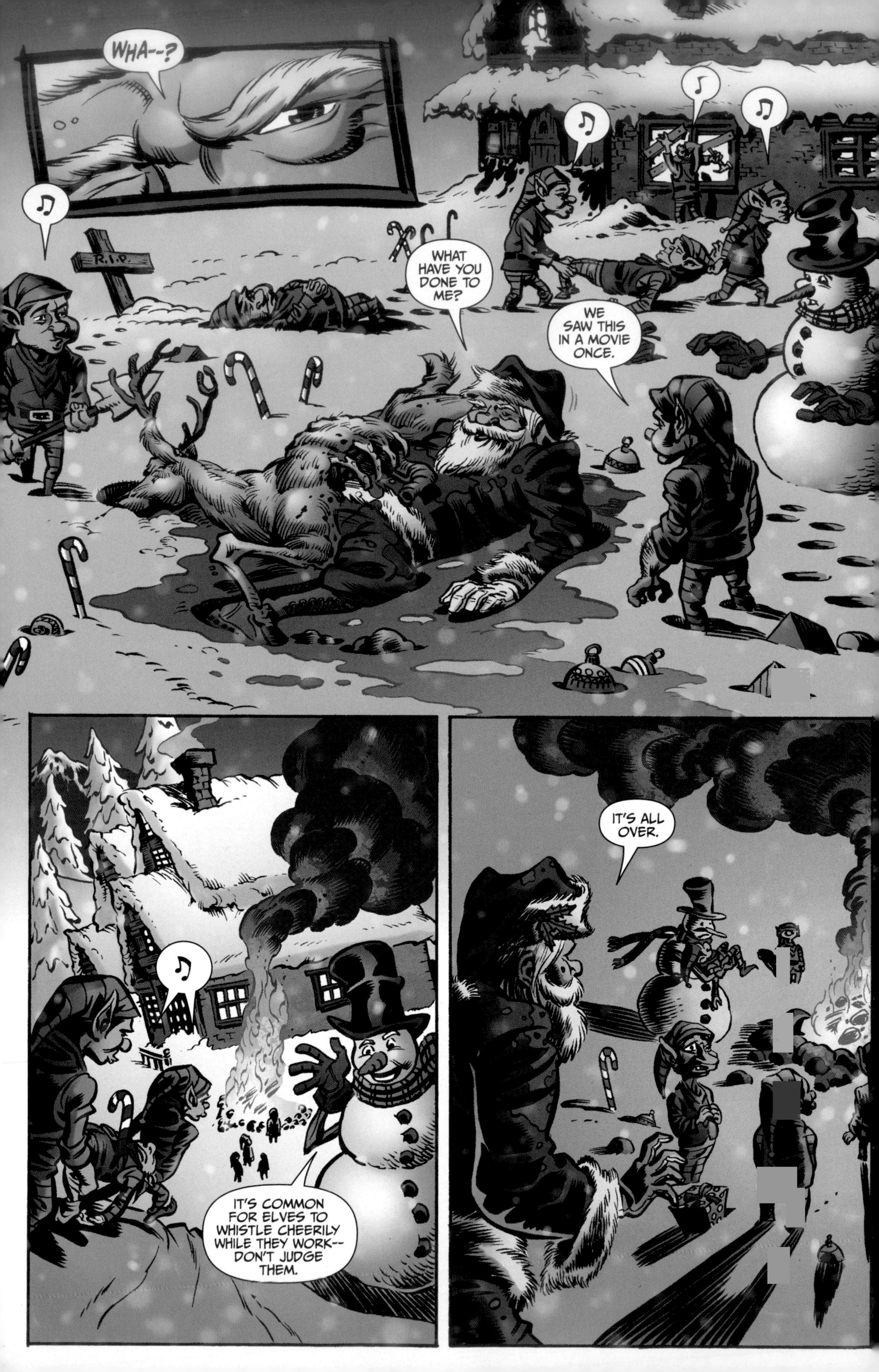
WHA--?
R.I.P.
WHAT HAVE YOU DONE TO ME?
WE SAW THIS IN A MOVIE ONCE.
IT'S COMMON FOR ELVES TO WHISTLE CHEERILY WHILE THEY WORK-- DON'T JUDGE THEM.
IT'S ALL OVER.

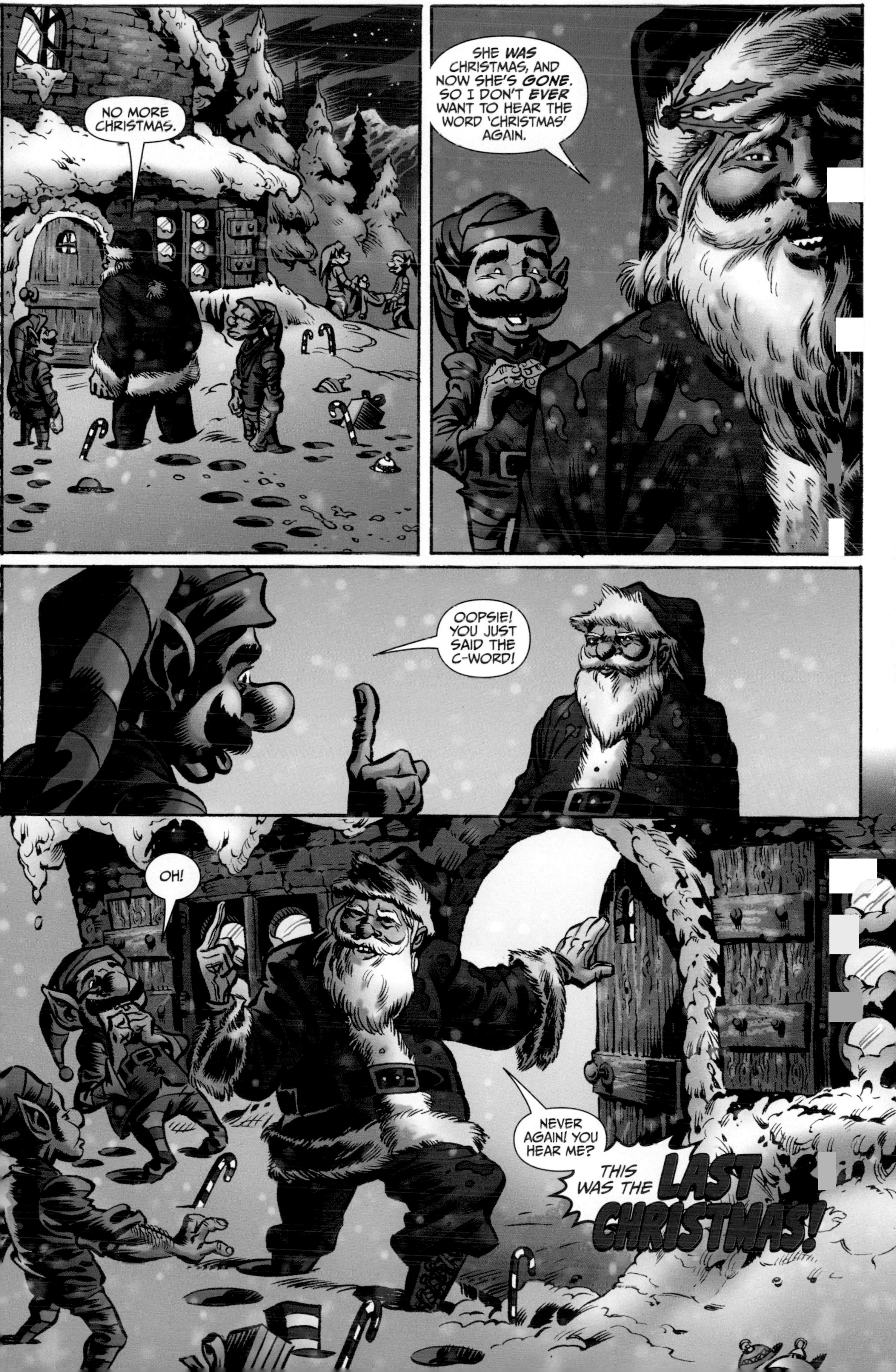
NO MORE CHRISTMAS.
SHE WAS CHRISTMAS, AND NOW SHE'S GONE. SO I DON'T EVER WANT TO HEAR THE WORD 'CHRISTMAS' AGAIN.
OOPSIE! YOU JUST SAID THE C-WORD!
OH!
NEVER AGAIN! YOU HEAR ME?
THIS WAS THE LAST CHRISTMAS!

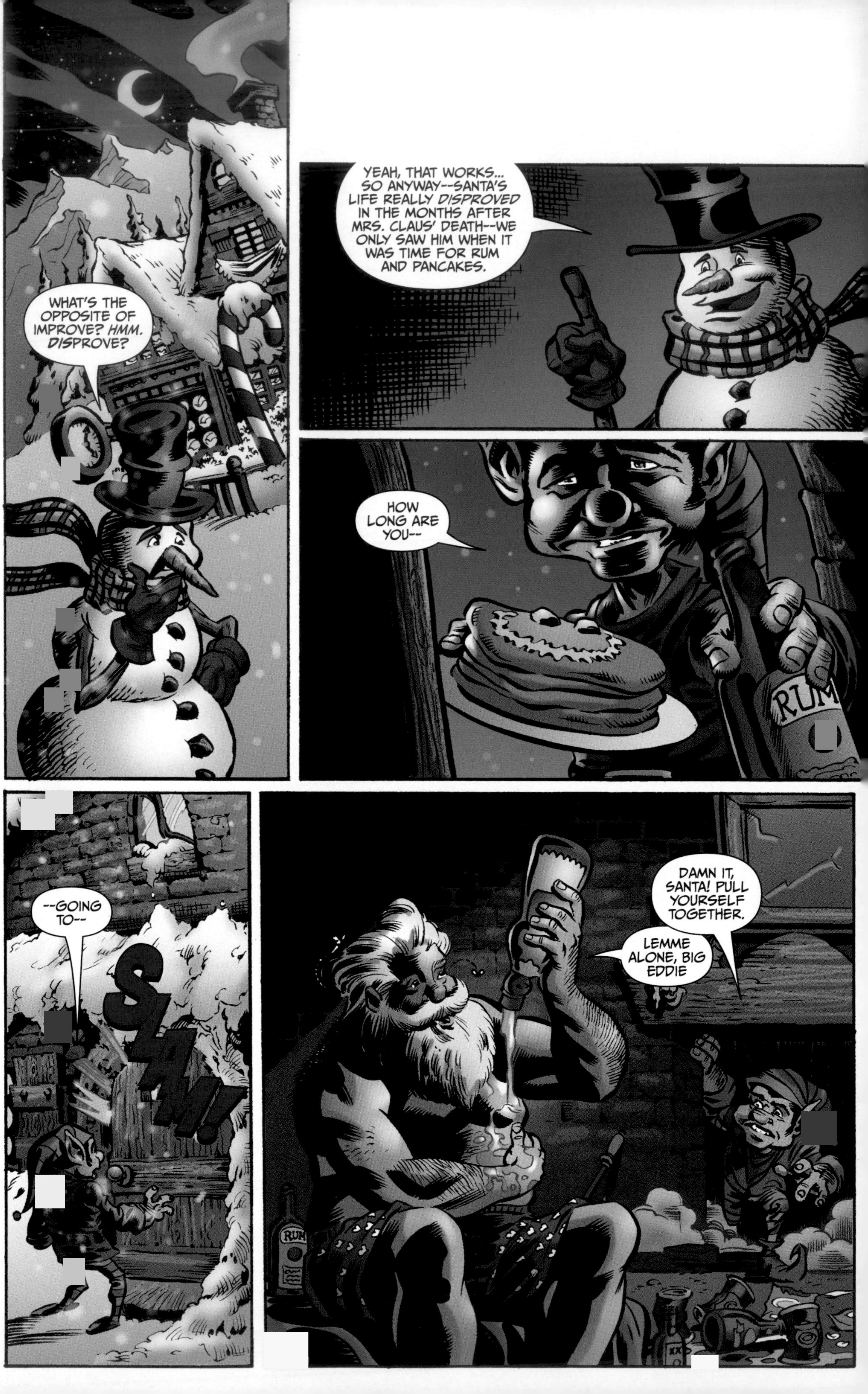
WHAT'S THE OPPOSITE OF IMPROVE? HMM. DISPROVE?
YEAH, THAT WORKS... SO ANYWAY--SANTA'S LIFE REALLY DISPROVED IN THE MONTHS AFTER MRS. CLAUS' DEATH--WE ONLY SAW HIM WHEN IT WAS TIME FOR RUM AND PANCAKES.
HOW LONG ARE YOU--
RUM
--GOING TO--
SLAM!
DAMN IT, SANTA! PULL YOURSELF TOGETHER.
LEMME ALONE, BIG EDDIE
RUM

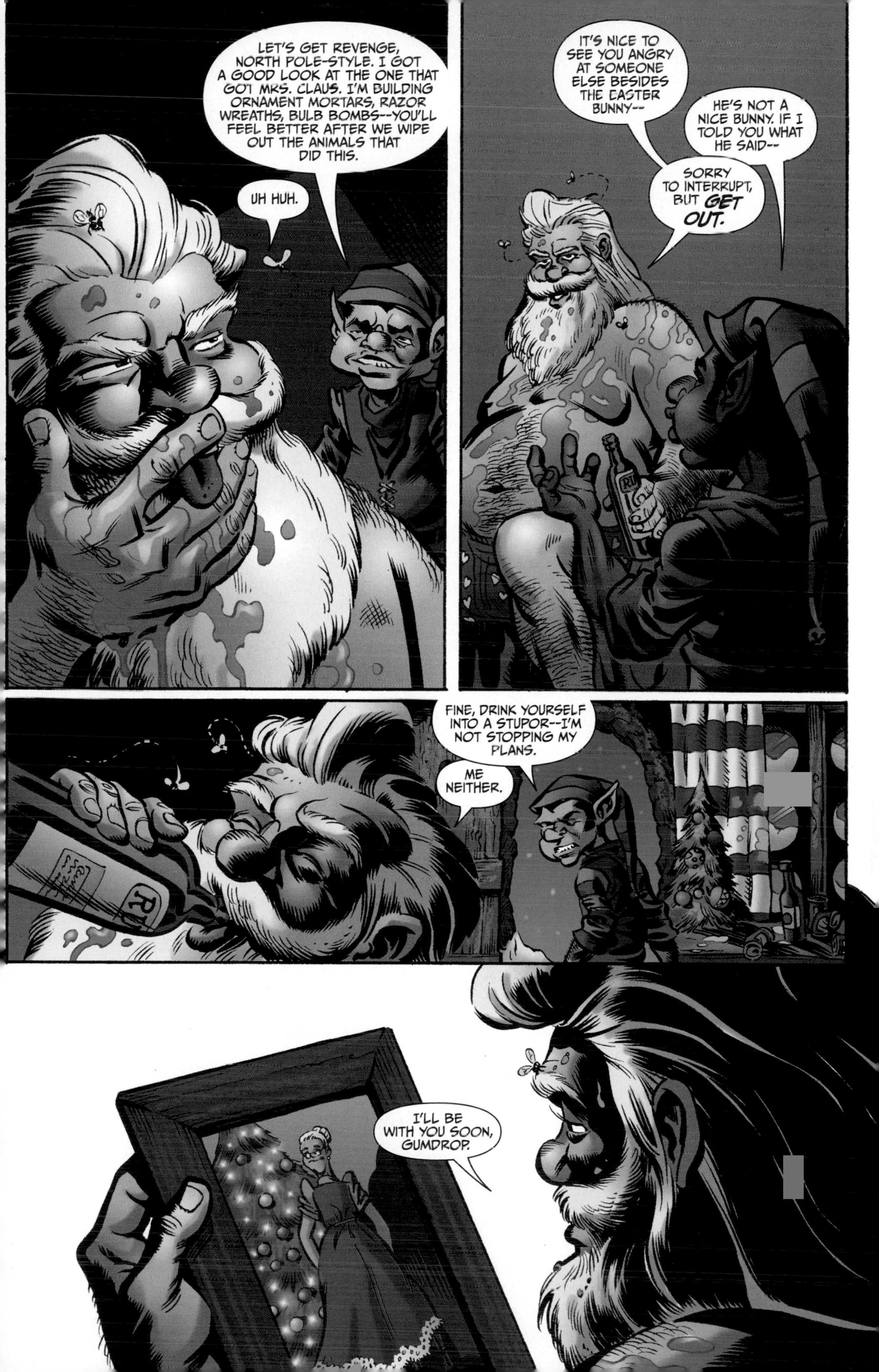
LET'S GET REVENGE, NORTH POLE-STYLE. I GOT A GOOD LOOK AT THE ONE THAT GOT MRS. CLAUS. I'M BUILDING ORNAMENT MORTARS, RAZOR WREATHS, BULB BOMBS--YOU'LL FEEL BETTER AFTER WE WIPE OUT THE ANIMALS THAT DID THIS.
UH HUH.
IT'S NICE TO SEE YOU ANGRY AT SOMEONE ELSE BESIDES THE EASTER BUNNY--
HE'S NOT A NICE BUNNY. IF I TOLD YOU WHAT HE SAID--
SORRY TO INTERRUPT, BUT GET OUT.
FINE, DRINK YOURSELF INTO A STUPOR--I'M NOT STOPPING MY PLANS.
ME NEITHER.
I'LL BE WITH YOU SOON, GUMDROP.

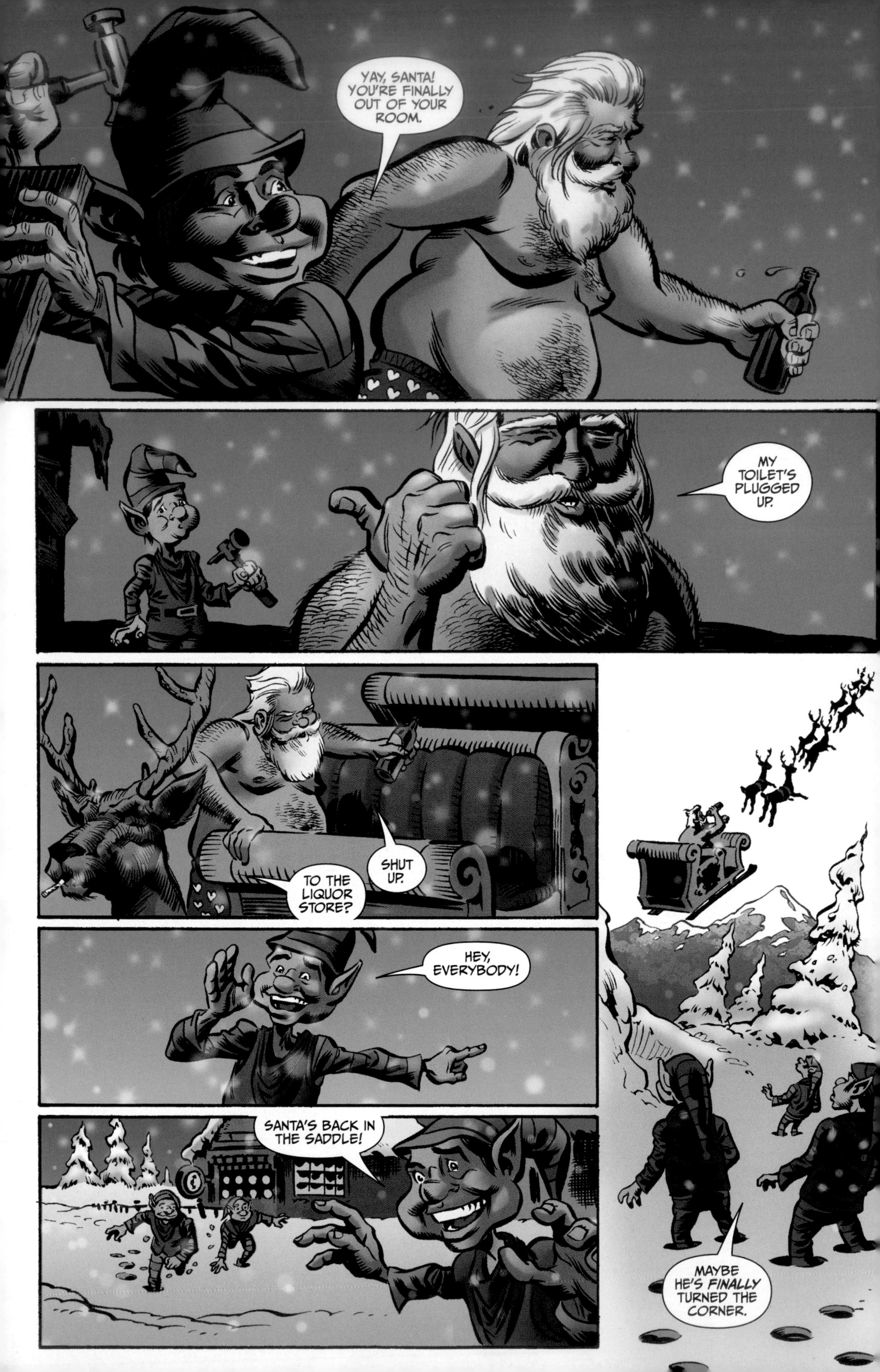
YAY, SANTA! YOU'RE FINALLY OUT OF YOUR ROOM.
MY TOILET'S PLUGGED UP.
TO THE LIQUOR STORE?
SHUT UP.
HEY, EVERYBODY!
SANTA'S BACK IN THE SADDLE!
MAYBE HE'S FINALLY TURNED THE CORNER.

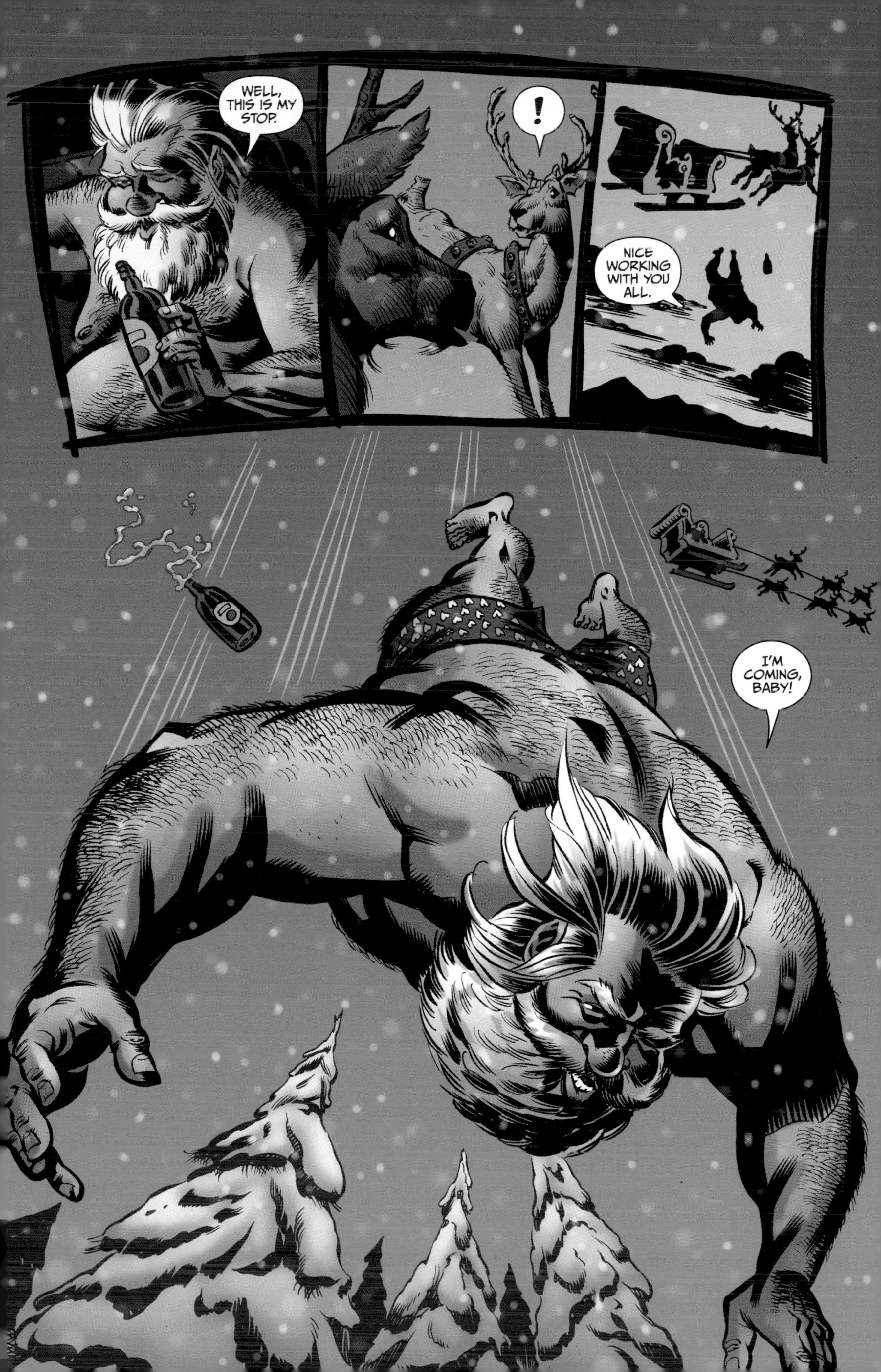
WELL, THIS IS MY STOP.
!
NICE WORKING WITH YOU ALL.
I'M COMING, BABY!

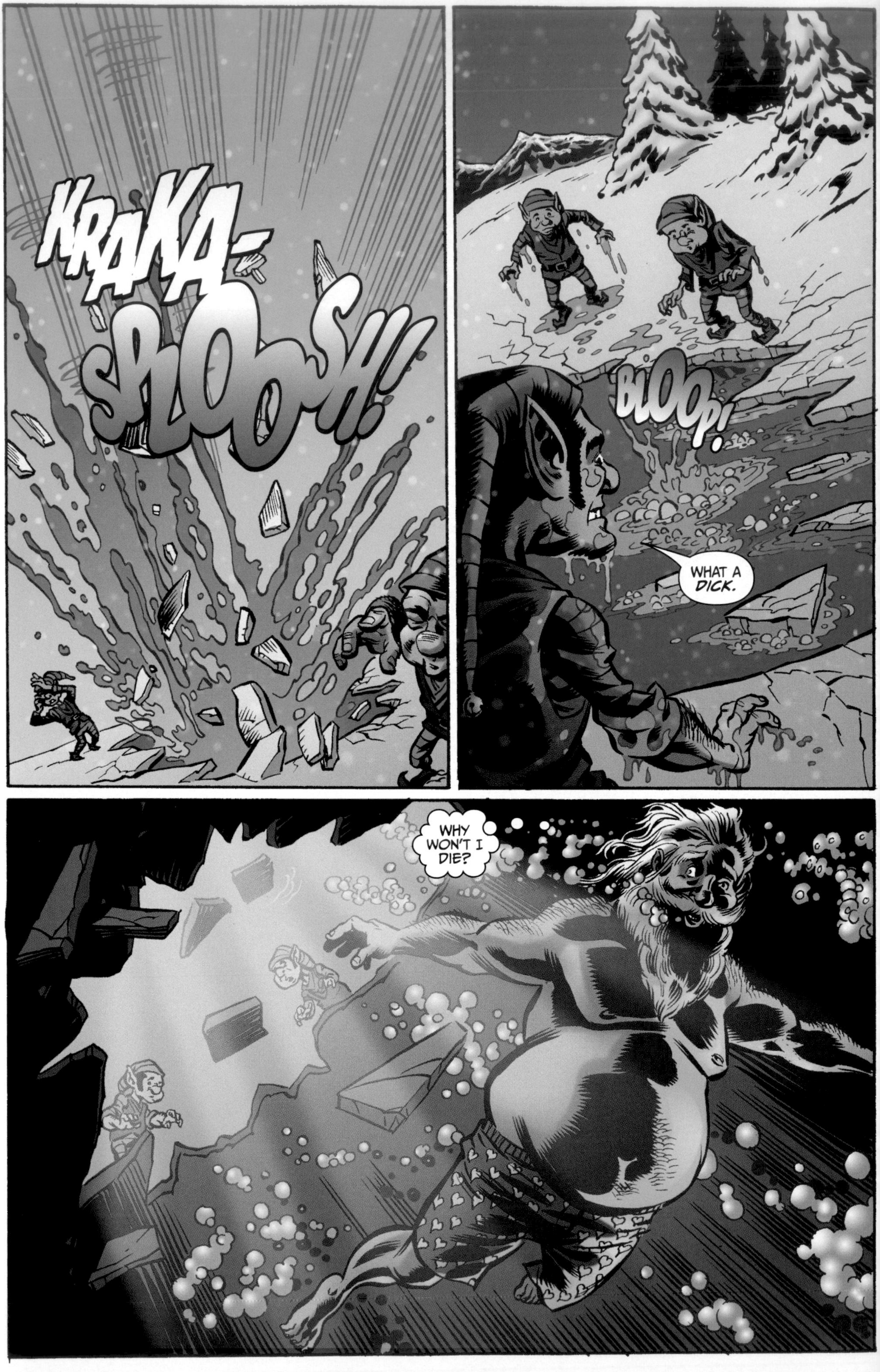
KRAKA-SPLOOSH!!
BLOOP!
WHAT A DICK.
WHY WON'T I DIE?

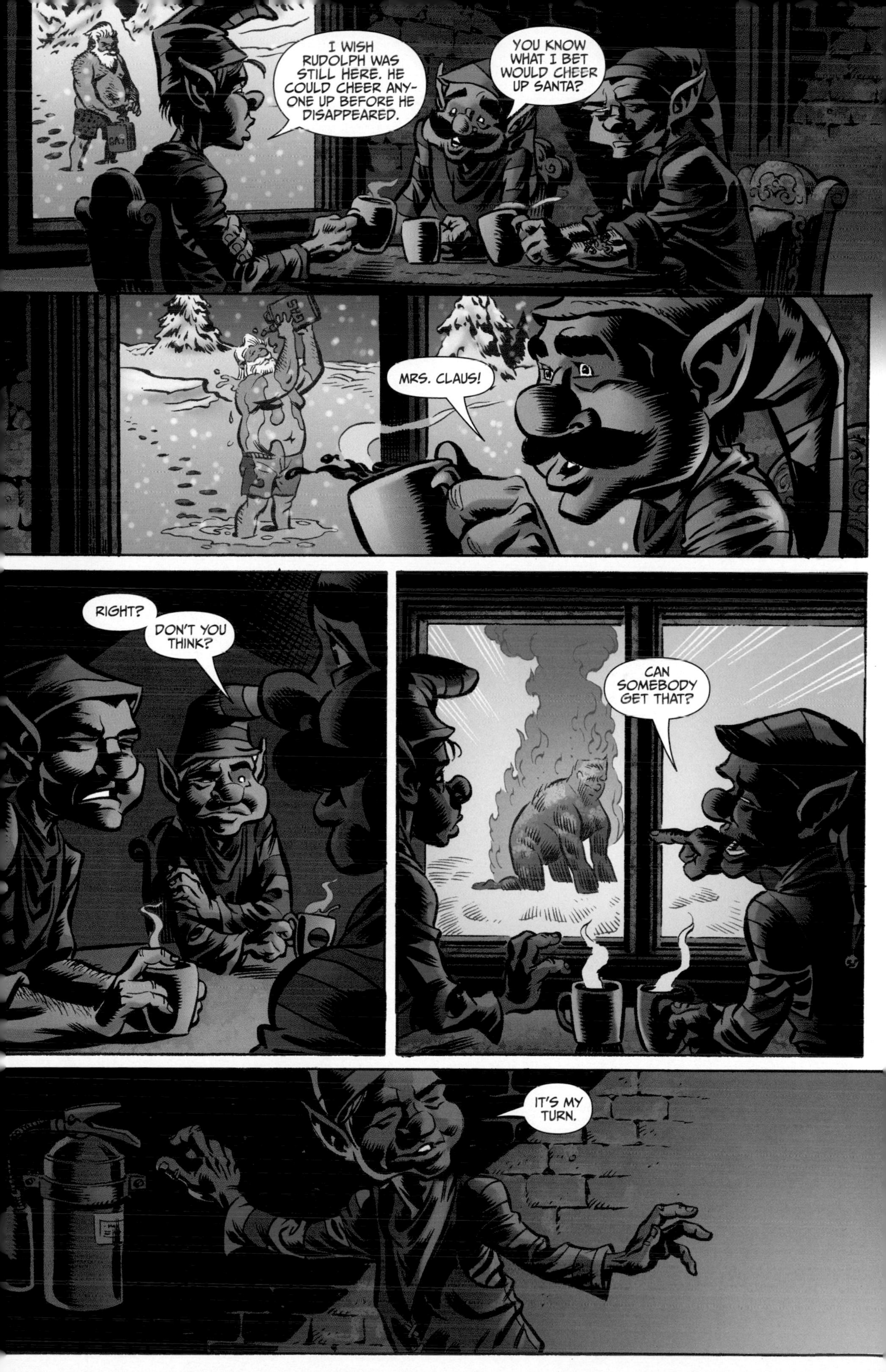
I WISH RUDOLPH WAS STILL HERE. HE COULD CHEER ANY-ONE UP BEFORE HE DISAPPEARED.
YOU KNOW WHAT I BET WOULD CHEER UP SANTA?
MRS. CLAUS!
RIGHT?
DON'T YOU THINK?
CAN SOMEBODY GET THAT?
IT'S MY TURN.

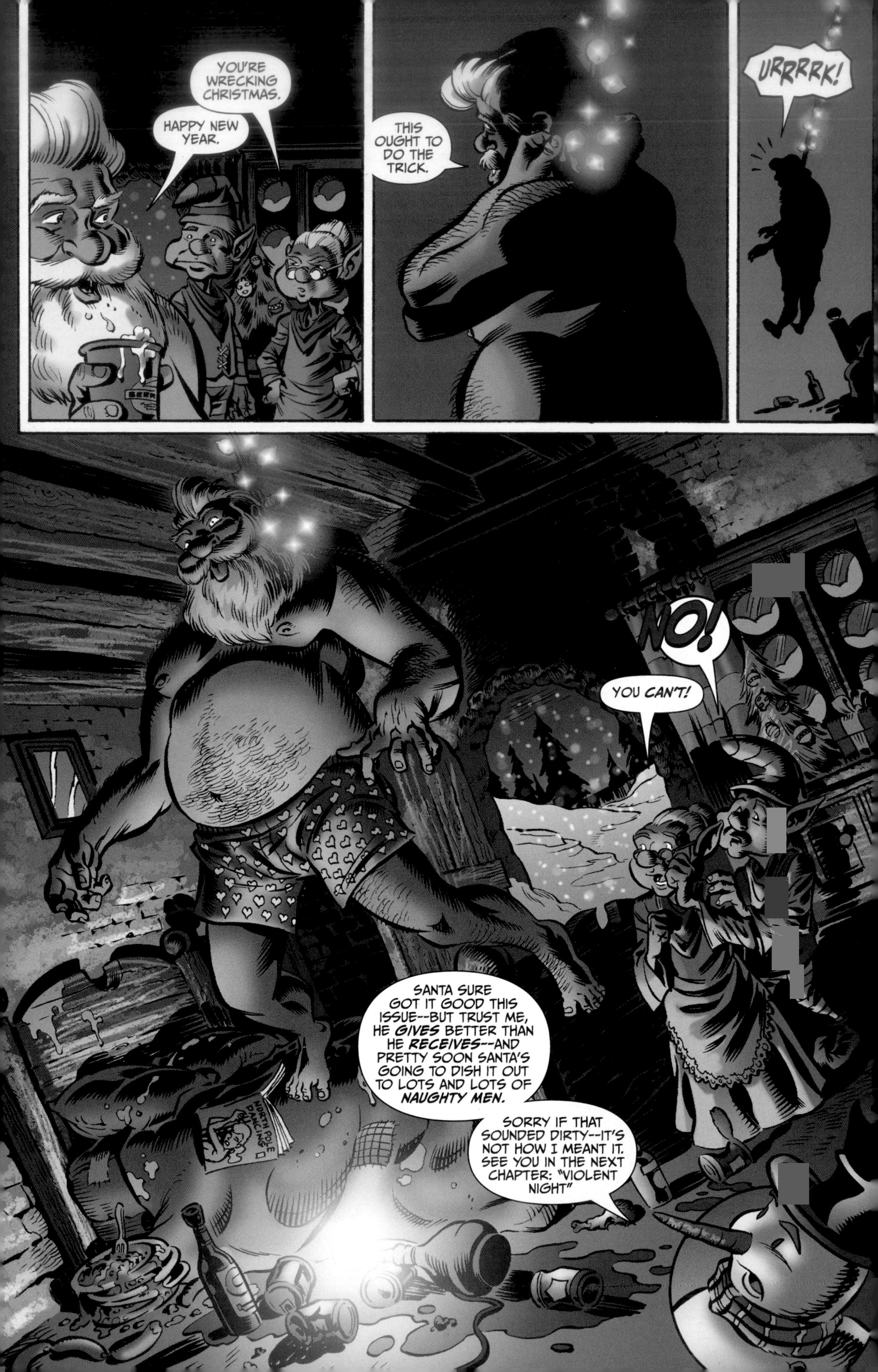
HAPPY NEW YEAR.
YOU'RE WRECKING CHRISTMAS.
BEER
THIS OUGHT TO DO THE TRICK.
URRRRK!
NO!
YOU CAN'T!
SANTA SURE GOT IT GOOD THIS ISSUE--BUT TRUST ME, HE GIVES BETTER THAN HE RECEIVES--AND PRETTY SOON SANTA'S GOING TO DISH IT OUT TO LOTS AND LOTS OF NAUGHTY MEN.
SORRY IF THAT SOUNDED DIRTY--IT'S NOT HOW I MEANT IT. SEE YOU IN THE NEXT CHAPTER: "VIOLENT NIGHT"
NORTH POLE DANCING

Chapter 2

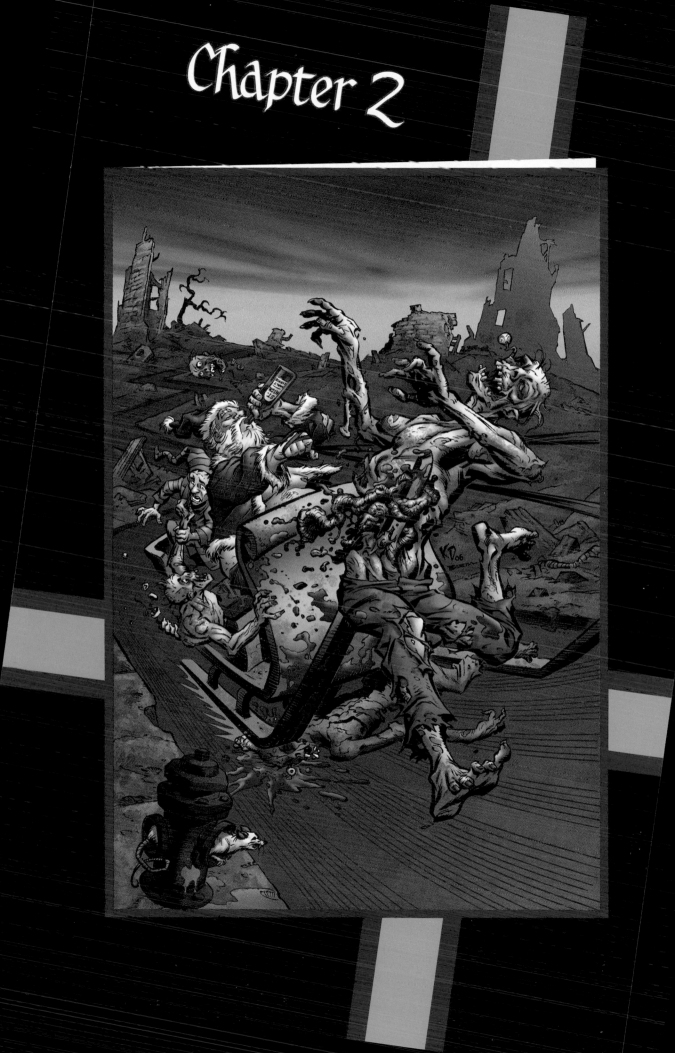

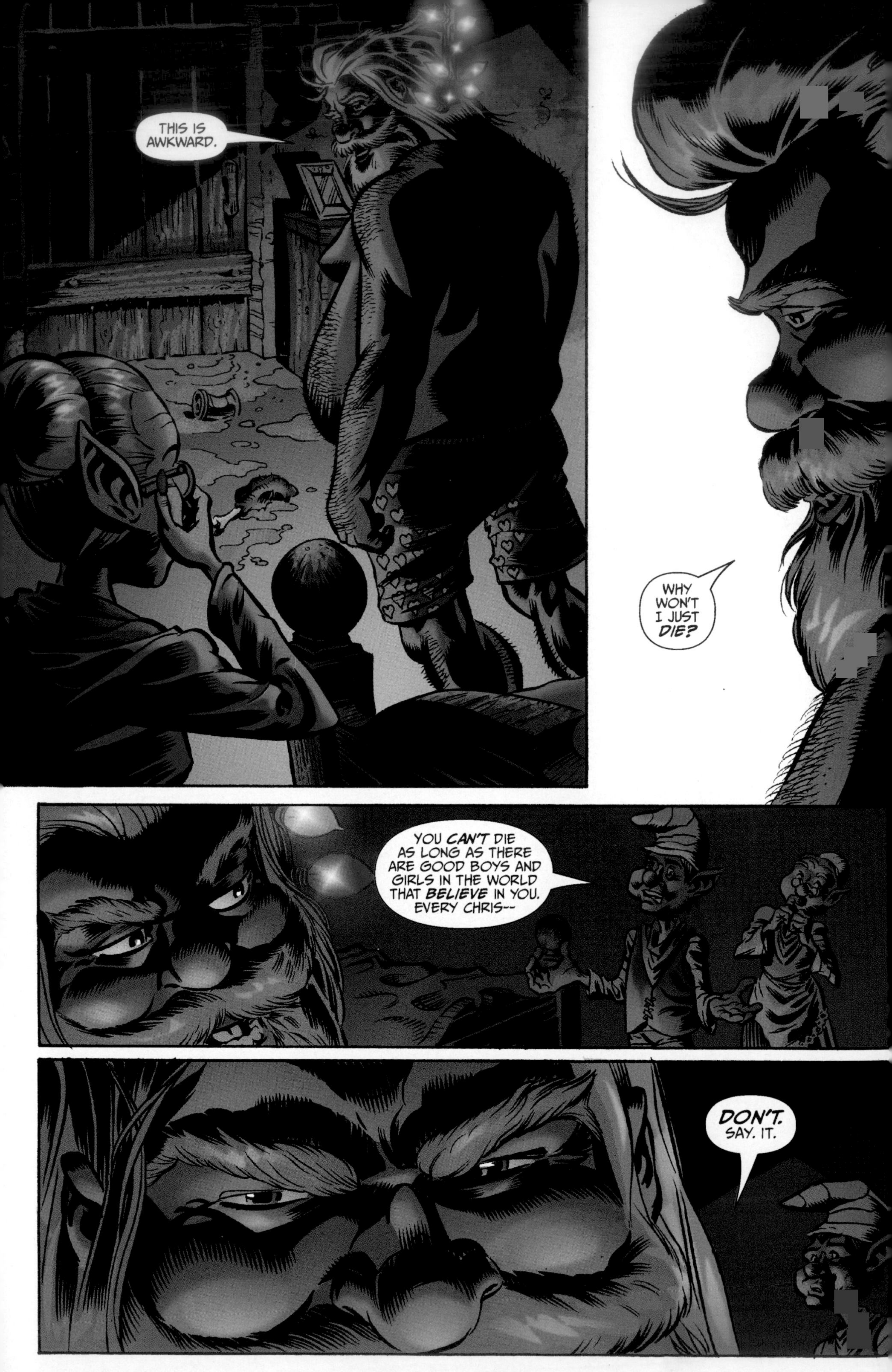

THIS IS AWKWARD.
WHY WON'T I JUST *DIE?*
YOU *CAN'T* DIE AS LONG AS THERE ARE GOOD BOYS AND GIRLS IN THE WORLD THAT *BELIEVE* IN YOU. EVERY CHRIS--
DON'T. SAY. IT.

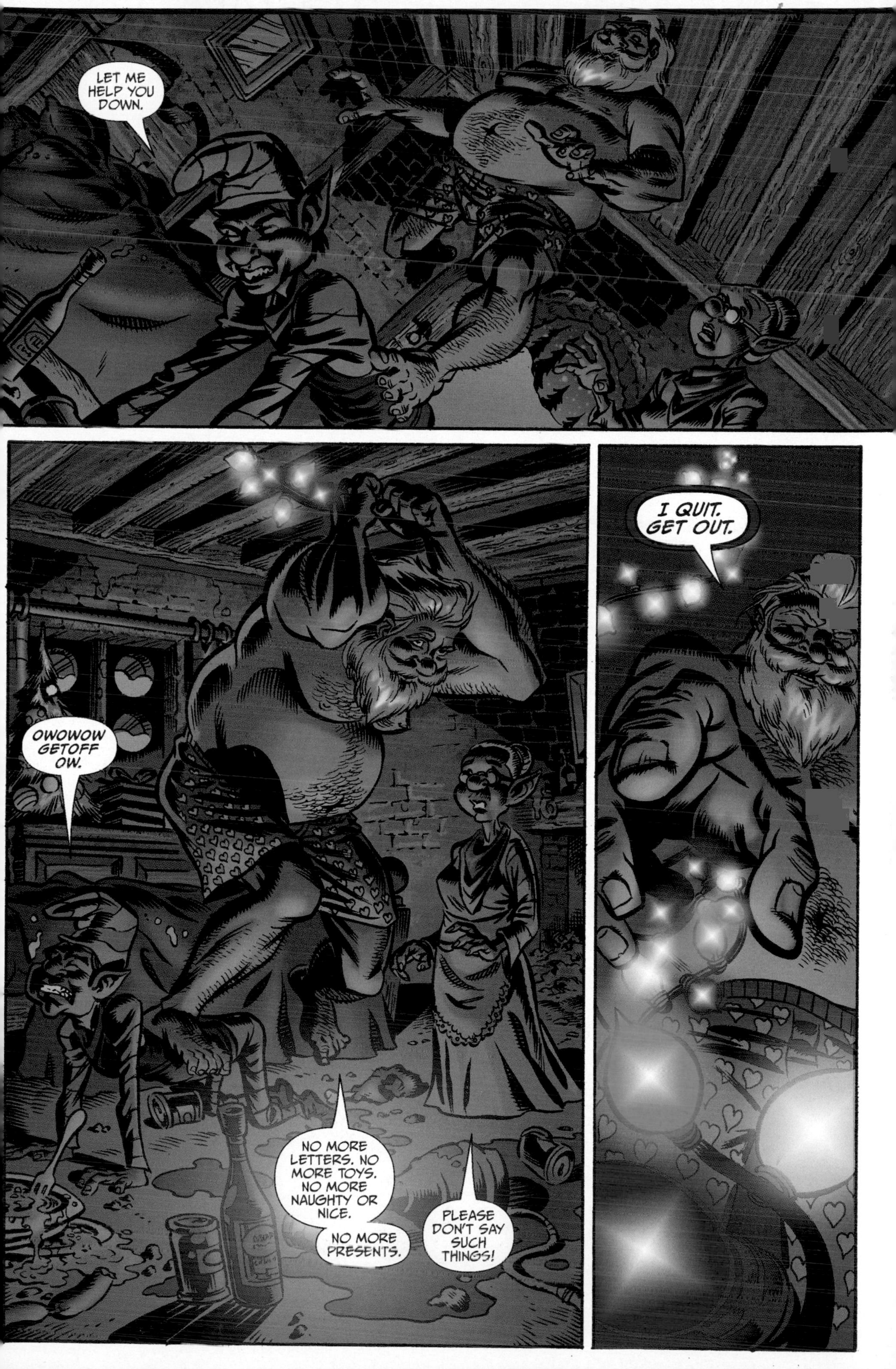
LET ME HELP YOU DOWN.
OWOWOW GETOFF OW.
NO MORE LETTERS. NO MORE TOYS. NO MORE NAUGHTY OR NICE.
NO MORE PRESENTS.
PLEASE DON'T SAY SUCH THINGS!
I QUIT. GET OUT.

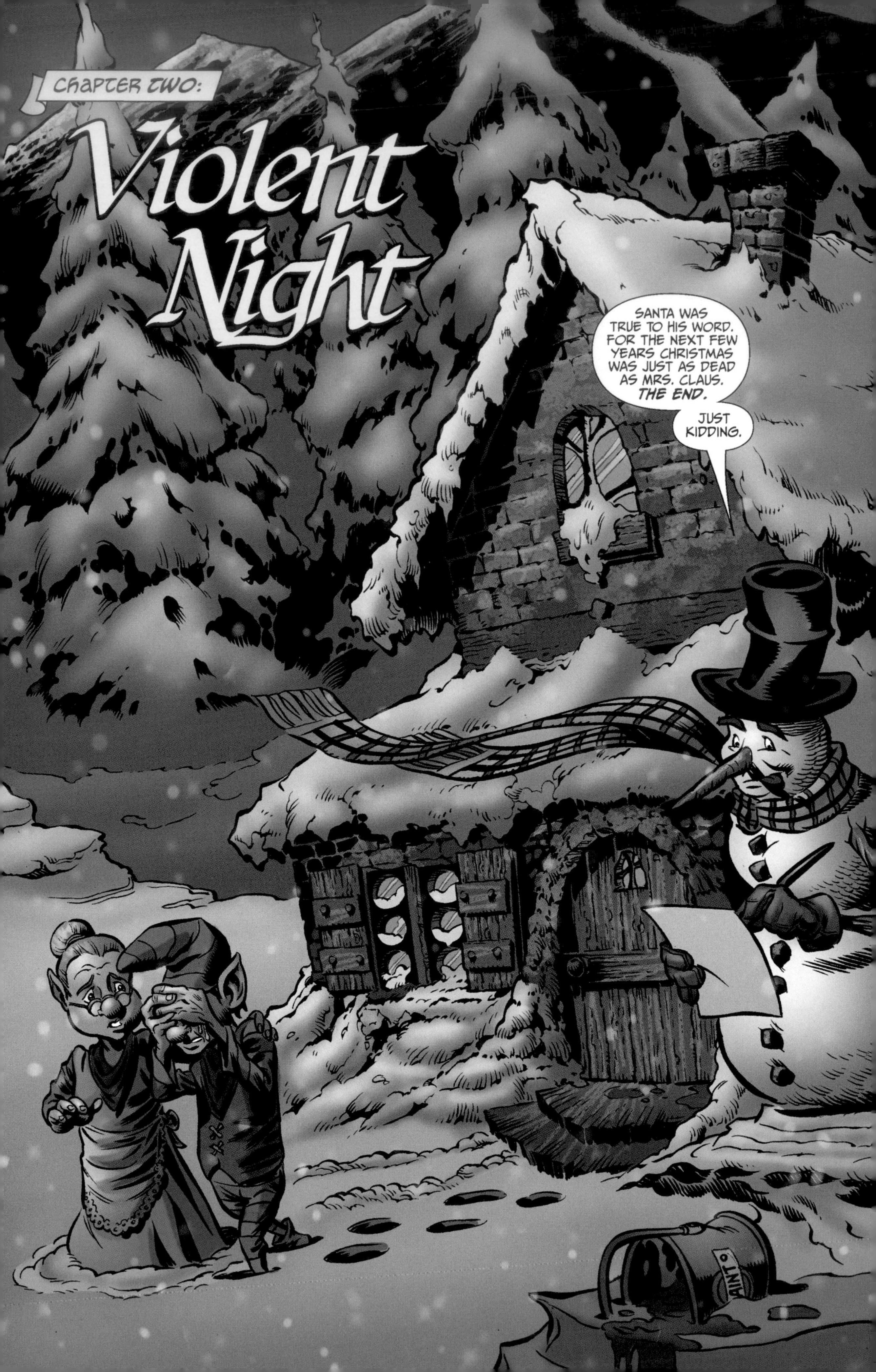
CHAPTER TWO:
Violent Night
SANTA WAS TRUE TO HIS WORD. FOR THE NEXT FEW YEARS CHRISTMAS WAS JUST AS DEAD AS MRS. CLAUS. THE END.
JUST KIDDING.

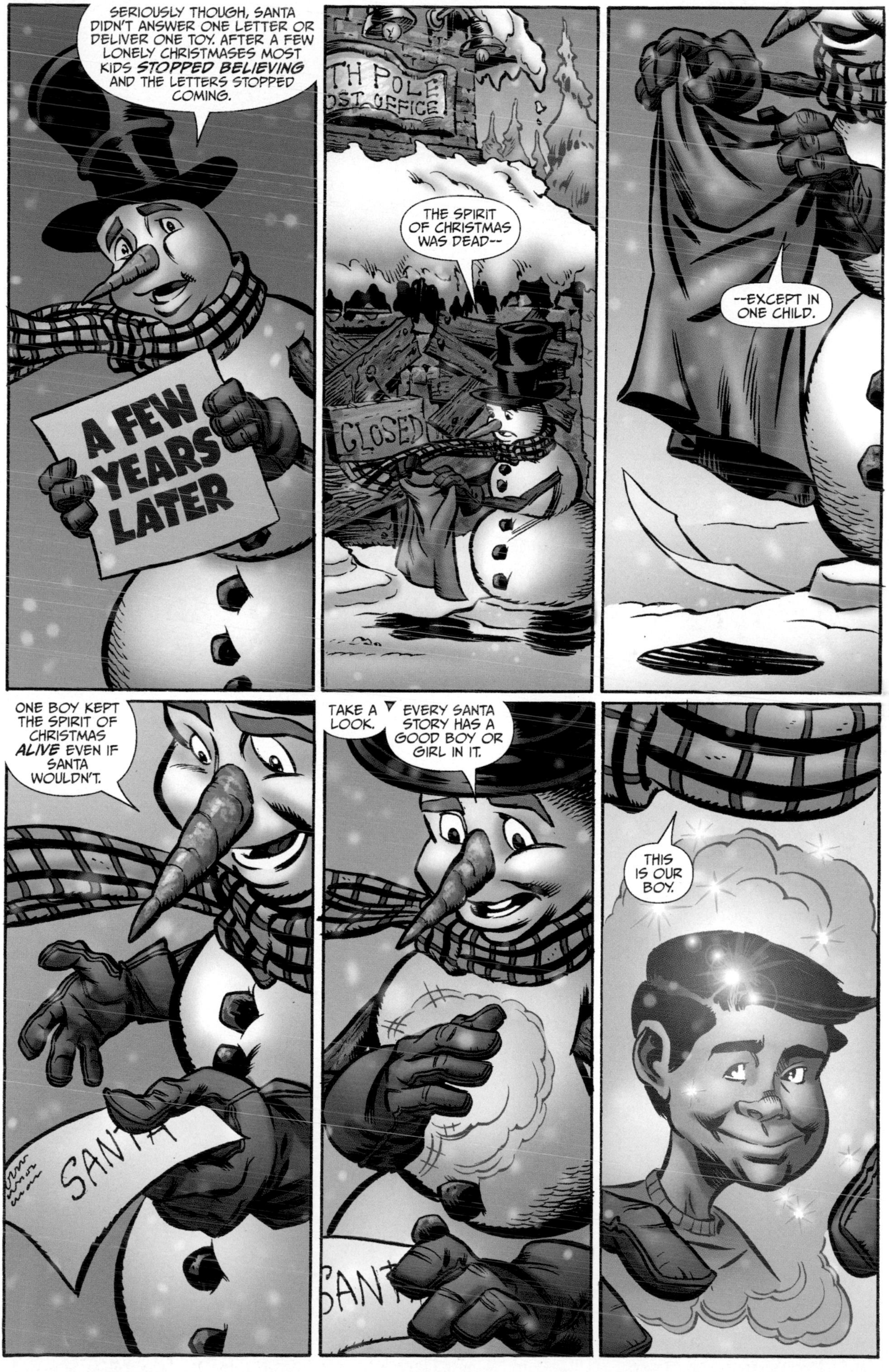
SERIOUSLY THOUGH, SANTA DIDN'T ANSWER ONE LETTER OR DELIVER ONE TOY. AFTER A FEW LONELY CHRISTMASES MOST KIDS STOPPED BELIEVING AND THE LETTERS STOPPED COMING.
A FEW YEARS LATER
TH POLE
OST OFFICE
THE SPIRIT OF CHRISTMAS WAS DEAD--
CLOSED
--EXCEPT IN ONE CHILD.
ONE BOY KEPT THE SPIRIT OF CHRISTMAS ALIVE EVEN IF SANTA WOULDN'T.
SANTA
TAKE A LOOK.
EVERY SANTA STORY HAS A GOOD BOY OR GIRL IN IT.
THIS IS OUR BOY.

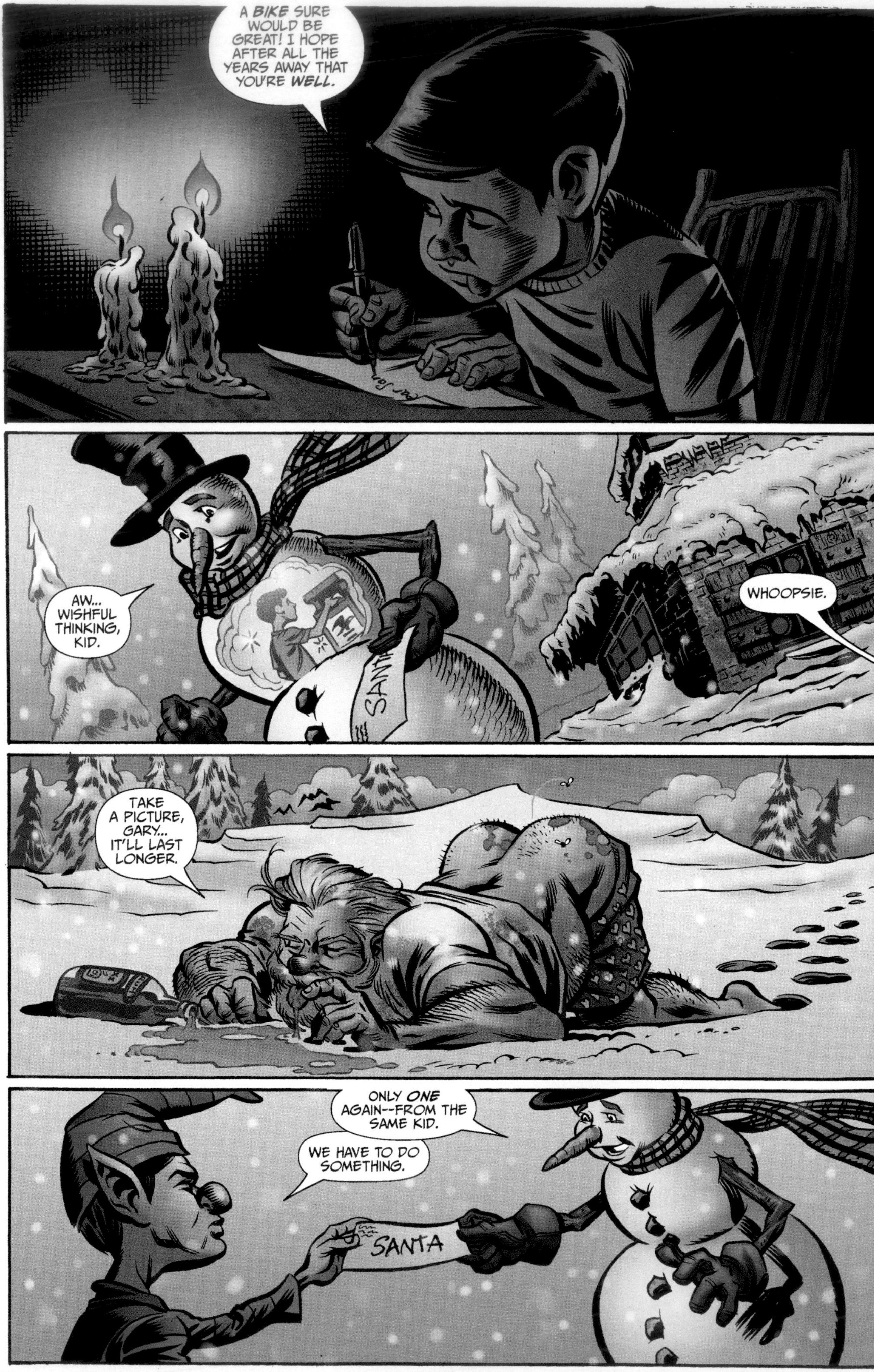
A BIKE SURE WOULD BE GREAT! I HOPE AFTER ALL THE YEARS AWAY THAT YOU'RE WELL.
AW... WISHFUL THINKING, KID.
WHOOPSIE.
SANTA
TAKE A PICTURE, GARY... IT'LL LAST LONGER.
ONLY ONE AGAIN--FROM THE SAME KID.
WE HAVE TO DO SOMETHING.
SANTA

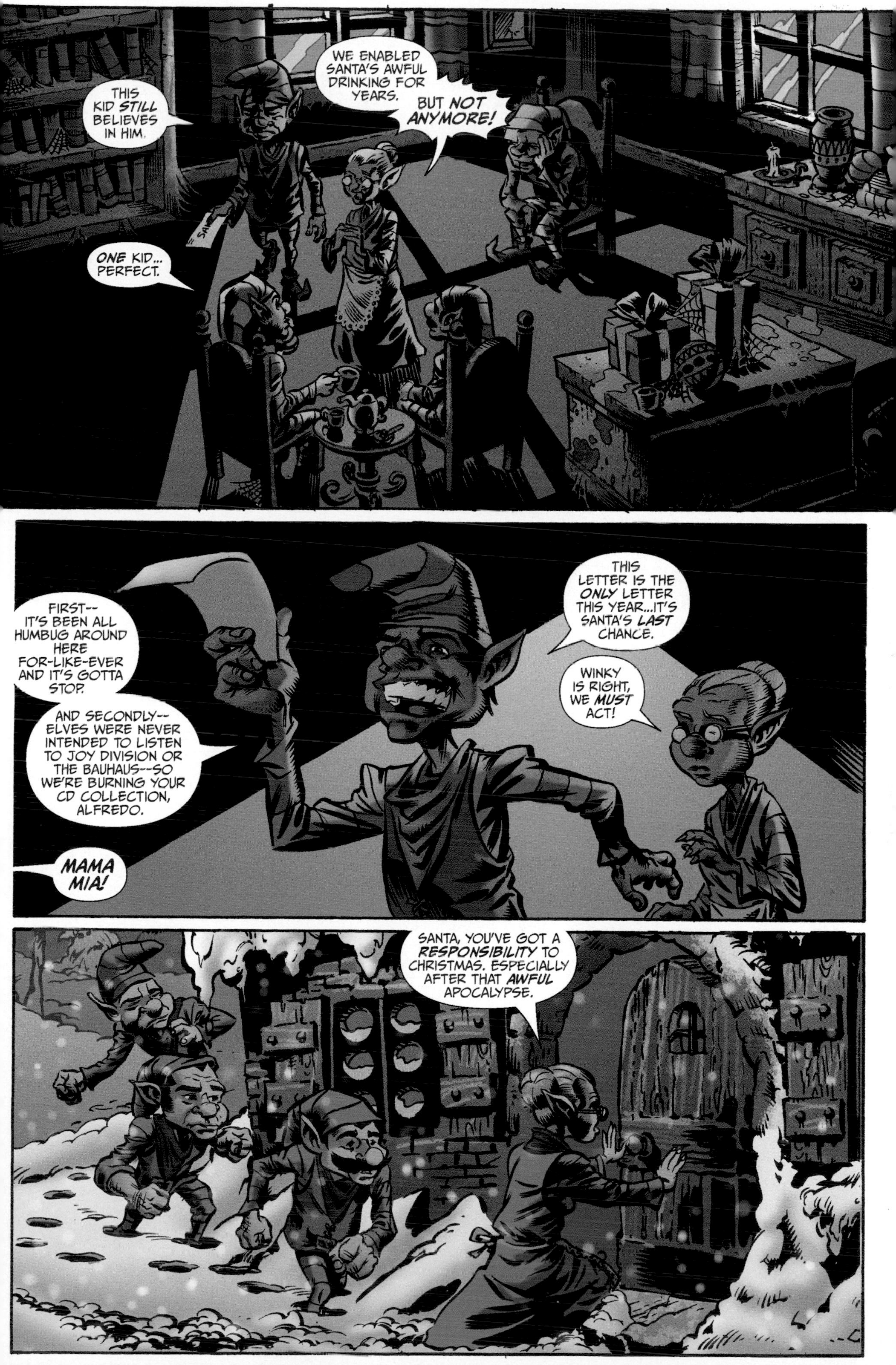
THIS KID STILL BELIEVES IN HIM.
WE ENABLED SANTA'S AWFUL DRINKING FOR YEARS.
BUT NOT ANYMORE!
ONE KID... PERFECT.
FIRST-- IT'S BEEN ALL HUMBUG AROUND HERE FOR-LIKE-EVER AND IT'S GOTTA STOP.
AND SECONDLY-- ELVES WERE NEVER INTENDED TO LISTEN TO JOY DIVISION OR THE BAUHAUS--SO WE'RE BURNING YOUR CD COLLECTION, ALFREDO.
MAMA MIA!
THIS LETTER IS THE ONLY LETTER THIS YEAR...IT'S SANTA'S LAST CHANCE.
WINKY IS RIGHT, WE MUST ACT!
SANTA, YOU'VE GOT A RESPONSIBILITY TO CHRISTMAS. ESPECIALLY AFTER THAT AWFUL APOCALYPSE.

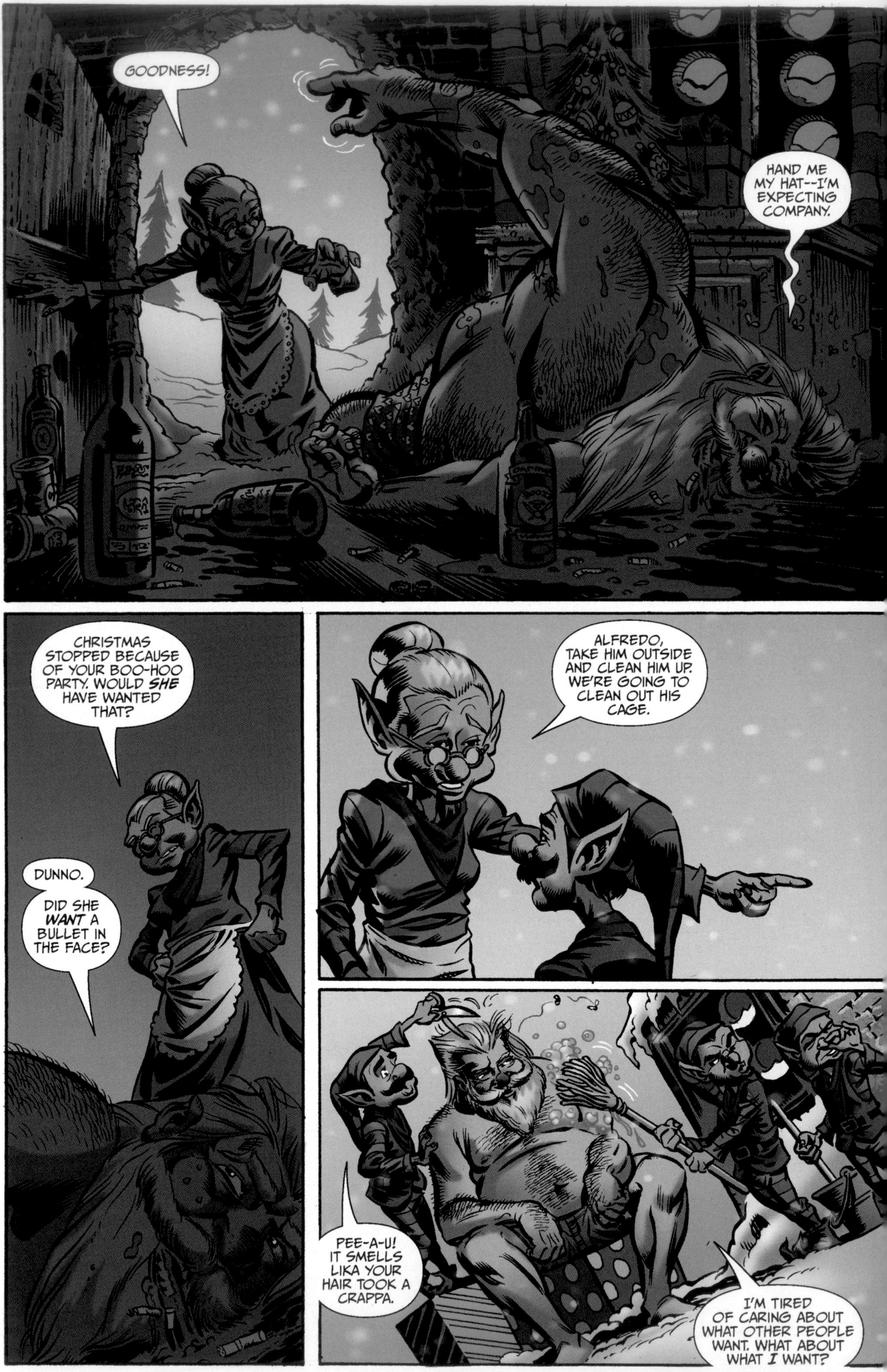
GOODNESS!
HAND ME MY HAT--I'M EXPECTING COMPANY.
CHRISTMAS STOPPED BECAUSE OF YOUR BOO-HOO PARTY. WOULD SHE HAVE WANTED THAT?
DUNNO.
DID SHE WANT A BULLET IN THE FACE?
ALFREDO, TAKE HIM OUTSIDE AND CLEAN HIM UP. WE'RE GOING TO CLEAN OUT HIS CAGE.
PEE-A-U! IT SMELLS LIKA YOUR HAIR TOOK A CRAPPA.
I'M TIRED OF CARING ABOUT WHAT OTHER PEOPLE WANT. WHAT ABOUT WHAT I WANT?

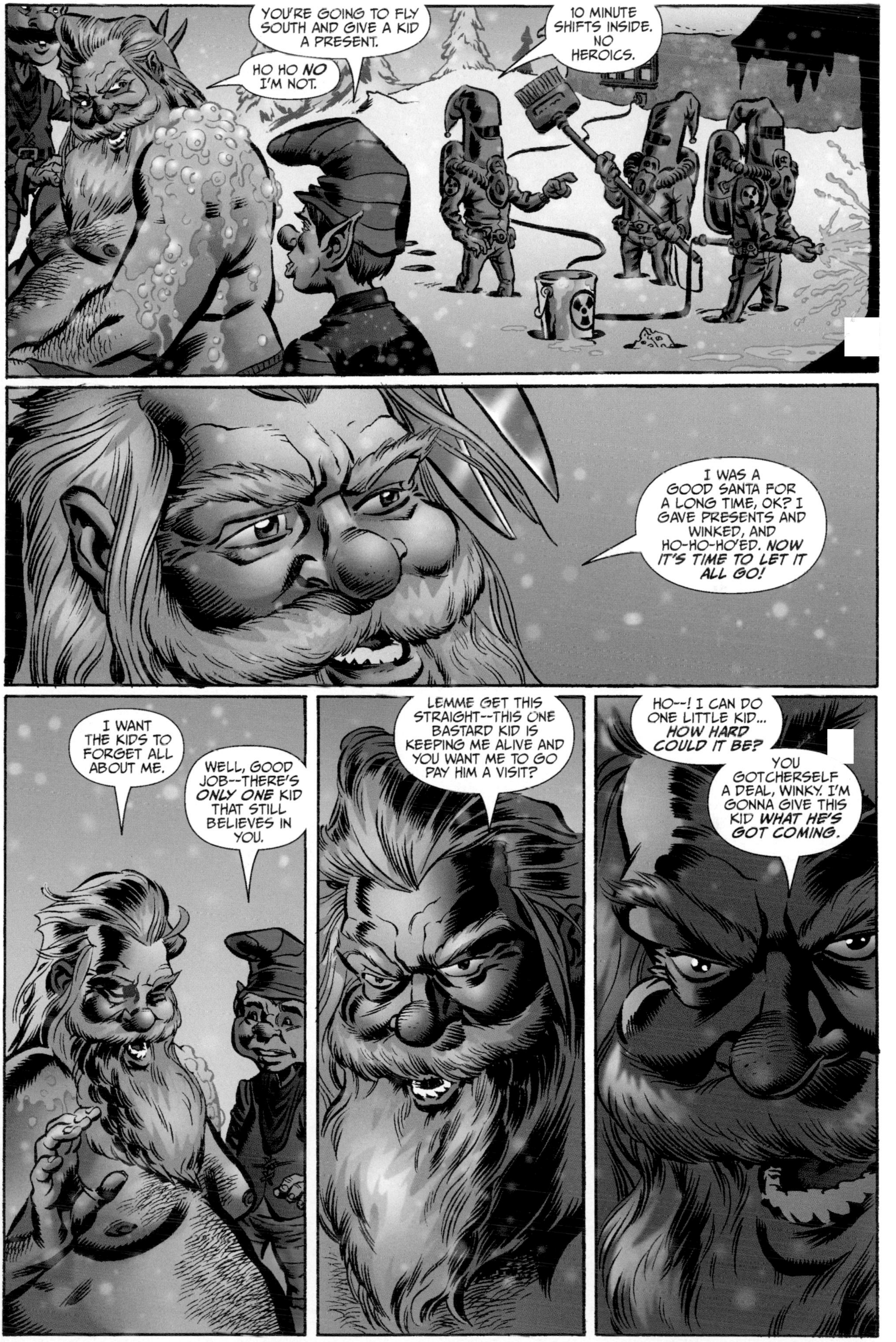
YOU'RE GOING TO FLY SOUTH AND GIVE A KID A PRESENT.
HO HO ***NO*** I'M NOT.
10 MINUTE SHIFTS INSIDE. NO HEROICS.
I WAS A GOOD SANTA FOR A LONG TIME, OK? I GAVE PRESENTS AND WINKED, AND HO-HO-HO'ED. ***NOW IT'S TIME TO LET IT ALL GO!***
I WANT THE KIDS TO FORGET ALL ABOUT ME.
WELL, GOOD JOB--THERE'S ***ONLY ONE*** KID THAT STILL BELIEVES IN YOU.
LEMME GET THIS STRAIGHT--THIS ONE BASTARD KID IS KEEPING ME ALIVE AND YOU WANT ME TO GO PAY HIM A VISIT?
HO--! I CAN DO ONE LITTLE KID... ***HOW HARD COULD IT BE?***
YOU GOTCHERSELF A DEAL, WINKY. I'M GONNA GIVE THIS KID ***WHAT HE'S GOT COMING.***

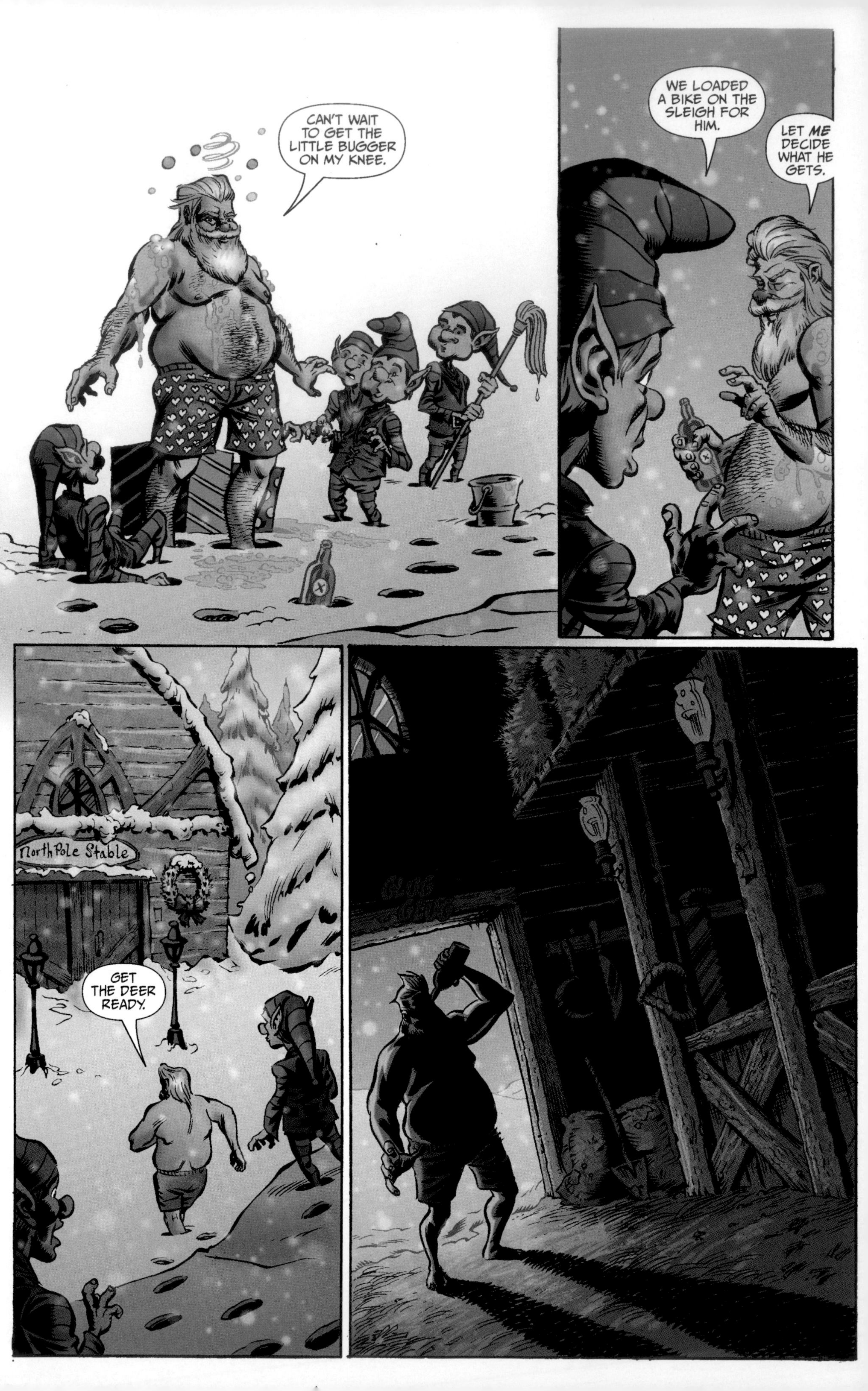
CAN'T WAIT TO GET THE LITTLE BUGGER ON MY KNEE.
WE LOADED A BIKE ON THE SLEIGH FOR HIM.
LET ME DECIDE WHAT HE GETS.
North Pole Stable
GET THE DEER READY.

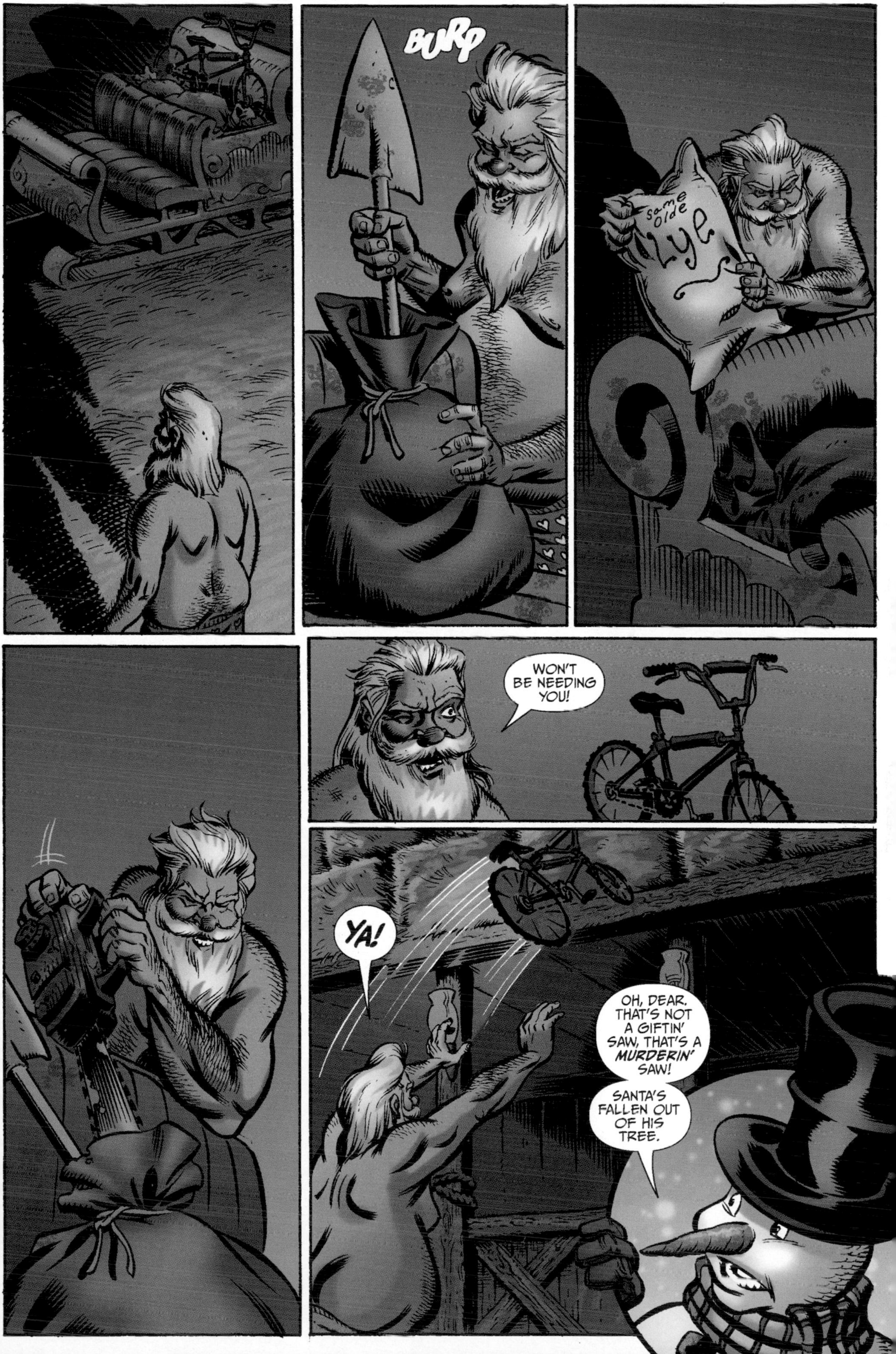
BURP
Same Olde Lye
WON'T BE NEEDING YOU!
YA!
OH, DEAR. THAT'S NOT A GIFTIN' SAW, THAT'S A *MURDERIN'* SAW!
SANTA'S FALLEN OUT OF HIS TREE.

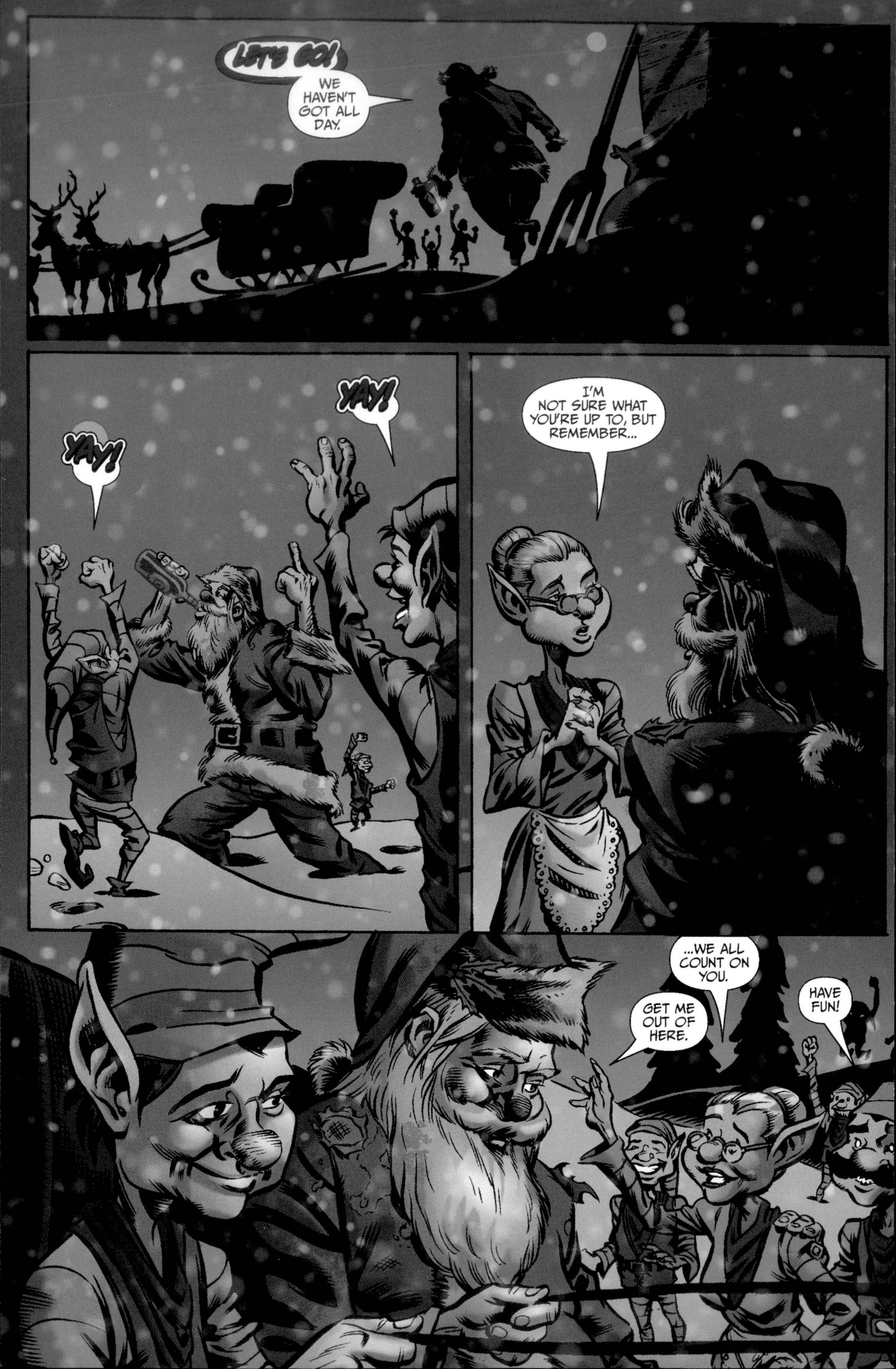
LET'S GO!
WE HAVEN'T GOT ALL DAY.
YAY!
YAY!
I'M NOT SURE WHAT YOU'RE UP TO, BUT REMEMBER...
...WE ALL COUNT ON YOU.
GET ME OUT OF HERE.
HAVE FUN!

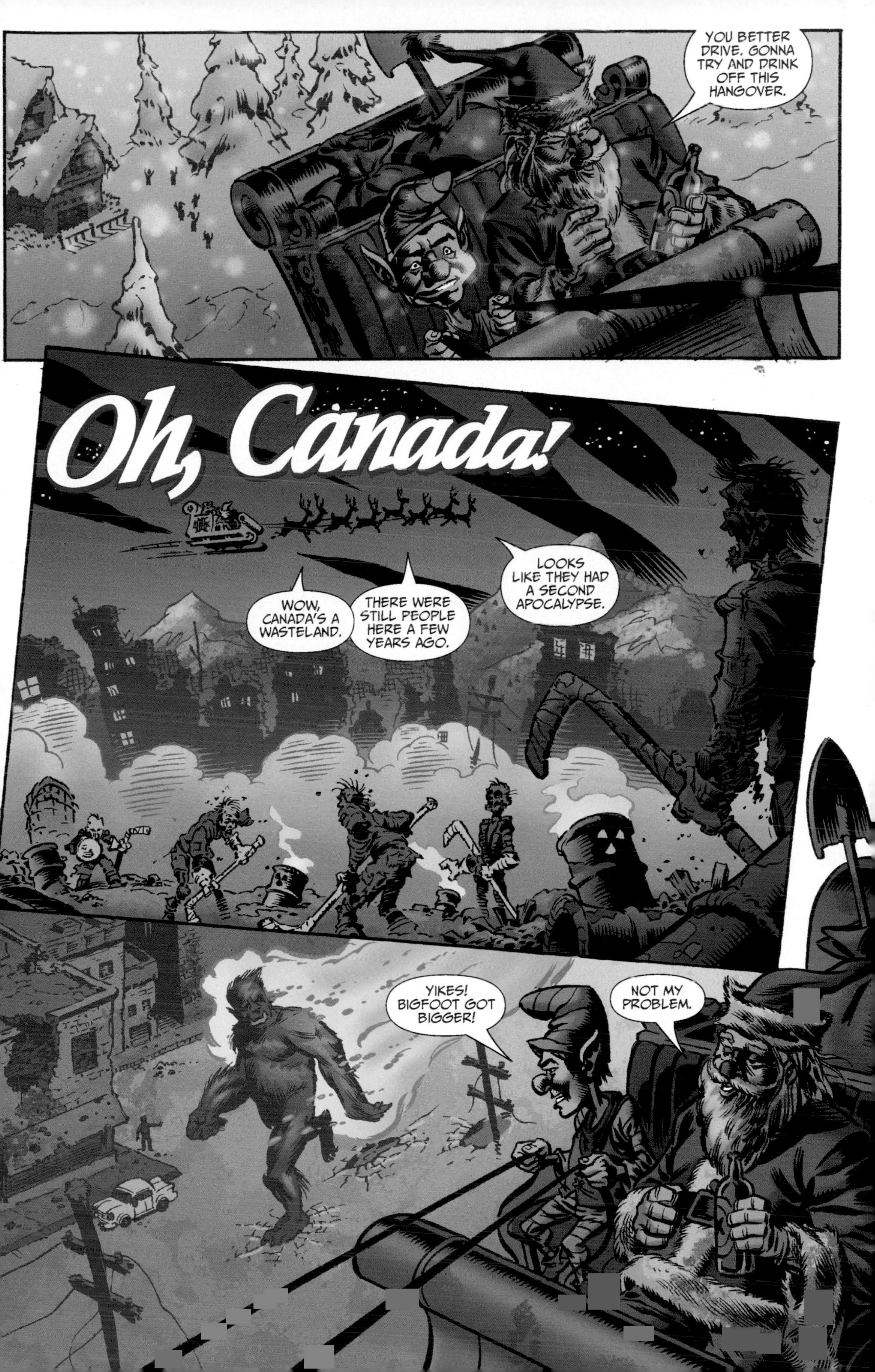
YOU BETTER DRIVE. GONNA TRY AND DRINK OFF THIS HANGOVER.
Oh, Canada!
WOW, CANADA'S A WASTELAND.
THERE WERE STILL PEOPLE HERE A FEW YEARS AGO.
LOOKS LIKE THEY HAD A SECOND APOCALYPSE.
YIKES! BIGFOOT GOT BIGGER!
NOT MY PROBLEM.

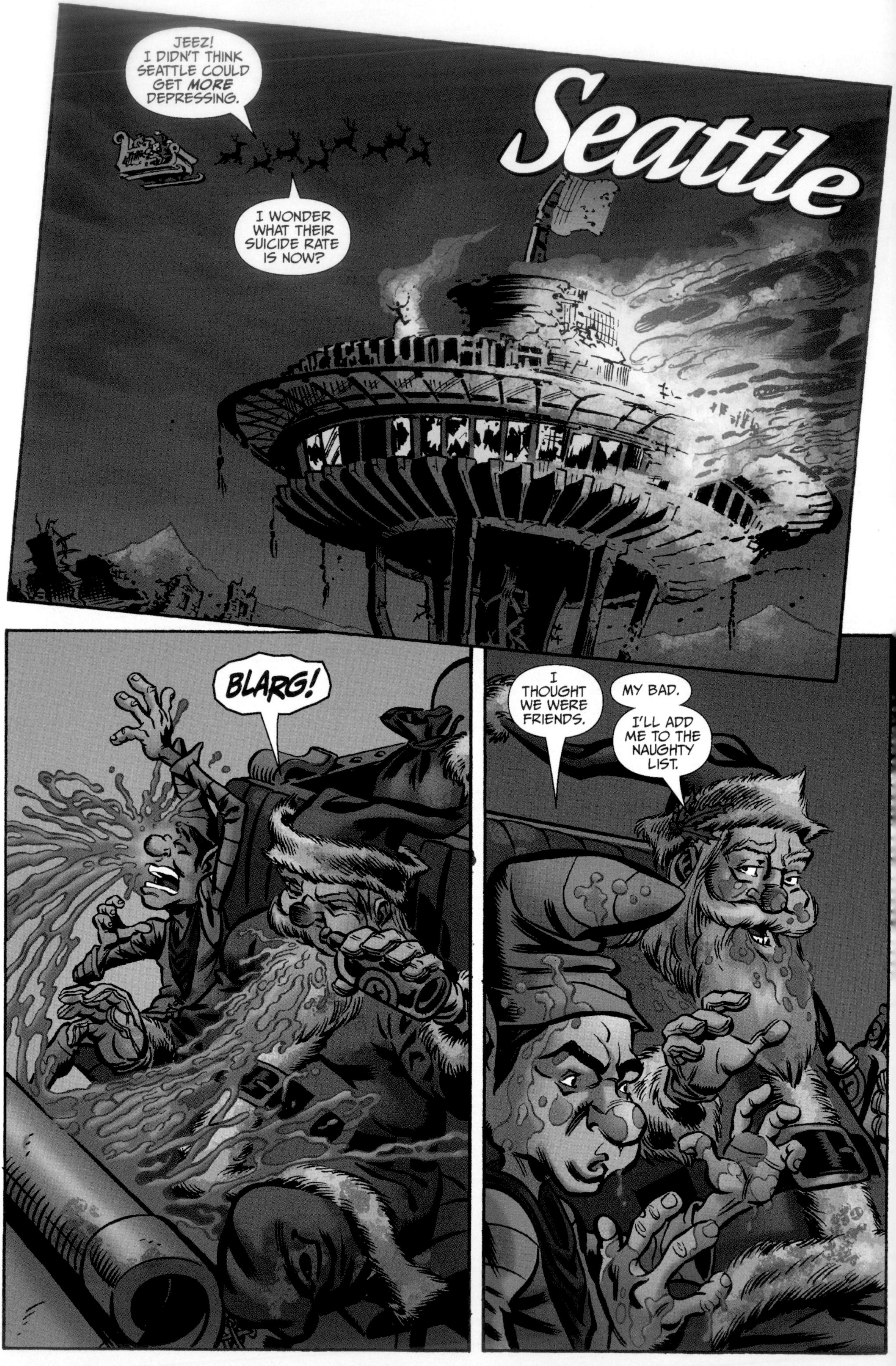

JEEZ! I DIDN'T THINK SEATTLE COULD GET *MORE* DEPRESSING.
Seattle
I WONDER WHAT THEIR SUICIDE RATE IS NOW?
BLARG!
I THOUGHT WE WERE FRIENDS.
MY BAD.
I'LL ADD ME TO THE NAUGHTY LIST.

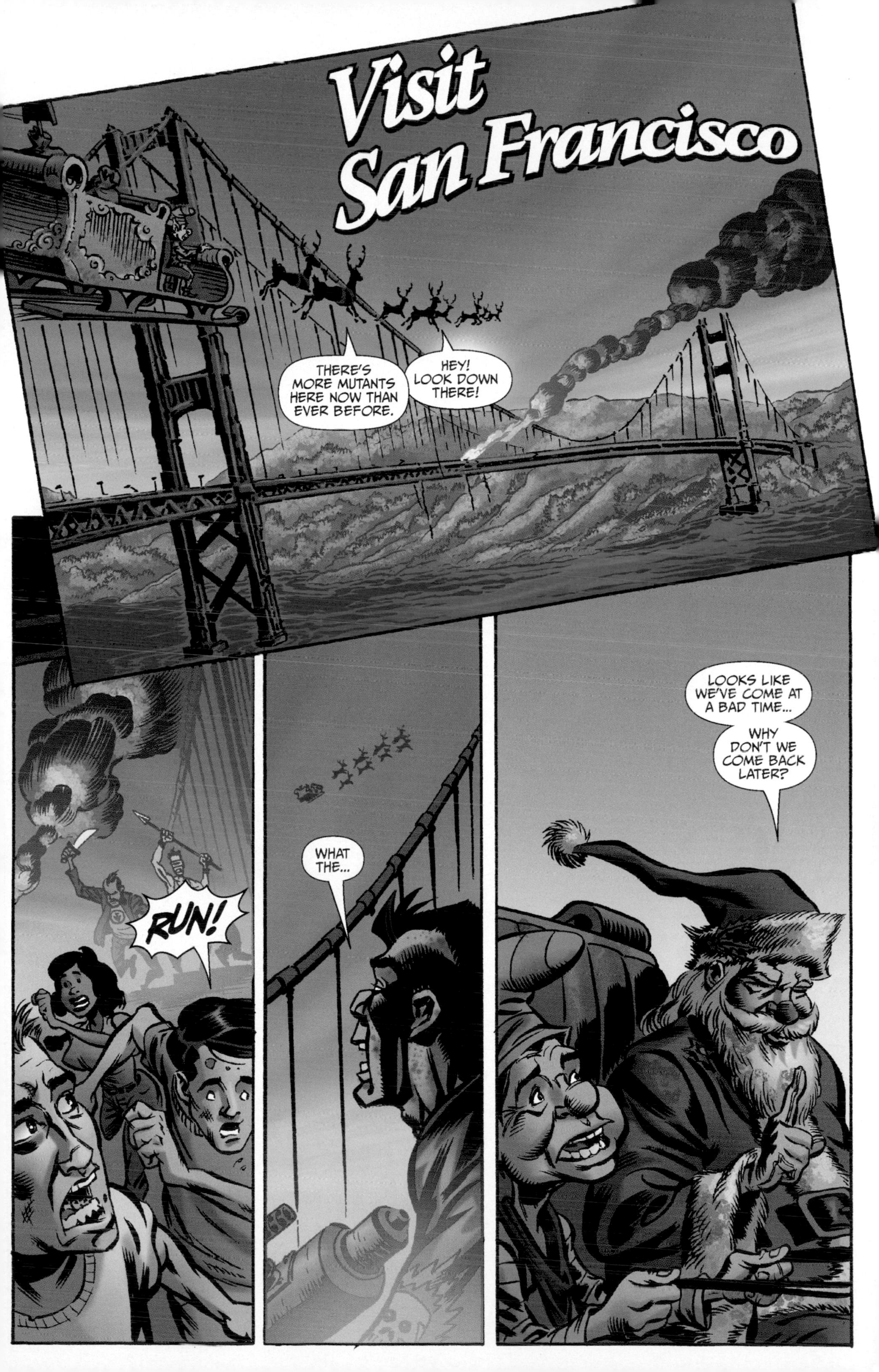
Visit San Francisco
THERE'S MORE MUTANTS HERE NOW THAN EVER BEFORE.
HEY! LOOK DOWN THERE!
RUN!
WHAT THE...
LOOKS LIKE WE'VE COME AT A BAD TIME...
WHY DON'T WE COME BACK LATER?

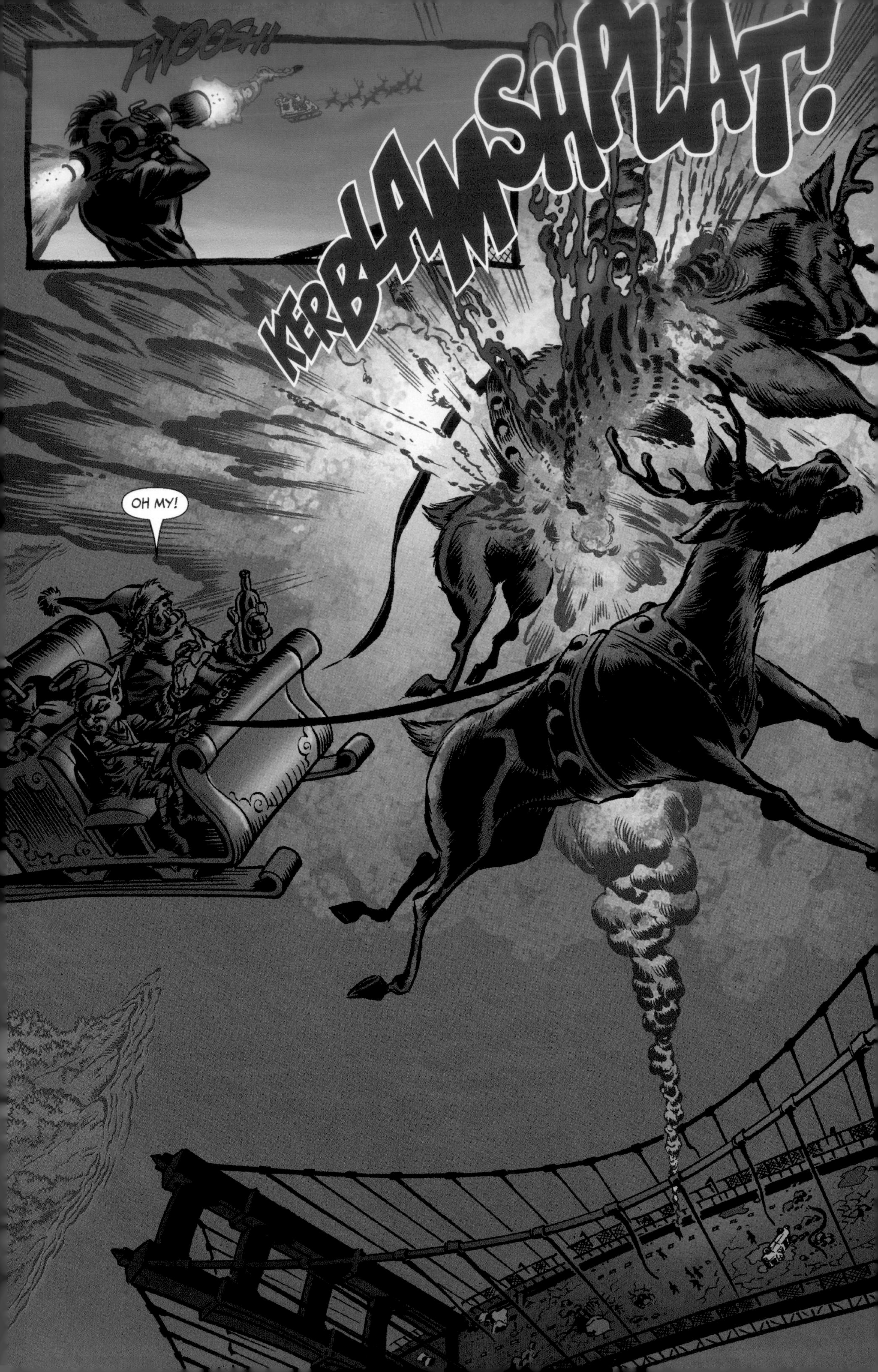
FWOOSH!
KERBLAM! SHPLAT!
OH MY!

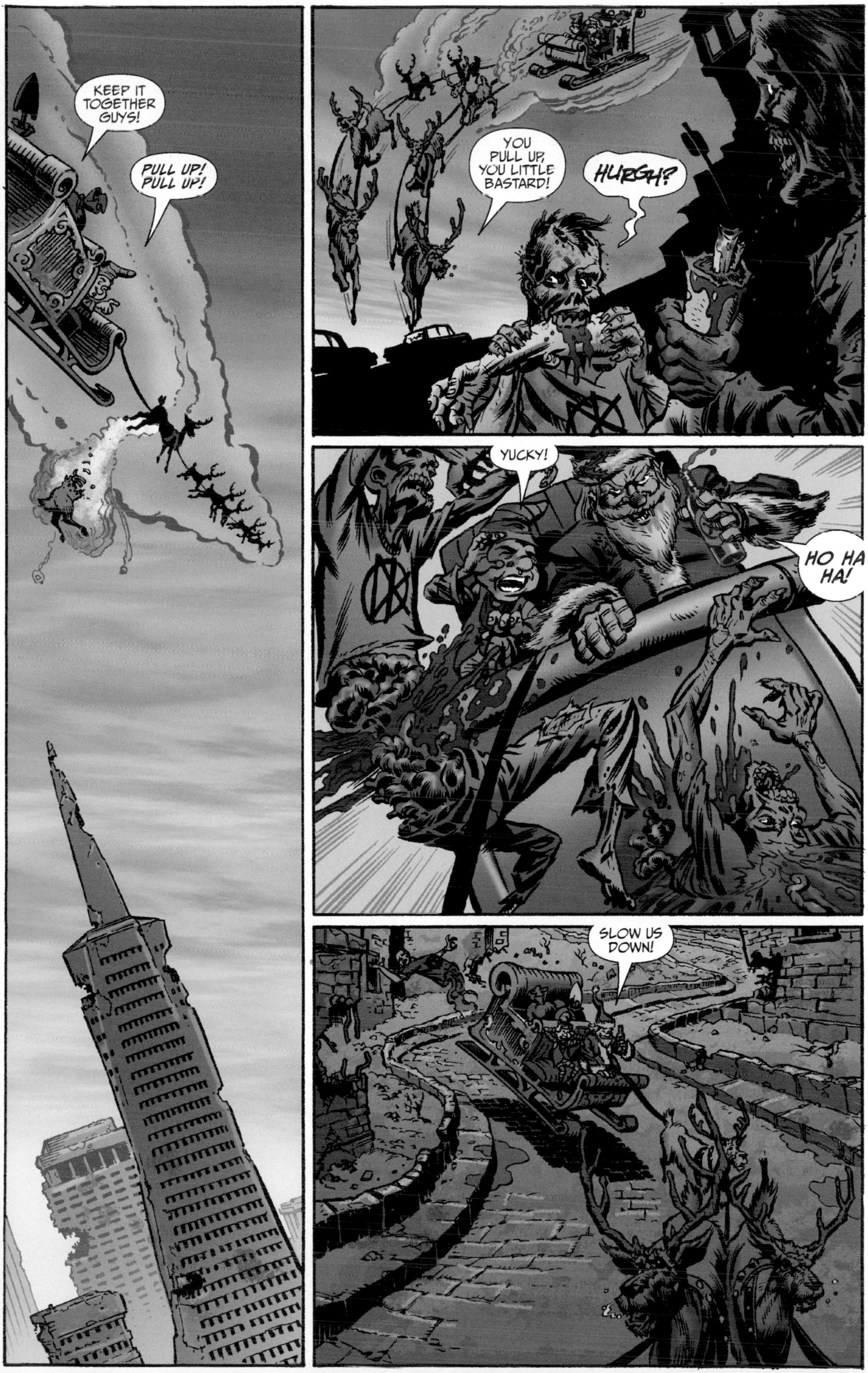
KEEP IT TOGETHER GUYS!
PULL UP! PULL UP!
YOU PULL UP, YOU LITTLE BASTARD!
HURGH?
YUCKY!
HO HA HA!
SLOW US DOWN!

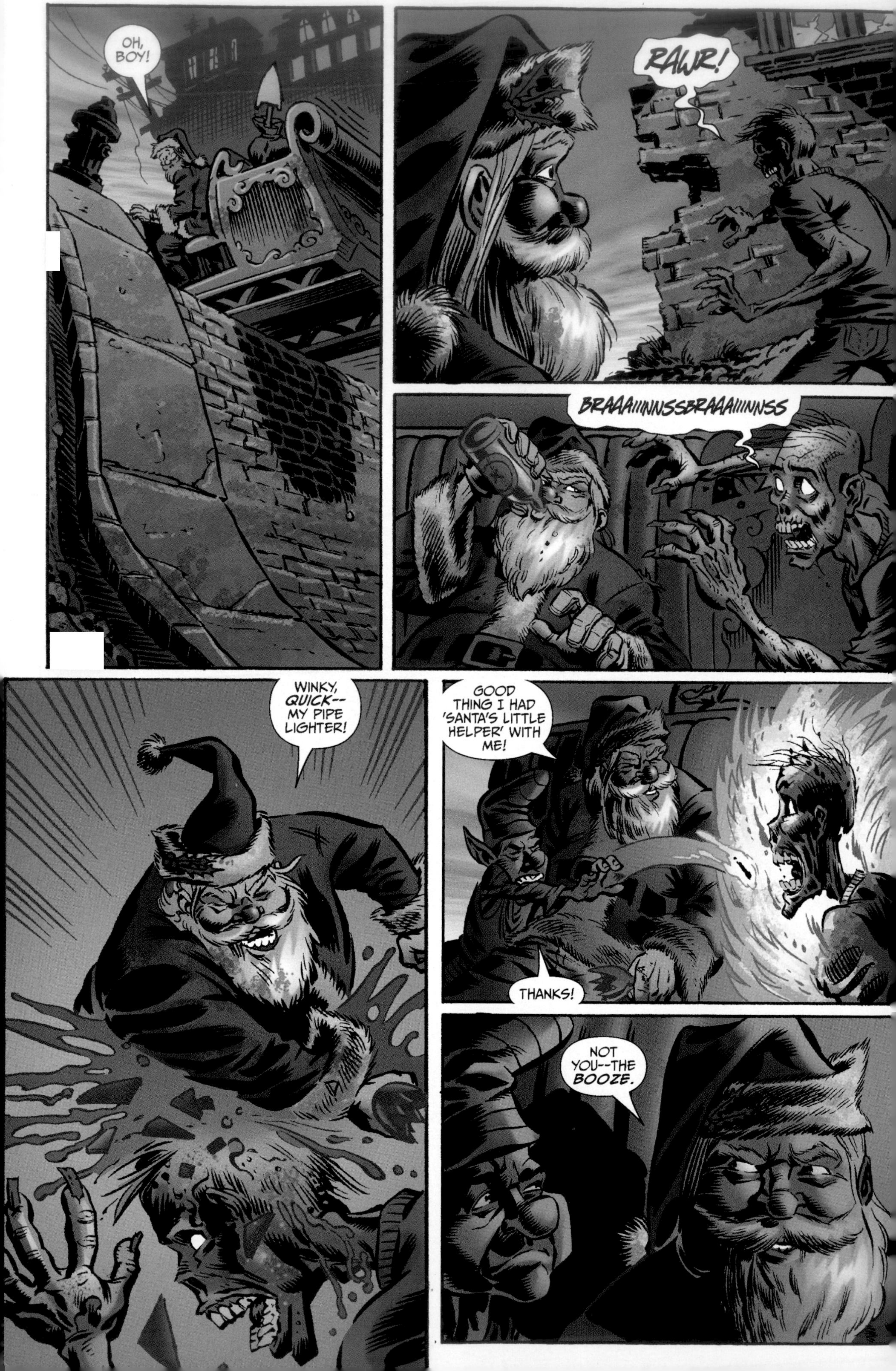
OH, BOY!
RAWR!
BRAAAIIINNSSBRAAAIIINNSS
WINKY, QUICK-- MY PIPE LIGHTER!
GOOD THING I HAD 'SANTA'S LITTLE HELPER' WITH ME!
THANKS!
NOT YOU--THE BOOZE.

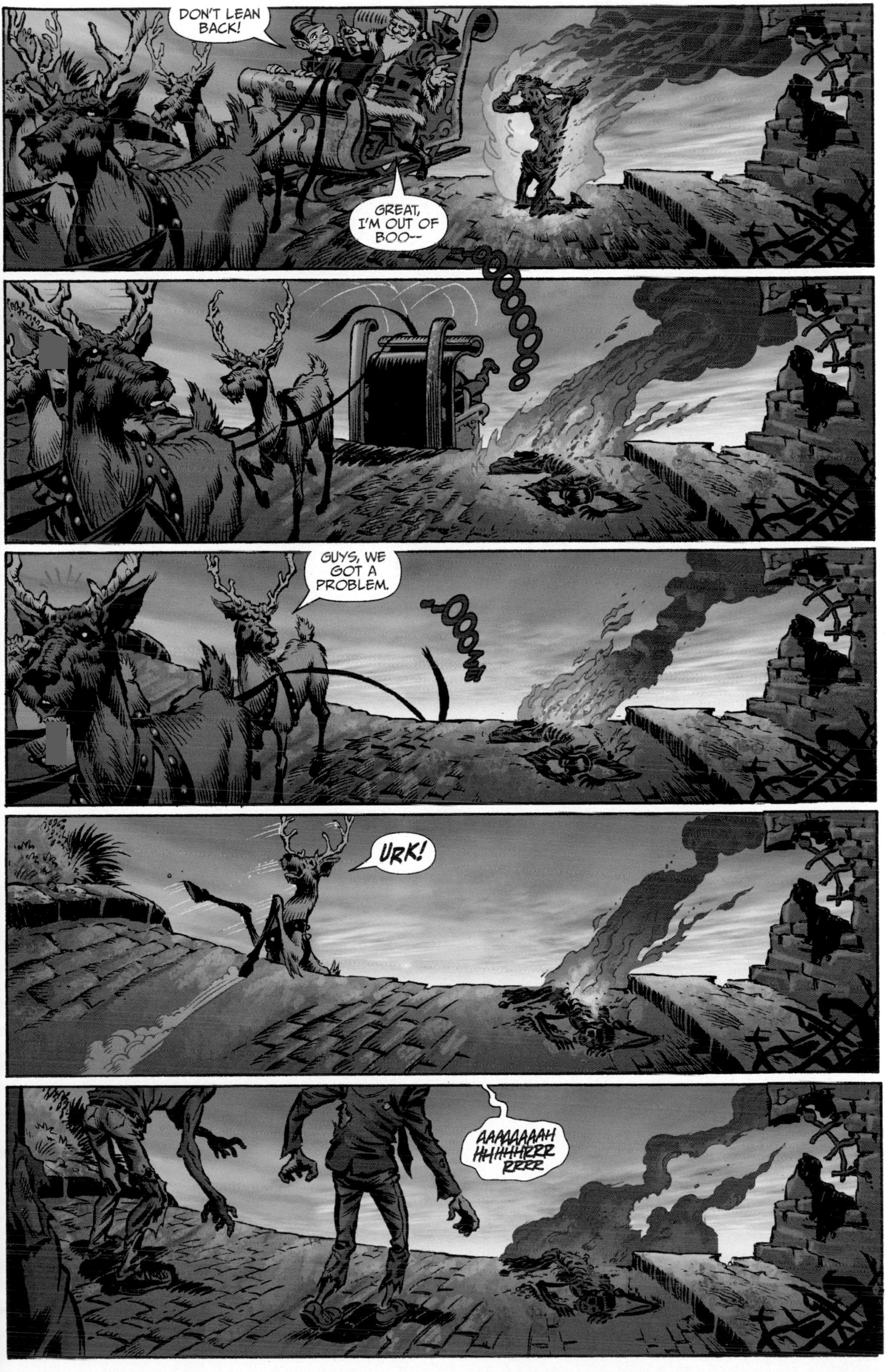
DON'T LEAN BACK!
GREAT, I'M OUT OF BOO--
GUYS, WE GOT A PROBLEM.
--OOOM!!
URK!
AAAAAAAAH HHHHHHRRR RRRR

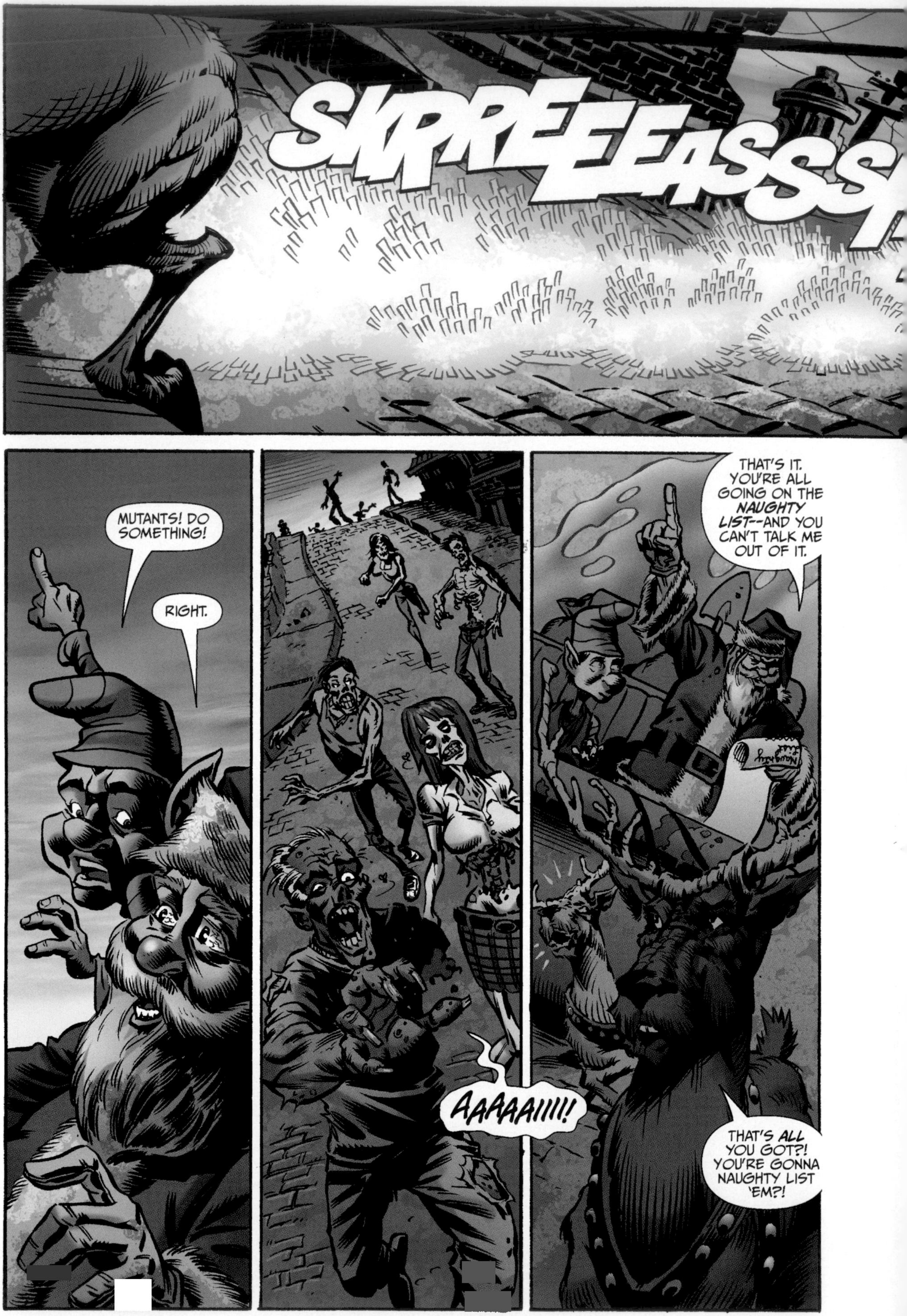
SKREEEASSS
MUTANTS! DO SOMETHING!
RIGHT.
AAAAIIIII!
THAT'S IT. YOU'RE ALL GOING ON THE *NAUGHTY LIST*--AND YOU CAN'T TALK ME OUT OF IT.
THAT'S *ALL* YOU GOT?! YOU'RE GONNA NAUGHTY LIST 'EM?!

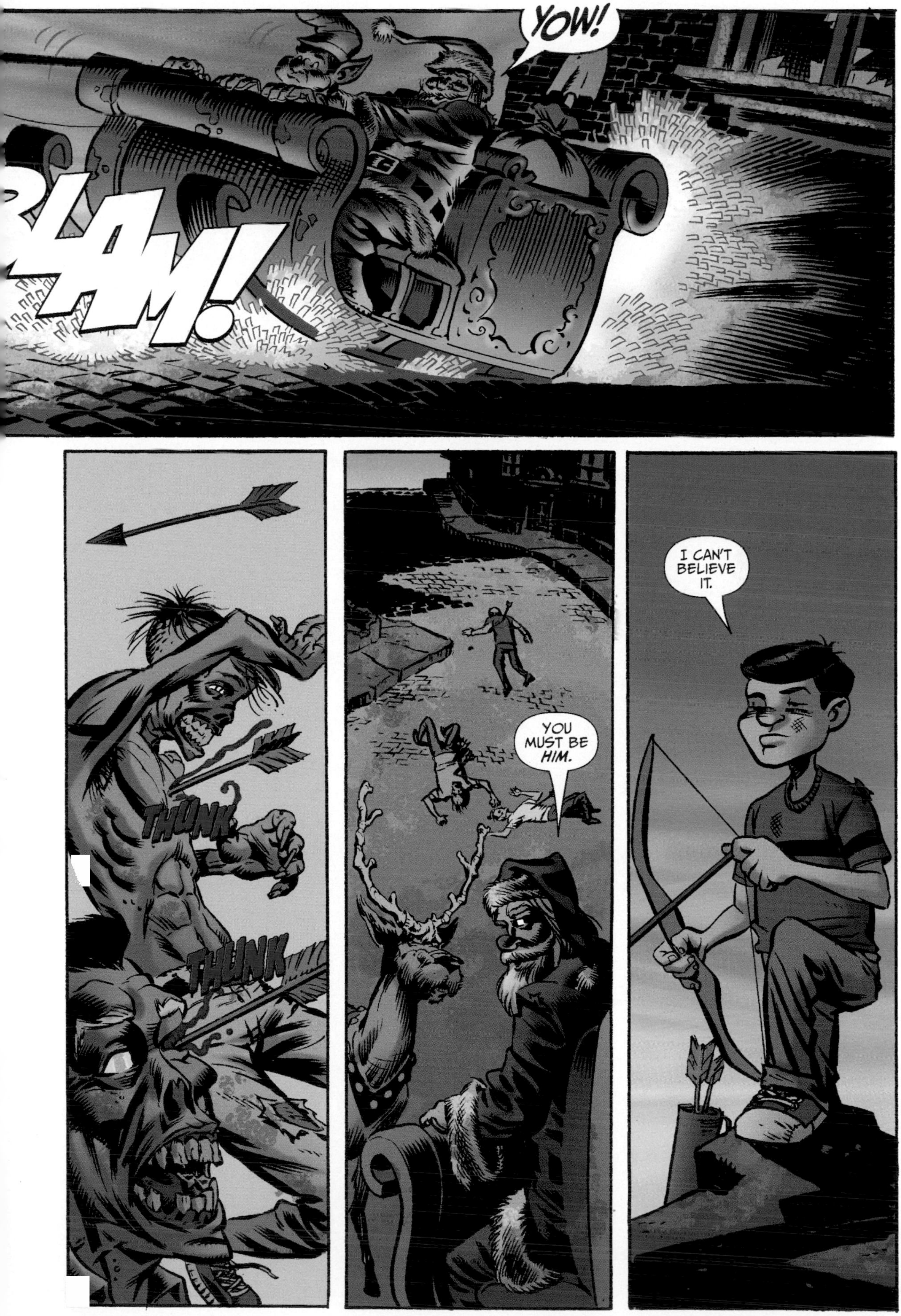
YOW!
BLAM!
THUNK
THUNK
YOU MUST BE HIM.
I CAN'T BELIEVE IT.

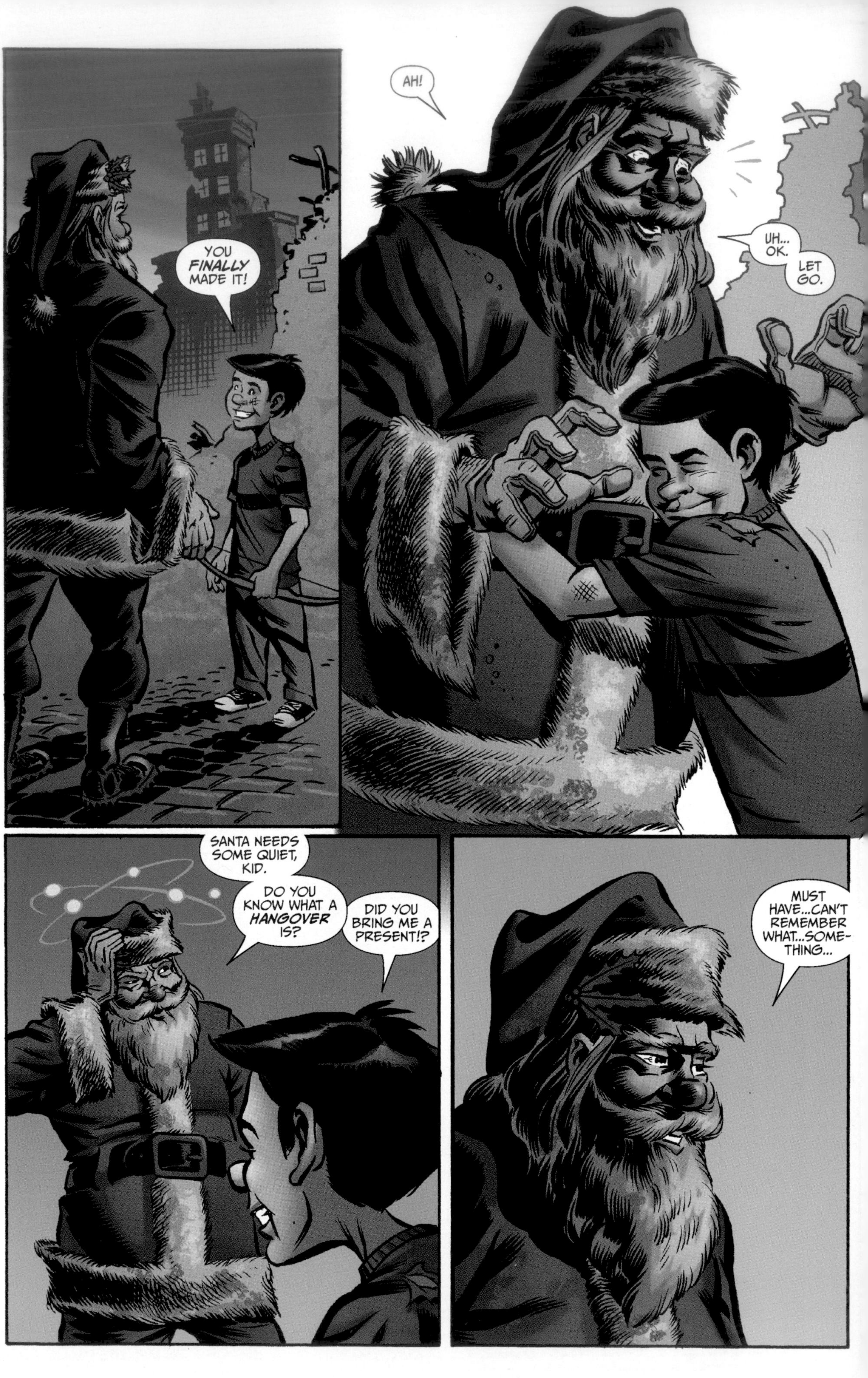
YOU FINALLY MADE IT!
AH!
UH... OK. LET GO.
SANTA NEEDS SOME QUIET, KID.
DO YOU KNOW WHAT A HANGOVER IS?
DID YOU BRING ME A PRESENT!?
MUST HAVE...CAN'T REMEMBER WHAT...SOME-THING...

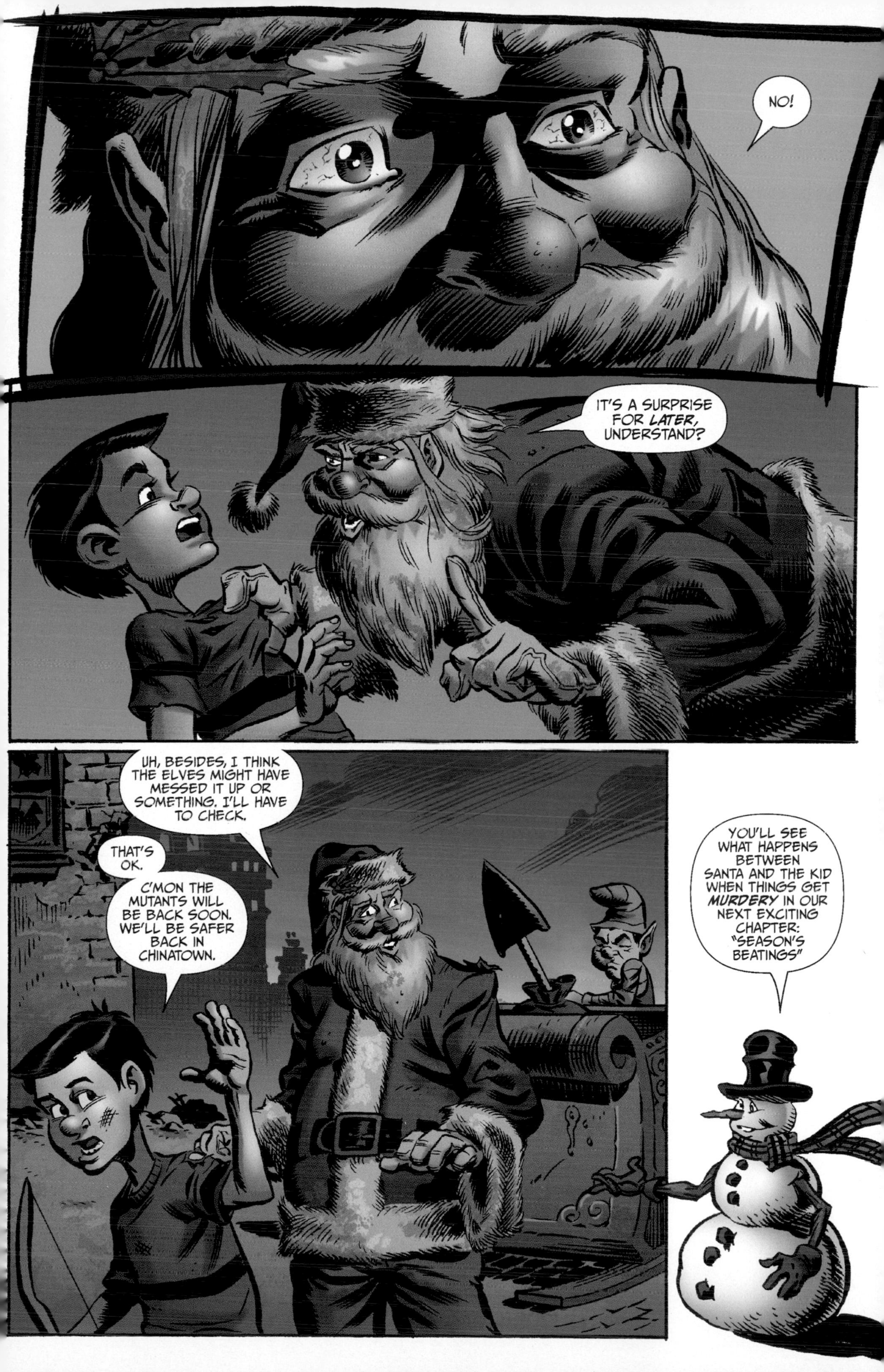
NO!
IT'S A SURPRISE FOR LATER, UNDERSTAND?
UH, BESIDES, I THINK THE ELVES MIGHT HAVE MESSED IT UP OR SOMETHING. I'LL HAVE TO CHECK.
THAT'S OK.
C'MON THE MUTANTS WILL BE BACK SOON. WE'LL BE SAFER BACK IN CHINATOWN.
YOU'LL SEE WHAT HAPPENS BETWEEN SANTA AND THE KID WHEN THINGS GET MURDERY IN OUR NEXT EXCITING CHAPTER: "SEASON'S BEATINGS"

Chapter 3

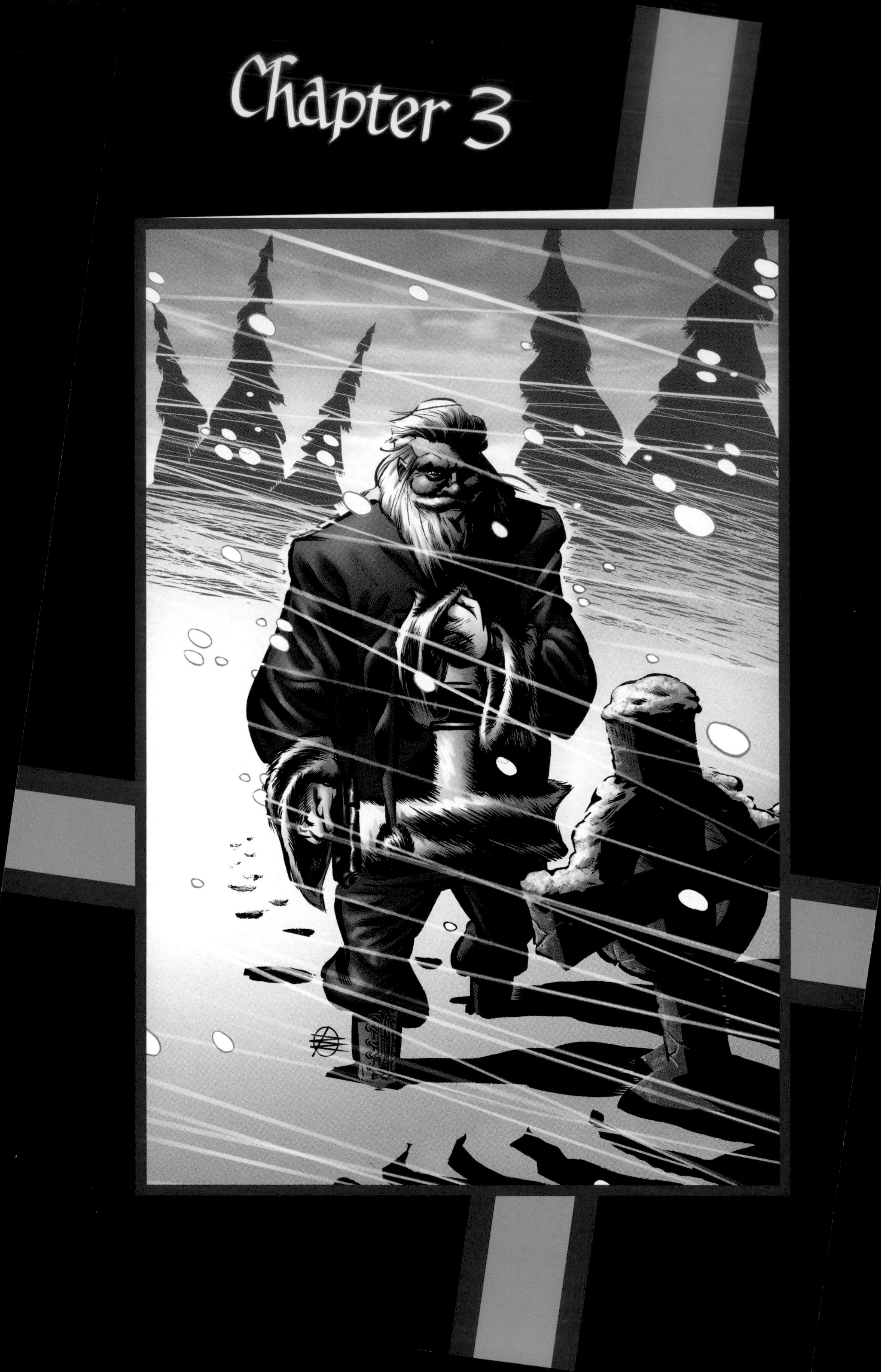

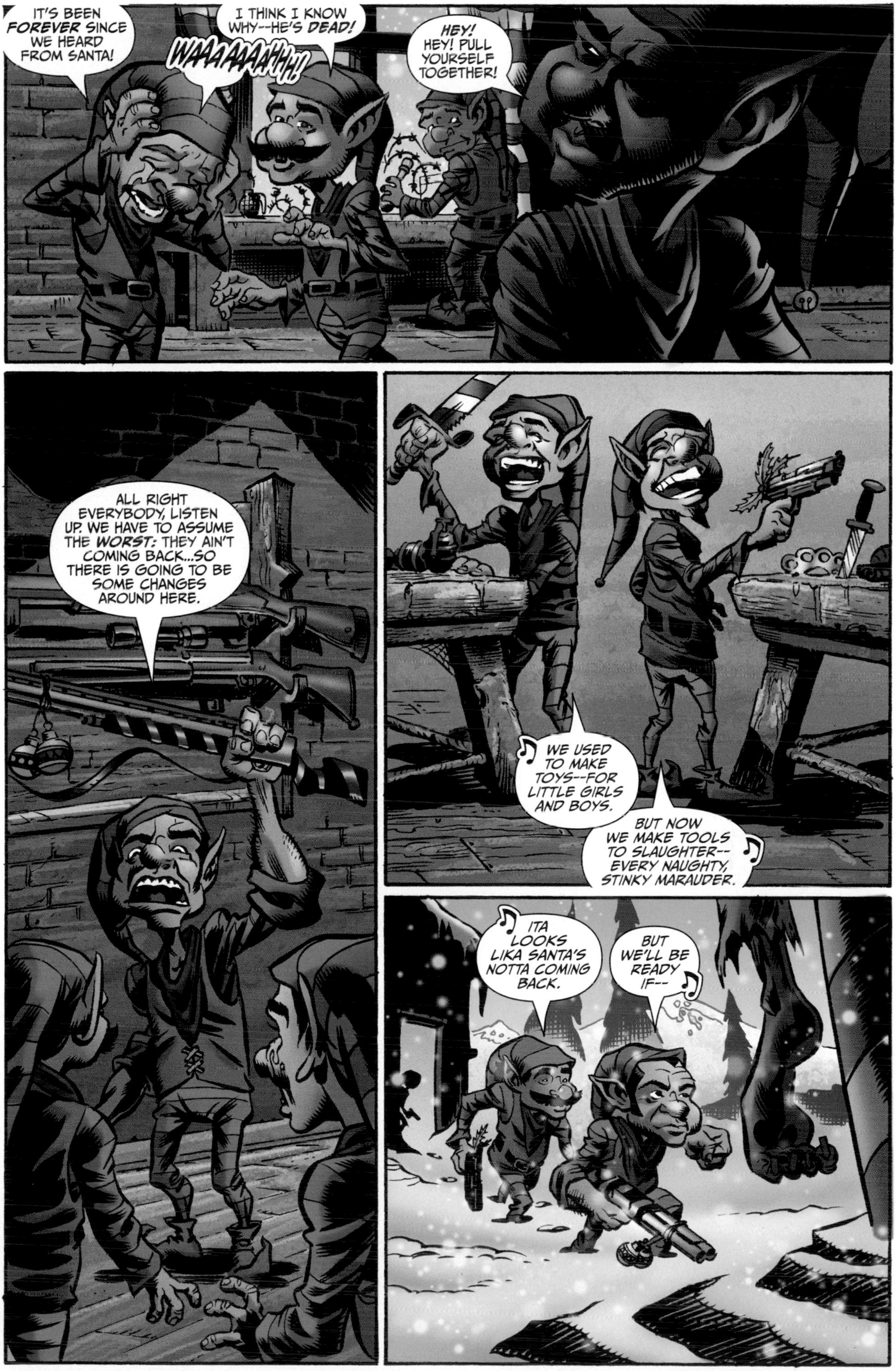

IT'S BEEN FOREVER SINCE WE HEARD FROM SANTA!
WAAAAAAAHHH!
I THINK I KNOW WHY--HE'S DEAD!
HEY! HEY! PULL YOURSELF TOGETHER!
ALL RIGHT EVERYBODY, LISTEN UP. WE HAVE TO ASSUME THE WORST: THEY AIN'T COMING BACK...SO THERE IS GOING TO BE SOME CHANGES AROUND HERE.
WE USED TO MAKE TOYS--FOR LITTLE GIRLS AND BOYS.
BUT NOW WE MAKE TOOLS TO SLAUGHTER-- EVERY NAUGHTY, STINKY MARAUDER.
ITA LOOKS LIKA SANTA'S NOTTA COMING BACK.
BUT WE'LL BE READY IF--

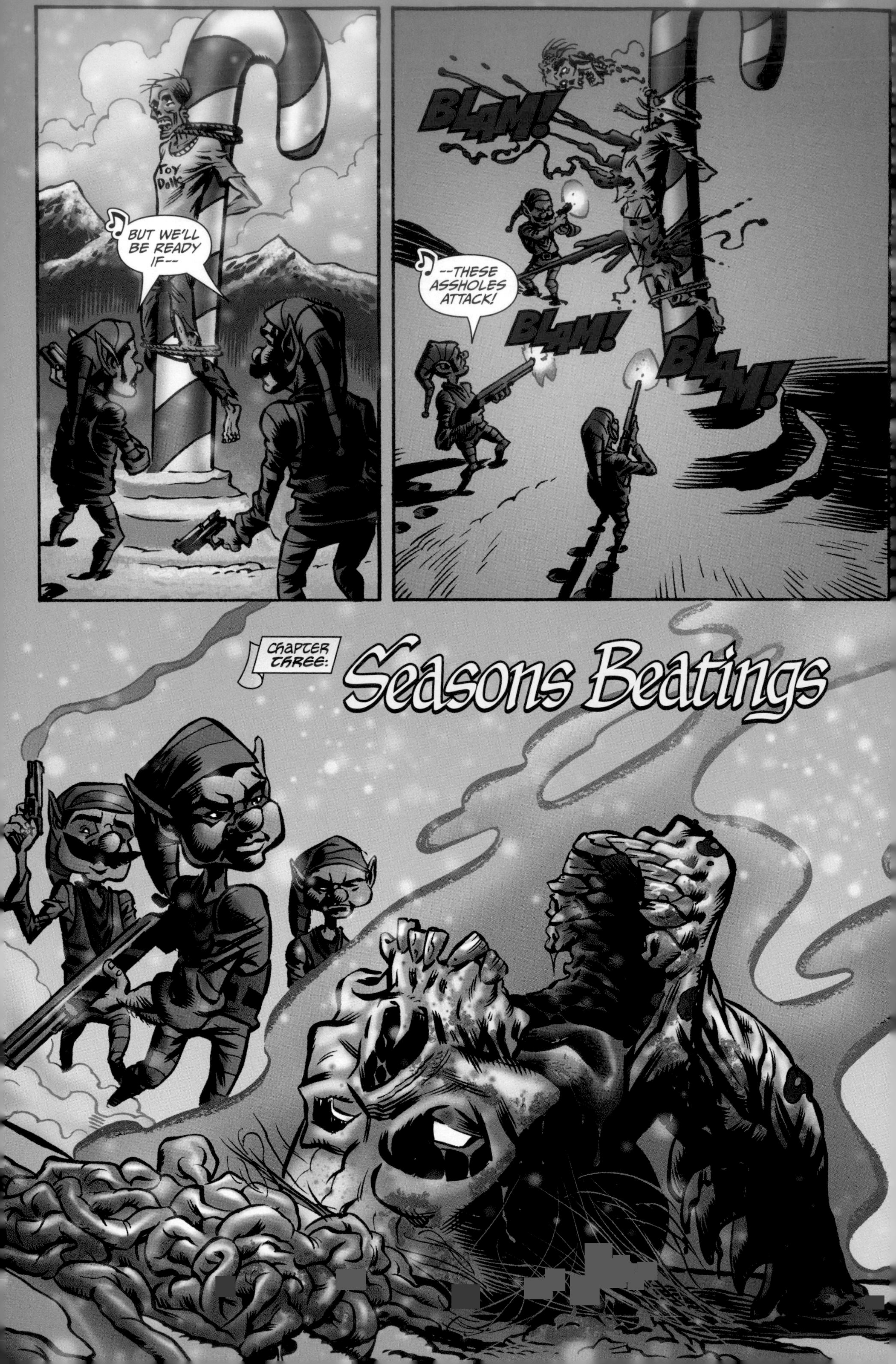
BUT WE'LL BE READY IF--
BLAM!
--THESE ASSHOLES ATTACK!
BLAM!
BLAM!
CHAPTER THREE:
Seasons Beatings

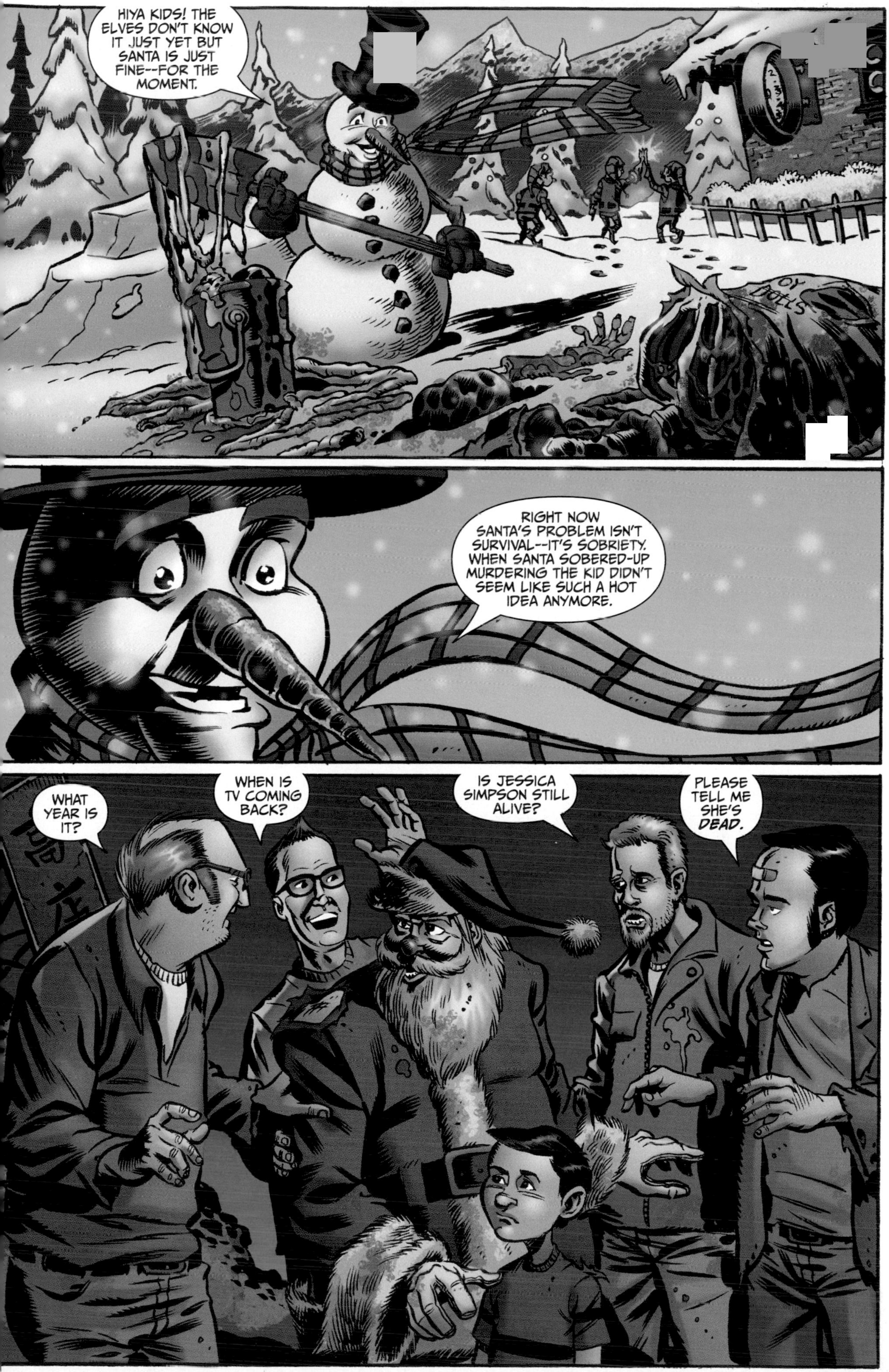
HIYA KIDS! THE ELVES DON'T KNOW IT JUST YET BUT SANTA IS JUST FINE--FOR THE MOMENT.
RIGHT NOW SANTA'S PROBLEM ISN'T SURVIVAL--IT'S SOBRIETY. WHEN SANTA SOBERED-UP MURDERING THE KID DIDN'T SEEM LIKE SUCH A HOT IDEA ANYMORE.
WHAT YEAR IS IT?
WHEN IS TV COMING BACK?
IS JESSICA SIMPSON STILL ALIVE?
PLEASE TELL ME SHE'S *DEAD*.

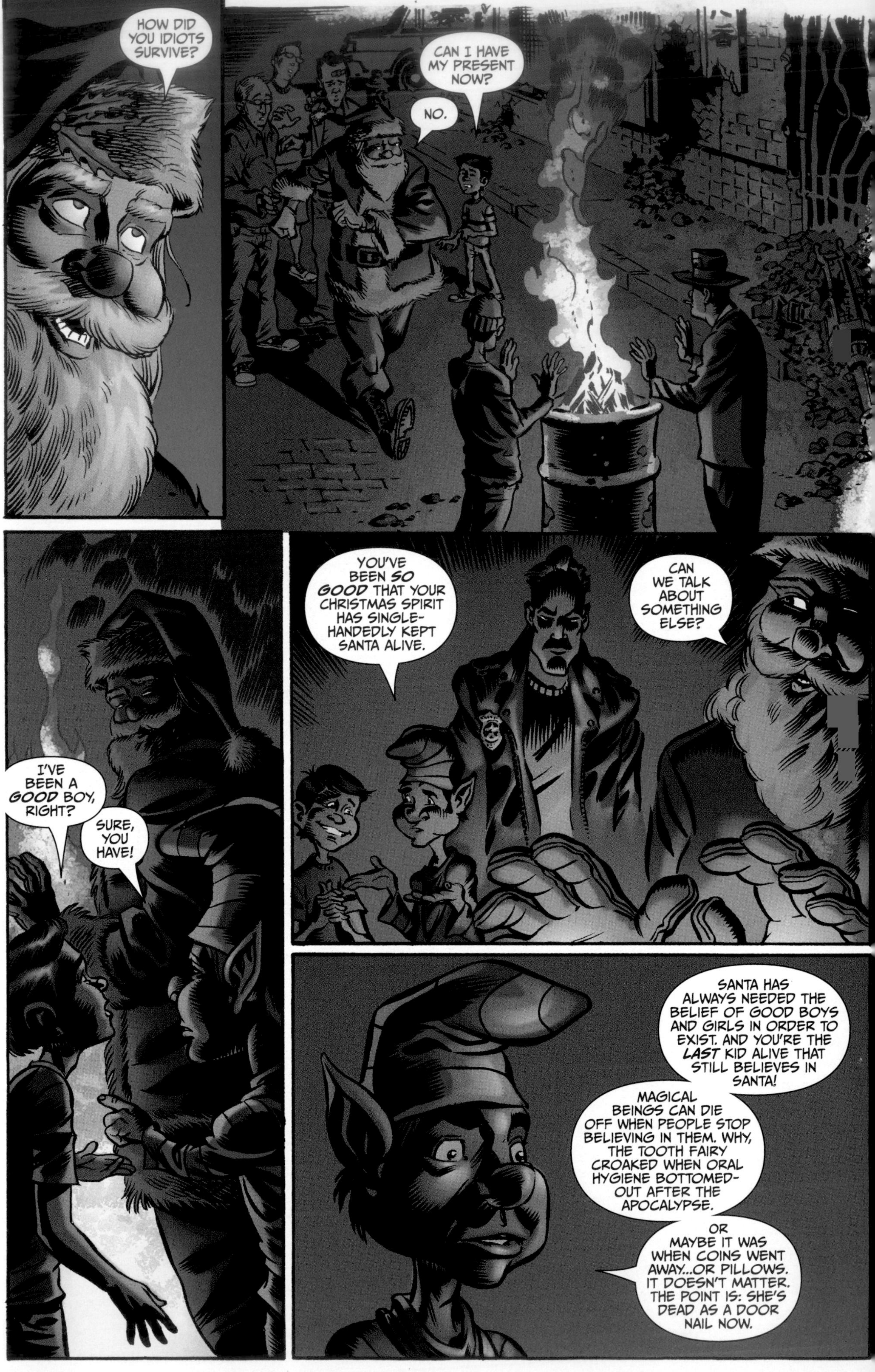
HOW DID YOU IDIOTS SURVIVE?
CAN I HAVE MY PRESENT NOW?
NO.
I'VE BEEN A *GOOD* BOY, RIGHT?
SURE, YOU HAVE!
YOU'VE BEEN *SO GOOD* THAT YOUR CHRISTMAS SPIRIT HAS SINGLE-HANDEDLY KEPT SANTA ALIVE.
CAN WE TALK ABOUT SOMETHING ELSE?
SANTA HAS ALWAYS NEEDED THE BELIEF OF GOOD BOYS AND GIRLS IN ORDER TO EXIST. AND YOU'RE THE *LAST* KID ALIVE THAT STILL BELIEVES IN SANTA!
MAGICAL BEINGS CAN DIE OFF WHEN PEOPLE STOP BELIEVING IN THEM. WHY, THE TOOTH FAIRY CROAKED WHEN ORAL HYGIENE BOTTOMED-OUT AFTER THE APOCALYPSE.
OR MAYBE IT WAS WHEN COINS WENT AWAY...OR PILLOWS. IT DOESN'T MATTER. THE POINT IS: SHE'S DEAD AS A DOOR NAIL NOW.

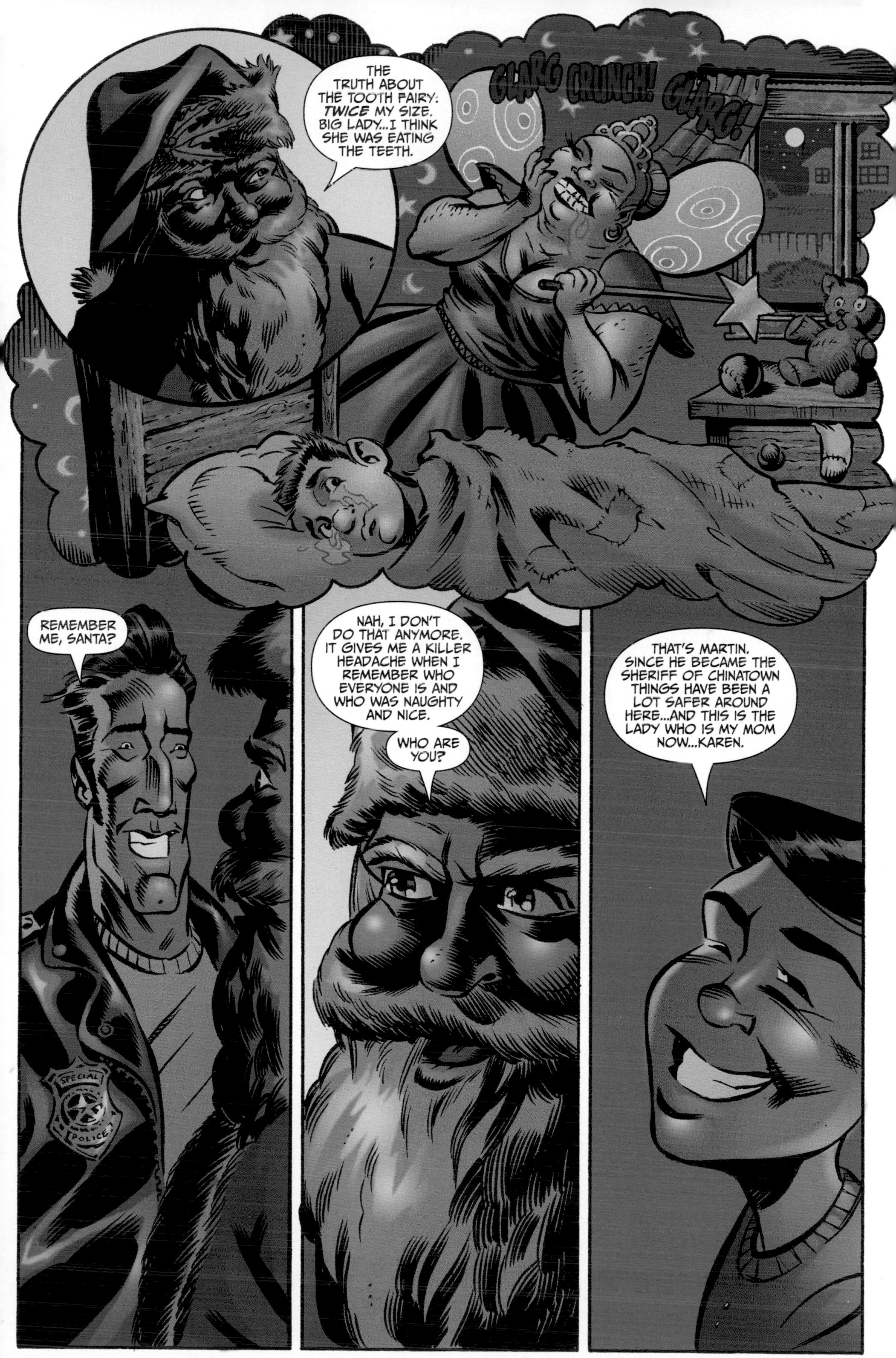
THE TRUTH ABOUT THE TOOTH FAIRY: *TWICE* MY SIZE. BIG LADY...I THINK SHE WAS EATING THE TEETH.
CLARG CRUNCH! CLARG!
REMEMBER ME, SANTA?
NAH, I DON'T DO THAT ANYMORE. IT GIVES ME A KILLER HEADACHE WHEN I REMEMBER WHO EVERYONE IS AND WHO WAS NAUGHTY AND NICE.
WHO ARE YOU?
THAT'S MARTIN. SINCE HE BECAME THE SHERIFF OF CHINATOWN THINGS HAVE BEEN A LOT SAFER AROUND HERE...AND THIS IS THE LADY WHO IS MY MOM NOW...KAREN.
SPECIAL POLICE

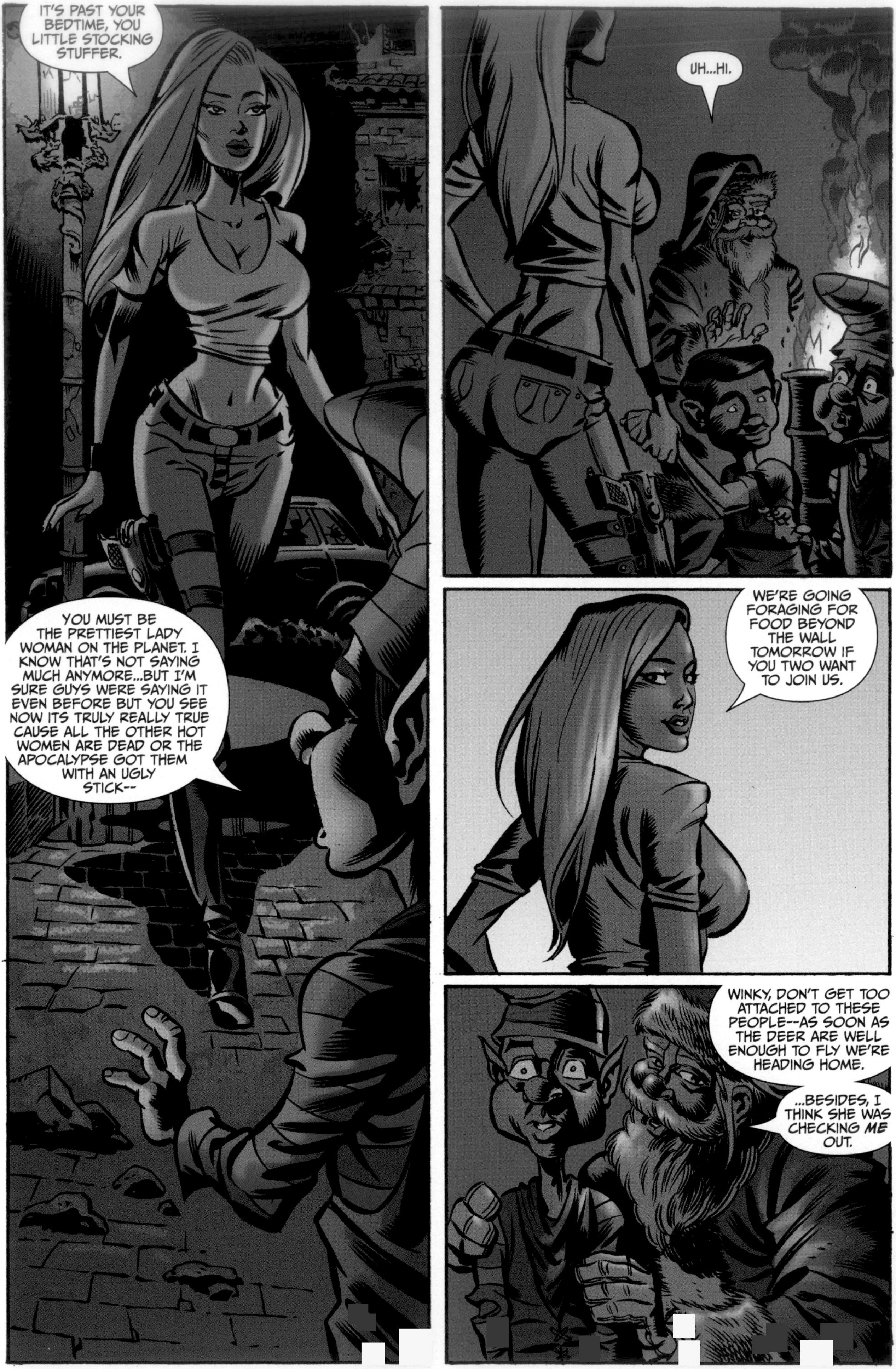
IT'S PAST YOUR BEDTIME, YOU LITTLE STOCKING STUFFER.
YOU MUST BE THE PRETTIEST LADY WOMAN ON THE PLANET. I KNOW THAT'S NOT SAYING MUCH ANYMORE...BUT I'M SURE GUYS WERE SAYING IT EVEN BEFORE BUT YOU SEE NOW ITS TRULY REALLY TRUE CAUSE ALL THE OTHER HOT WOMEN ARE DEAD OR THE APOCALYPSE GOT THEM WITH AN UGLY STICK--
UH...HI.
WE'RE GOING FORAGING FOR FOOD BEYOND THE WALL TOMORROW IF YOU TWO WANT TO JOIN US.
WINKY, DON'T GET TOO ATTACHED TO THESE PEOPLE--AS SOON AS THE DEER ARE WELL ENOUGH TO FLY WE'RE HEADING HOME.
...BESIDES, I THINK SHE WAS CHECKING *ME* OUT.

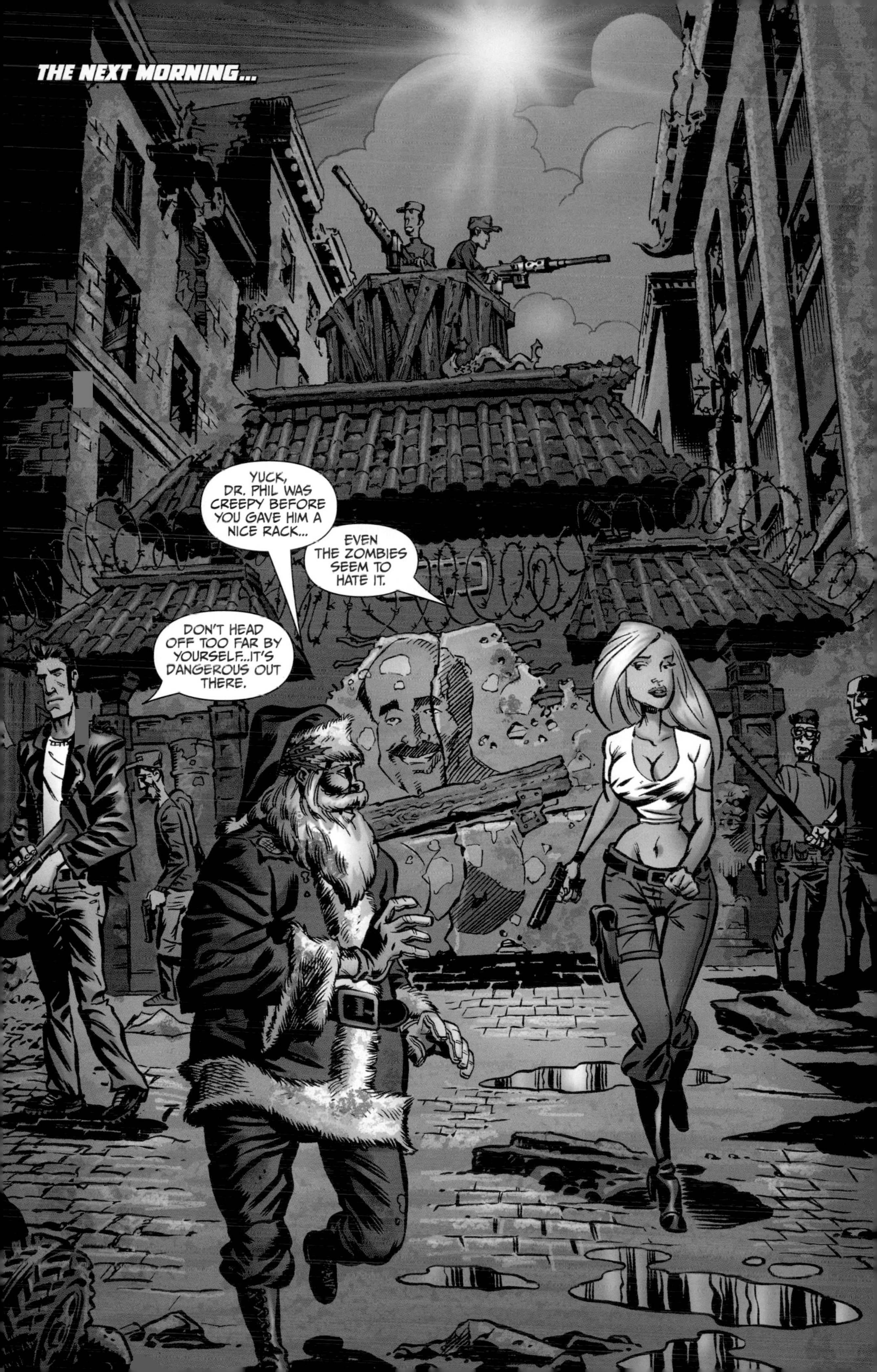
THE NEXT MORNING...
YUCK, DR. PHIL WAS CREEPY BEFORE YOU GAVE HIM A NICE RACK...
EVEN THE ZOMBIES SEEM TO HATE IT.
DON'T HEAD OFF TOO FAR BY YOURSELF...IT'S DANGEROUS OUT THERE.

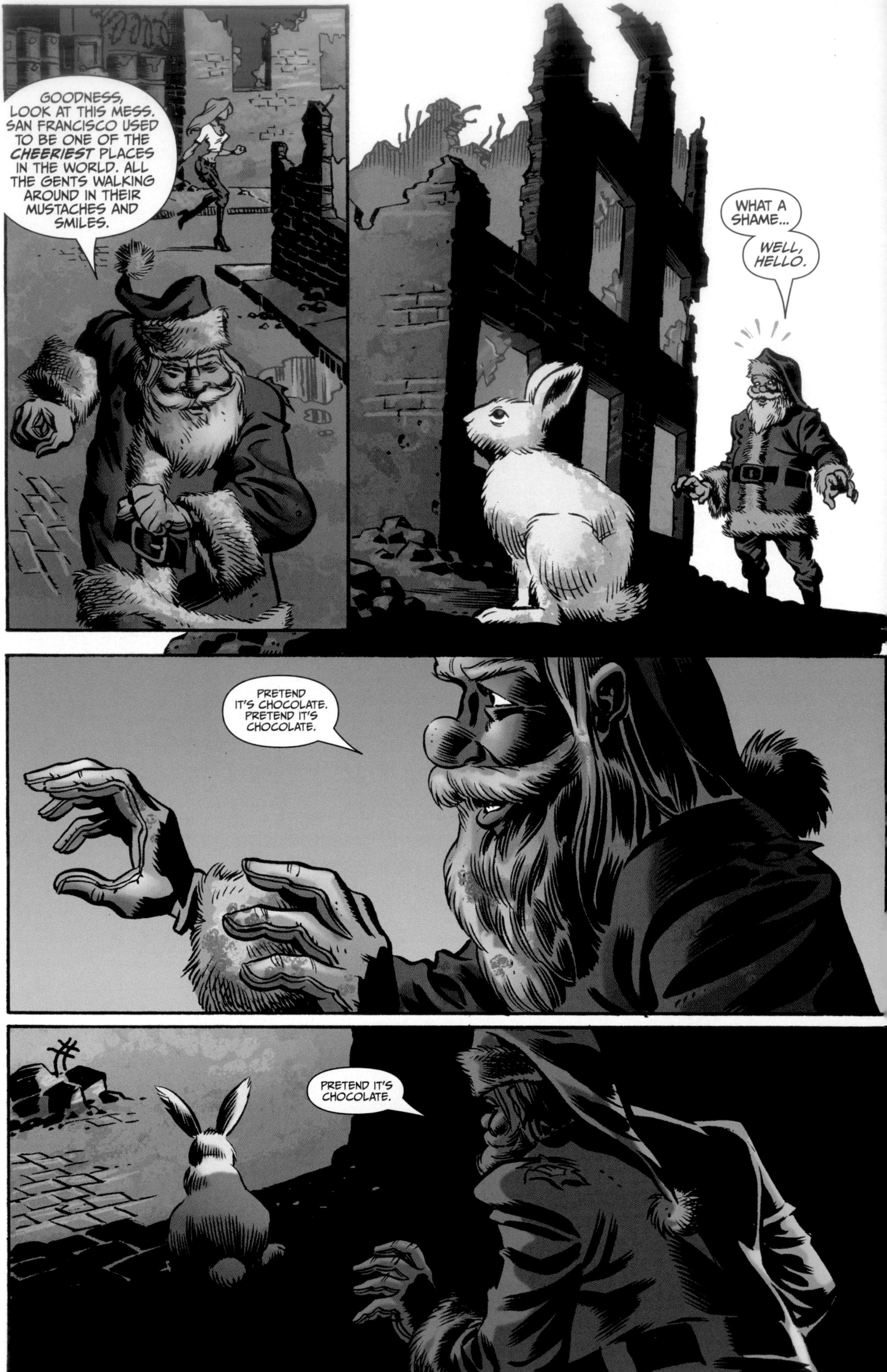
GOODNESS, LOOK AT THIS MESS. SAN FRANCISCO USED TO BE ONE OF THE CHEERIEST PLACES IN THE WORLD. ALL THE GENTS WALKING AROUND IN THEIR MUSTACHES AND SMILES.
WHAT A SHAME...
WELL, HELLO.
PRETEND IT'S CHOCOLATE. PRETEND IT'S CHOCOLATE.
PRETEND IT'S CHOCOLATE.

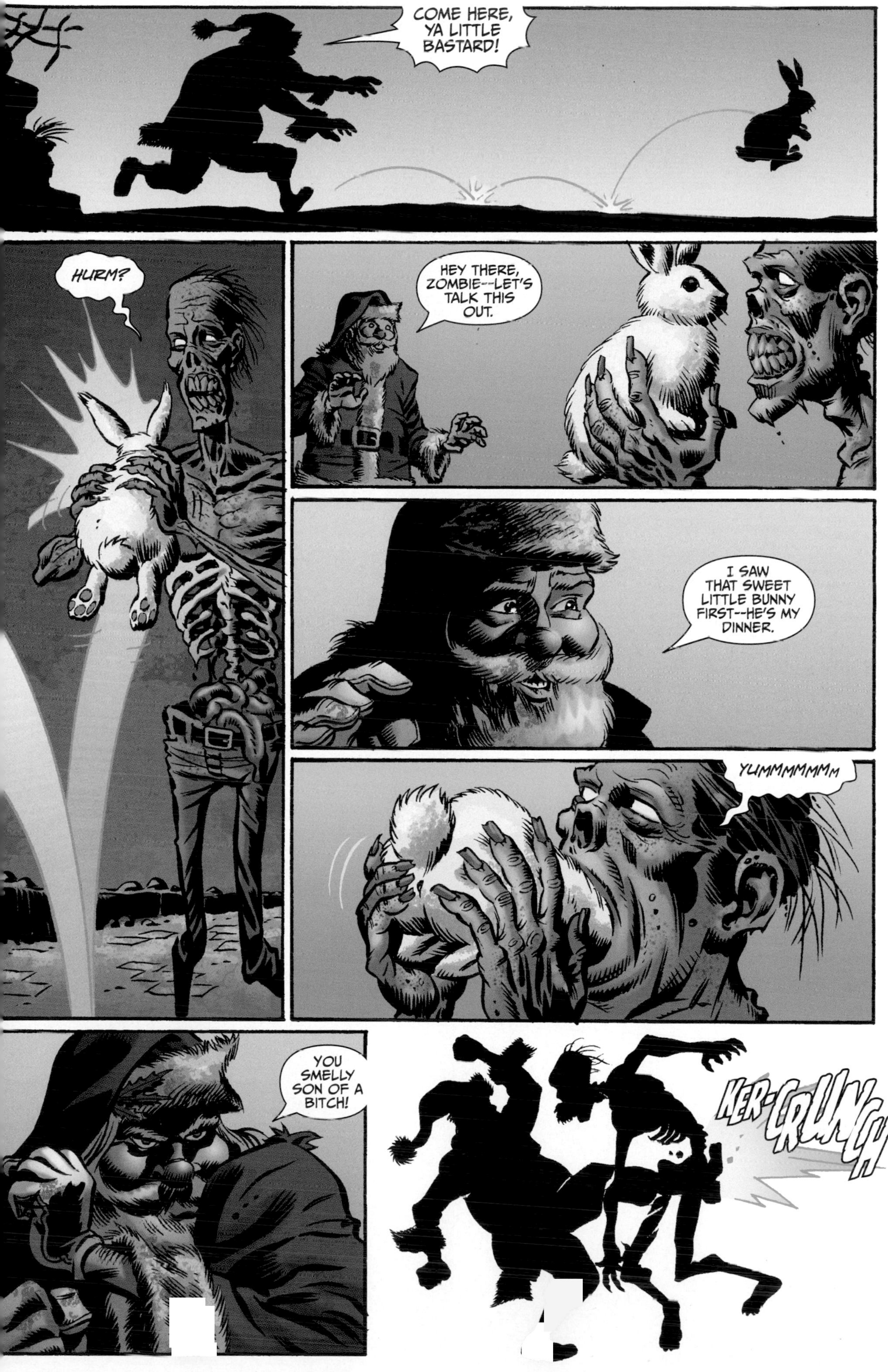
COME HERE, YA LITTLE BASTARD!
HURM?
HEY THERE, ZOMBIE--LET'S TALK THIS OUT.
I SAW THAT SWEET LITTLE BUNNY FIRST--HE'S MY DINNER.
YUMMMMMMM
YOU SMELLY SON OF A BITCH!
KER-CRUNCH

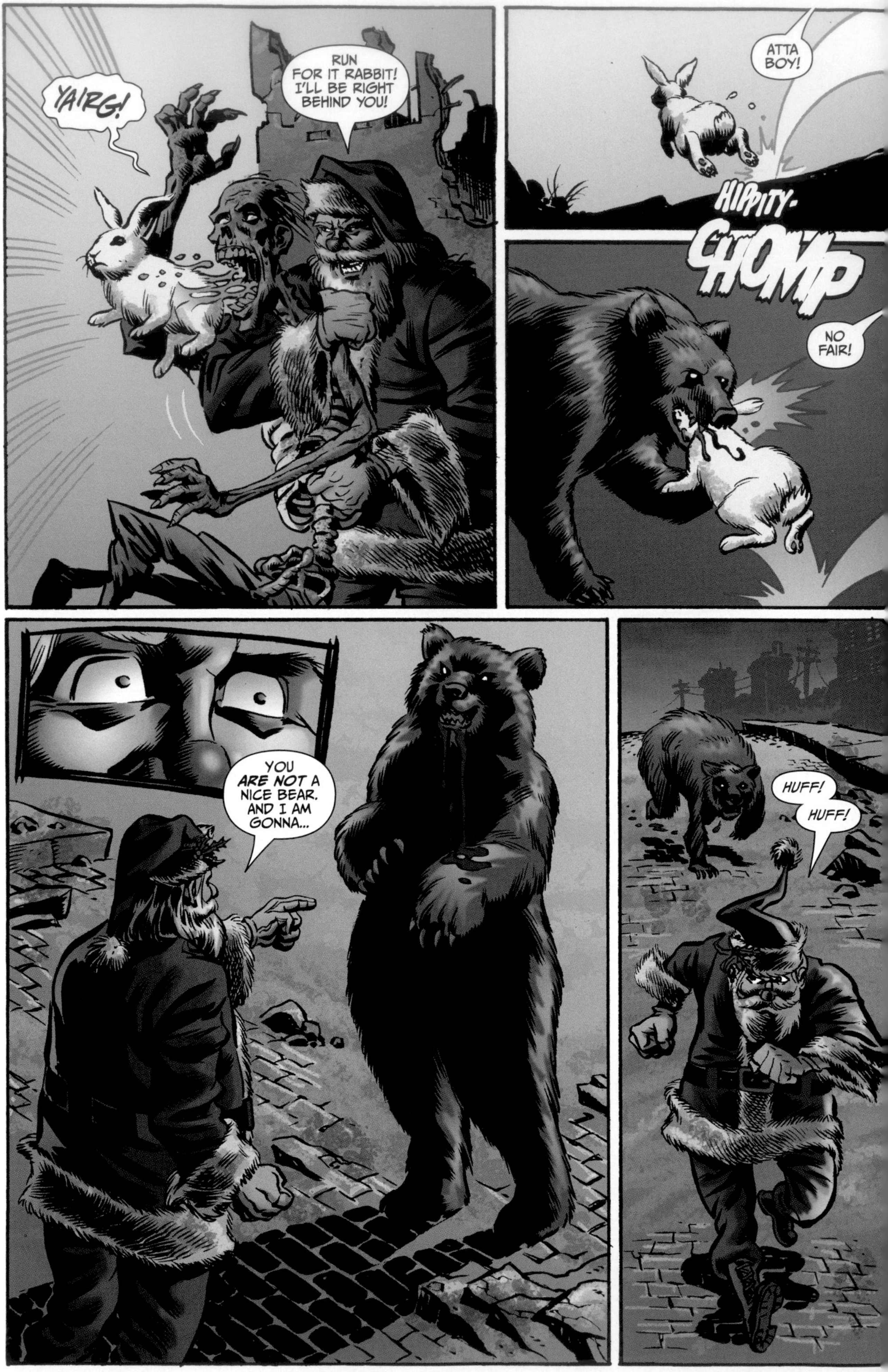
YAIRG!
RUN FOR IT RABBIT! I'LL BE RIGHT BEHIND YOU!
ATTA BOY!
HIPPITY-
CHOMP
NO FAIR!
YOU ARE NOT A NICE BEAR. AND I AM GONNA...
HUFF!
HUFF!

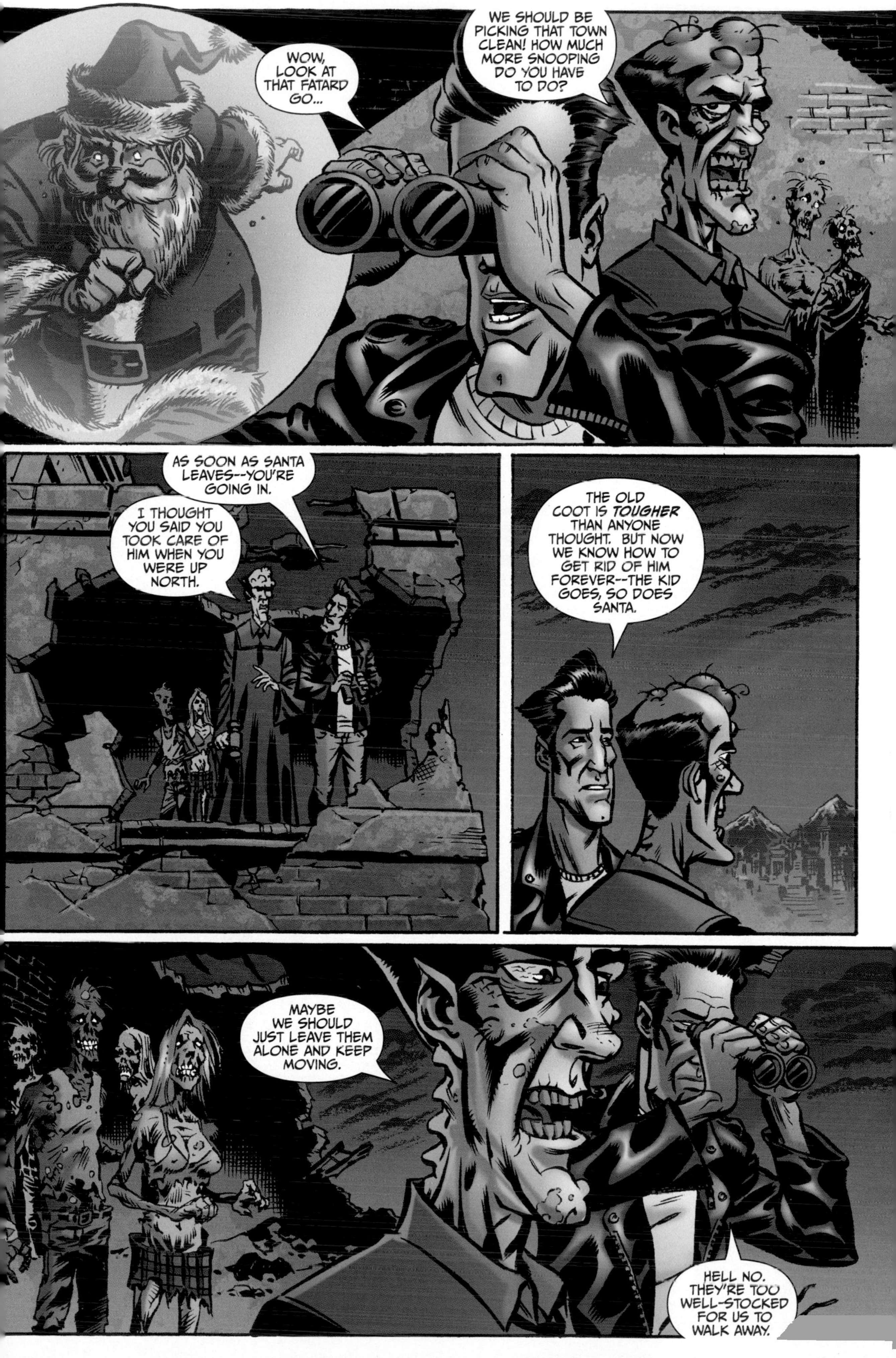
WOW, LOOK AT THAT FATARD GO...
WE SHOULD BE PICKING THAT TOWN CLEAN! HOW MUCH MORE SNOOPING DO YOU HAVE TO DO?
AS SOON AS SANTA LEAVES--YOU'RE GOING IN.
I THOUGHT YOU SAID YOU TOOK CARE OF HIM WHEN YOU WERE UP NORTH.
THE OLD COOT IS TOUGHER THAN ANYONE THOUGHT. BUT NOW WE KNOW HOW TO GET RID OF HIM FOREVER--THE KID GOES, SO DOES SANTA.
MAYBE WE SHOULD JUST LEAVE THEM ALONE AND KEEP MOVING.
HELL NO. THEY'RE TOO WELL-STOCKED FOR US TO WALK AWAY.

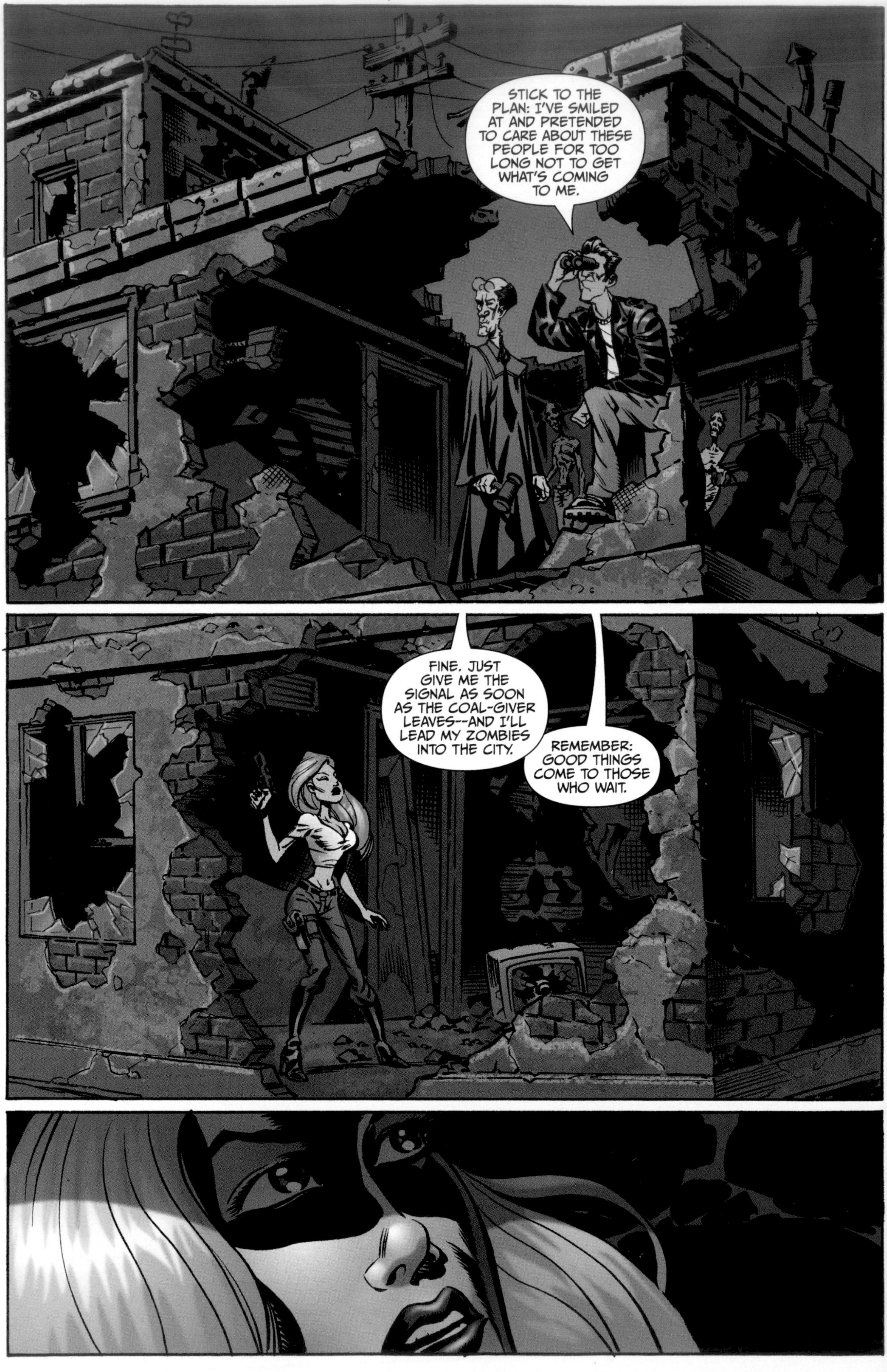
STICK TO THE PLAN: I'VE SMILED AT AND PRETENDED TO CARE ABOUT THESE PEOPLE FOR TOO LONG NOT TO GET WHAT'S COMING TO ME.
FINE. JUST GIVE ME THE SIGNAL AS SOON AS THE COAL-GIVER LEAVES--AND I'LL LEAD MY ZOMBIES INTO THE CITY.
REMEMBER: GOOD THINGS COME TO THOSE WHO WAIT.

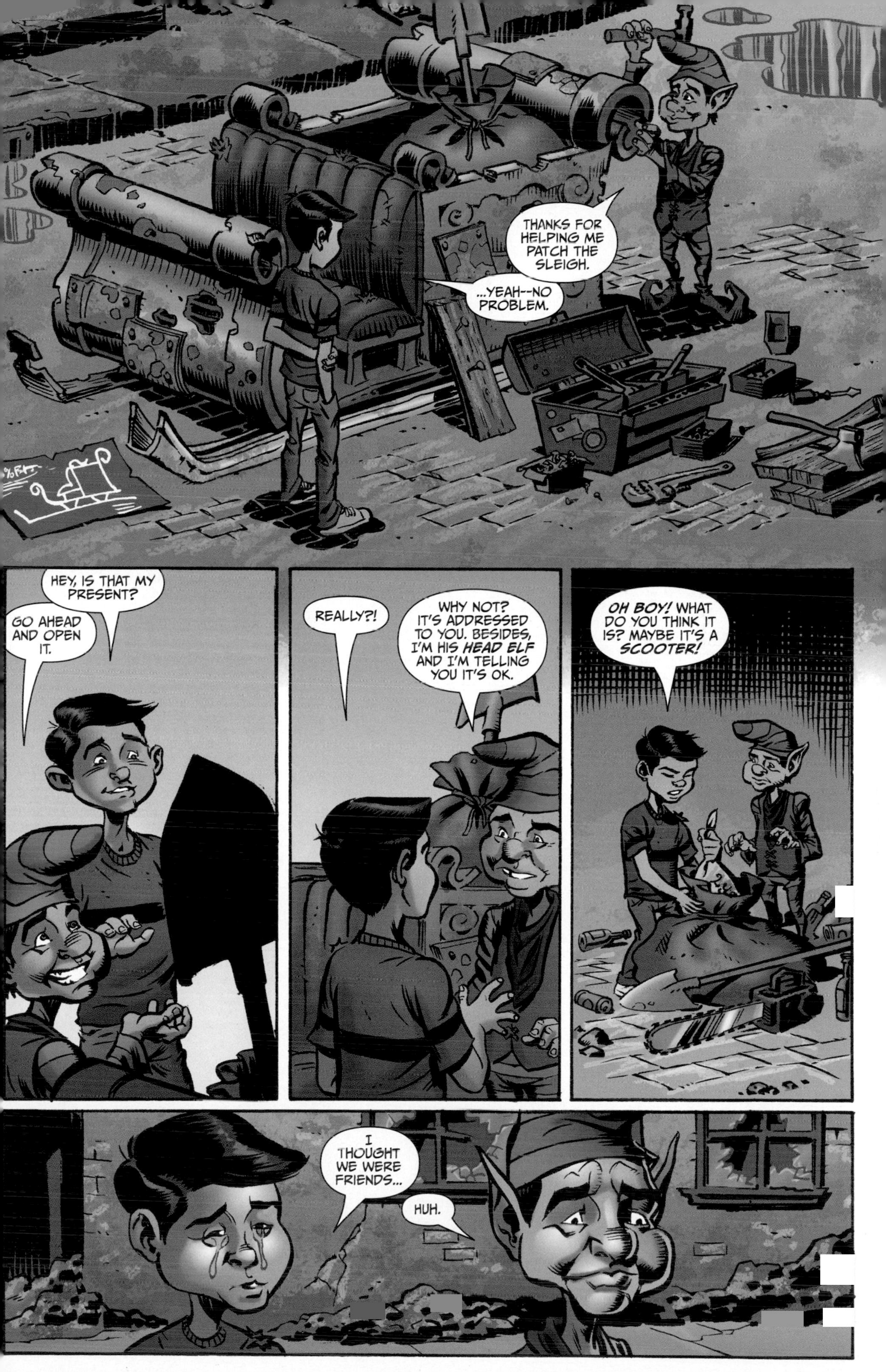
THANKS FOR HELPING ME PATCH THE SLEIGH.
...YEAH--NO PROBLEM.
HEY, IS THAT MY PRESENT?
GO AHEAD AND OPEN IT.
REALLY?!
WHY NOT? IT'S ADDRESSED TO YOU. BESIDES, I'M HIS **HEAD ELF** AND I'M TELLING YOU IT'S OK.
OH BOY! WHAT DO YOU THINK IT IS? MAYBE IT'S A ***SCOOTER!***
I THOUGHT WE WERE FRIENDS...
HUH.

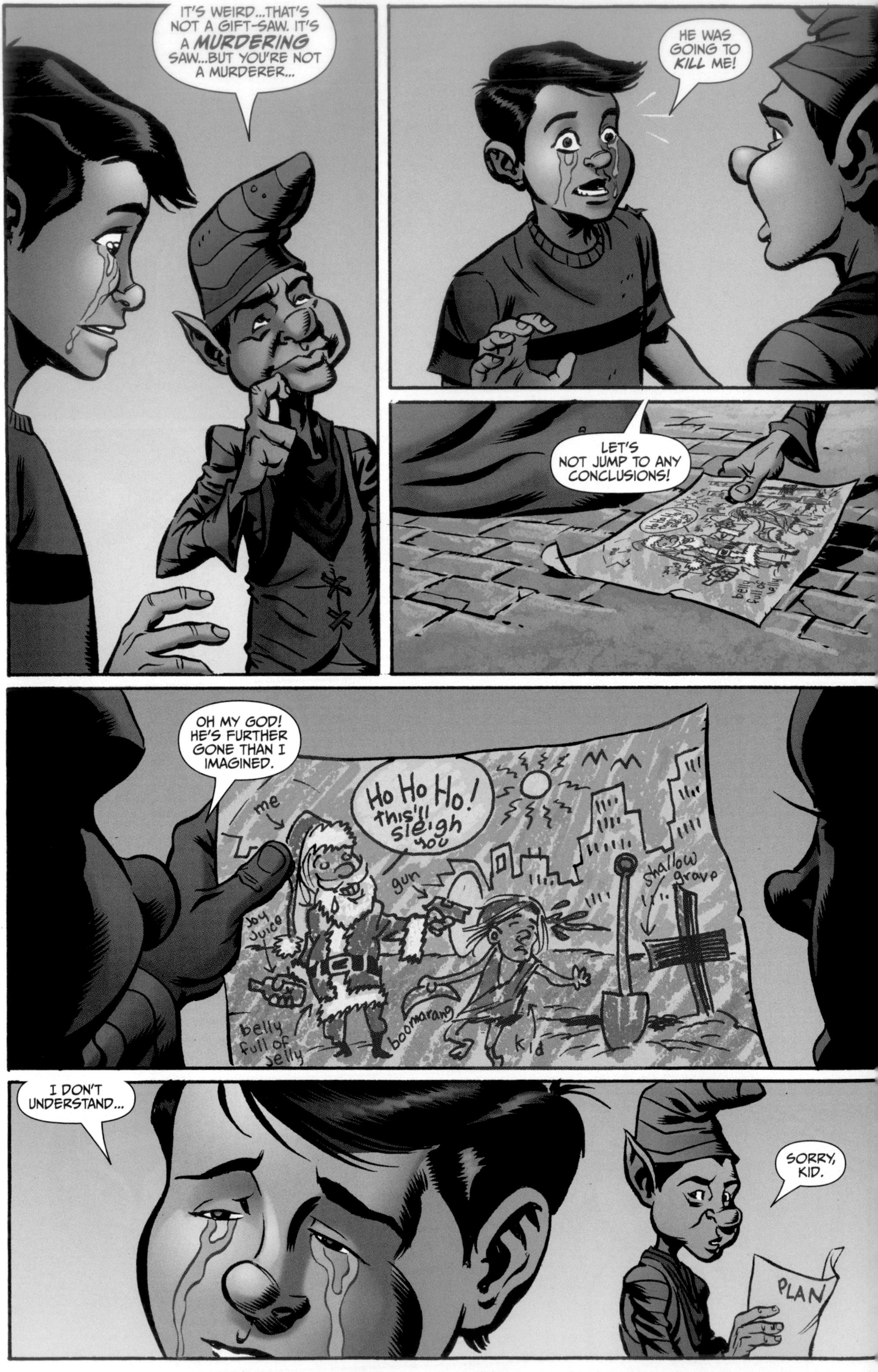
IT'S WEIRD...THAT'S NOT A GIFT-SAW. IT'S A MURDERING SAW...BUT YOU'RE NOT A MURDERER...
HE WAS GOING TO KILL ME!
LET'S NOT JUMP TO ANY CONCLUSIONS!
OH MY GOD! HE'S FURTHER GONE THAN I IMAGINED.
Ho Ho Ho! this'll sleigh you
me
gun
joy juice
belly full of jelly
boomarang
kid
shallow grave
I DON'T UNDERSTAND...
SORRY, KID.
PLAN

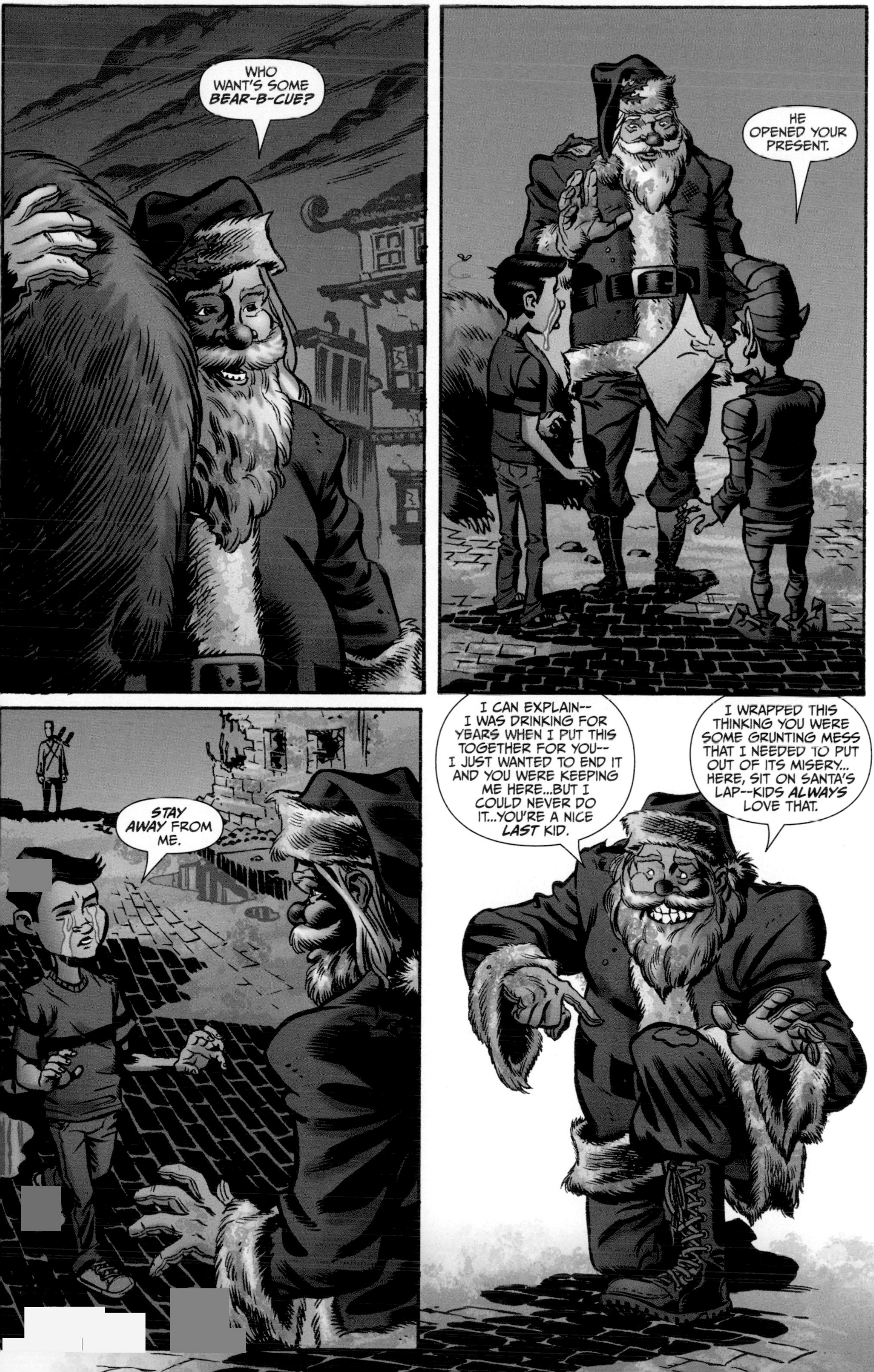
WHO WANT'S SOME BEAR-B-CUE?
HE OPENED YOUR PRESENT.
STAY AWAY FROM ME.
I CAN EXPLAIN-- I WAS DRINKING FOR YEARS WHEN I PUT THIS TOGETHER FOR YOU-- I JUST WANTED TO END IT AND YOU WERE KEEPING ME HERE...BUT I COULD NEVER DO IT...YOU'RE A NICE LAST KID.
I WRAPPED THIS THINKING YOU WERE SOME GRUNTING MESS THAT I NEEDED TO PUT OUT OF ITS MISERY... HERE, SIT ON SANTA'S LAP--KIDS ALWAYS LOVE THAT.

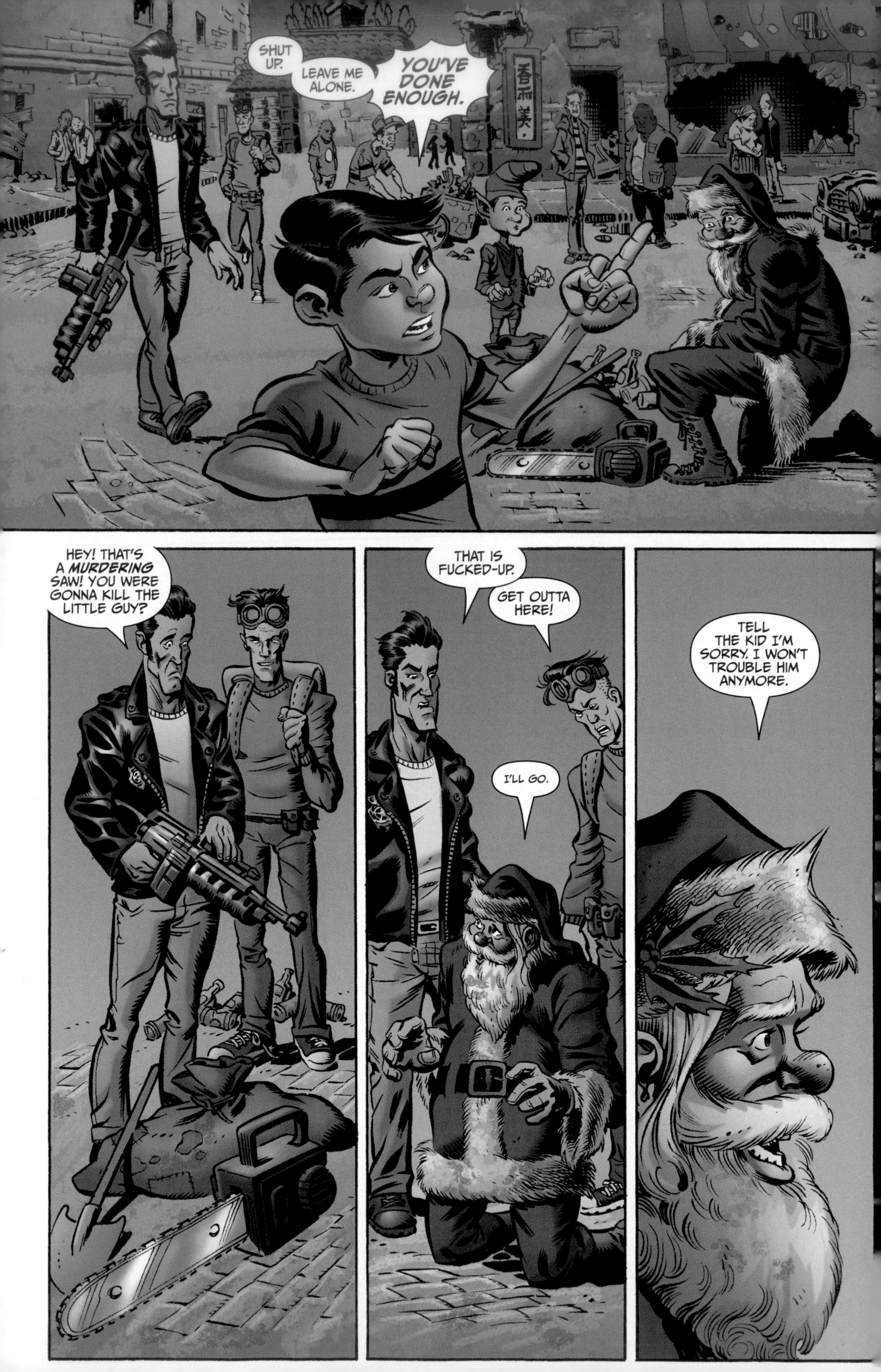
SHUT UP.
LEAVE ME ALONE.
YOU'VE DONE ENOUGH.
HEY! THAT'S A MURDERING SAW! YOU WERE GONNA KILL THE LITTLE GUY?
THAT IS FUCKED-UP.
GET OUTTA HERE!
I'LL GO.
TELL THE KID I'M SORRY. I WON'T TROUBLE HIM ANYMORE.

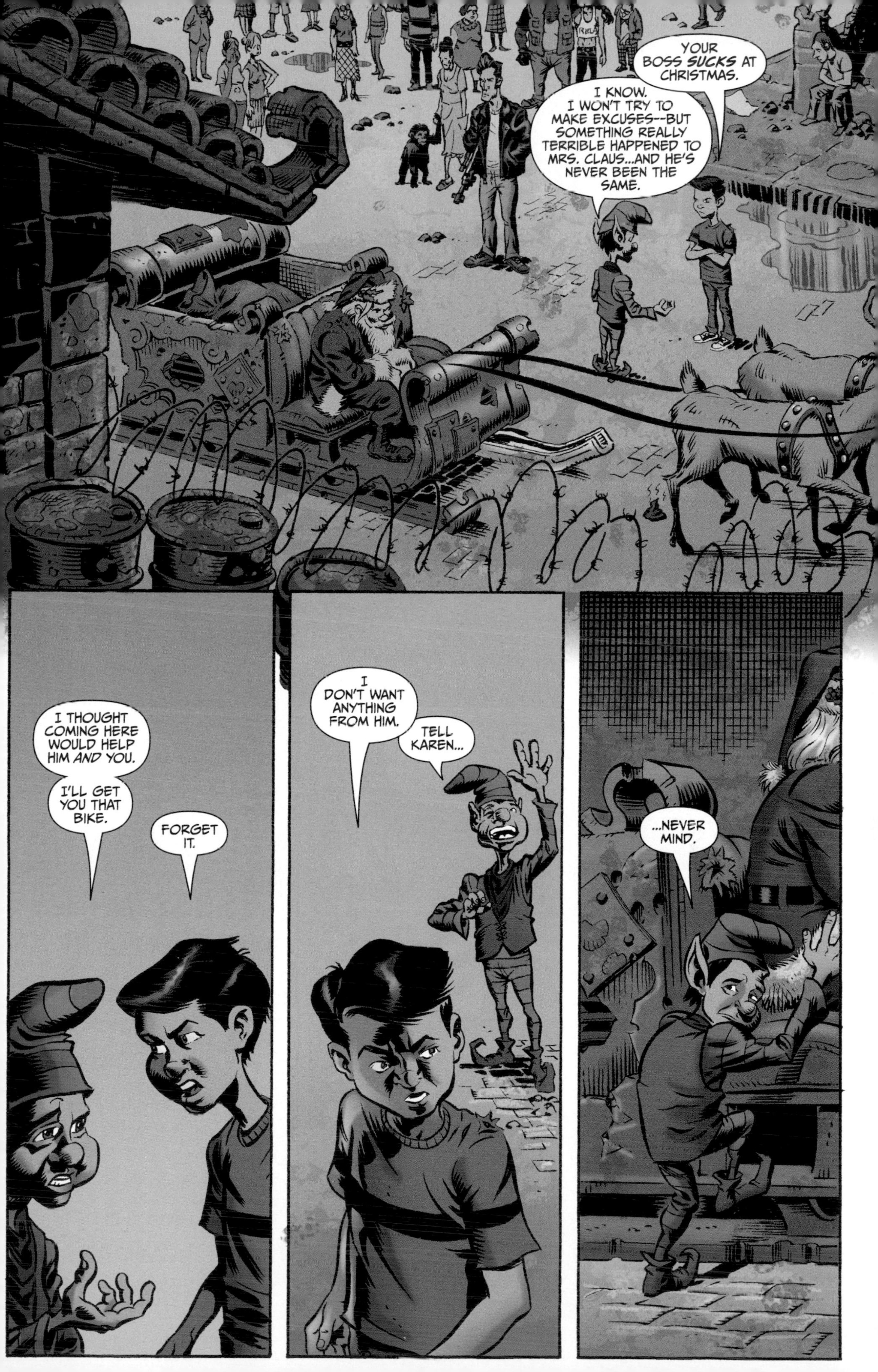
YOUR BOSS SUCKS AT CHRISTMAS.
I KNOW. I WON'T TRY TO MAKE EXCUSES--BUT SOMETHING REALLY TERRIBLE HAPPENED TO MRS. CLAUS...AND HE'S NEVER BEEN THE SAME.
I THOUGHT COMING HERE WOULD HELP HIM AND YOU.
I'LL GET YOU THAT BIKE.
FORGET IT.
I DON'T WANT ANYTHING FROM HIM.
TELL KAREN...
...NEVER MIND.

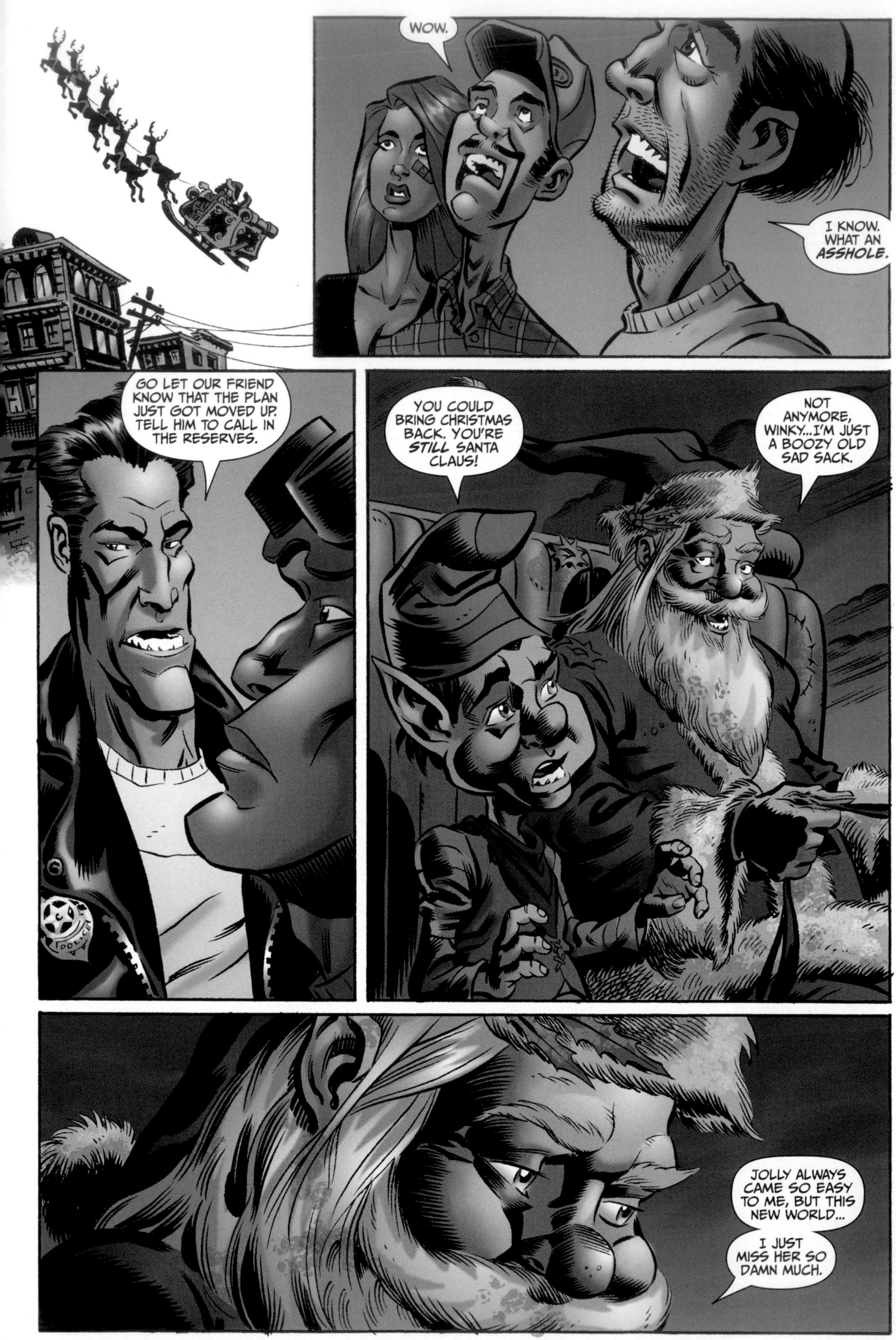
WOW.
I KNOW. WHAT AN ASSHOLE.
GO LET OUR FRIEND KNOW THAT THE PLAN JUST GOT MOVED UP. TELL HIM TO CALL IN THE RESERVES.
YOU COULD BRING CHRISTMAS BACK. YOU'RE STILL SANTA CLAUS!
NOT ANYMORE, WINKY...I'M JUST A BOOZY OLD SAD SACK.
JOLLY ALWAYS CAME SO EASY TO ME, BUT THIS NEW WORLD...
I JUST MISS HER SO DAMN MUCH.

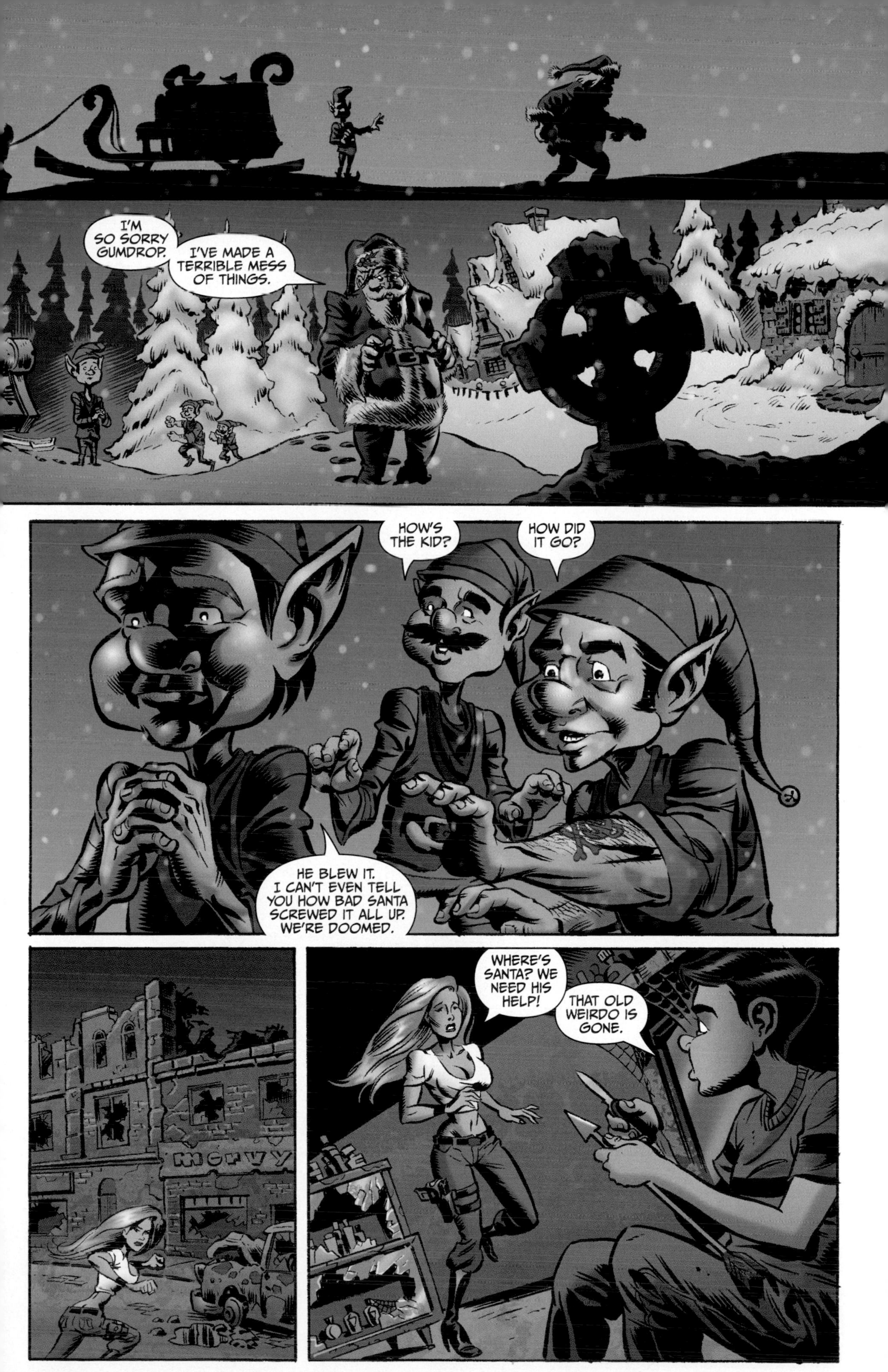
I'M SO SORRY GUMDROP.
I'VE MADE A TERRIBLE MESS OF THINGS.
HOW'S THE KID?
HOW DID IT GO?
HE BLEW IT. I CAN'T EVEN TELL YOU HOW BAD SANTA SCREWED IT ALL UP. WE'RE DOOMED.
WHERE'S SANTA? WE NEED HIS HELP!
THAT OLD WEIRDO IS GONE.

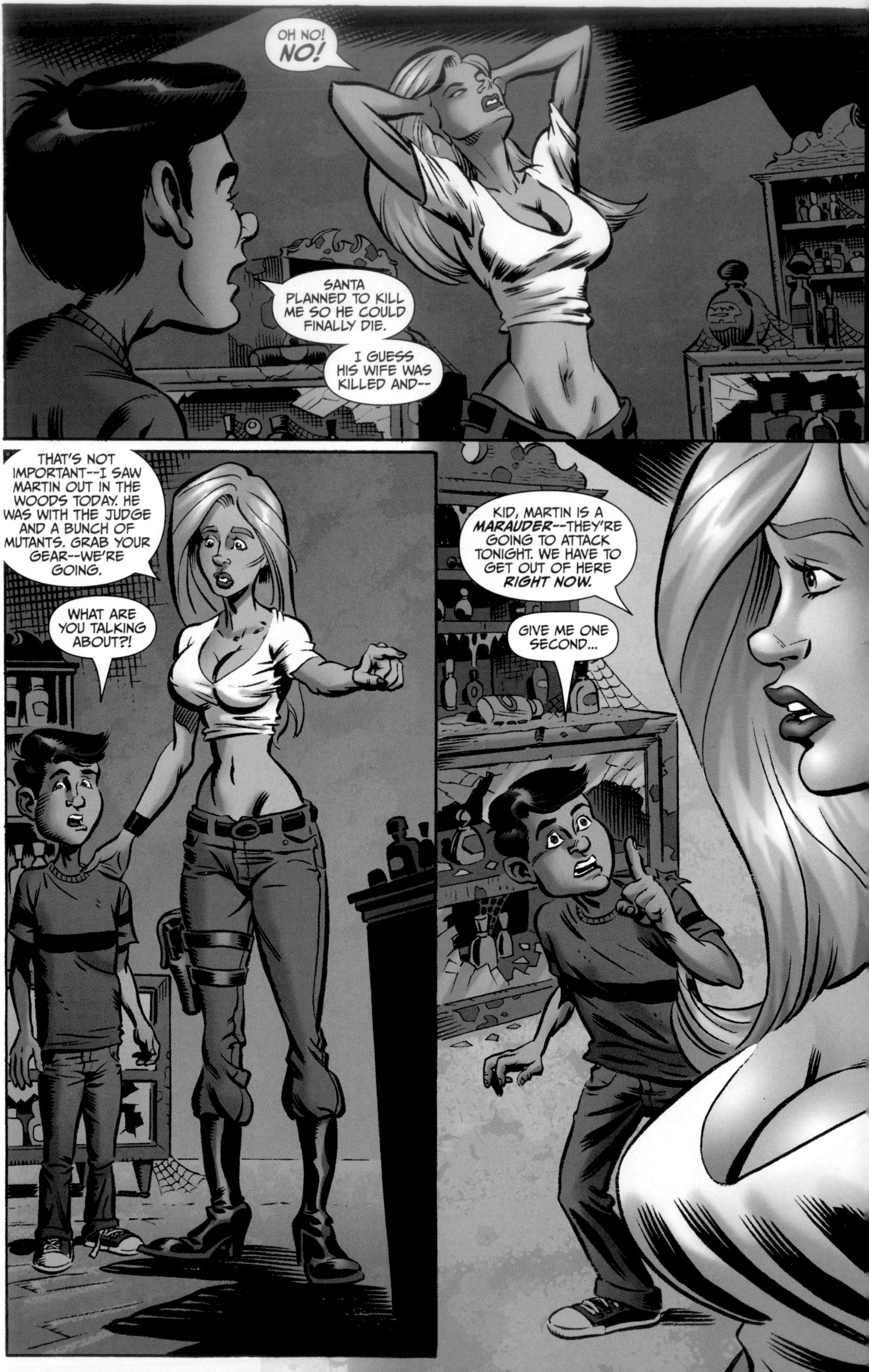
OH NO! NO!
SANTA PLANNED TO KILL ME SO HE COULD FINALLY DIE.
I GUESS HIS WIFE WAS KILLED AND--
THAT'S NOT IMPORTANT--I SAW MARTIN OUT IN THE WOODS TODAY. HE WAS WITH THE JUDGE AND A BUNCH OF MUTANTS. GRAB YOUR GEAR--WE'RE GOING.
WHAT ARE YOU TALKING ABOUT?!
KID, MARTIN IS A MARAUDER--THEY'RE GOING TO ATTACK TONIGHT. WE HAVE TO GET OUT OF HERE RIGHT NOW.
GIVE ME ONE SECOND...

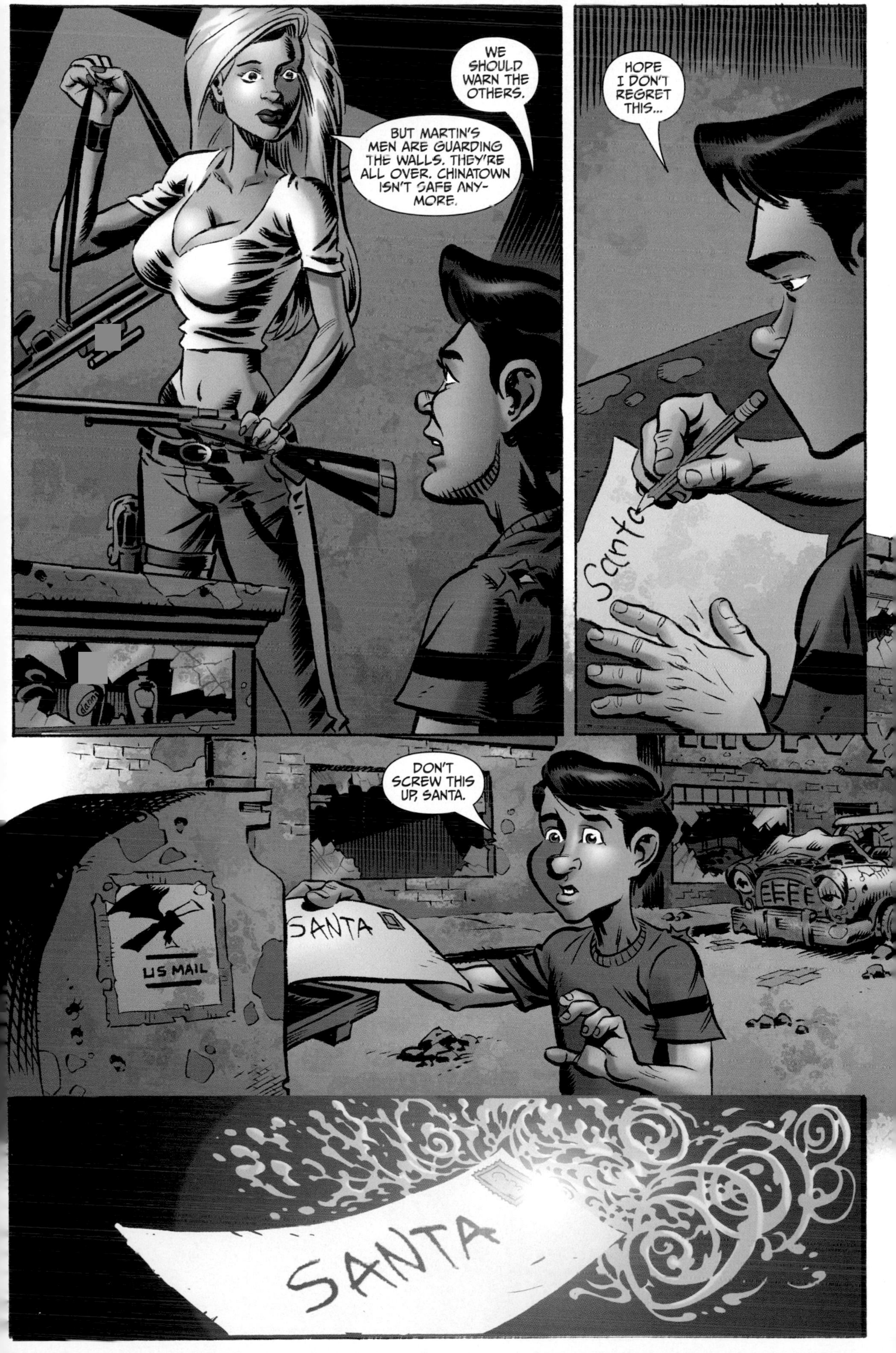

WE SHOULD WARN THE OTHERS.
BUT MARTIN'S MEN ARE GUARDING THE WALLS. THEY'RE ALL OVER. CHINATOWN ISN'T SAFE ANY-MORE.
HOPE I DON'T REGRET THIS...
Santa
DON'T SCREW THIS UP, SANTA.
SANTA
US MAIL
SANTA

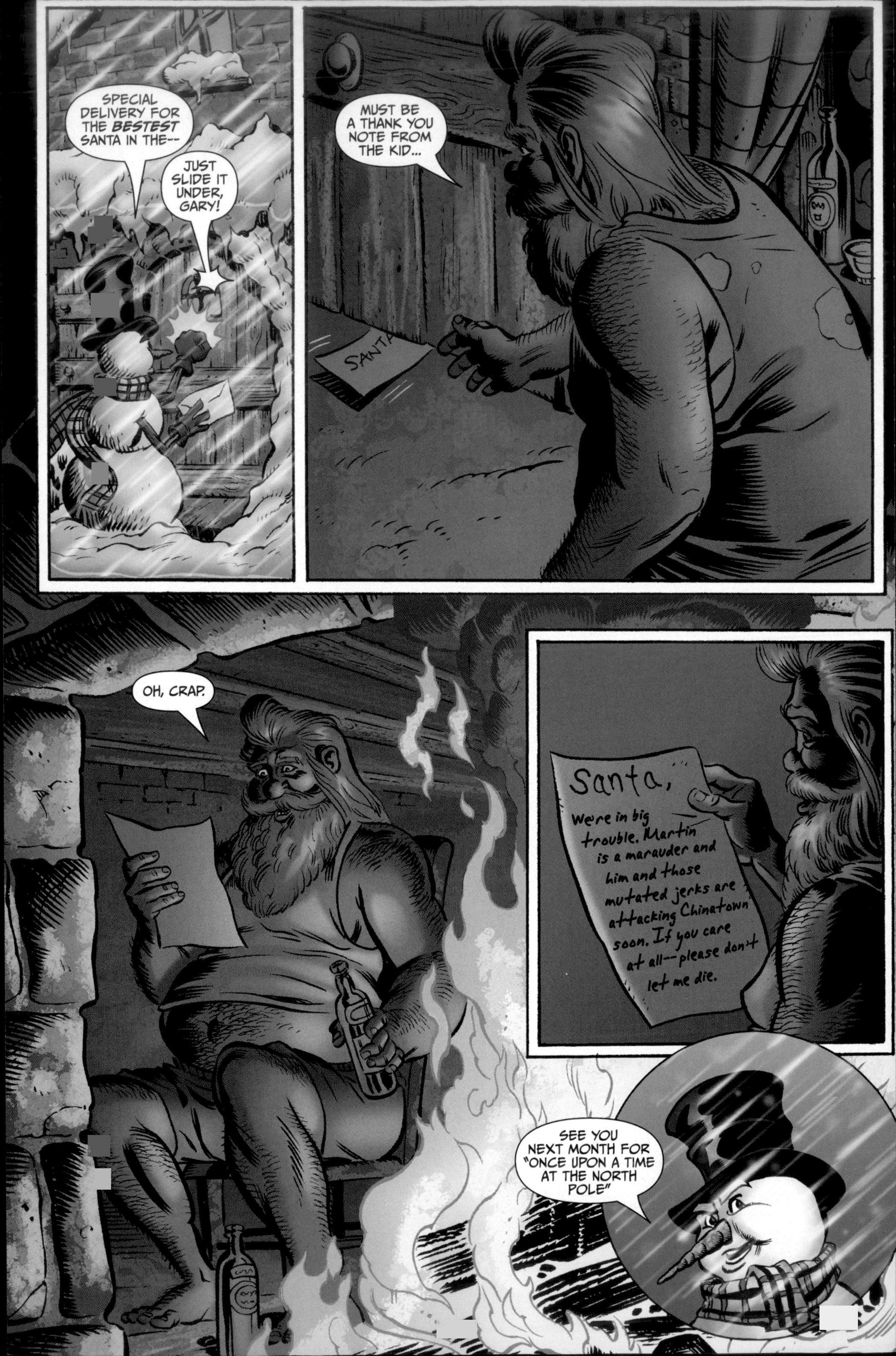
SPECIAL DELIVERY FOR THE **BESTEST** SANTA IN THE--
JUST SLIDE IT UNDER, GARY!
MUST BE A THANK YOU NOTE FROM THE KID...
SANTA
OH, CRAP.
Santa,
We're in big trouble. Martin is a marauder and him and those mutated jerks are attacking Chinatown soon. If you care at all--please don't let me die.
SEE YOU NEXT MONTH FOR "ONCE UPON A TIME AT THE NORTH POLE"

Chapter 4

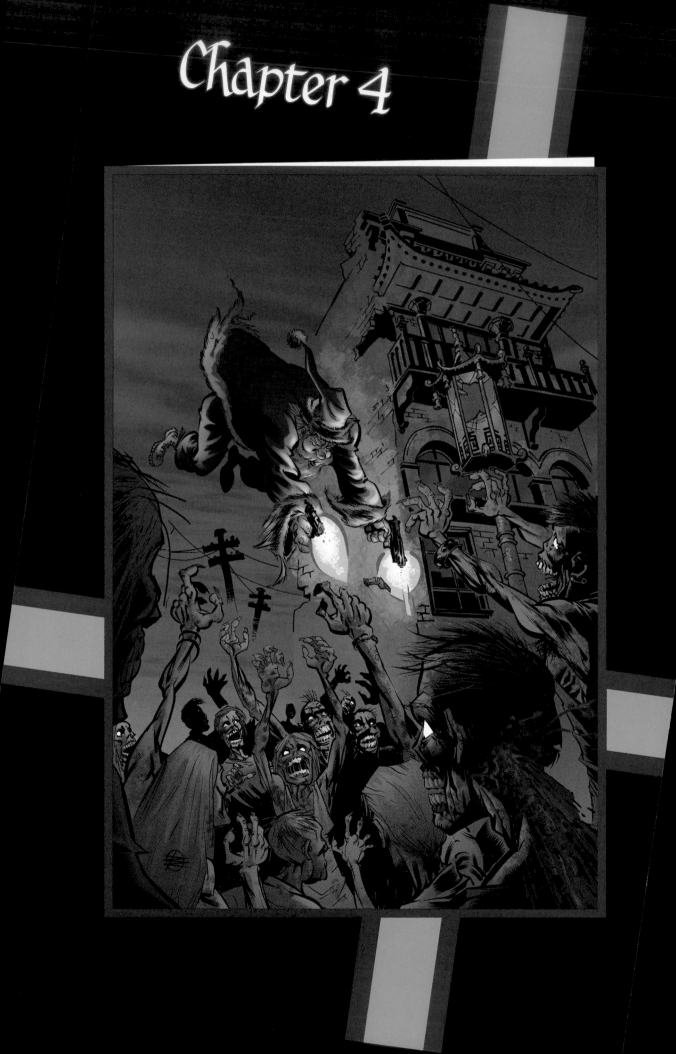

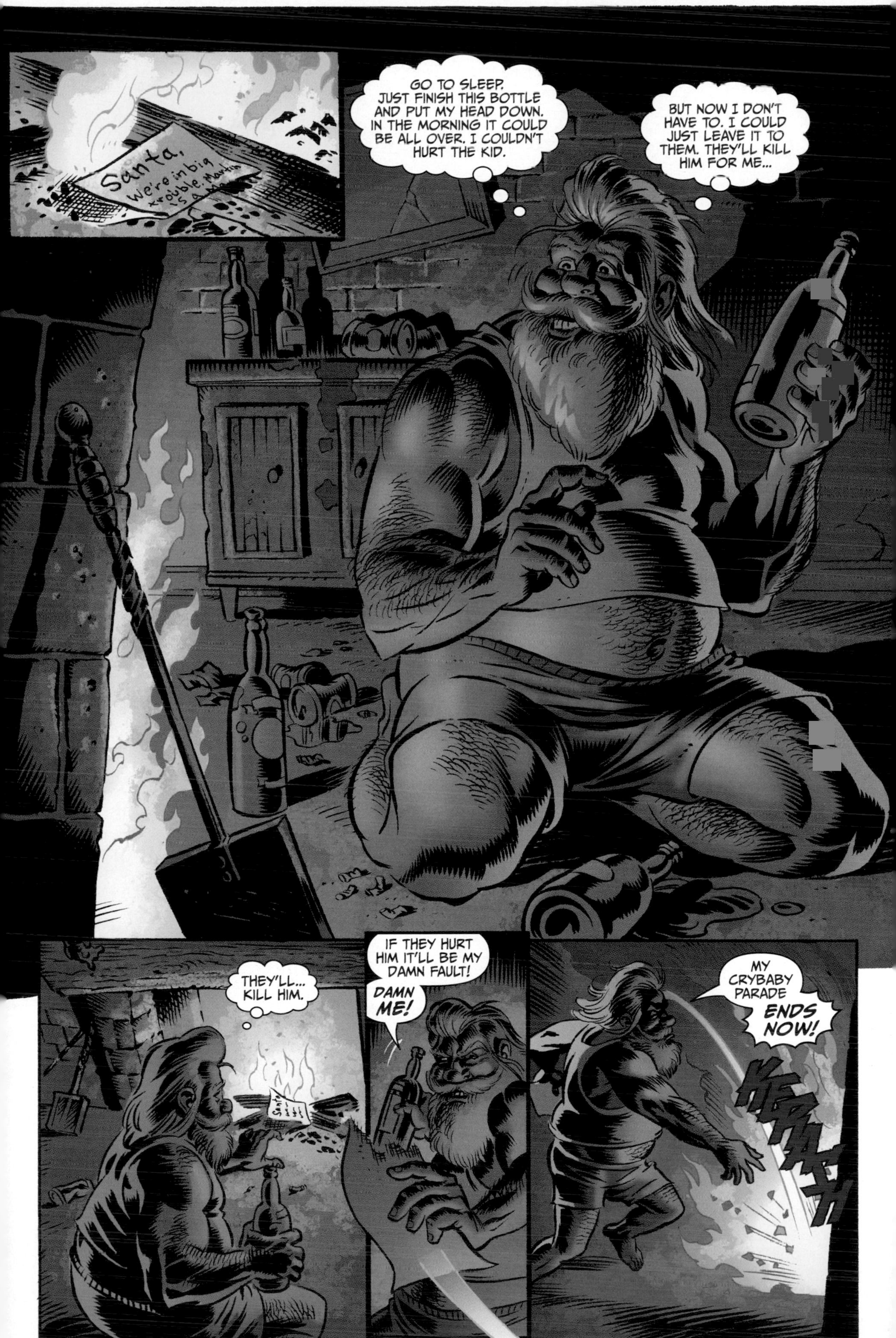
Santa,
We're in big
GO TO SLEEP. JUST FINISH THIS BOTTLE AND PUT MY HEAD DOWN. IN THE MORNING IT COULD BE ALL OVER. I COULDN'T HURT THE KID.
BUT NOW I DON'T HAVE TO. I COULD JUST LEAVE IT TO THEM. THEY'LL KILL HIM FOR ME...
THEY'LL... KILL HIM.
IF THEY HURT HIM IT'LL BE MY DAMN FAULT!
DAMN ME!
MY CRYBABY PARADE ENDS NOW!

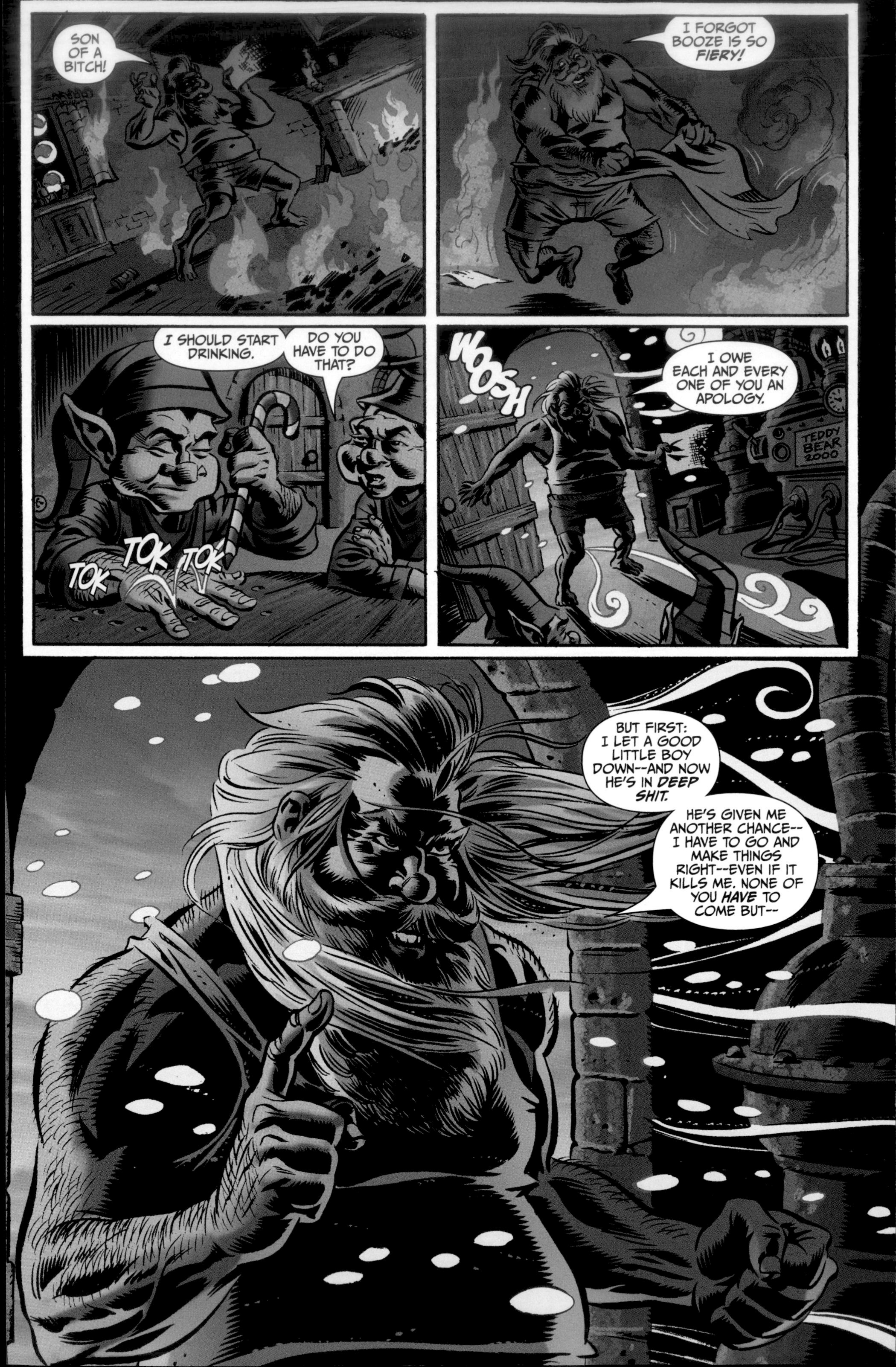
SON OF A BITCH!
I FORGOT BOOZE IS SO FIERY!
I SHOULD START DRINKING.
DO YOU HAVE TO DO THAT?
TOK TOK TOK
WOOSH
I OWE EACH AND EVERY ONE OF YOU AN APOLOGY.
TEDDY BEAR 2000
BUT FIRST: I LET A GOOD LITTLE BOY DOWN--AND NOW HE'S IN DEEP SHIT.
HE'S GIVEN ME ANOTHER CHANCE--I HAVE TO GO AND MAKE THINGS RIGHT--EVEN IF IT KILLS ME. NONE OF YOU HAVE TO COME BUT--

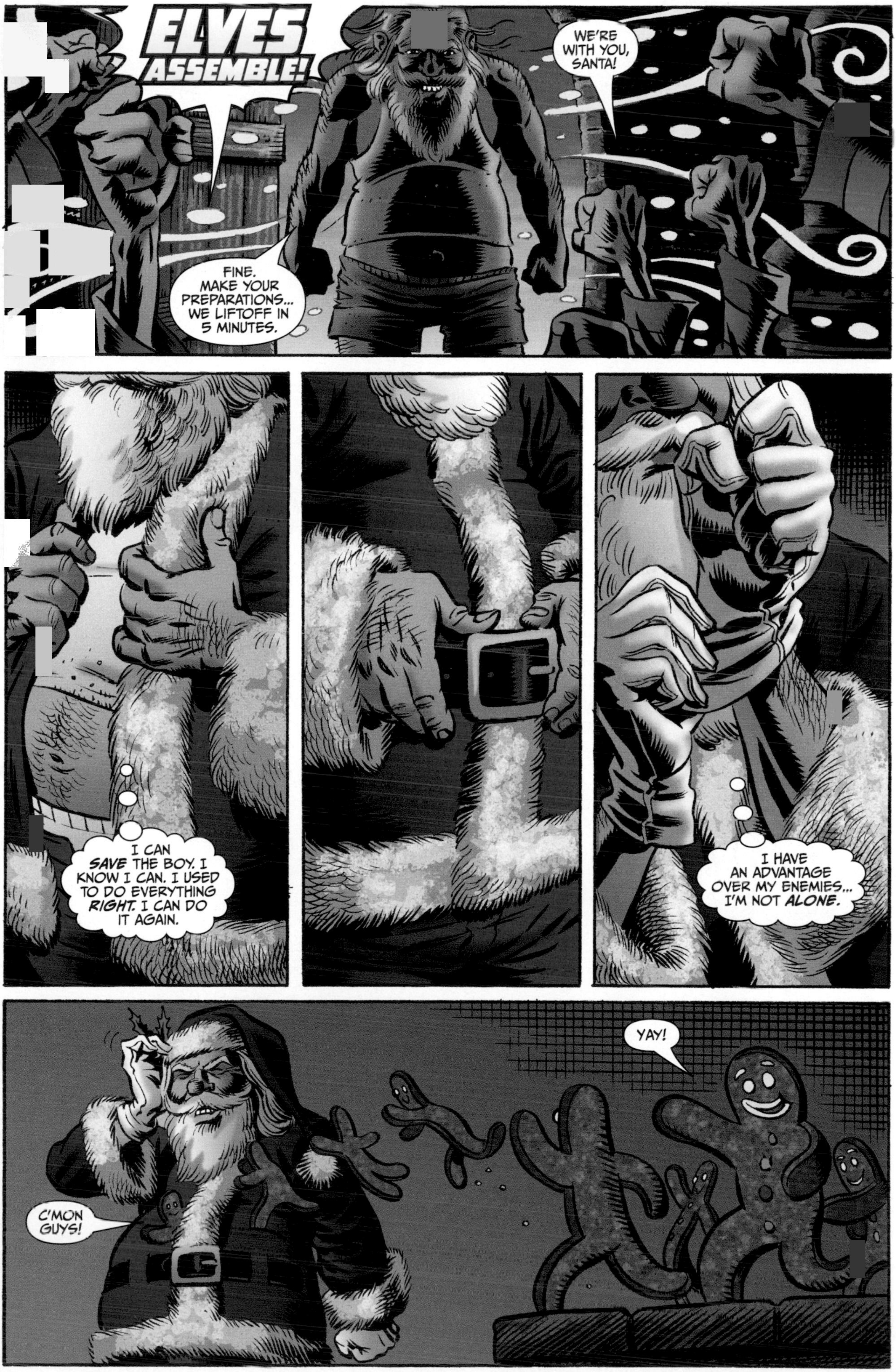
ELVES ASSEMBLE!
WE'RE WITH YOU, SANTA!
FINE. MAKE YOUR PREPARATIONS... WE LIFTOFF IN 5 MINUTES.
I CAN SAVE THE BOY. I KNOW I CAN. I USED TO DO EVERYTHING RIGHT. I CAN DO IT AGAIN.
I HAVE AN ADVANTAGE OVER MY ENEMIES... I'M NOT ALONE.
C'MON GUYS!
YAY!

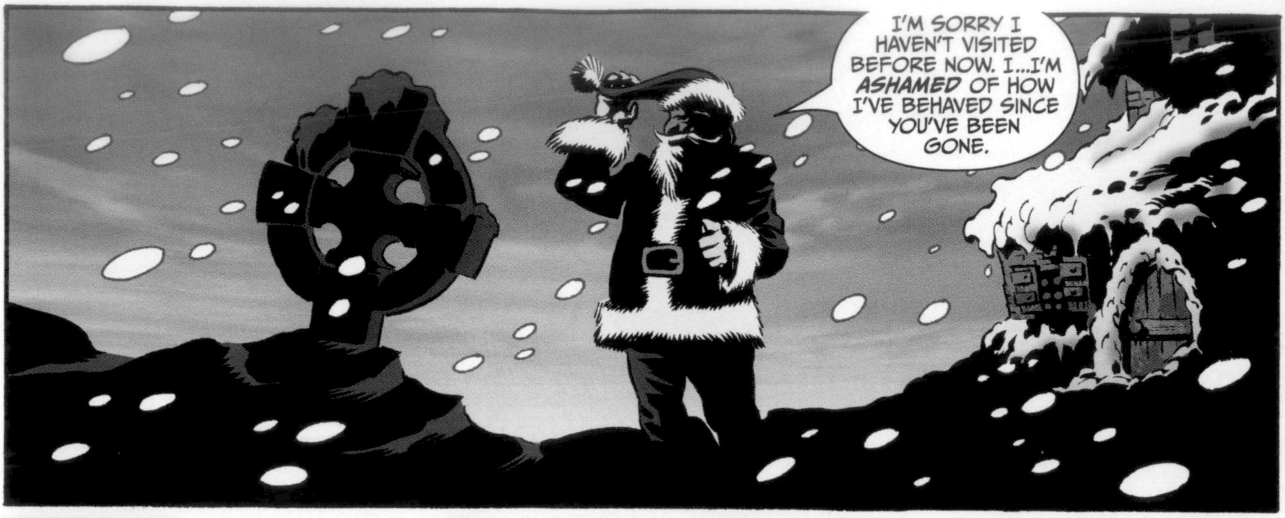
I'M SORRY I HAVEN'T VISITED BEFORE NOW. I...I'M ASHAMED OF HOW I'VE BEHAVED SINCE YOU'VE BEEN GONE.

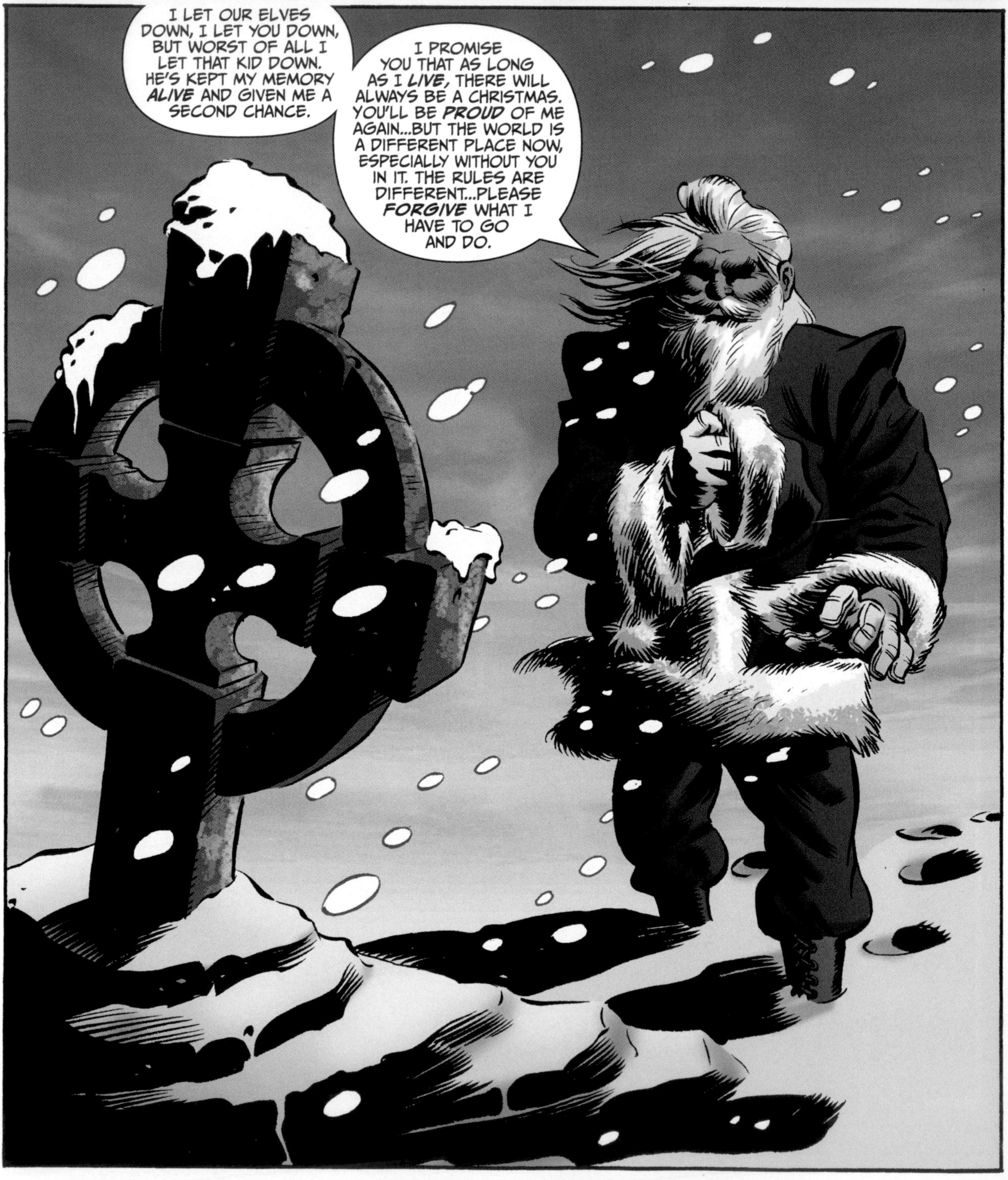
I LET OUR ELVES DOWN, I LET YOU DOWN, BUT WORST OF ALL I LET THAT KID DOWN. HE'S KEPT MY MEMORY ALIVE AND GIVEN ME A SECOND CHANCE.
I PROMISE YOU THAT AS LONG AS I LIVE, THERE WILL ALWAYS BE A CHRISTMAS. YOU'LL BE PROUD OF ME AGAIN...BUT THE WORLD IS A DIFFERENT PLACE NOW, ESPECIALLY WITHOUT YOU IN IT. THE RULES ARE DIFFERENT...PLEASE FORGIVE WHAT I HAVE TO GO AND DO.

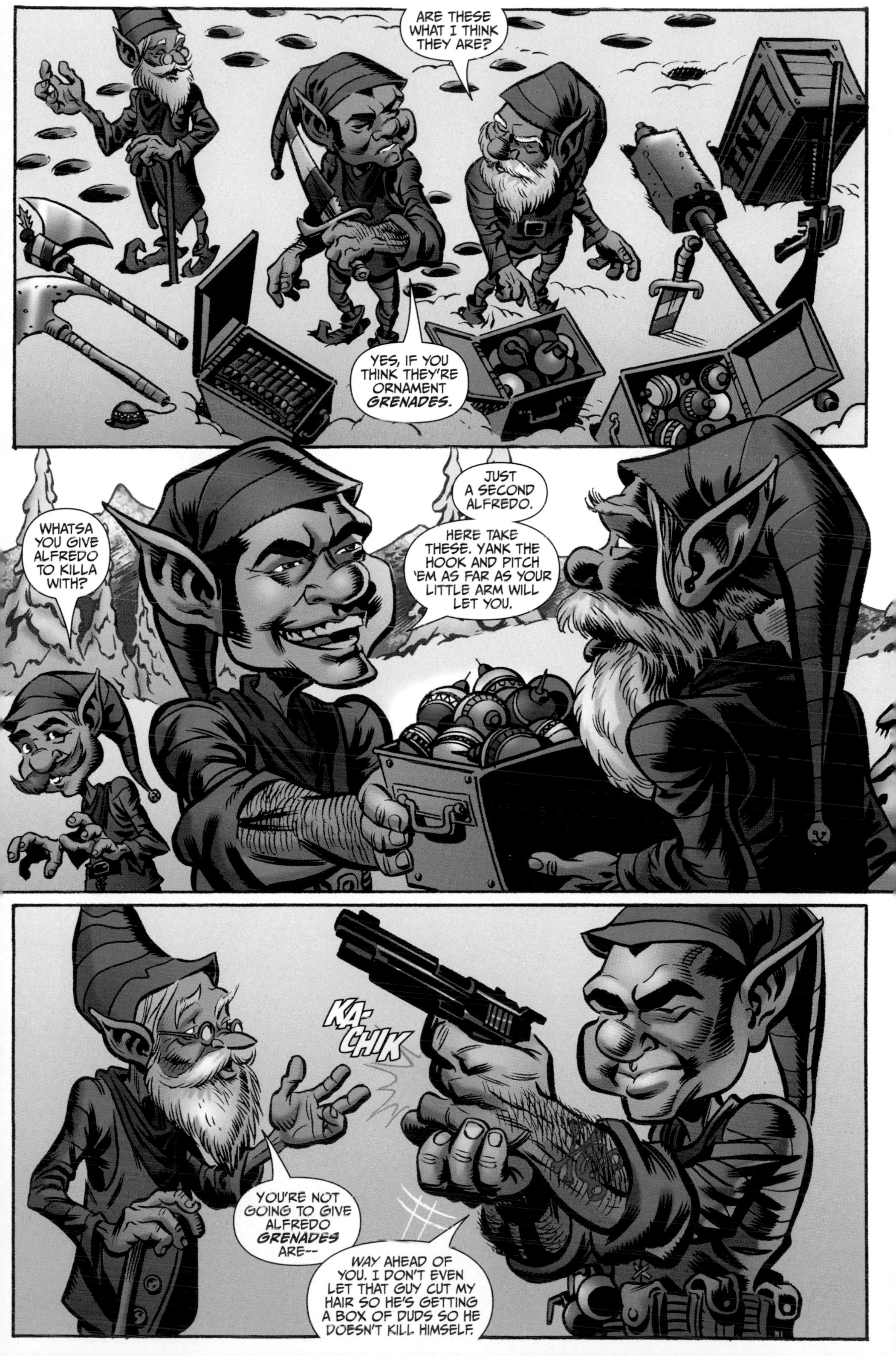
ARE THESE WHAT I THINK THEY ARE?
YES, IF YOU THINK THEY'RE ORNAMENT GRENADES.
WHATSA YOU GIVE ALFREDO TO KILLA WITH?
JUST A SECOND ALFREDO.
HERE TAKE THESE. YANK THE HOOK AND PITCH 'EM AS FAR AS YOUR LITTLE ARM WILL LET YOU.
KA-CHIK
YOU'RE NOT GOING TO GIVE ALFREDO GRENADES ARE--
WAY AHEAD OF YOU. I DON'T EVEN LET THAT GUY CUT MY HAIR SO HE'S GETTING A BOX OF DUDS SO HE DOESN'T KILL HIMSELF.

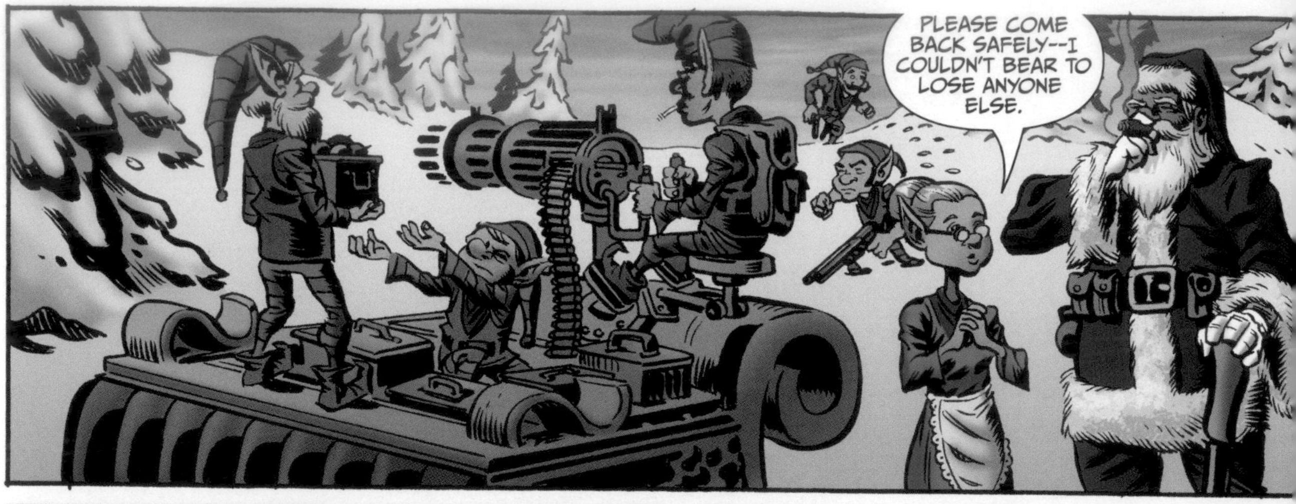
PLEASE COME BACK SAFELY--I COULDN'T BEAR TO LOSE ANYONE ELSE.

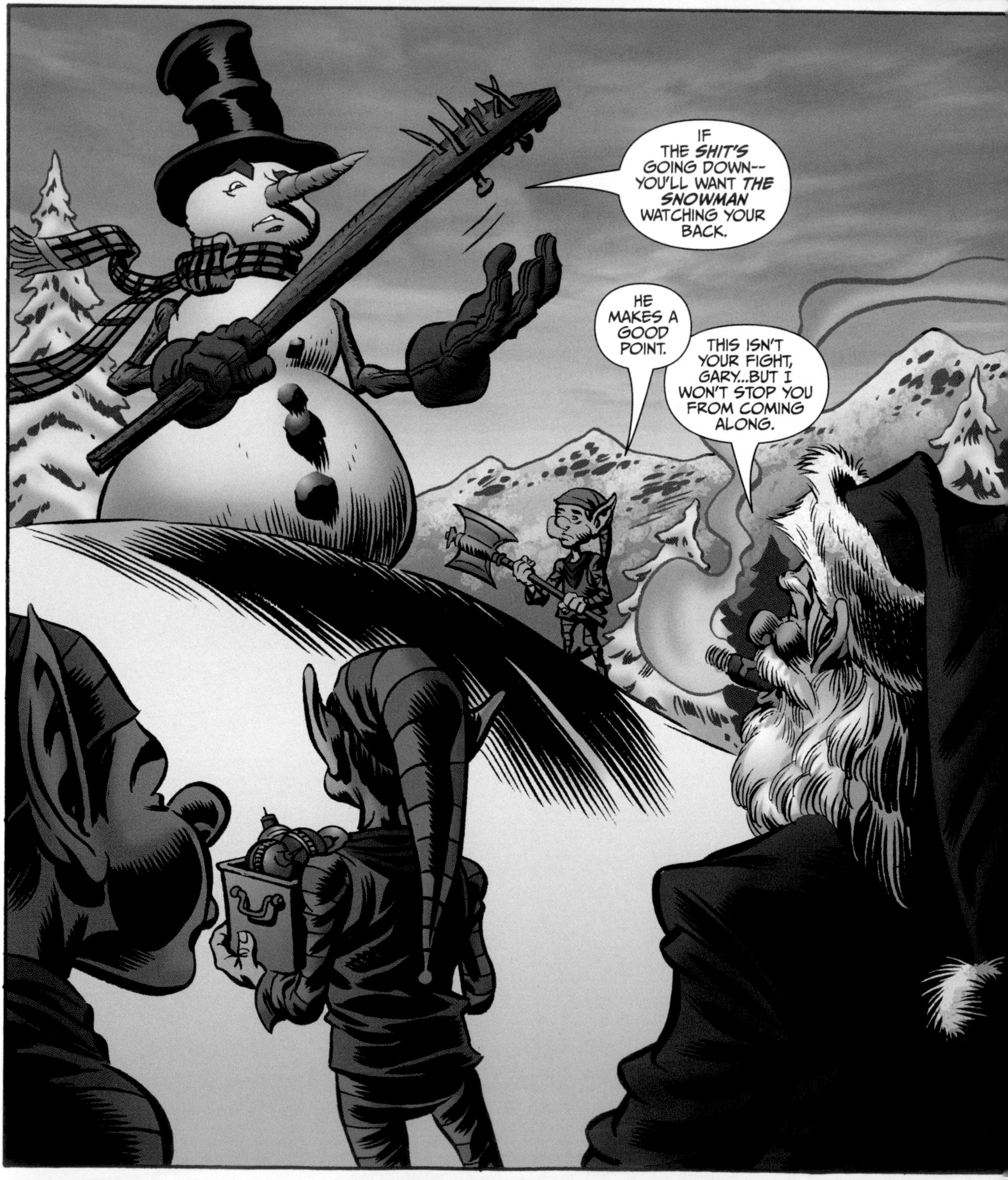
IF THE SHIT'S GOING DOWN-- YOU'LL WANT THE SNOWMAN WATCHING YOUR BACK.
HE MAKES A GOOD POINT.
THIS ISN'T YOUR FIGHT, GARY...BUT I WON'T STOP YOU FROM COMING ALONG.

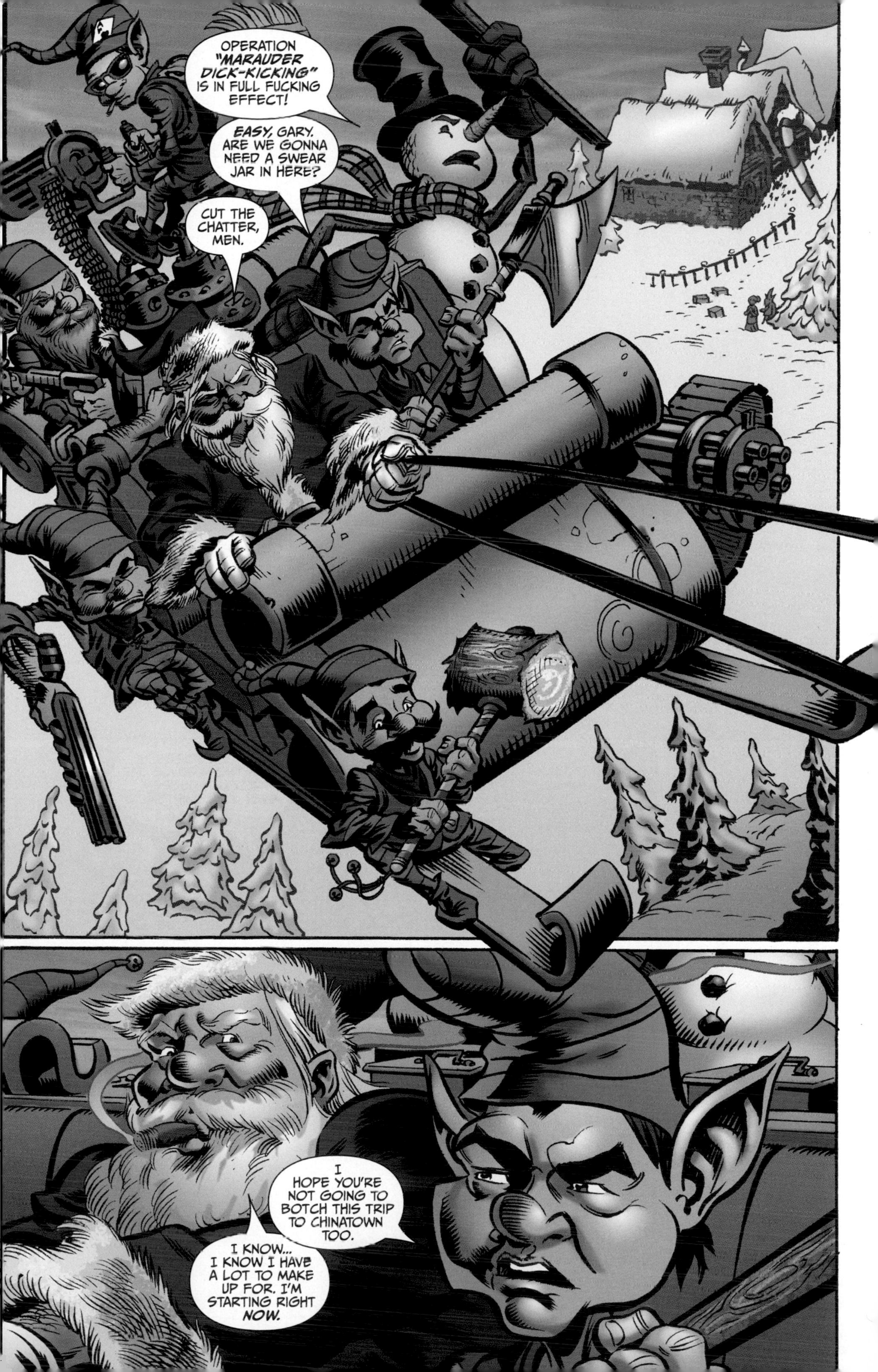

OPERATION "MARAUDER DICK-KICKING" IS IN FULL FUCKING EFFECT!
EASY, GARY. ARE WE GONNA NEED A SWEAR JAR IN HERE?
CUT THE CHATTER, MEN.
I HOPE YOU'RE NOT GOING TO BOTCH THIS TRIP TO CHINATOWN TOO.
I KNOW... I KNOW I HAVE A LOT TO MAKE UP FOR. I'M STARTING RIGHT NOW.

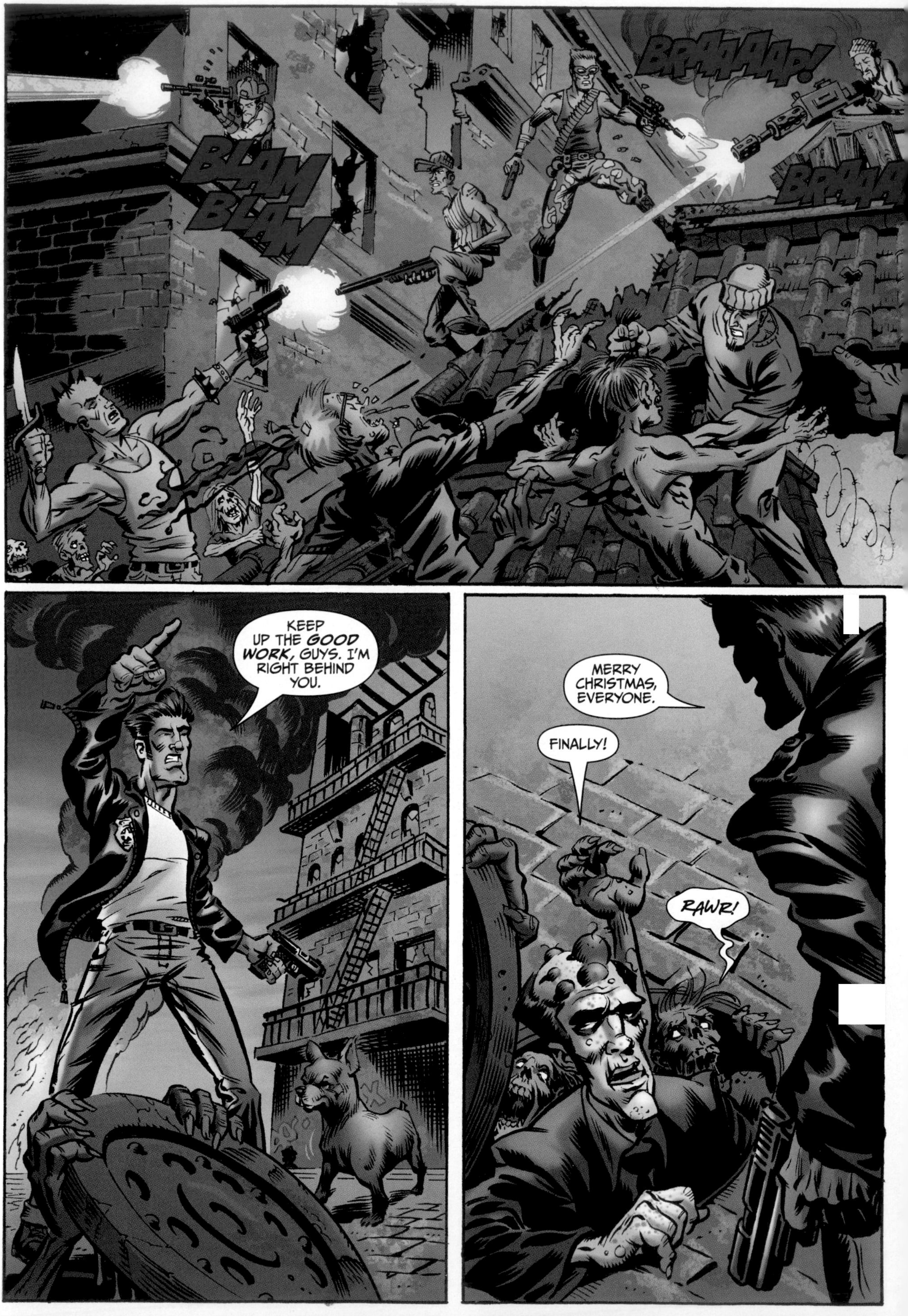
BLAM
BLAM
BRAAAAP!
BRAAA
KEEP UP THE GOOD WORK, GUYS. I'M RIGHT BEHIND YOU.
MERRY CHRISTMAS, EVERYONE.
FINALLY!
RAWR!

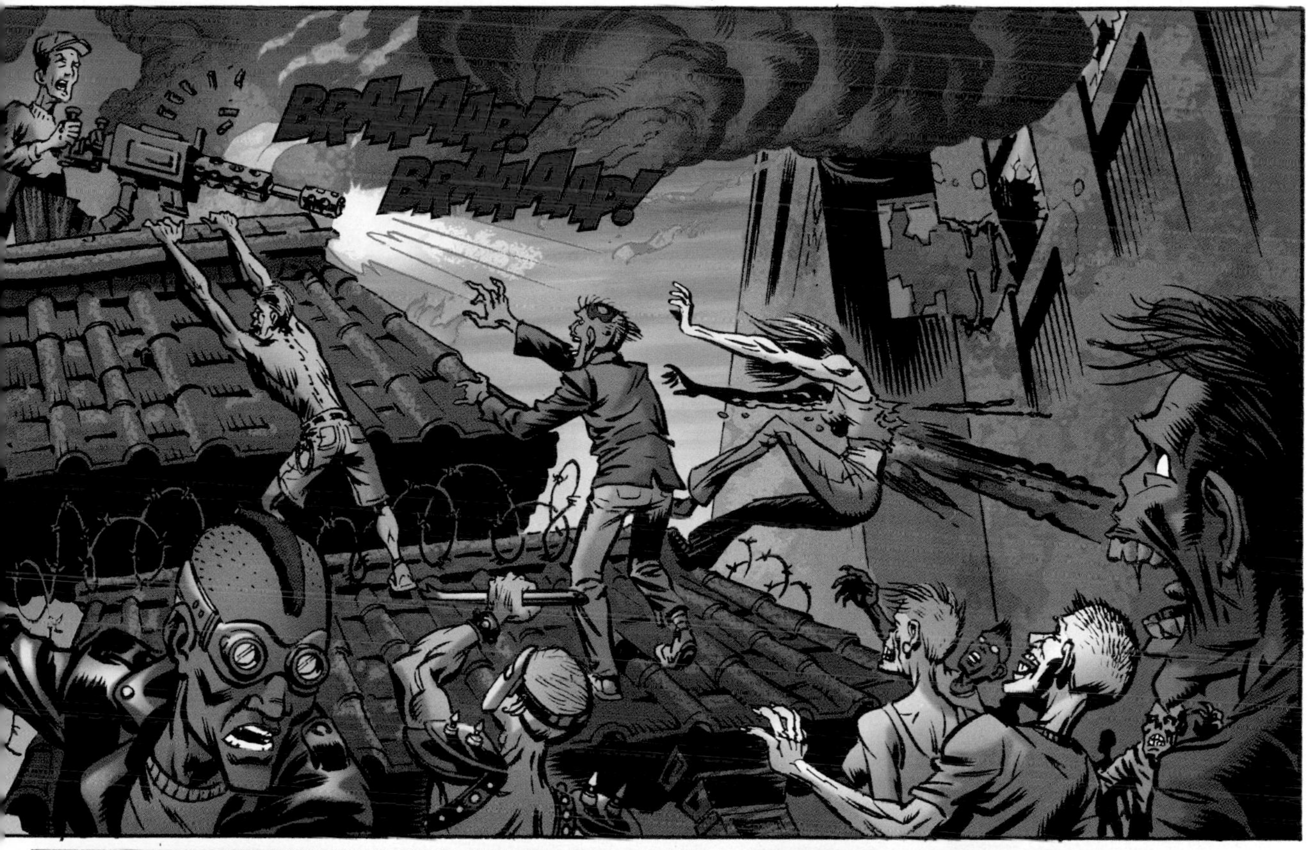
BRAAAAP!
BRAAAAP!

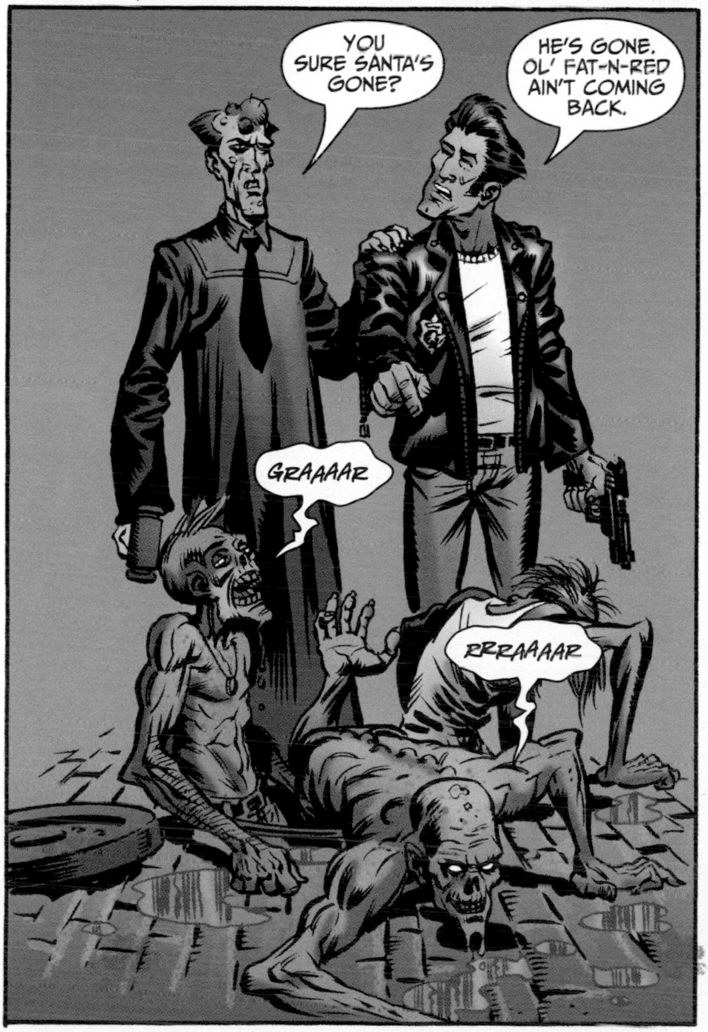
YOU SURE SANTA'S GONE?
HE'S GONE. OL' FAT-N-RED AIN'T COMING BACK.
GRAAAAR
RRRAAAAR

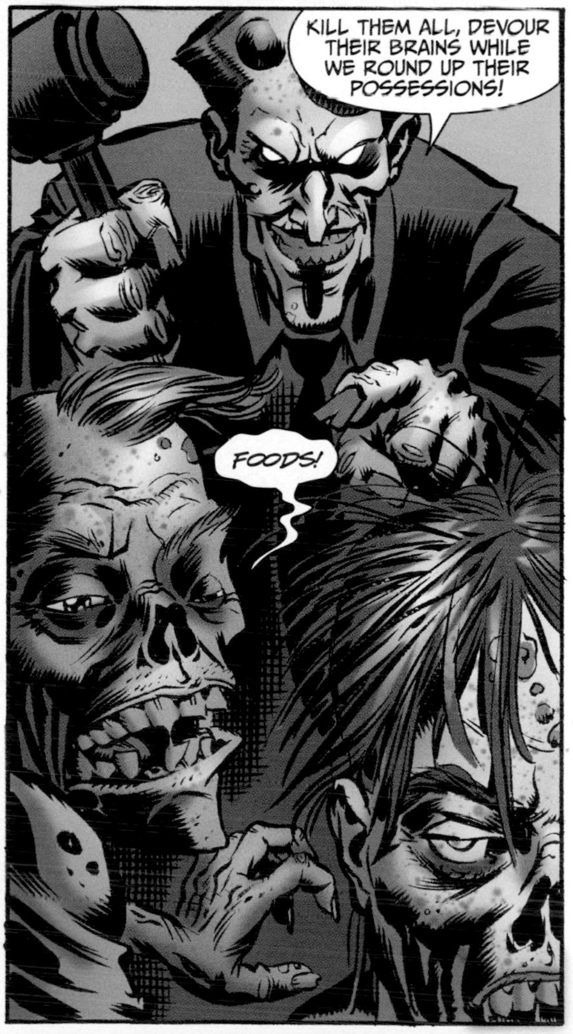
KILL THEM ALL, DEVOUR THEIR BRAINS WHILE WE ROUND UP THEIR POSSESSIONS!
FOODS!

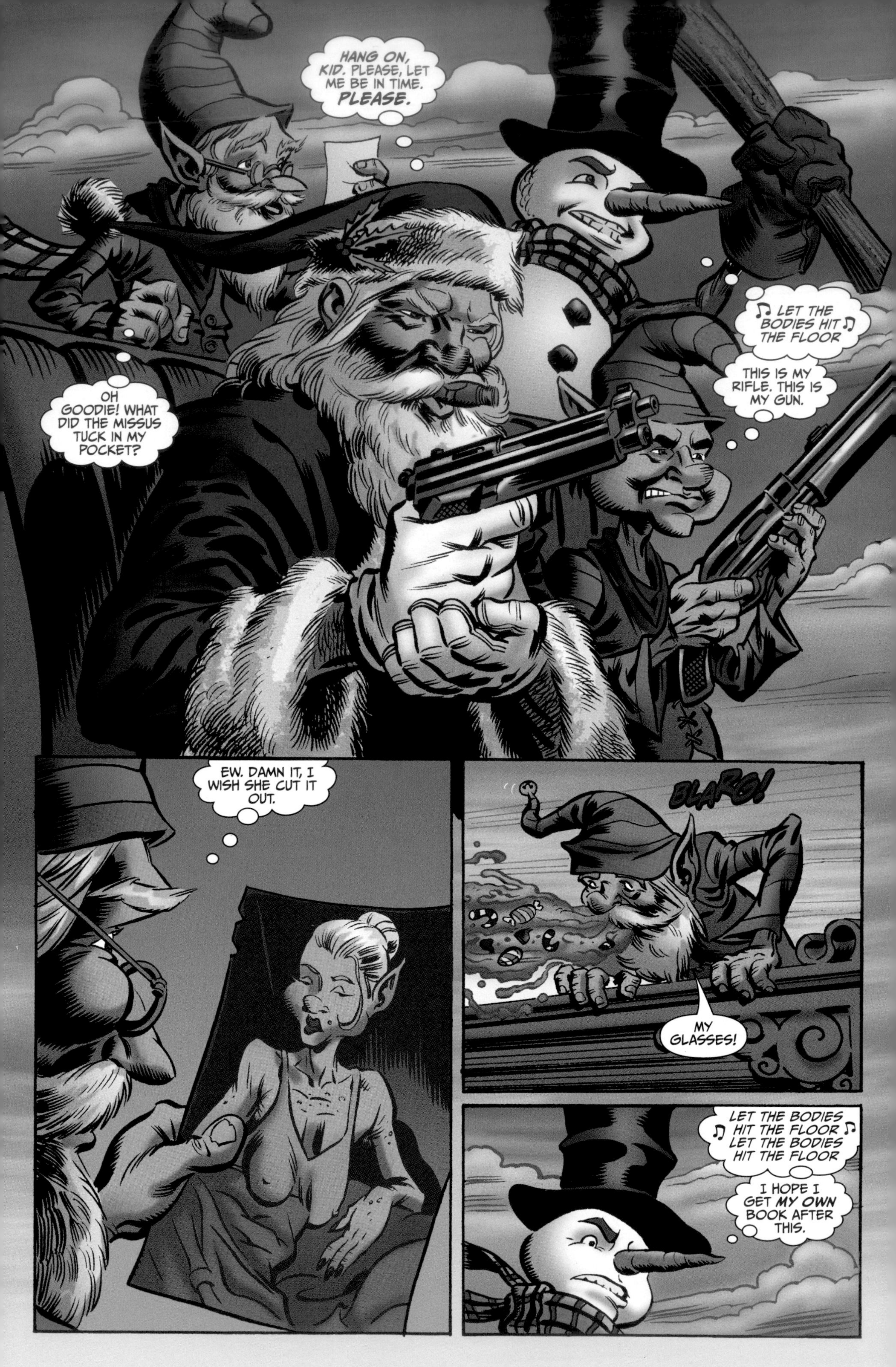
HANG ON, KID. PLEASE, LET ME BE IN TIME. PLEASE.
♫ LET THE BODIES HIT ♫ THE FLOOR
THIS IS MY RIFLE. THIS IS MY GUN.
OH GOODIE! WHAT DID THE MISSUS TUCK IN MY POCKET?
EW. DAMN IT, I WISH SHE CUT IT OUT.
BLARG!
MY GLASSES!
LET THE BODIES HIT THE FLOOR ♫ LET THE BODIES HIT THE FLOOR ♫
I HOPE I GET MY OWN BOOK AFTER THIS.

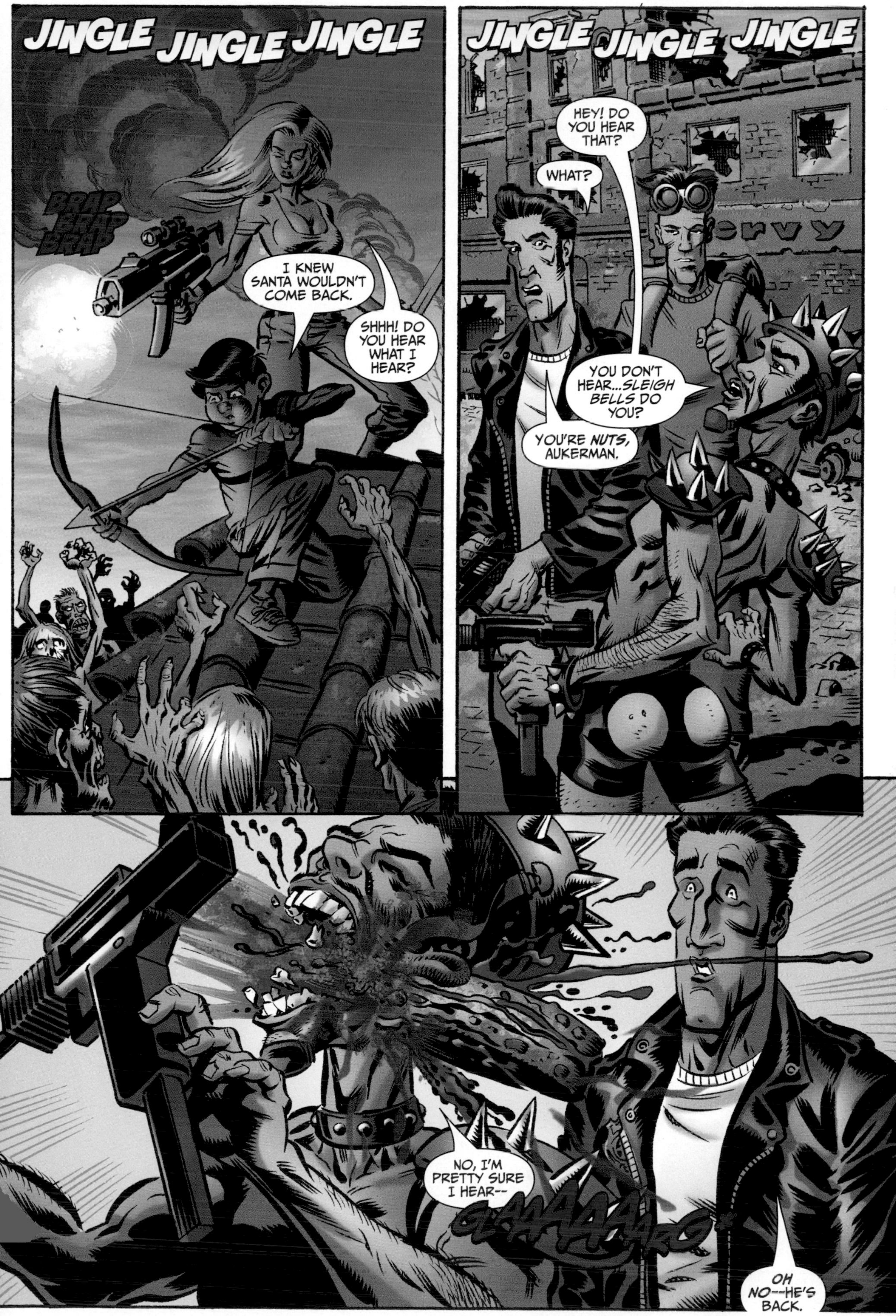

JINGLE JINGLE JINGLE
BRAP BRAP BRAP
I KNEW SANTA WOULDN'T COME BACK.
SHHH! DO YOU HEAR WHAT I HEAR?
JINGLE JINGLE JINGLE
HEY! DO YOU HEAR THAT?
WHAT?
YOU DON'T HEAR...SLEIGH BELLS DO YOU?
YOU'RE *NUTS*, AUKERMAN.
NO, I'M PRETTY SURE I HEAR--
OH NO--HE'S BACK.

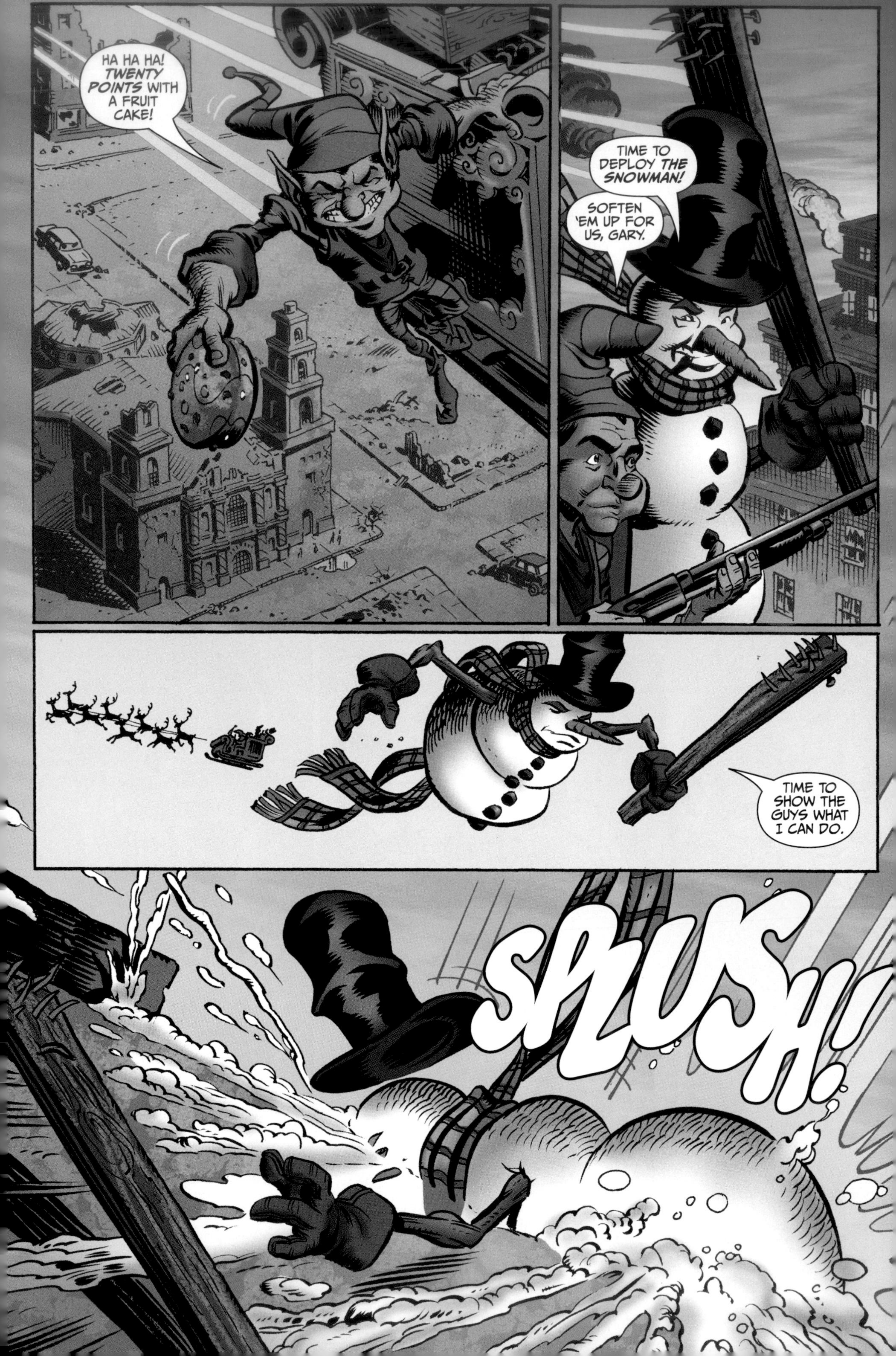
HA HA HA! TWENTY POINTS WITH A FRUIT CAKE!
TIME TO DEPLOY THE SNOWMAN!
SOFTEN 'EM UP FOR US, GARY.
TIME TO SHOW THE GUYS WHAT I CAN DO.
SPLUSH!

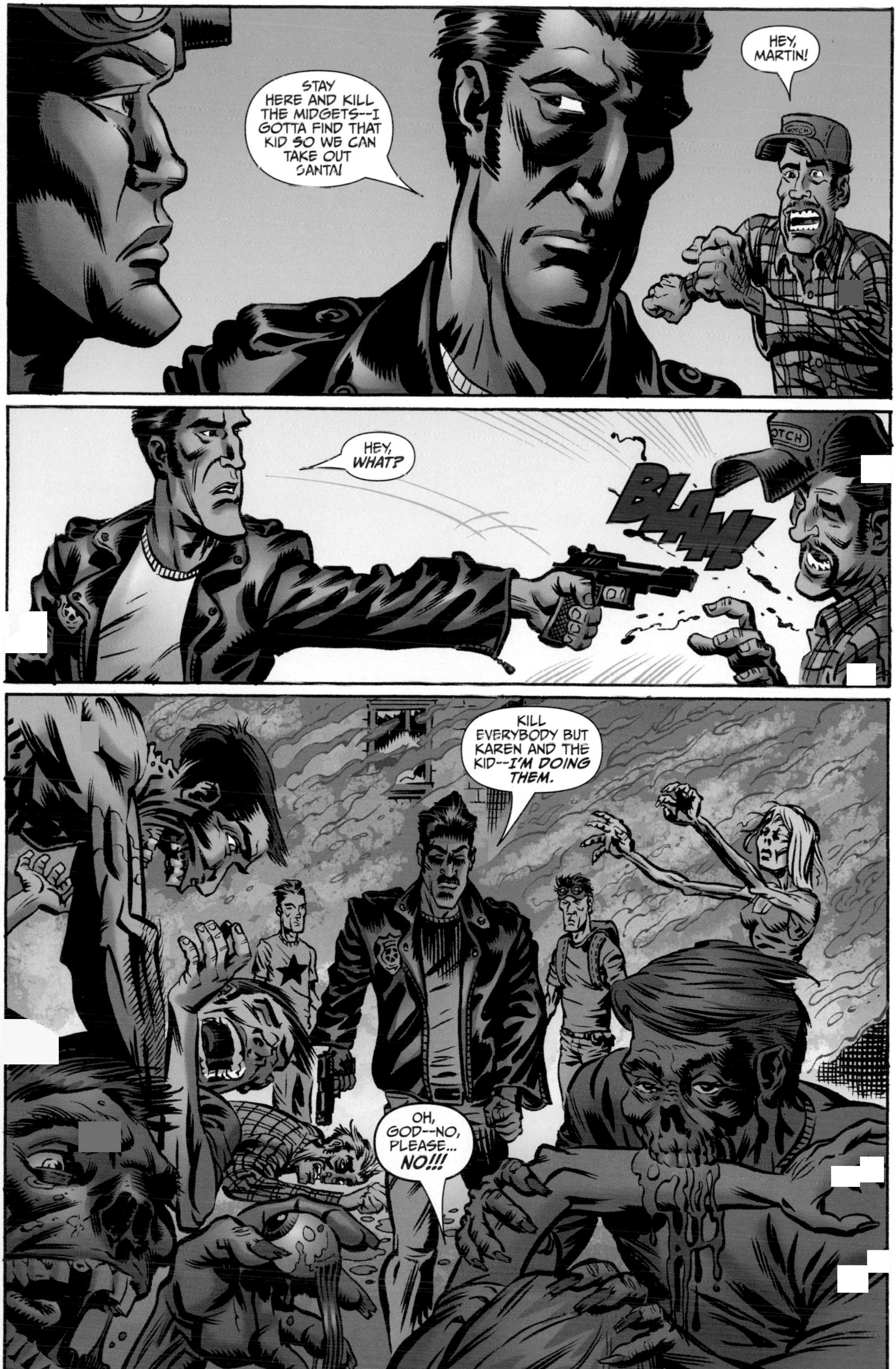
STAY HERE AND KILL THE MIDGETS--I GOTTA FIND THAT KID SO WE CAN TAKE OUT SANTA!
HEY, MARTIN!
HEY, WHAT?
BLAM!
KILL EVERYBODY BUT KAREN AND THE KID--I'M DOING THEM.
OH, GOD--NO, PLEASE... NO!!!

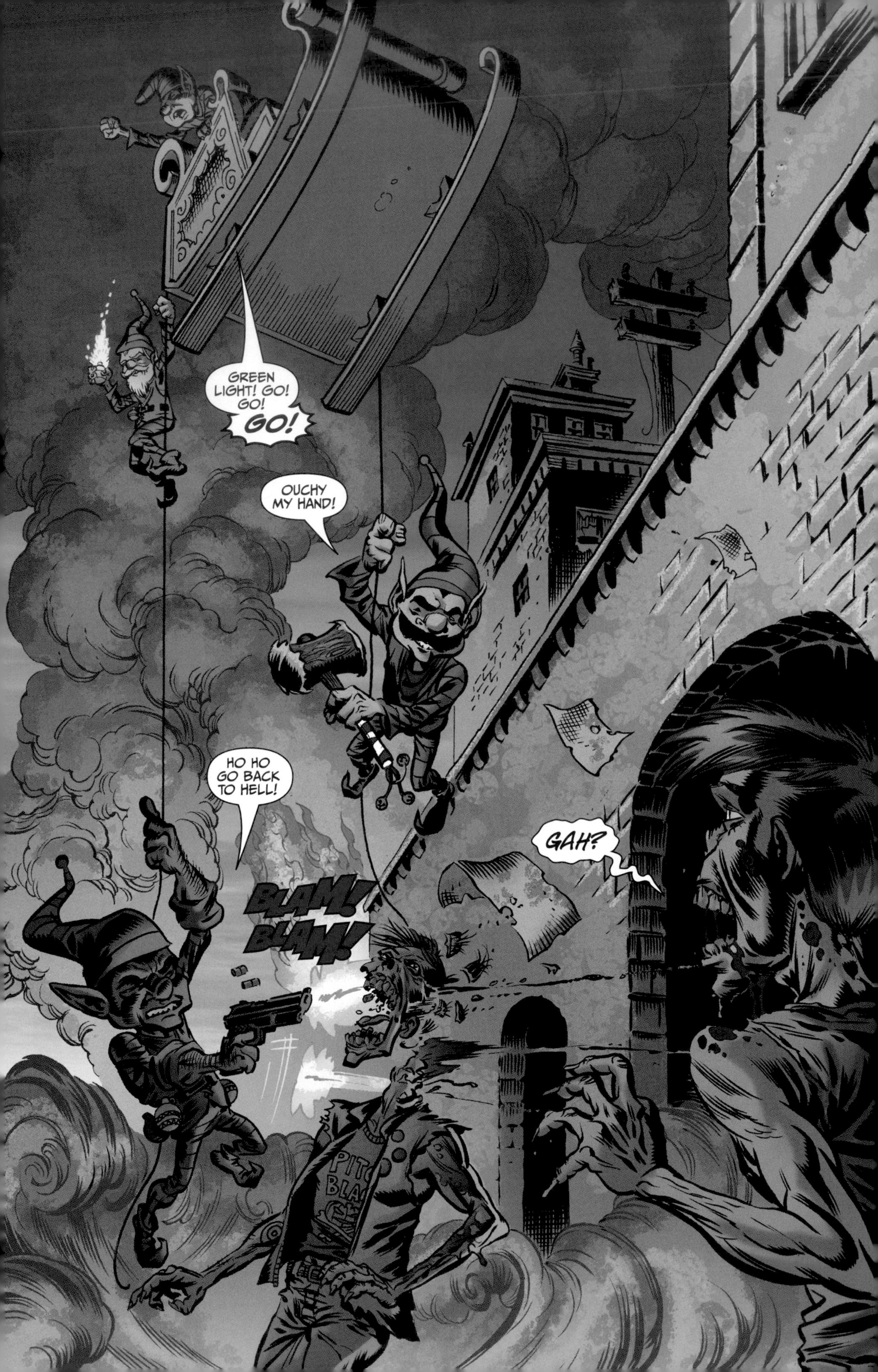
GREEN LIGHT! GO! GO! GO!
OUCHY MY HAND!
HO HO GO BACK TO HELL!
BLAM! BLAM!
GAH?

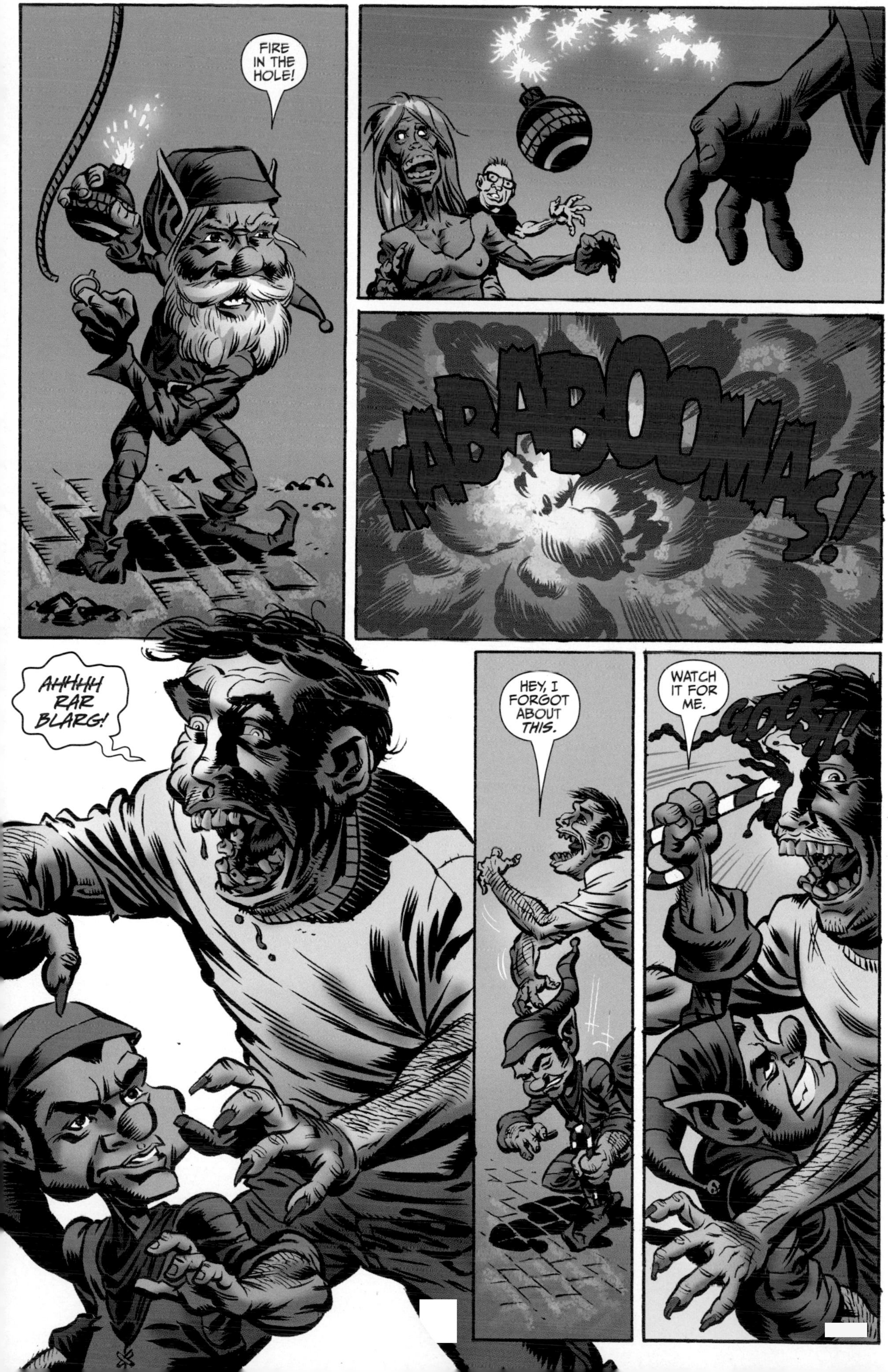
FIRE IN THE HOLE!
KABABOOMAS!
AHHHH RAR BLARG!
HEY, I FORGOT ABOUT THIS.
WATCH IT FOR ME.
GOOSH!

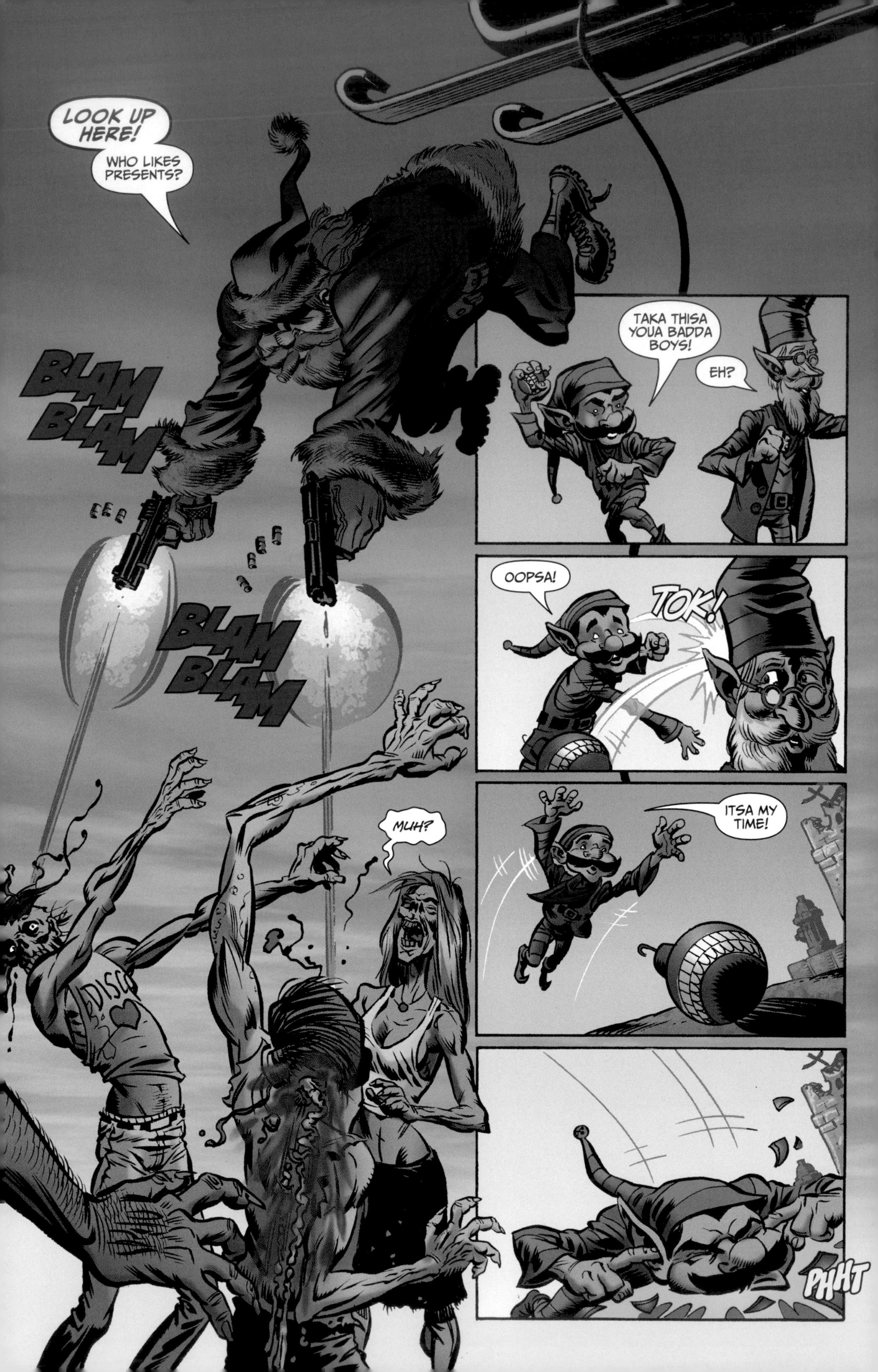
LOOK UP HERE!
WHO LIKES PRESENTS?
BLAM BLAM
BLAM BLAM
MUH?
TAKA THISA YOUA BADDA BOYS!
EH?
OOPSA!
TOK!
ITSA MY TIME!
PHHT

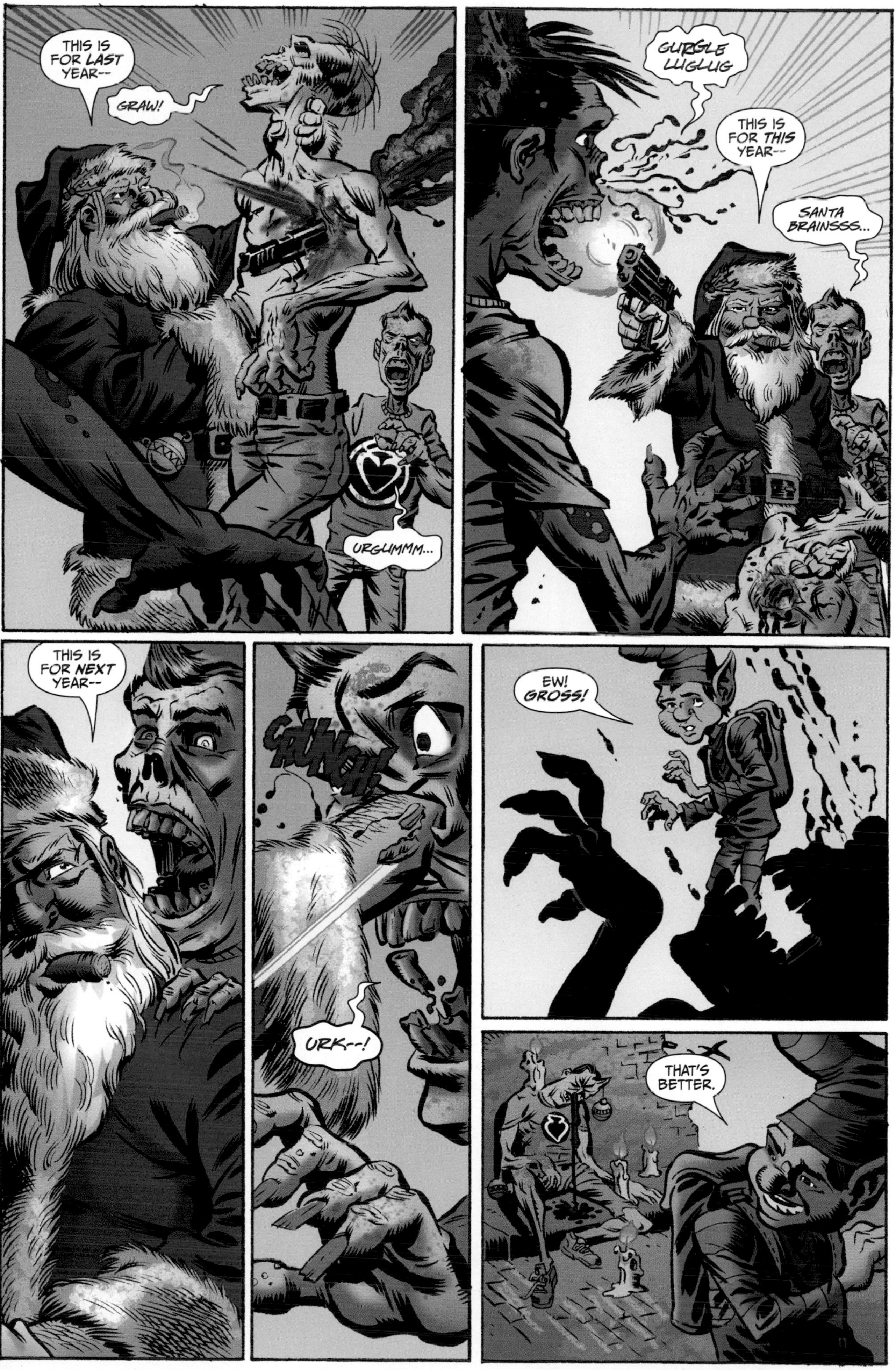

THIS IS FOR LAST YEAR--
GRAW!
URGUMMM...
GURGLE LUGLUG
THIS IS FOR THIS YEAR--
SANTA BRAINSSS...
THIS IS FOR NEXT YEAR--
CRUNCH!
URK--!
EW! GROSS!
THAT'S BETTER.

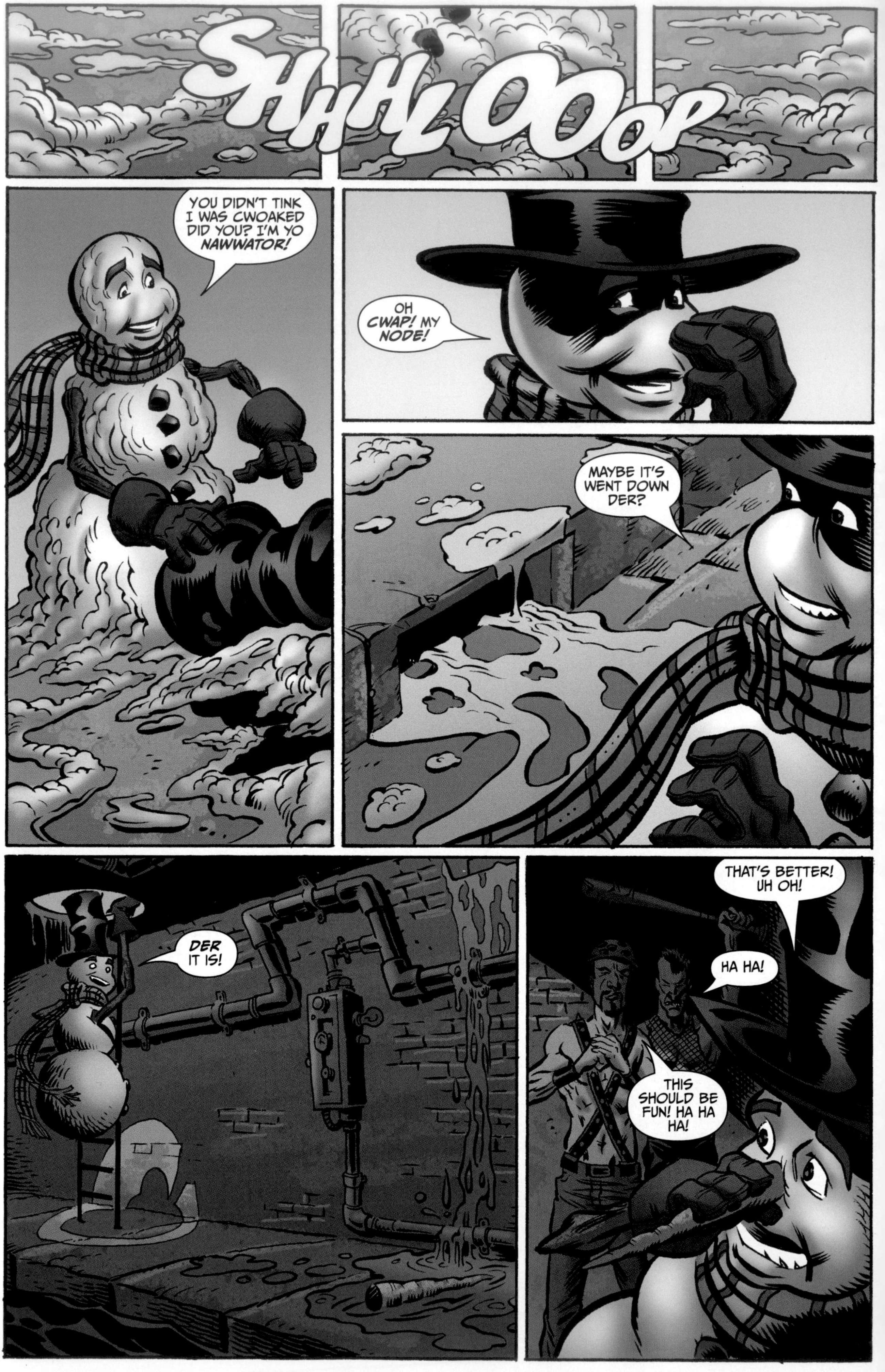
SHHLOOOP
YOU DIDN'T TINK I WAS CWOAKED DID YOU? I'M YO NAWWATOR!
OH CWAP! MY NODE!
MAYBE IT'S WENT DOWN DER?
DER IT IS!
THAT'S BETTER! UH OH!
HA HA!
THIS SHOULD BE FUN! HA HA HA!

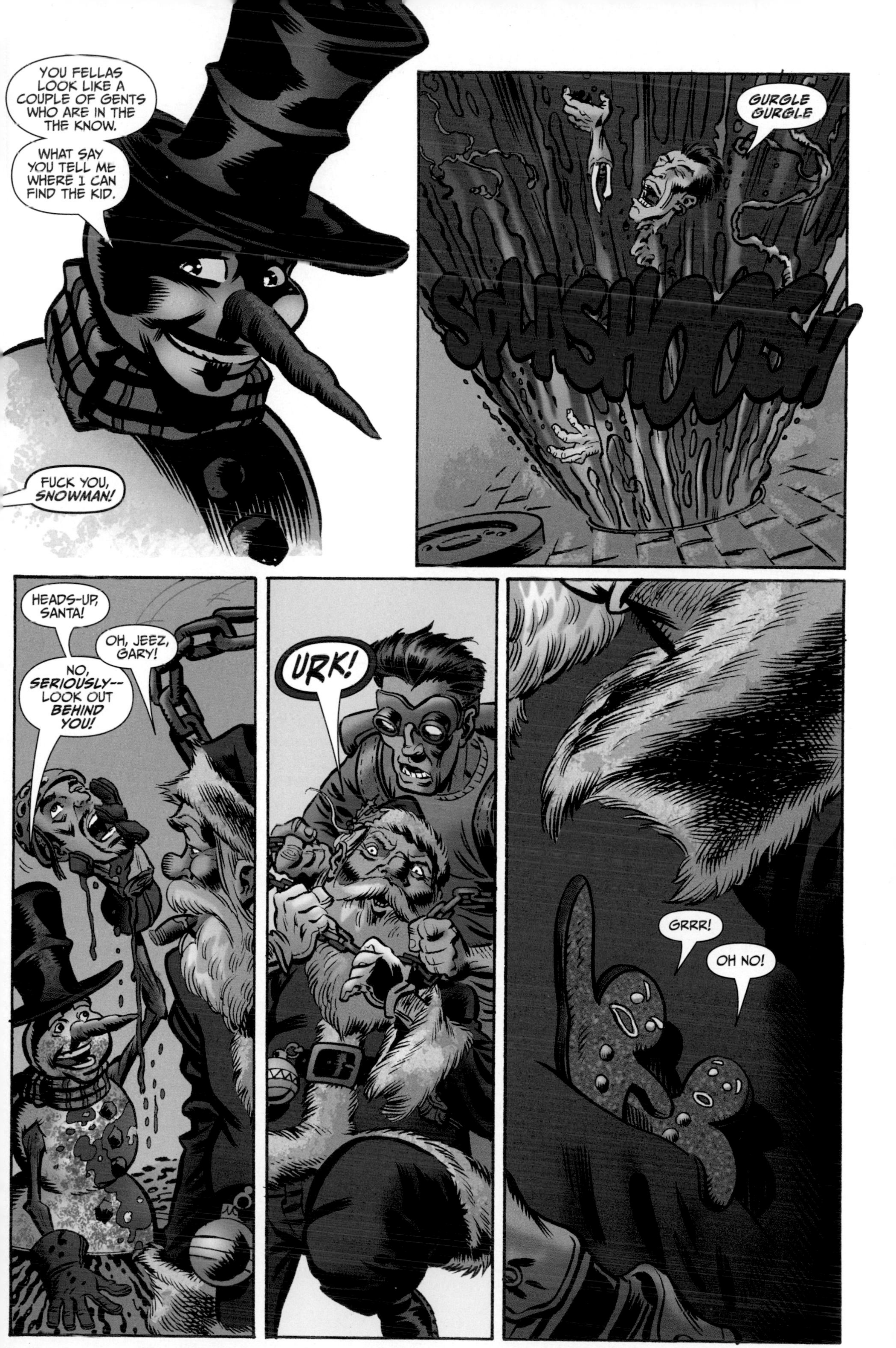
YOU FELLAS LOOK LIKE A COUPLE OF GENTS WHO ARE IN THE THE KNOW.
WHAT SAY YOU TELL ME WHERE I CAN FIND THE KID.
FUCK YOU, SNOWMAN!
GURGLE GURGLE
SPLASHOOOSH
HEADS-UP, SANTA!
OH, JEEZ, GARY!
NO, SERIOUSLY-- LOOK OUT BEHIND YOU!
URK!
GRRR!
OH NO!

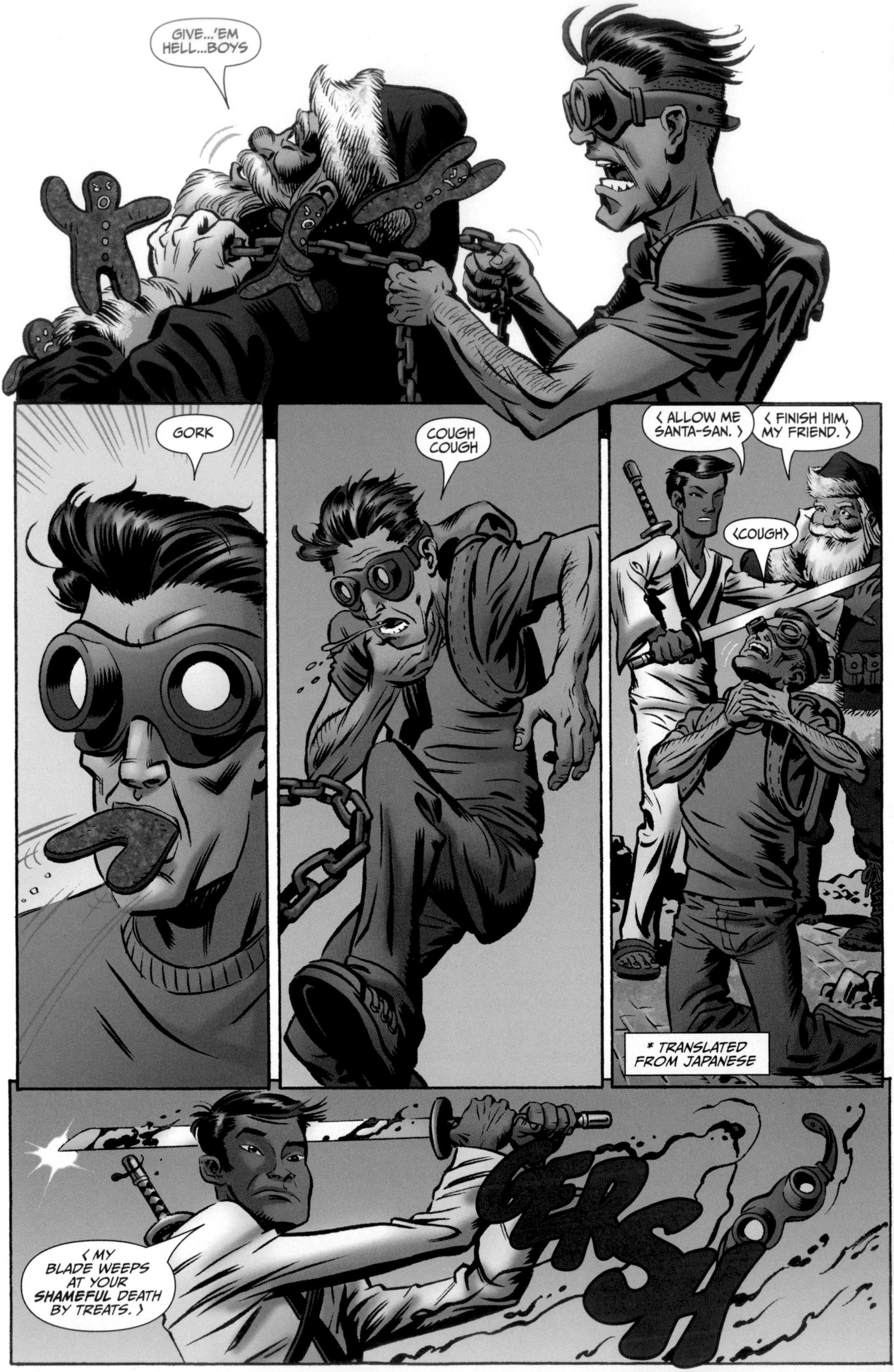
GIVE...'EM HELL...BOYS
GORK
COUGH COUGH
‹ ALLOW ME SANTA-SAN. ›
‹ FINISH HIM, MY FRIEND. ›
‹COUGH›
* TRANSLATED FROM JAPANESE
‹ MY BLADE WEEPS AT YOUR SHAMEFUL DEATH BY TREATS. ›
GERSSH

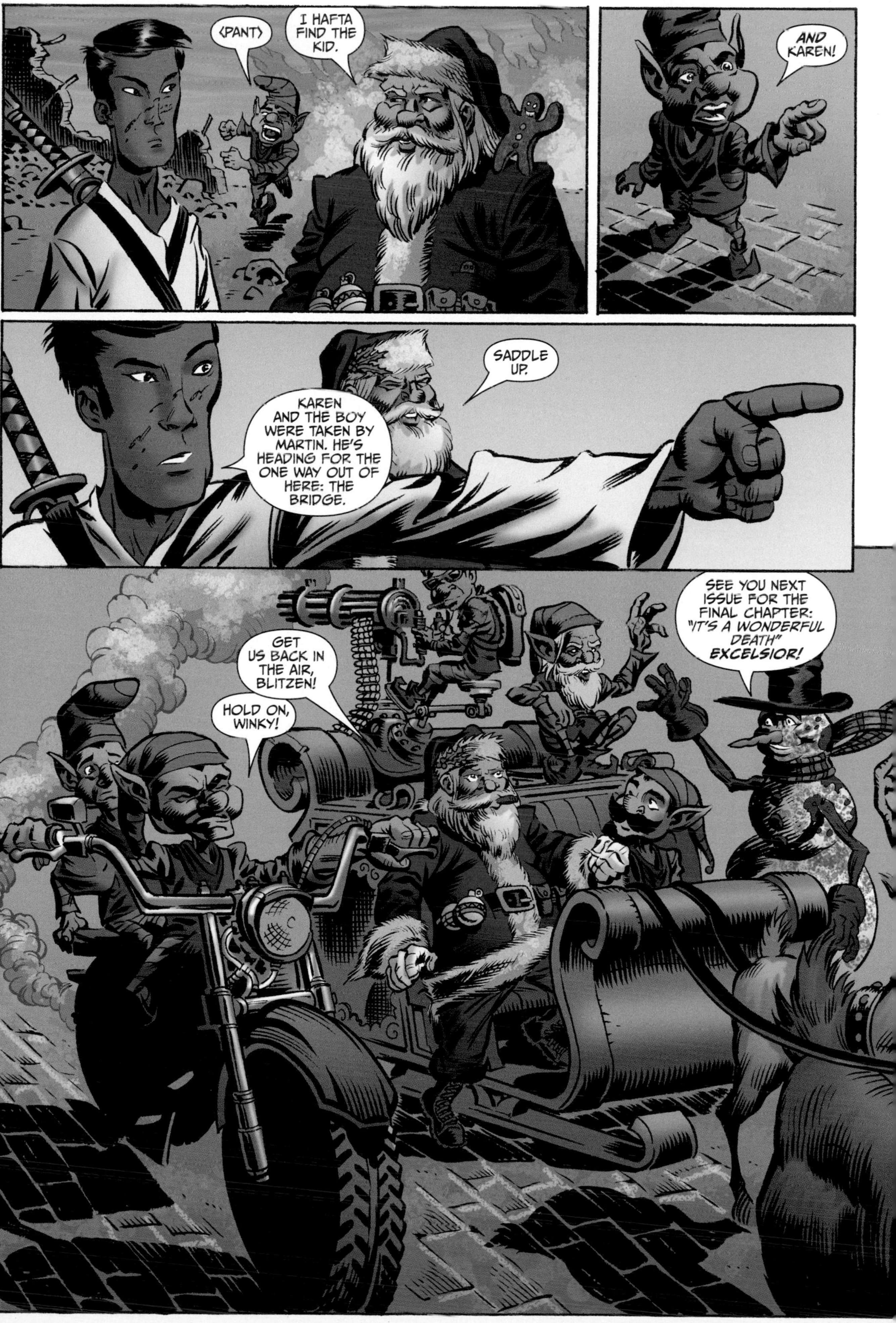

‹PANT›
I HAFTA FIND THE KID.
AND KAREN!
SADDLE UP.
KAREN AND THE BOY WERE TAKEN BY MARTIN. HE'S HEADING FOR THE ONE WAY OUT OF HERE: THE BRIDGE.
GET US BACK IN THE AIR, BLITZEN!
HOLD ON, WINKY!
SEE YOU NEXT ISSUE FOR THE FINAL CHAPTER: "IT'S A WONDERFUL DEATH" EXCELSIOR!

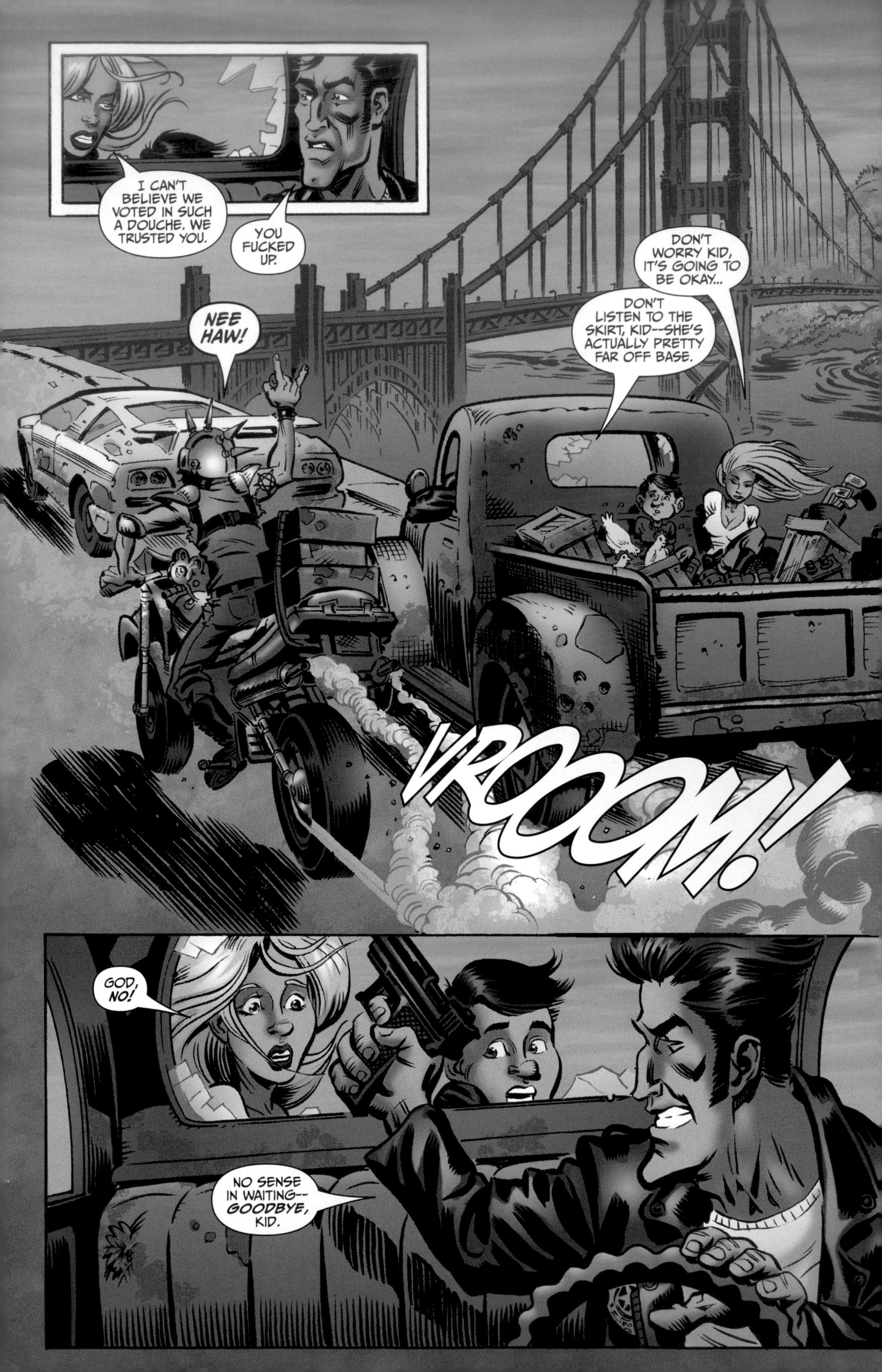
I CAN'T BELIEVE WE VOTED IN SUCH A DOUCHE. WE TRUSTED YOU.
YOU FUCKED UP.
NEE HAW!
DON'T WORRY KID, IT'S GOING TO BE OKAY...
DON'T LISTEN TO THE SKIRT, KID--SHE'S ACTUALLY PRETTY FAR OFF BASE.
VROOOM!!
GOD, NO!
NO SENSE IN WAITING-- GOODBYE, KID.

Chapter 5

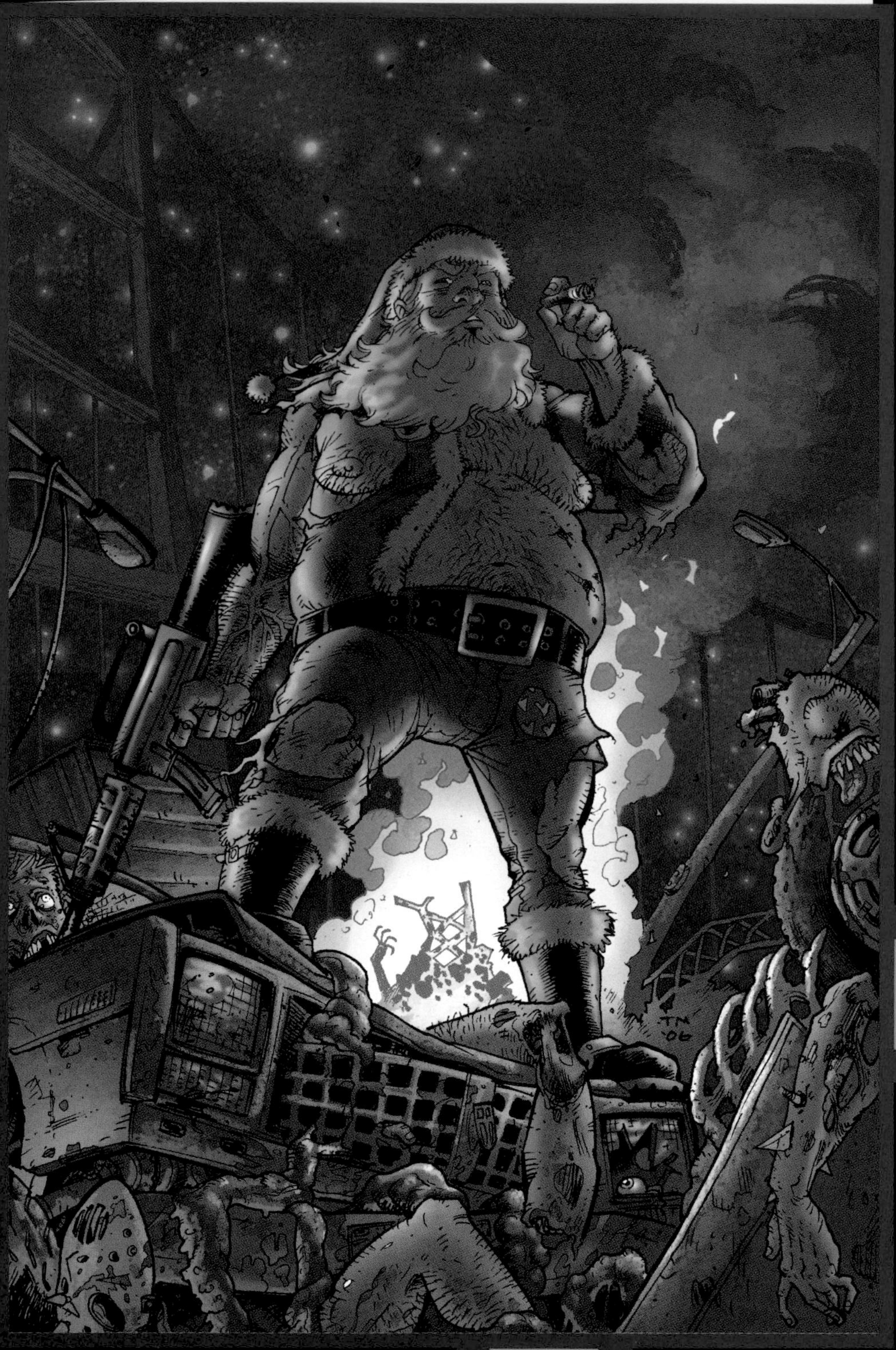

TM '06

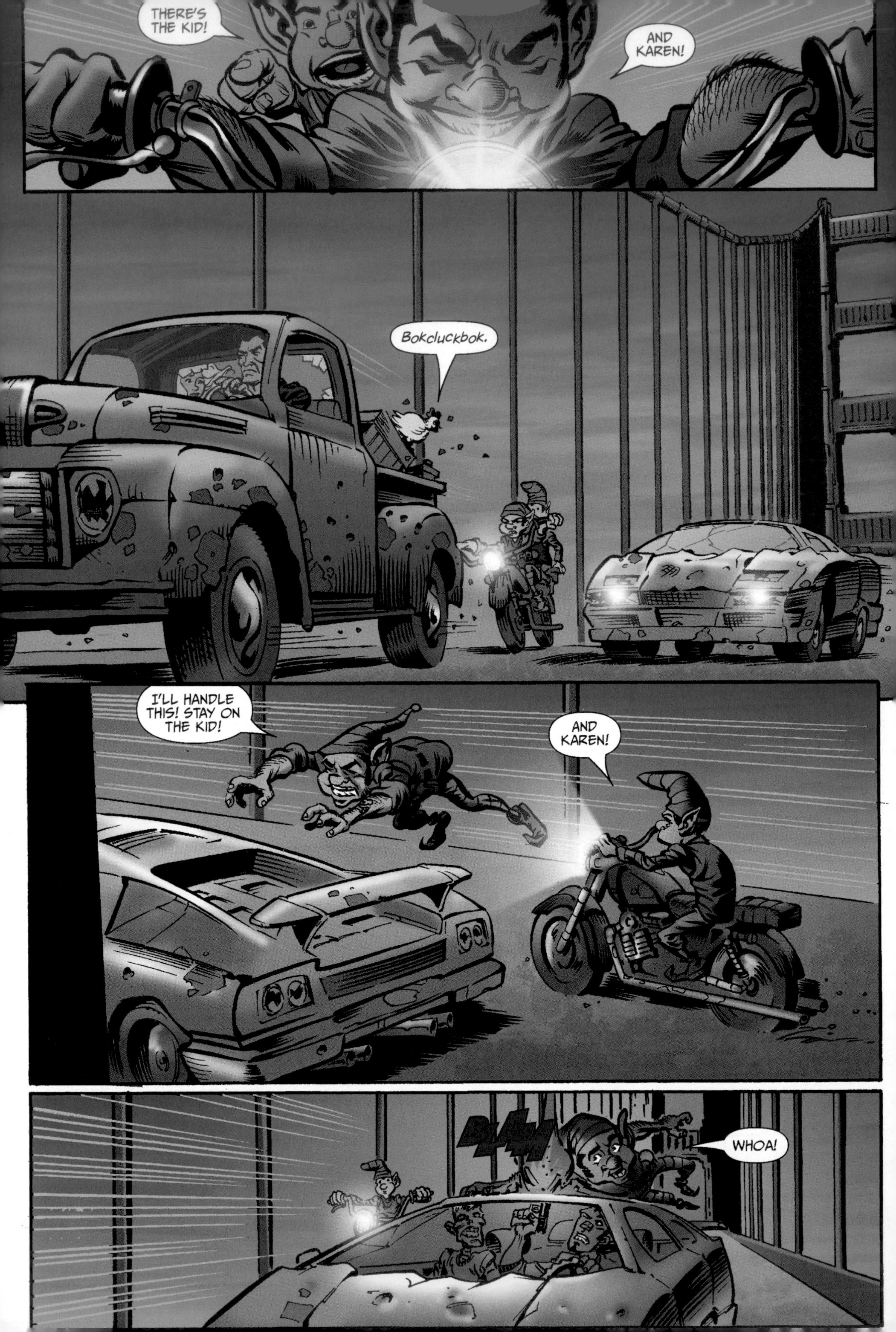
THERE'S THE KID!
AND KAREN!
Bokcluckbok.
I'LL HANDLE THIS! STAY ON THE KID!
AND KAREN!
WHOA!

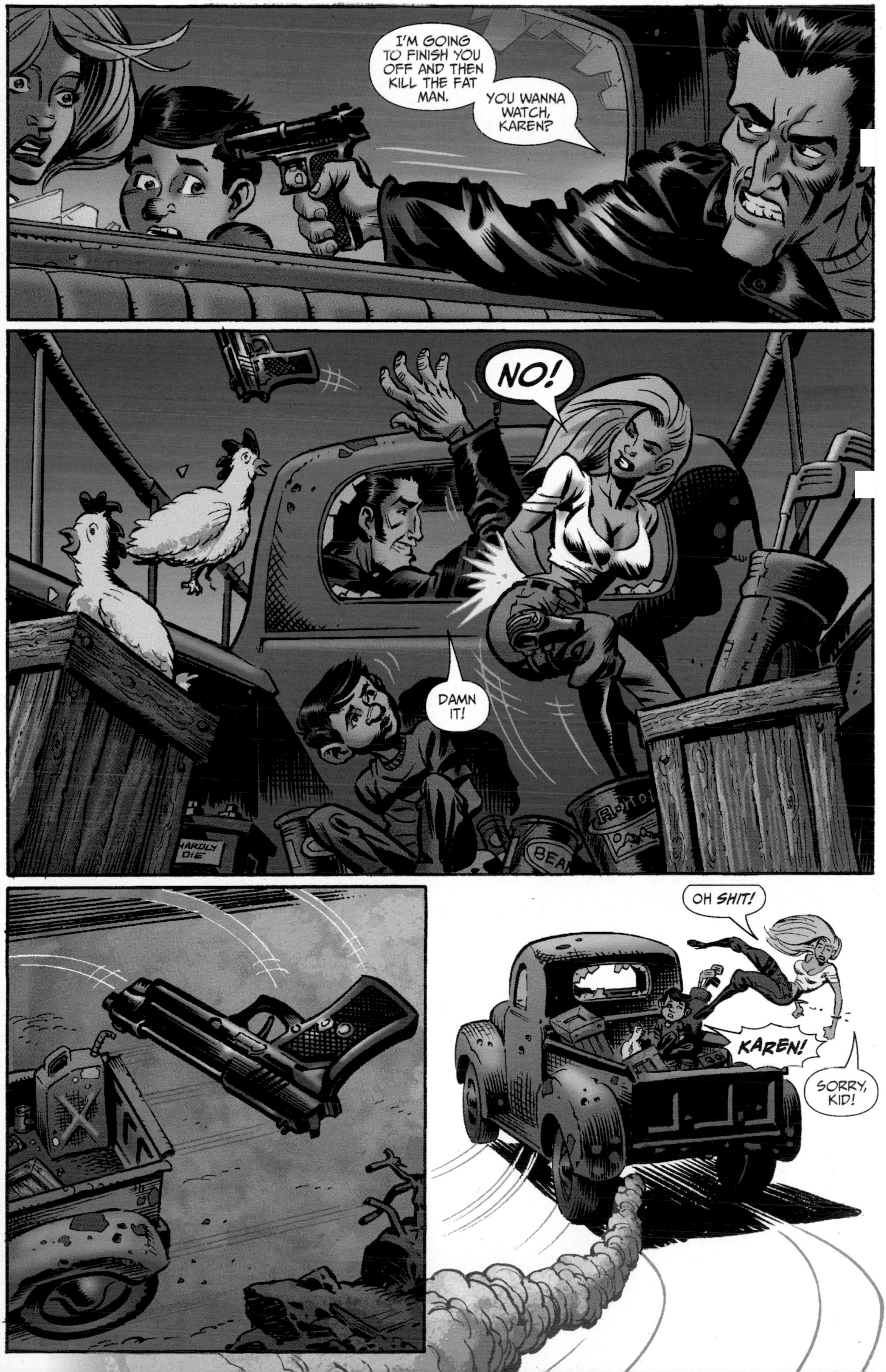
I'M GOING TO FINISH YOU OFF AND THEN KILL THE FAT MAN.
YOU WANNA WATCH, KAREN?
NO!
DAMN IT!
HARDLY DIE
BEAN
OH SHIT!
KAREN!
SORRY, KID!

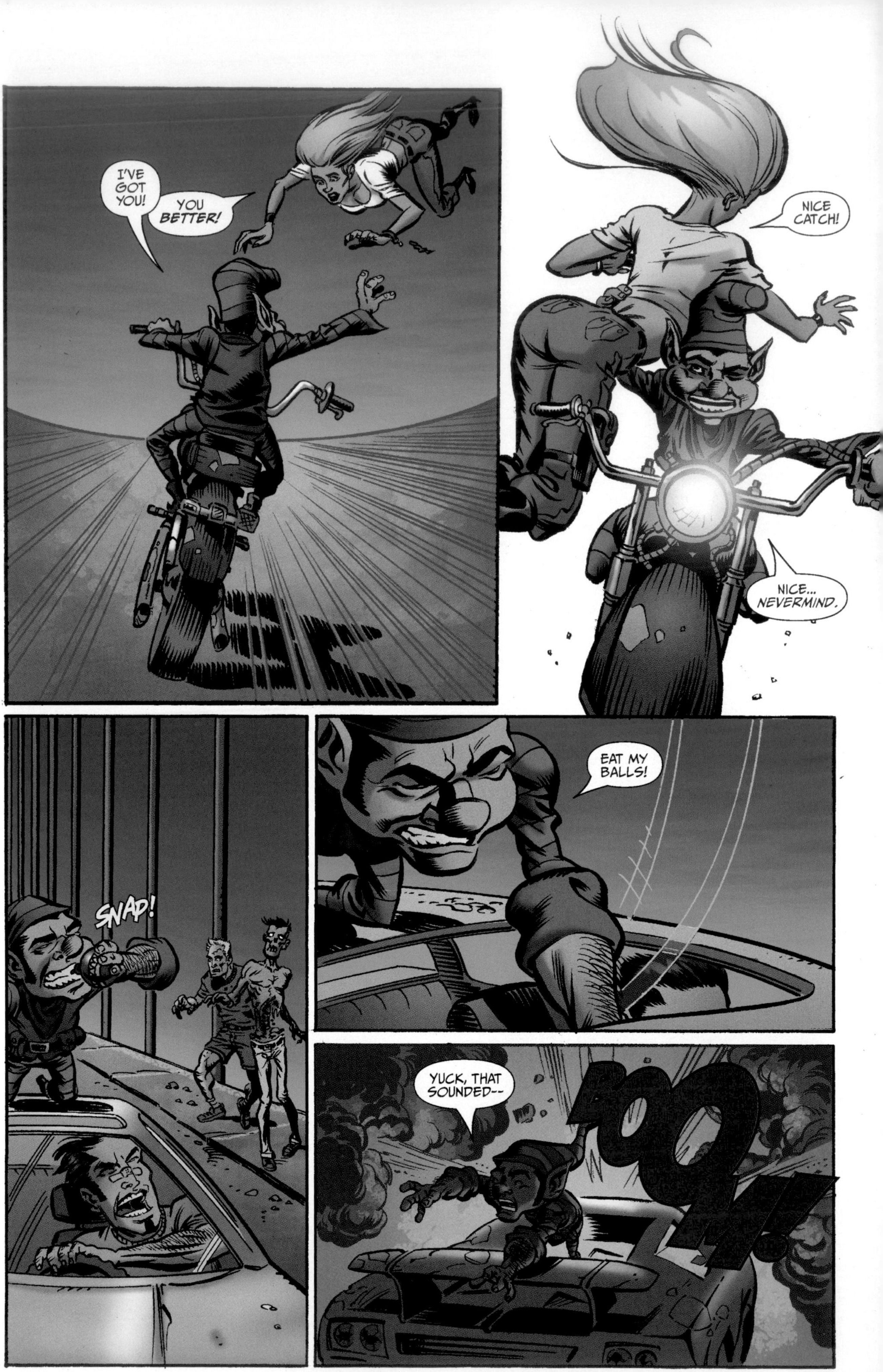
I'VE GOT YOU!
YOU BETTER!
NICE CATCH!
NICE... NEVERMIND.
SNAP!
EAT MY BALLS!
YUCK, THAT SOUNDED--
BOOM!!

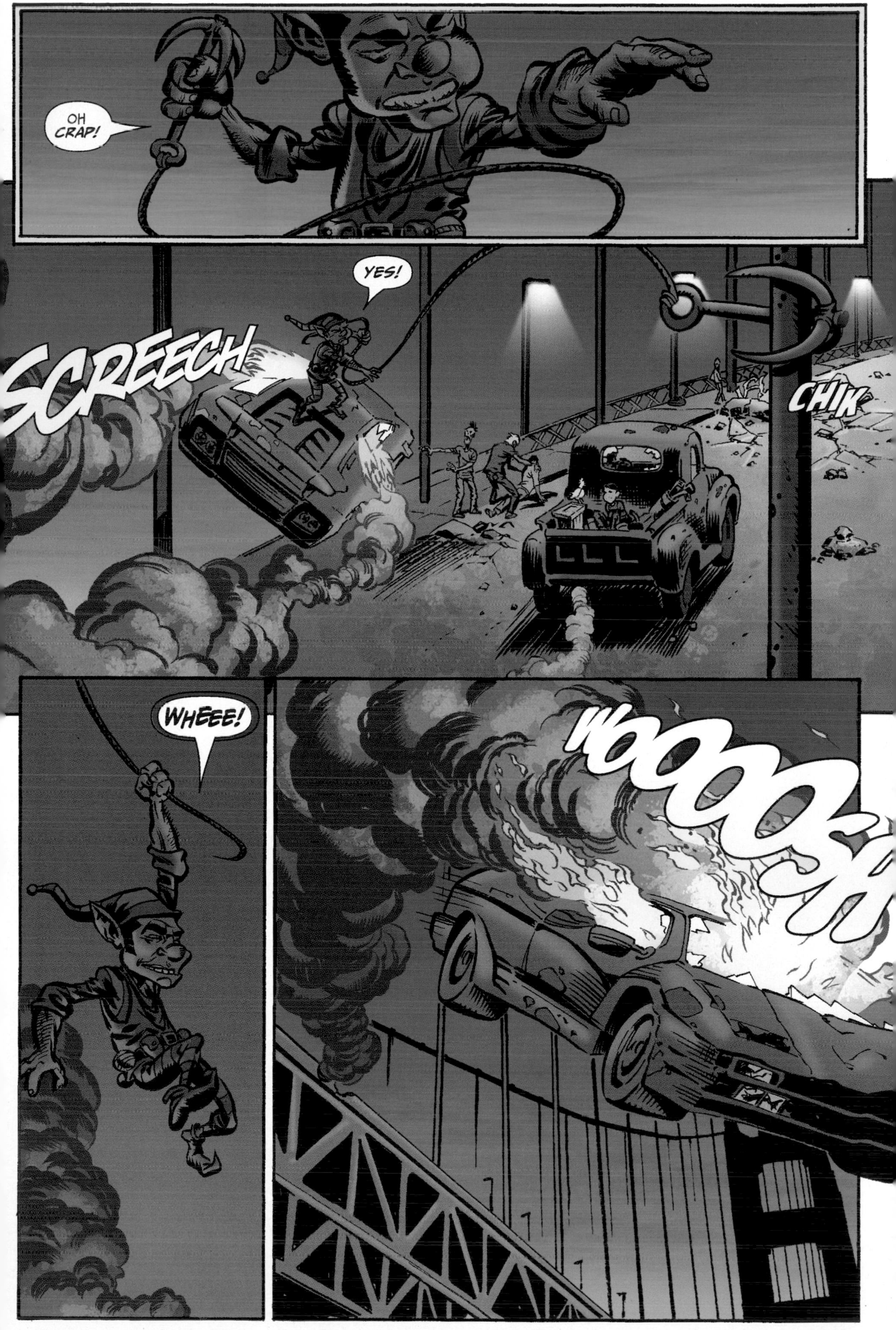
OH CRAP!
YES!
SCREECH
CHIK
WHEEE!
WOOOOSH

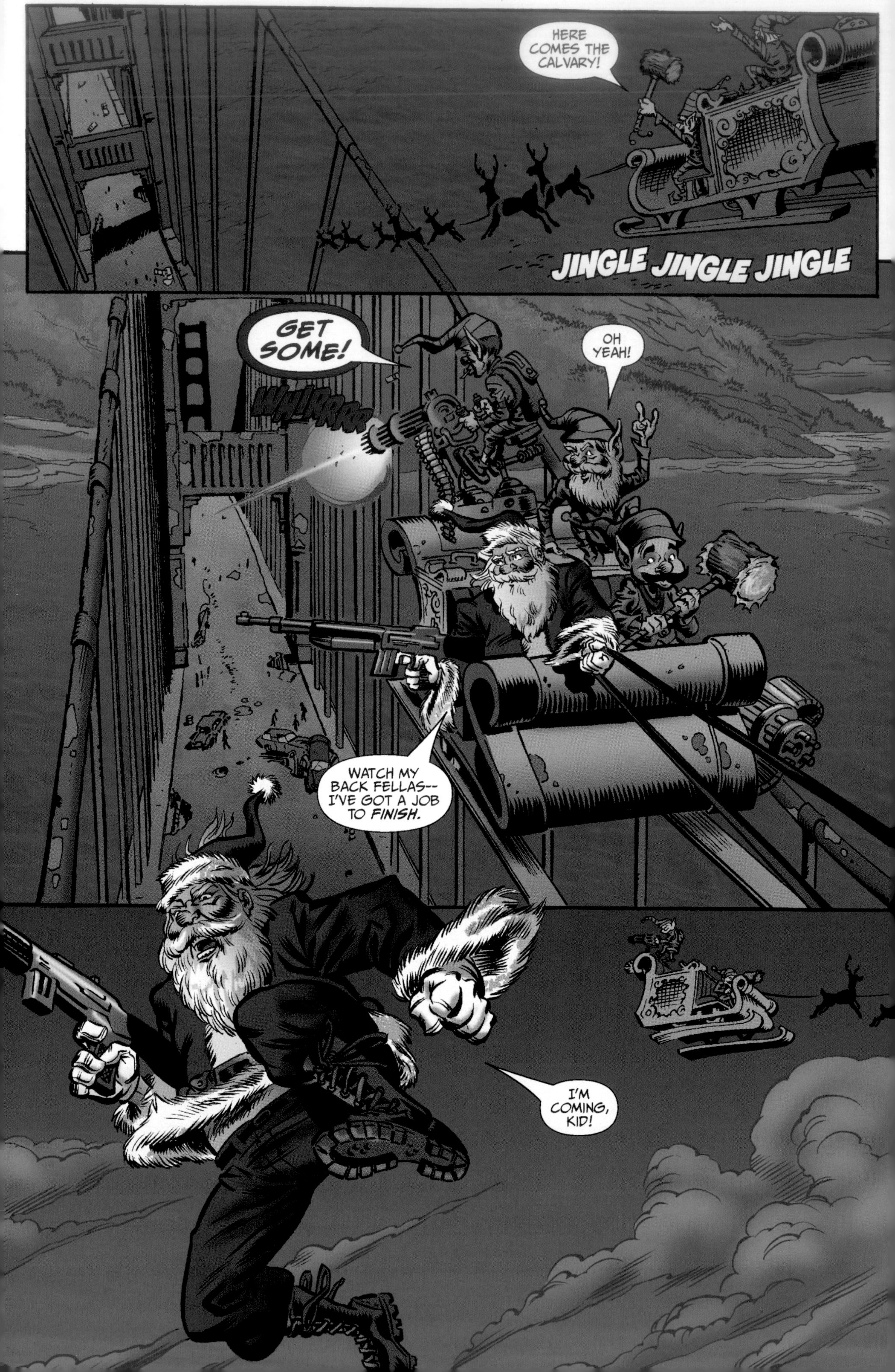
HERE COMES THE CALVARY!
JINGLE JINGLE JINGLE
GET SOME!
WHIRRRR
OH YEAH!
WATCH MY BACK FELLAS-- I'VE GOT A JOB TO *FINISH.*
I'M COMING, KID!

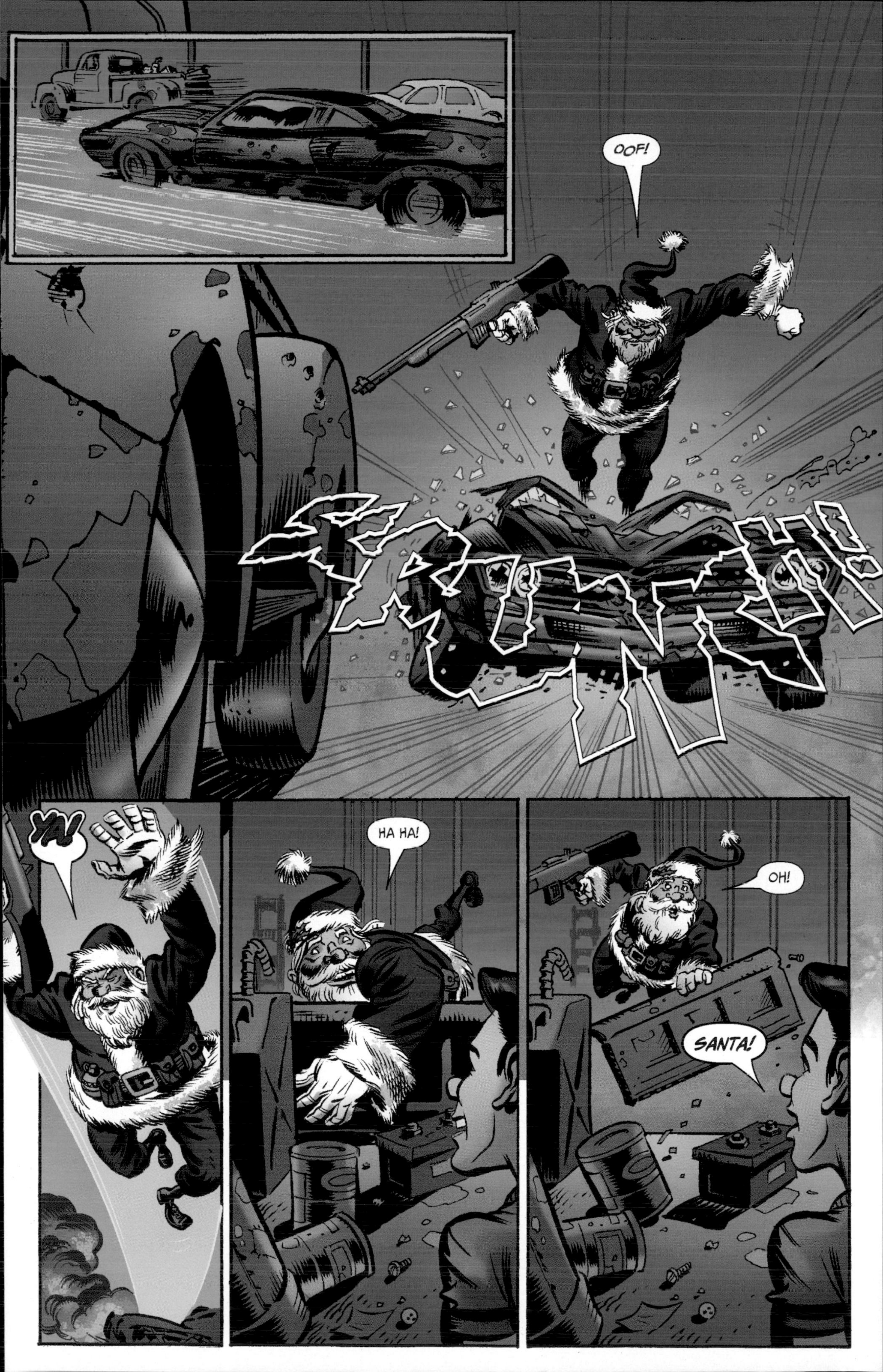
OOF!
KRUNCH!!
YA!
HA HA!
OH!
SANTA!

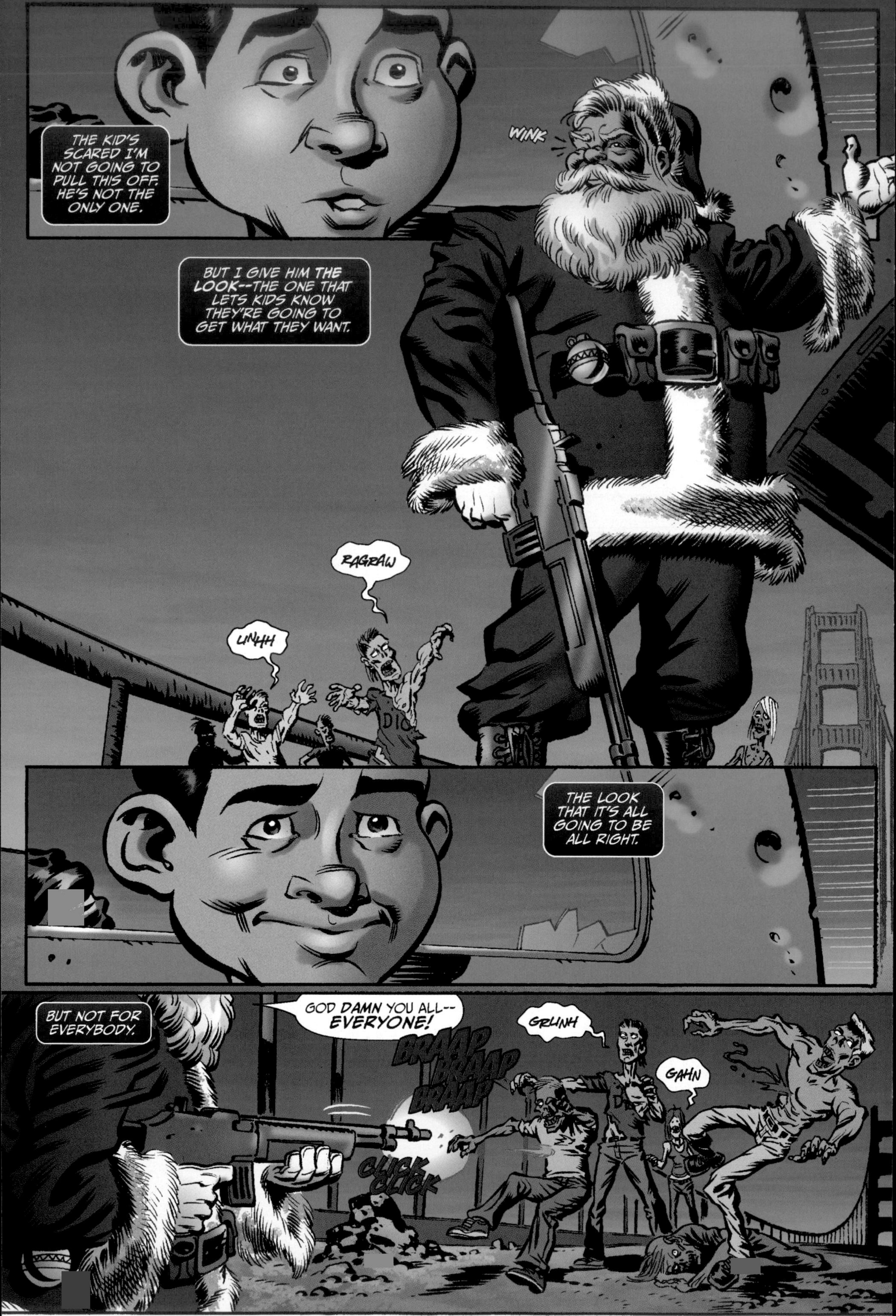
THE KID'S SCARED I'M NOT GOING TO PULL THIS OFF. HE'S NOT THE ONLY ONE.
WINK
BUT I GIVE HIM THE LOOK--THE ONE THAT LETS KIDS KNOW THEY'RE GOING TO GET WHAT THEY WANT.
RAGRAW
UNHH
THE LOOK THAT IT'S ALL GOING TO BE ALL RIGHT.
BUT NOT FOR EVERYBODY.
GOD DAMN YOU ALL-- EVERYONE!
GRUNH
BRAAP BRAAP BRAAP
GAHN
CLICK CLICK

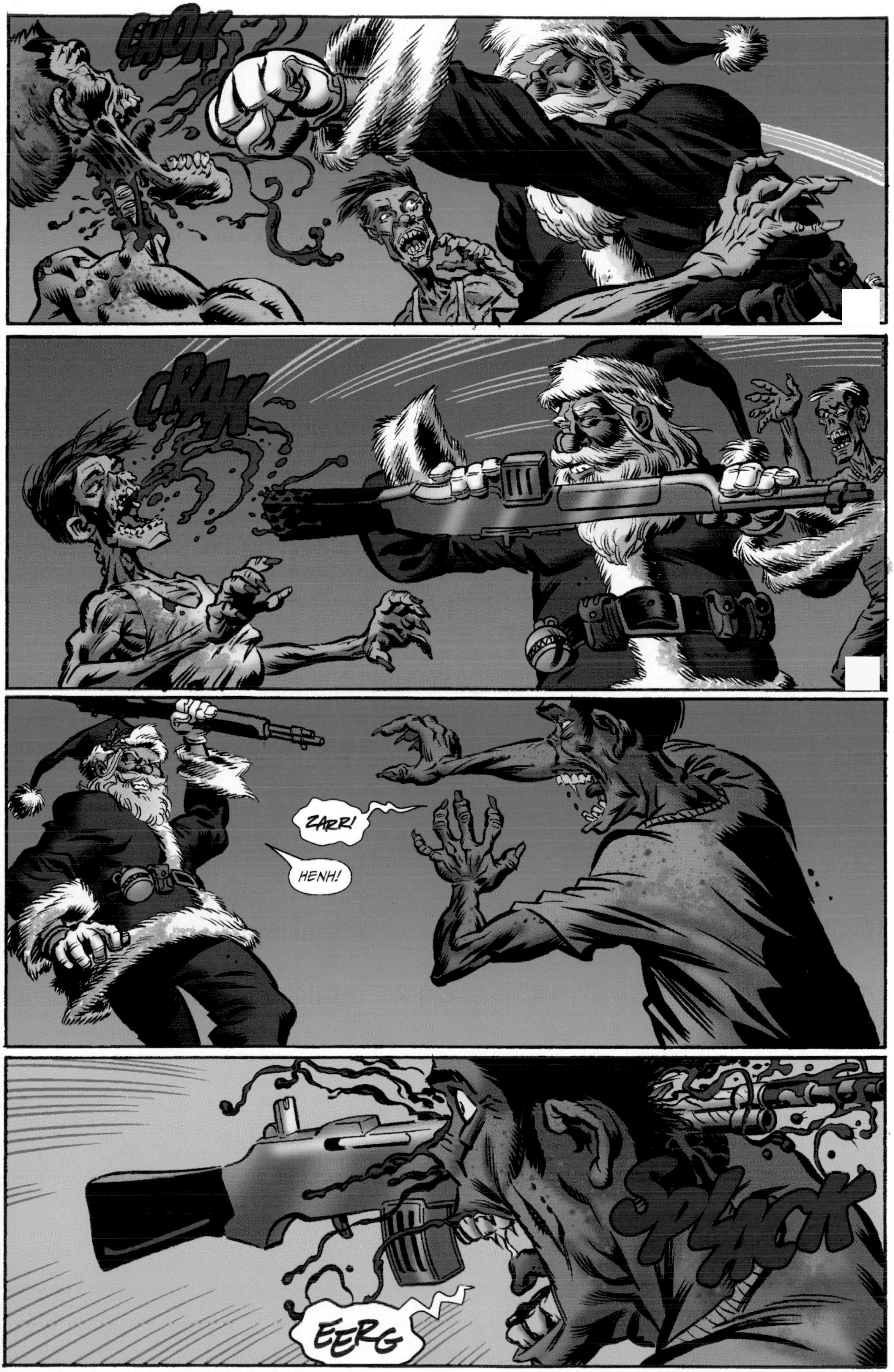
CHOK
CRAK
ZARR!
HENH!
SPLACK
EERG

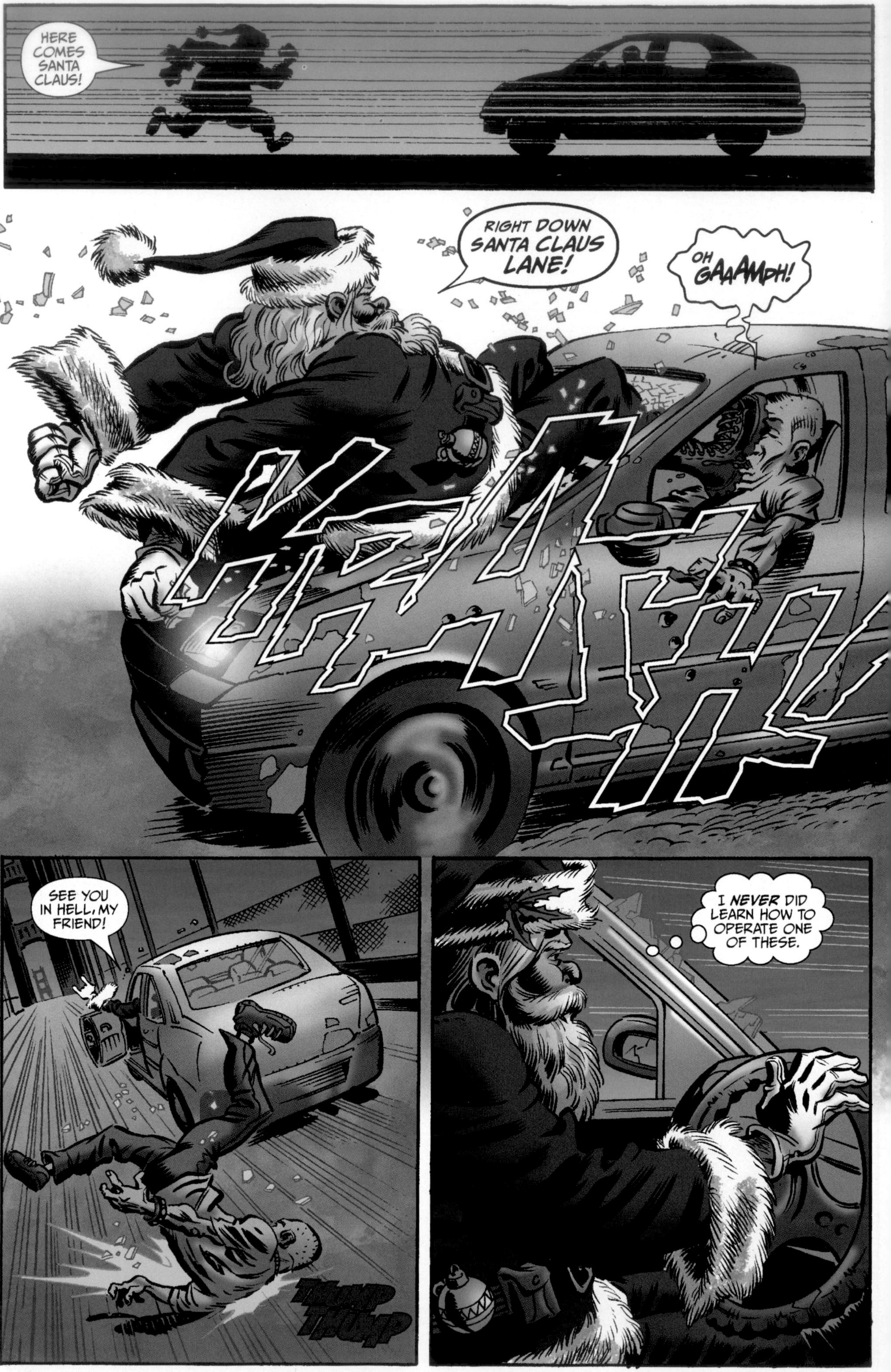
HERE COMES SANTA CLAUS!
RIGHT DOWN SANTA CLAUS LANE!
OH GAAAMPH!
SEE YOU IN HELL, MY FRIEND!
THUMP THUMP
I NEVER DID LEARN HOW TO OPERATE ONE OF THESE.

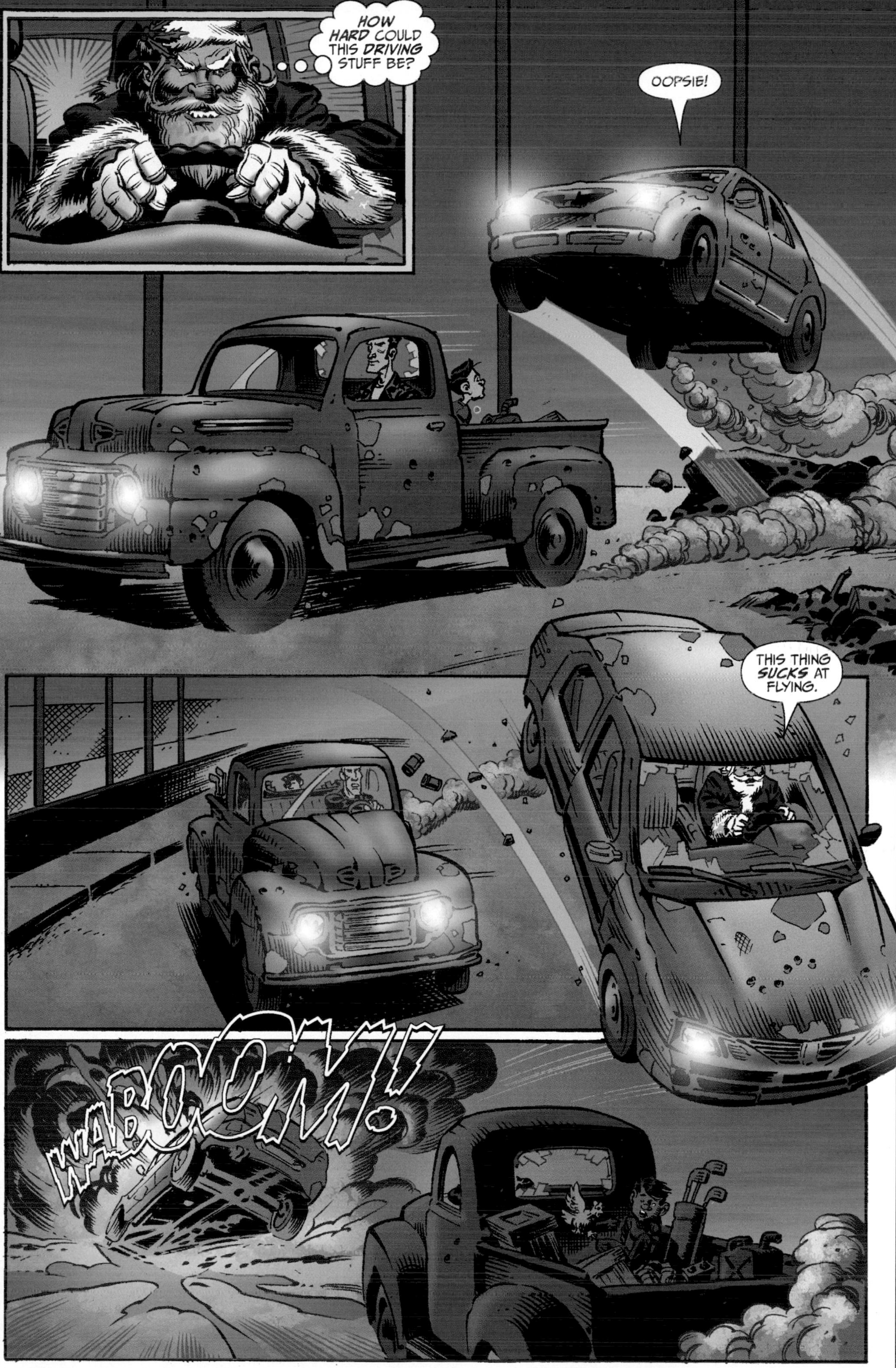
HOW HARD COULD THIS DRIVING STUFF BE?
OOPSIE!
THIS THING SUCKS AT FLYING.
WABOOM!

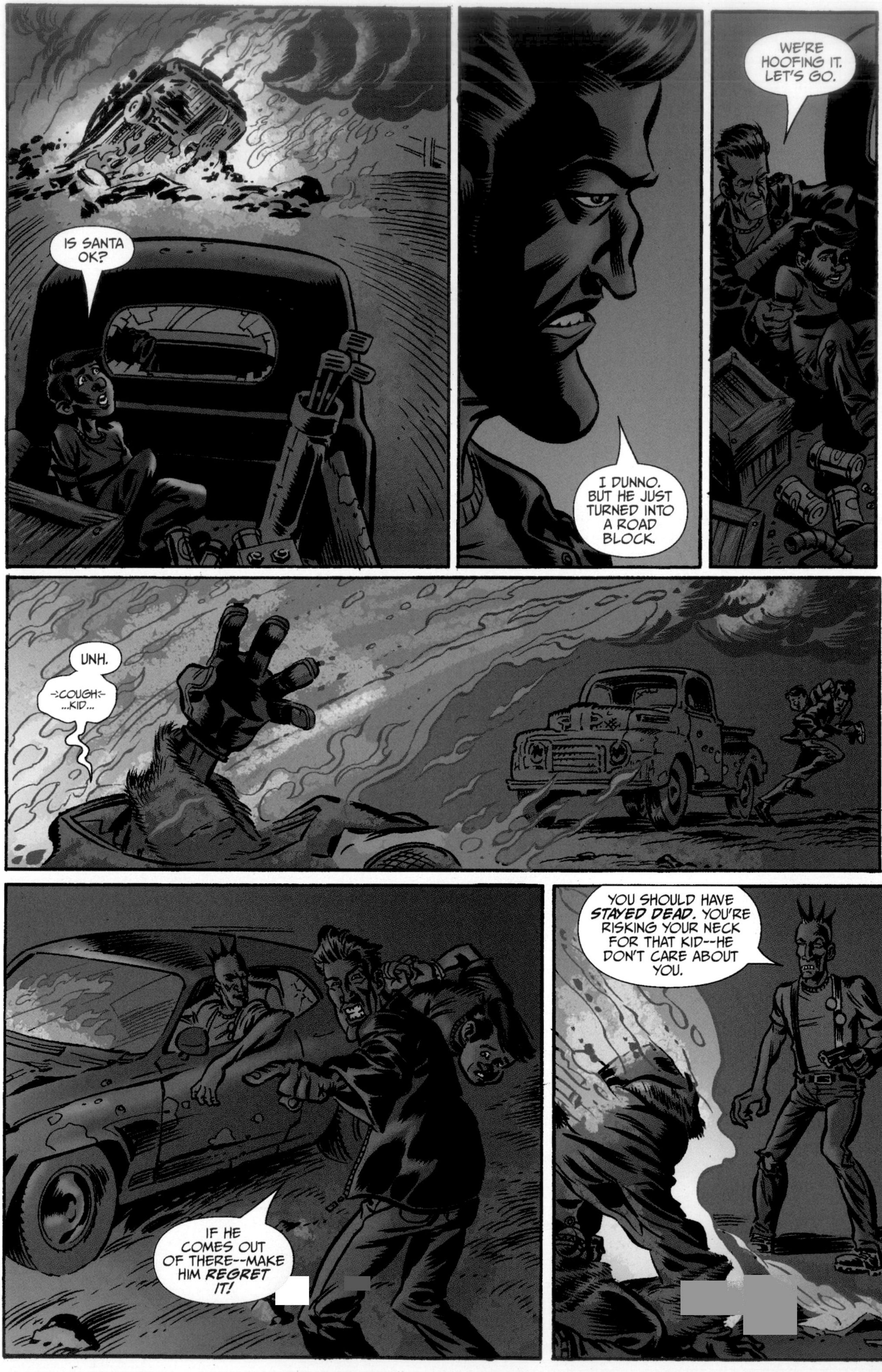
IS SANTA OK?
I DUNNO. BUT HE JUST TURNED INTO A ROAD BLOCK.
WE'RE HOOFING IT. LET'S GO.
UNH.
-COUGH- ...KID...
IF HE COMES OUT OF THERE--MAKE HIM REGRET IT!
YOU SHOULD HAVE STAYED DEAD. YOU'RE RISKING YOUR NECK FOR THAT KID--HE DON'T CARE ABOUT YOU.

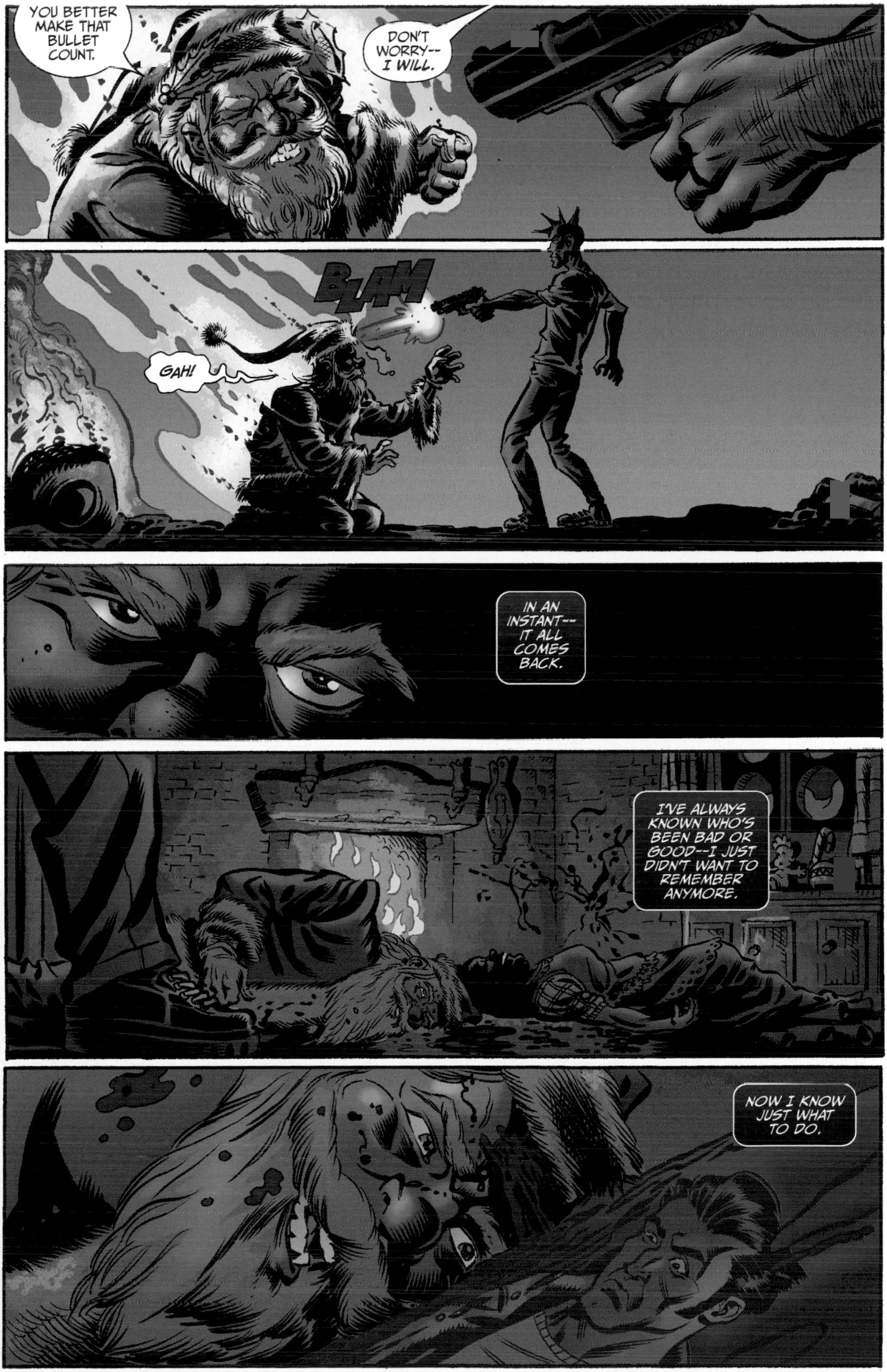

YOU BETTER MAKE THAT BULLET COUNT.
DON'T WORRY-- I WILL.
BLAM
GAH!
IN AN INSTANT-- IT ALL COMES BACK.
I'VE ALWAYS KNOWN WHO'S BEEN BAD OR GOOD--I JUST DIDN'T WANT TO REMEMBER ANYMORE.
NOW I KNOW JUST WHAT TO DO.

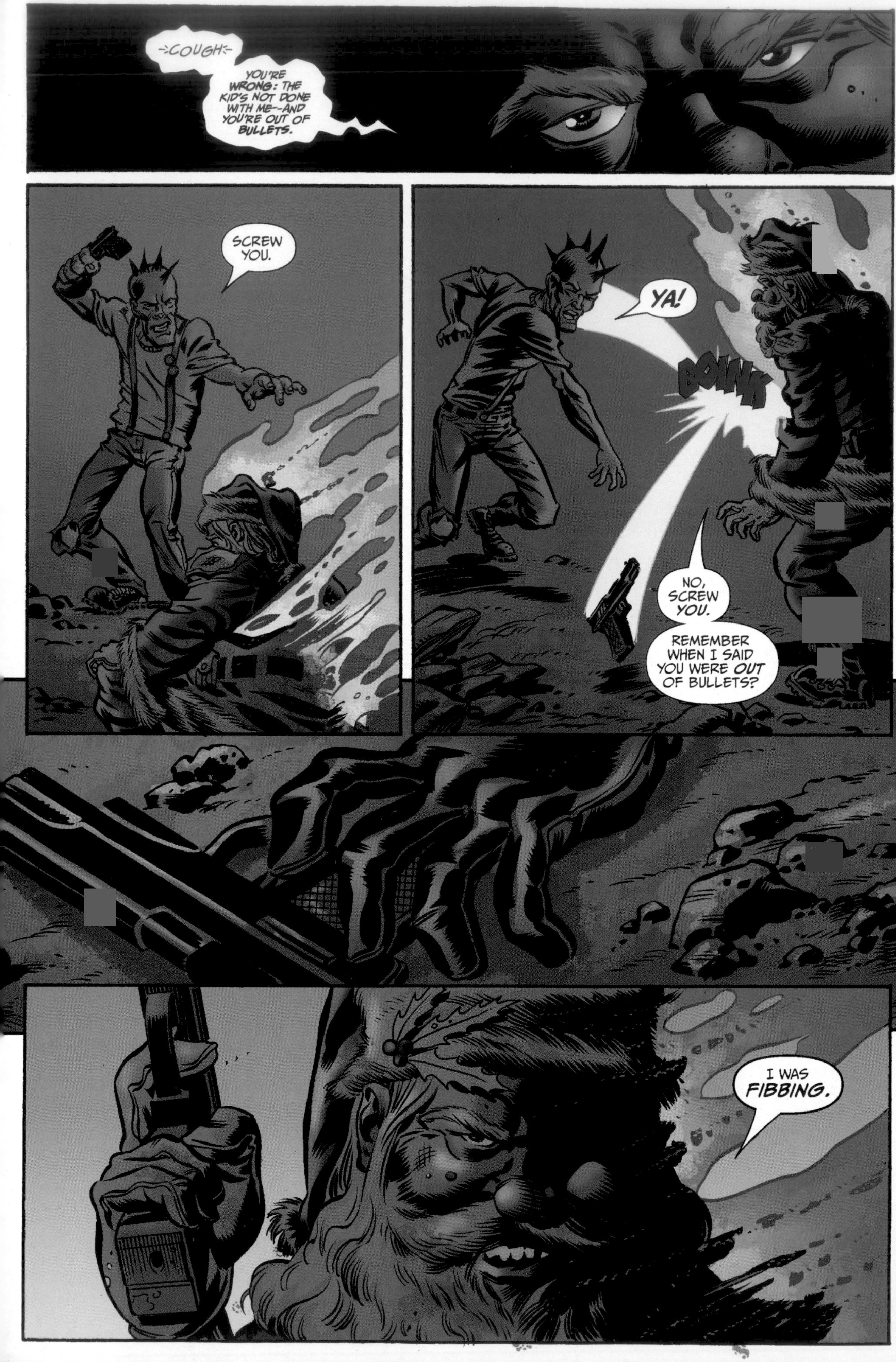
-COUGH-
YOU'RE WRONG: THE KID'S NOT DONE WITH ME--AND YOU'RE OUT OF BULLETS.
SCREW YOU.
YA!
BOINK
NO, SCREW YOU.
REMEMBER WHEN I SAID YOU WERE OUT OF BULLETS?
I WAS FIBBING.

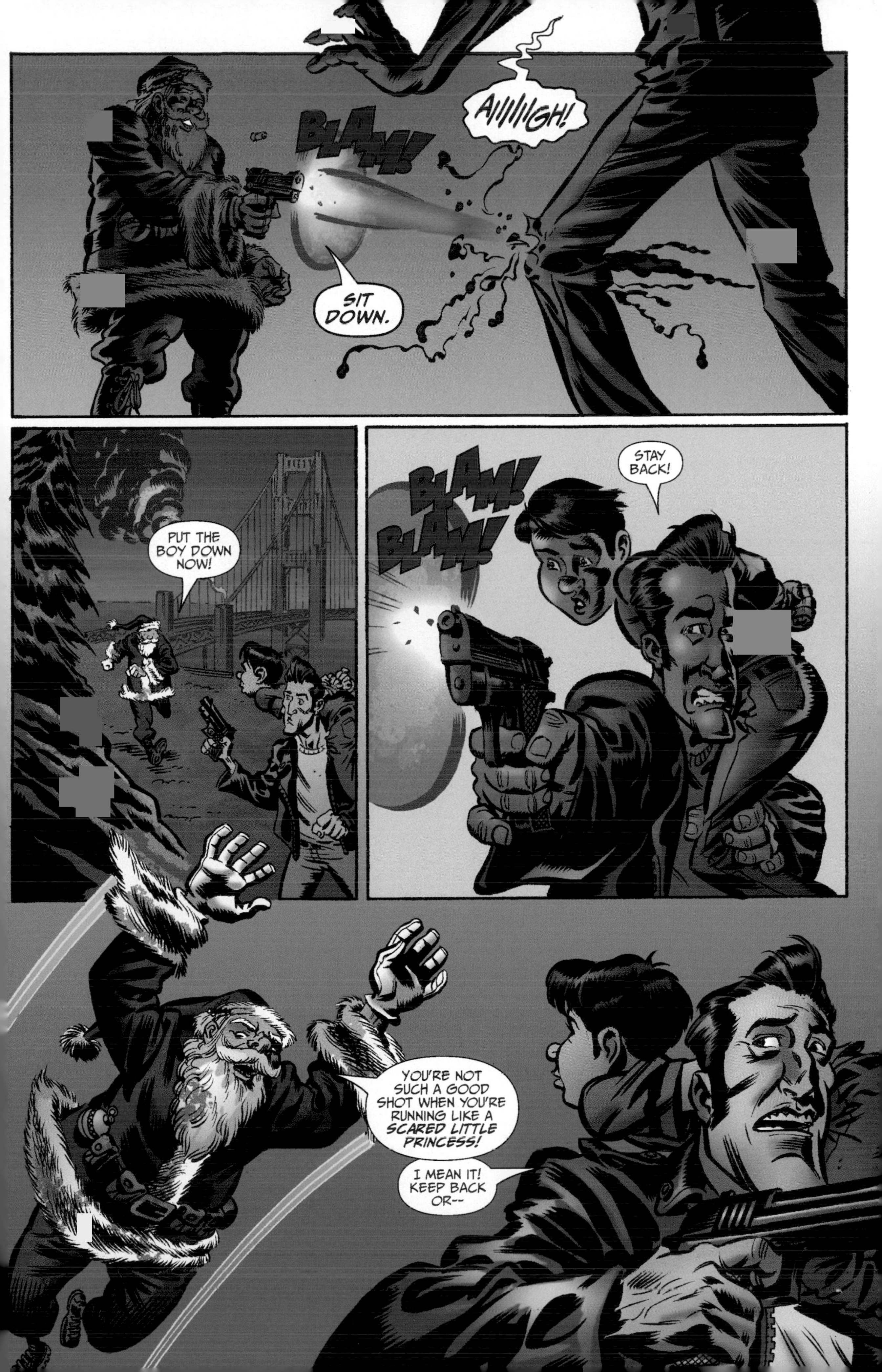
BLAM!
AIIIIIGH!
SIT DOWN.
PUT THE BOY DOWN NOW!
BLAM! BLAM!
STAY BACK!
YOU'RE NOT SUCH A GOOD SHOT WHEN YOU'RE RUNNING LIKE A SCARED LITTLE PRINCESS!
I MEAN IT! KEEP BACK OR--

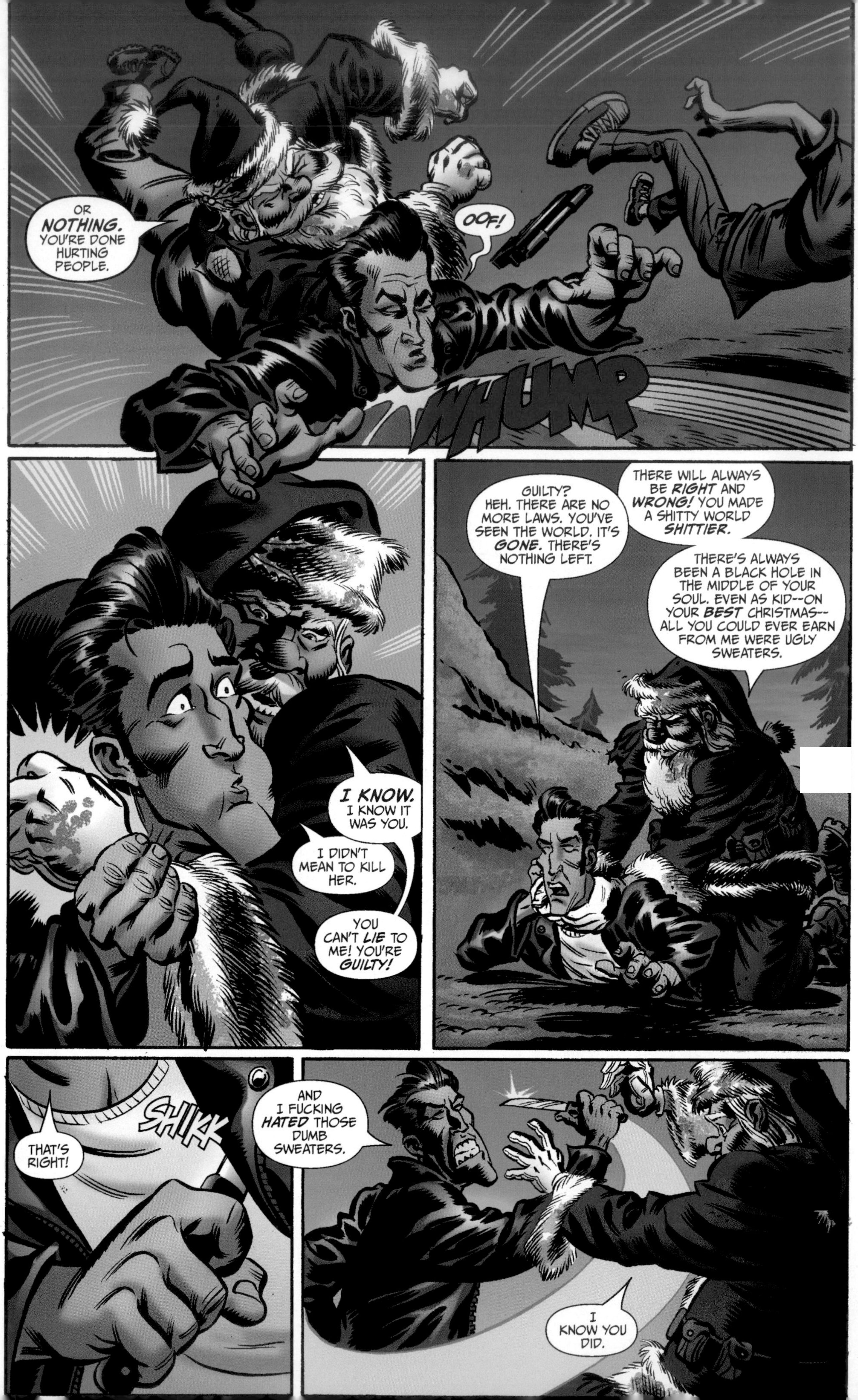
OR NOTHING. YOU'RE DONE HURTING PEOPLE.
OOF!
WHUMP
I KNOW. I KNOW IT WAS YOU.
I DIDN'T MEAN TO KILL HER.
YOU CAN'T LIE TO ME! YOU'RE GUILTY!
GUILTY? HEH. THERE ARE NO MORE LAWS. YOU'VE SEEN THE WORLD. IT'S GONE. THERE'S NOTHING LEFT.
THERE WILL ALWAYS BE RIGHT AND WRONG! YOU MADE A SHITTY WORLD SHITTIER.
THERE'S ALWAYS BEEN A BLACK HOLE IN THE MIDDLE OF YOUR SOUL. EVEN AS KID--ON YOUR BEST CHRISTMAS--ALL YOU COULD EVER EARN FROM ME WERE UGLY SWEATERS.
SHIKK
THAT'S RIGHT!
AND I FUCKING HATED THOSE DUMB SWEATERS.
I KNOW YOU DID.

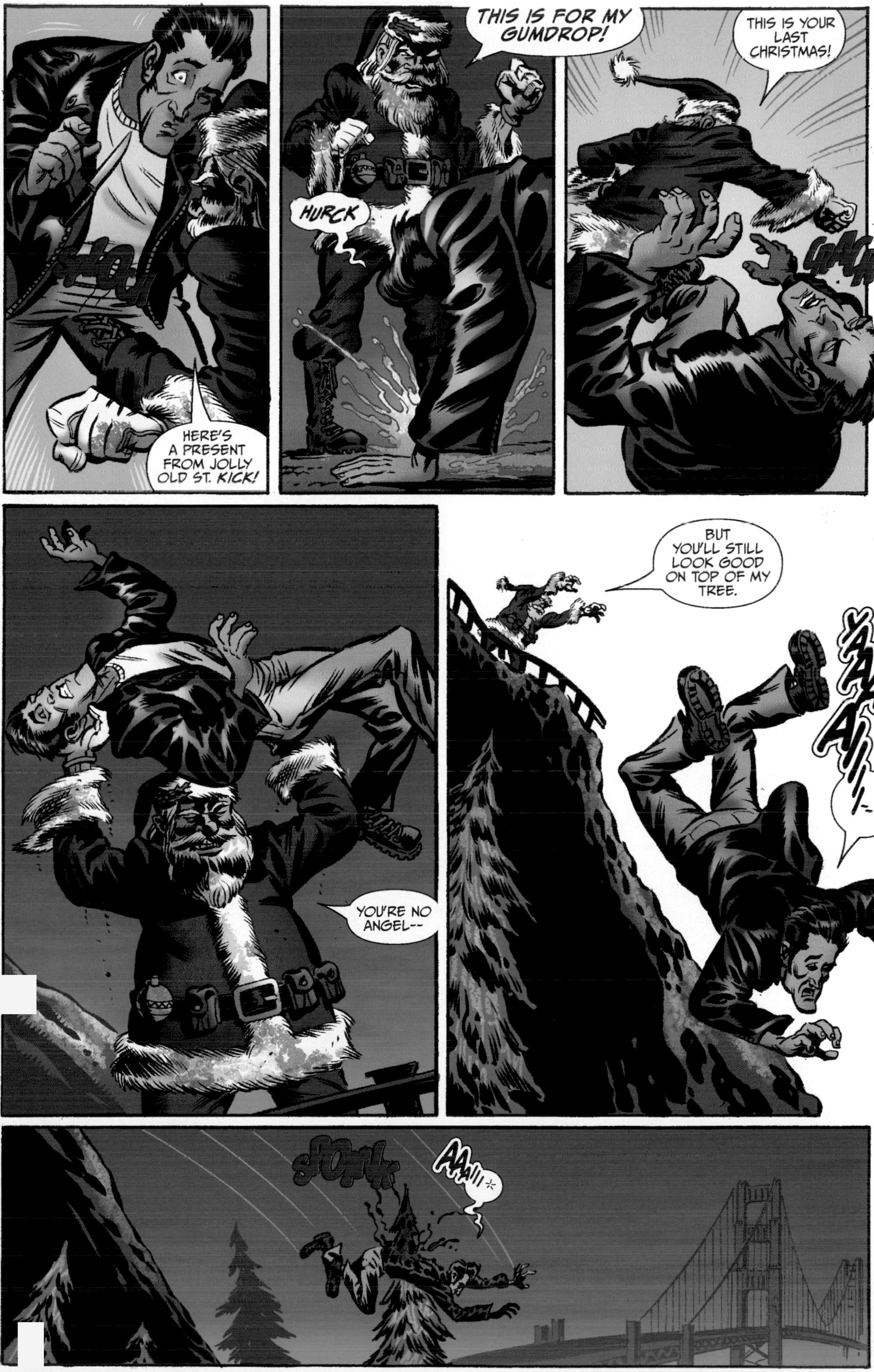
HERE'S A PRESENT FROM JOLLY OLD ST. KICK!
THIS IS FOR MY GUMDROP!
HURCK
THIS IS YOUR LAST CHRISTMAS!
YOU'RE NO ANGEL--
BUT YOU'LL STILL LOOK GOOD ON TOP OF MY TREE.
YAAAAAIII--
AAAIII

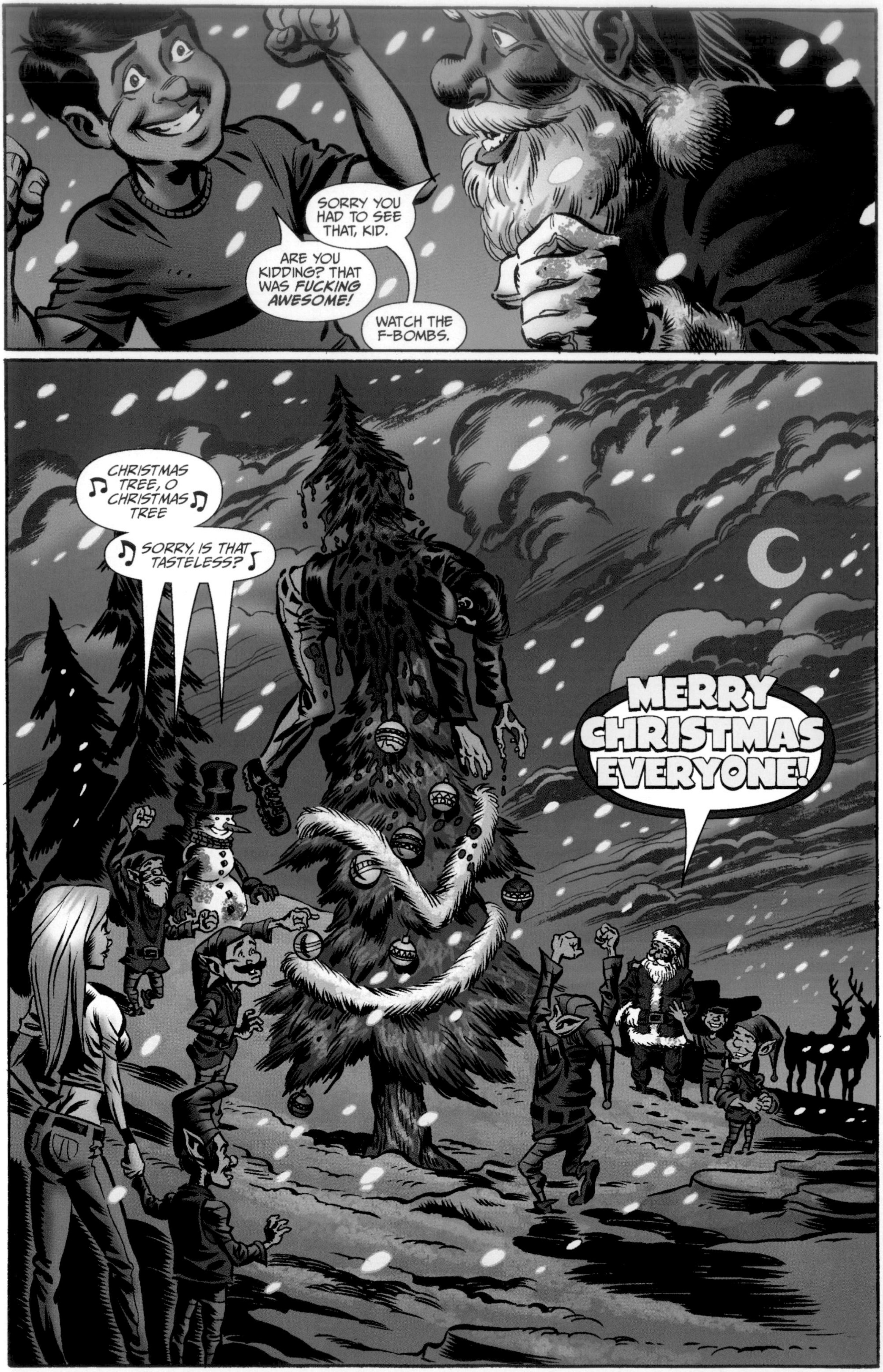
SORRY YOU HAD TO SEE THAT, KID.
ARE YOU KIDDING? THAT WAS *FUCKING AWESOME!*
WATCH THE F-BOMBS.
♪ CHRISTMAS TREE, O CHRISTMAS TREE ♪
♪ SORRY, IS THAT TASTELESS? ♪
MERRY CHRISTMAS EVERYONE!

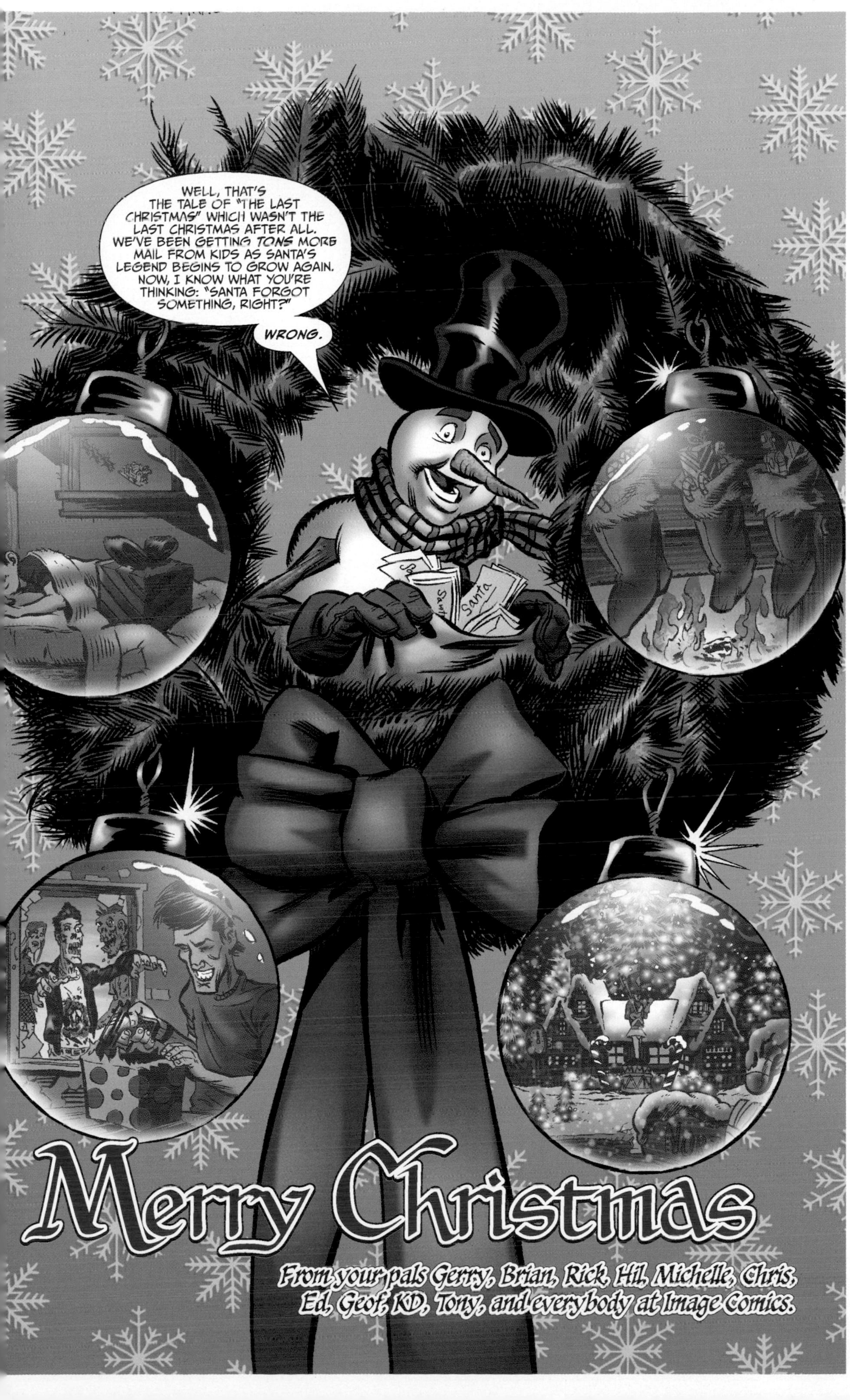
WELL, THAT'S THE TALE OF "THE LAST CHRISTMAS" WHICH WASN'T THE LAST CHRISTMAS AFTER ALL. WE'VE BEEN GETTING TONS MORE MAIL FROM KIDS AS SANTA'S LEGEND BEGINS TO GROW AGAIN. NOW, I KNOW WHAT YOU'RE THINKING: "SANTA FORGOT SOMETHING, RIGHT?"
WRONG.
Santa
Merry Christmas
From your pals Gerry, Brian, Rick, Hil, Michelle, Chris, Ed, Geof, KD, Tony, and everybody at Image Comics.

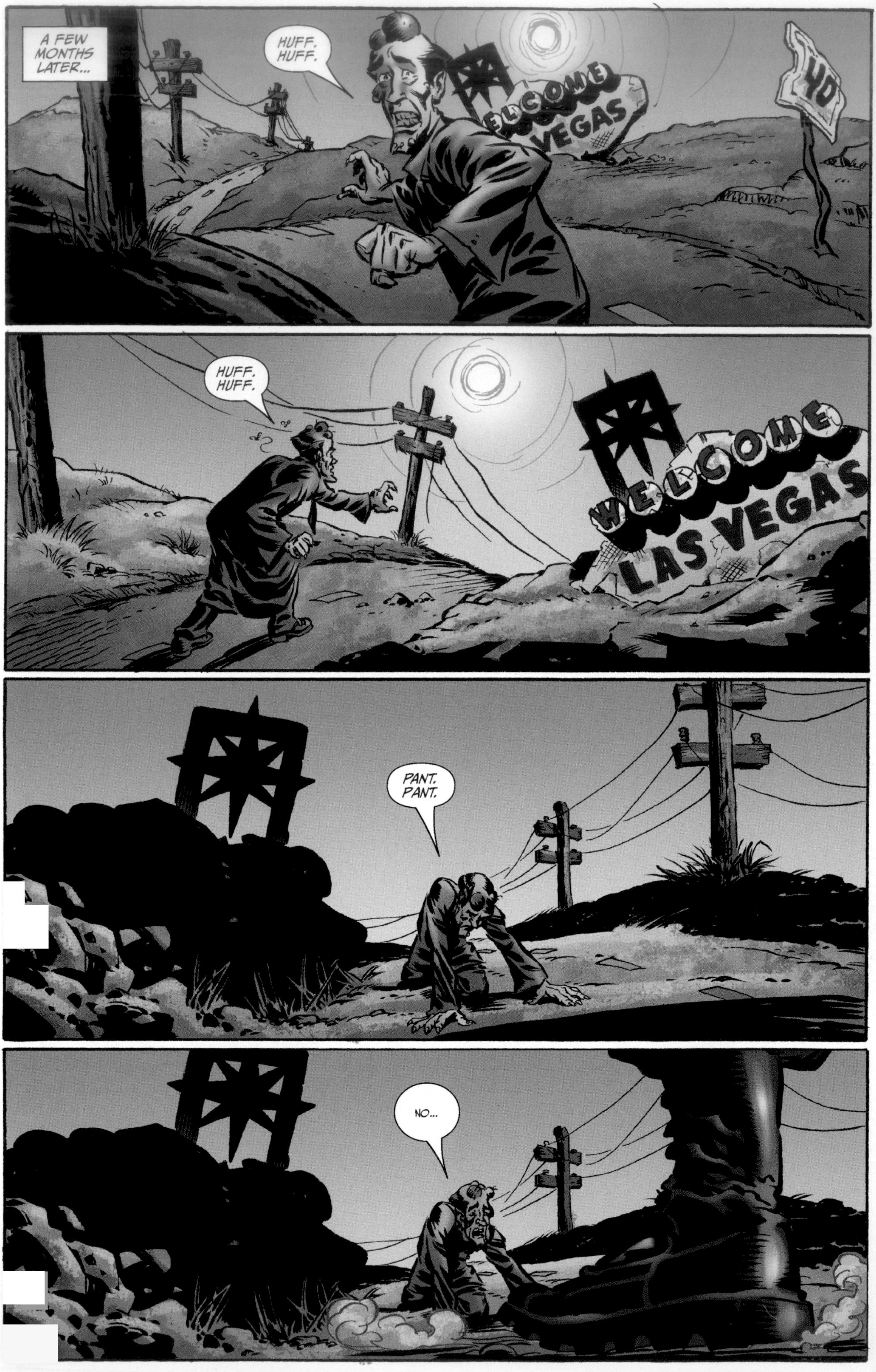

A FEW MONTHS LATER...
HUFF. HUFF.
WELCOME VEGAS
40
HUFF. HUFF.
WELCOME LAS VEGAS
PANT. PANT.
NO...

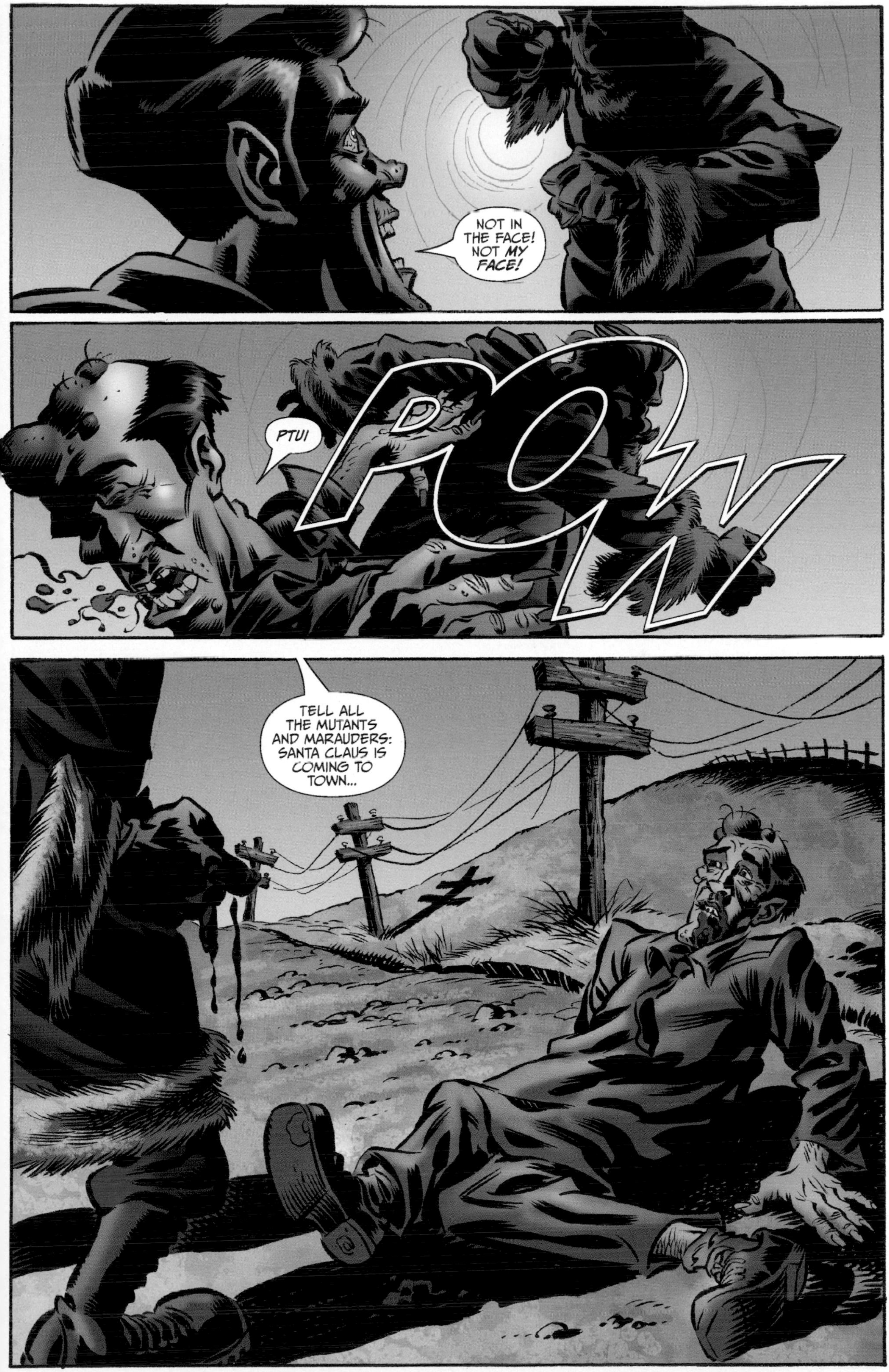
NOT IN THE FACE! NOT MY FACE!
PTUI
POW
TELL ALL THE MUTANTS AND MARAUDERS: SANTA CLAUS IS COMING TO TOWN...

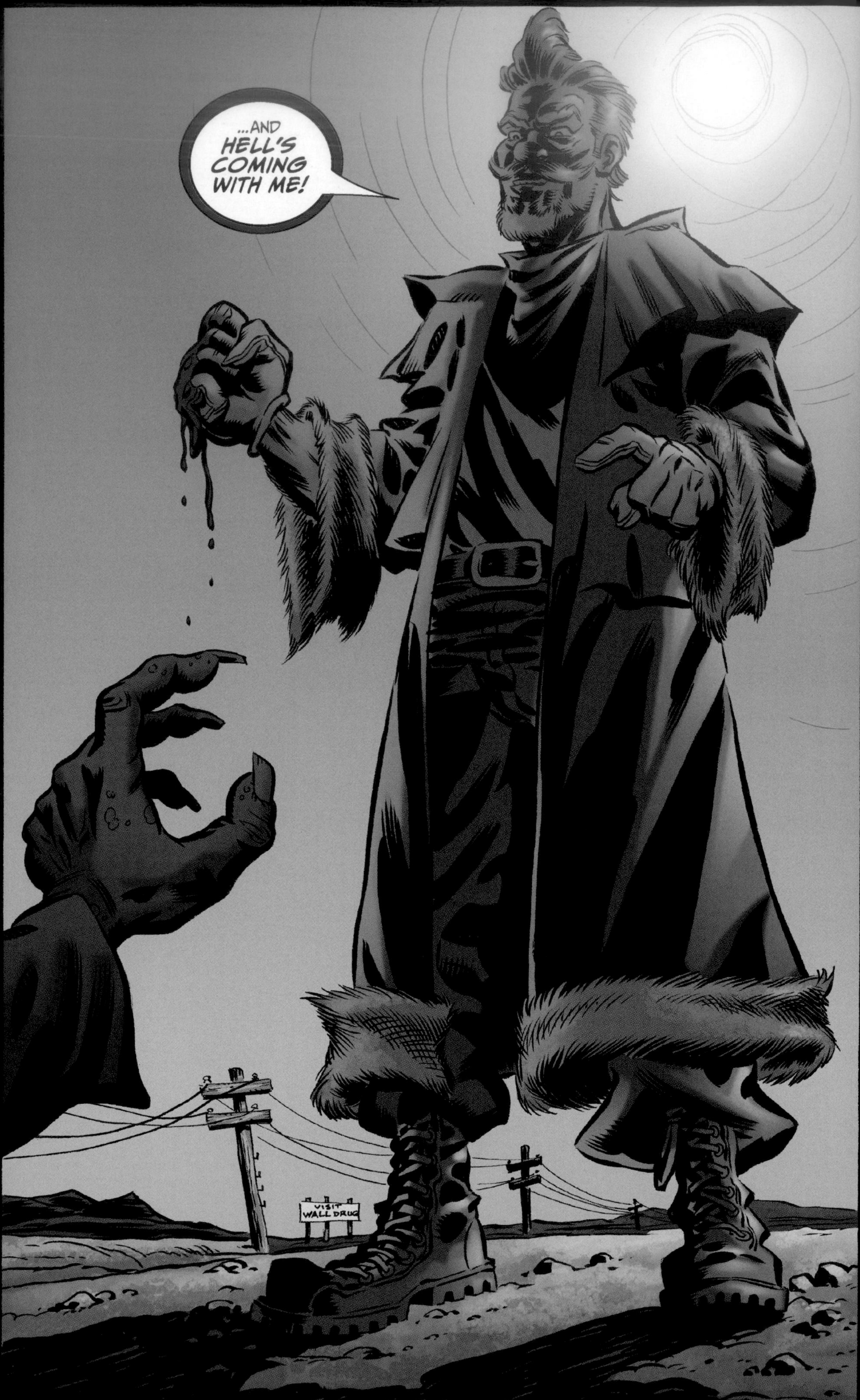
...AND HELL'S COMING WITH ME!
VISIT WALL DRUG

NOT
THE END

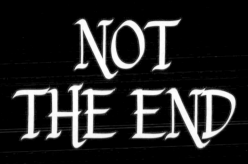

You just finished the sad, funny, true tale of Santa after the apocalypse – we hope that you enjoyed it.

An idea hatched by two idiots playing Halo turned into one of the most fun and fulfilling creative experiences of said idiots' lives. Those idiots were us. "Santa meets the Road Warrior" was the germ of the idea that made us laugh and put down our X-Box controllers and jump in front of the computer and start writing. We took our life-long love of the apocalypse, EC comics and old-timey funny books, horror and action movies, Eastwood westerns and comedy and threw them in a blender that Brian's wife Melanie, got at Williams Sonoma.

We will always be indebted to our artists. The two of us had wanted to make The Last Christmas our first comic book for a long time – and we waited a little longer for the art team that we wanted. Rick, Hil and Michelle had just wrapped up Man With The Screaming Brain when they began work on Christmas. Their collaboration made this comic better than we ever dared hope. Brian feels that his management skills also helped. When we received new pages Gerry would send an e-mail to Rick and Hil thanking them and applauding their art. Brian would send an e-mail like this: "Dear Rick, nice try. You can be replaced by a dumb-tard that paints with their foot. But foot brushes are really expensive. Love, Bri-Bri." These e-mails, Brian claims, helped keep them in line.

Rick possesses the perfect eye for both comedy and action. His experience writing and penciling his own exceptional comics made the production of this book so much easier on two first-time comic writers. Rick's pencils gave our goofy story life and depth. Hilary's inks and uncanny ability to ink dynamic lighting made Rick's world pop even brighter and had us ecstatic since the first page of issue one came in.

We had a good laugh when Brian recently recalled that we were considering making this book black and white. Michelle Madsen's color work on Christmas is among the best in all of comics. She made the North Pole magical and the apocalyptic landscape of a ravaged San Francisco menacing and real with her spot-on color choices.

You're going to need a lot of good help when your dream is to tell a post-apocalyptic western starring Santa. So, to Ed, Chris Carmen, Digital Webbing and everyone at Image Comics – we thank you for helping us make some crazy deadlines – and ensuring the book looked so damn good.

And lastly to our guest cover artists – Geof Darrow, Kieron Dwyer and Tony Moore (issues 1, 2 and 5 respectively) who each took time away from their families and busy schedules to turn in fantastic work – we'll always be grateful for your superb contributions.

We would also like to thank Virginia Vanover, Melanie Truhett-Posehn, David Mandel, Kelvin Mao, Scott Aukerman, the Duggan and Posehn families (for encouraging us to read comics as kids and for the undying support of everything we've done since), Harris Miller III, Patton Oswalt, Ed Brubaker, Gail Simone, Dave Rath and of course everyone that picked up our comic. Support your local comic shops, we do!

Seasons Beatings, Brian and Gerry

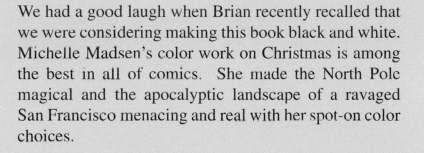

EXTRAS

(well, aren't you lucky)

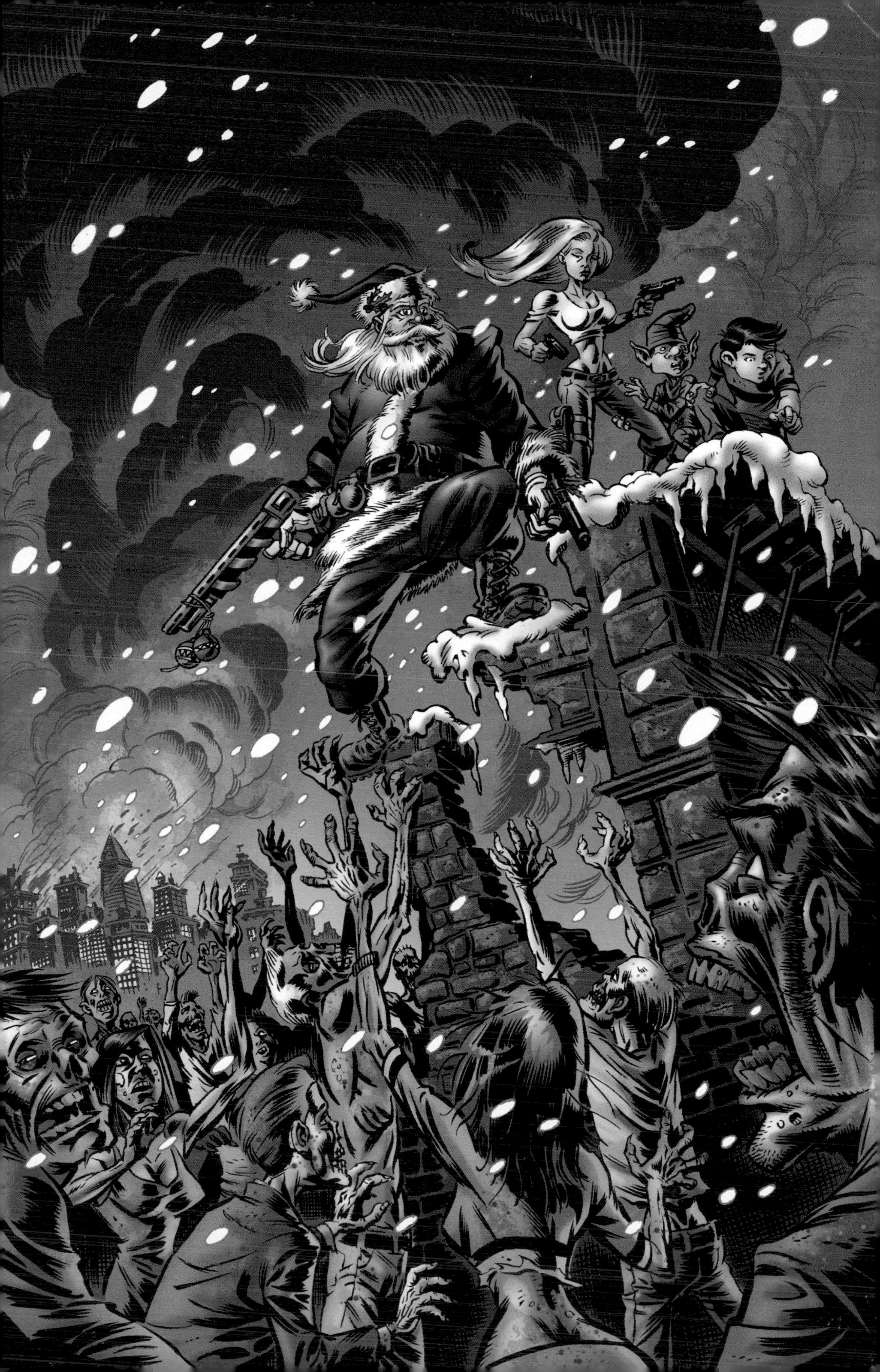

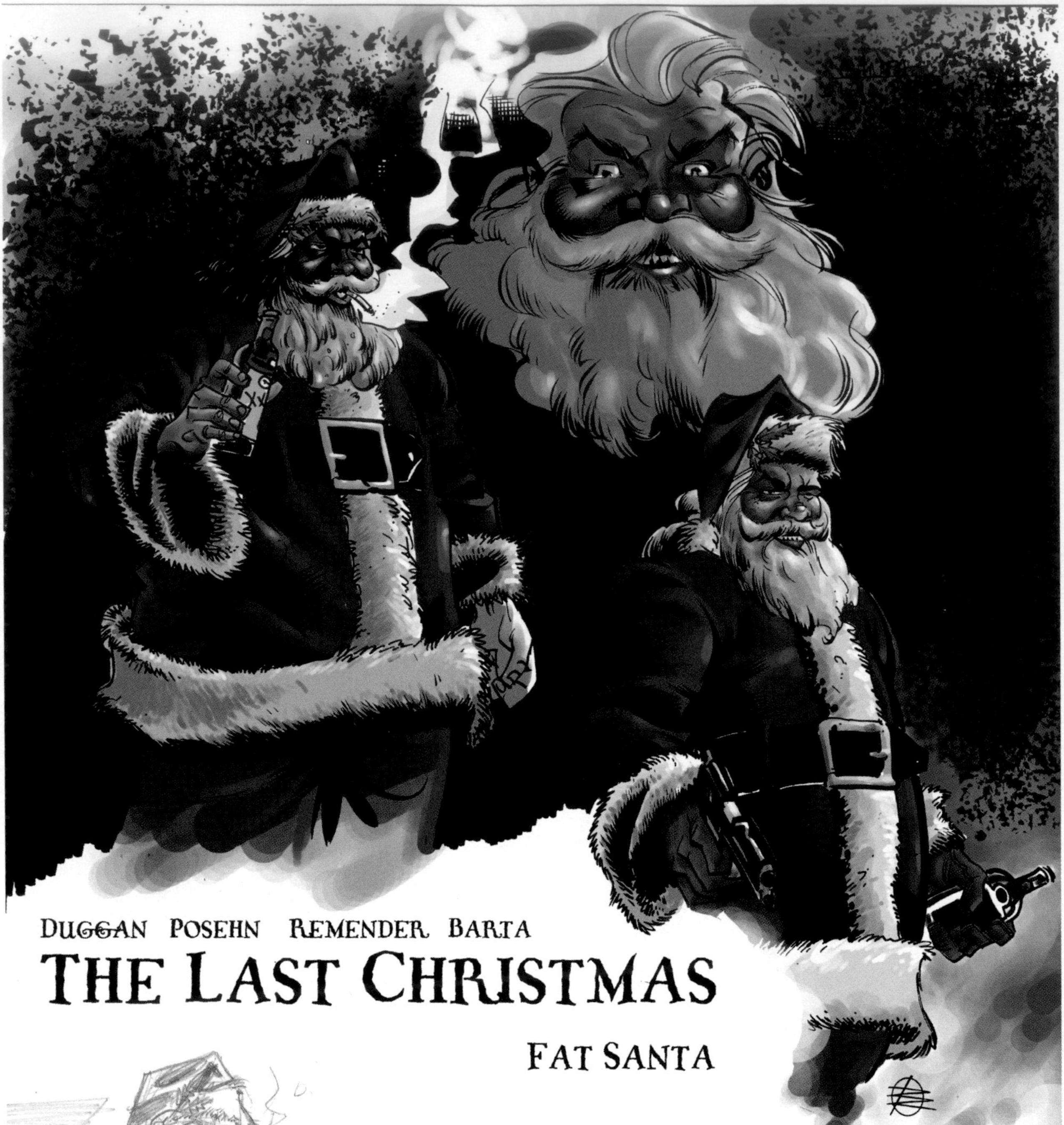
DUGGAN POSEHN REMENDER BARTA
THE LAST CHRISTMAS
FAT SANTA

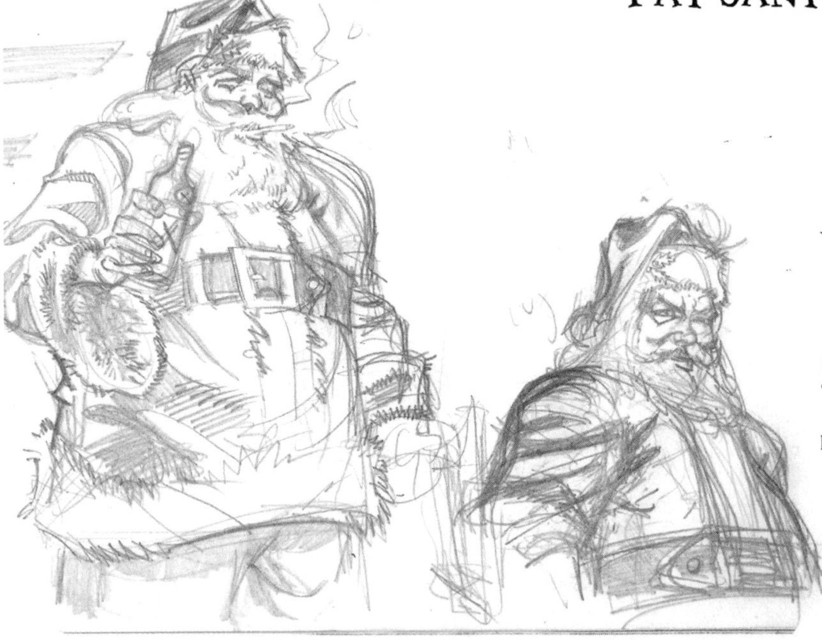

HI, RICK THE ART-MONKEY HERE. THE GUYS GAVE ME A FEW PAGES AT THE BACK OF THE BOOK TO SHOW SOME OF MY SKETCHBOOK STUFF. YIPPEE. LIKE YOU'VE GOT NOTHING BETTER TO DO THAN READ SOME WINDBAG, EGOTIST PONTIFICATING ABOUT HIS MEDIOCRE SKETCHES, THAT HE ONLY DID TO SHUT GERRY AND BRIAN THE HELL UP SO HE COULD PROCRASTINATE ACTUALLY STARTING WORK ON THE BOOK. WELL, HERE WE ARE. THESE ARE SOME DRAWINGS I DID OF DRUNK AND VIOLENT SANTA CLAUS. WHO FUCKING CARES.

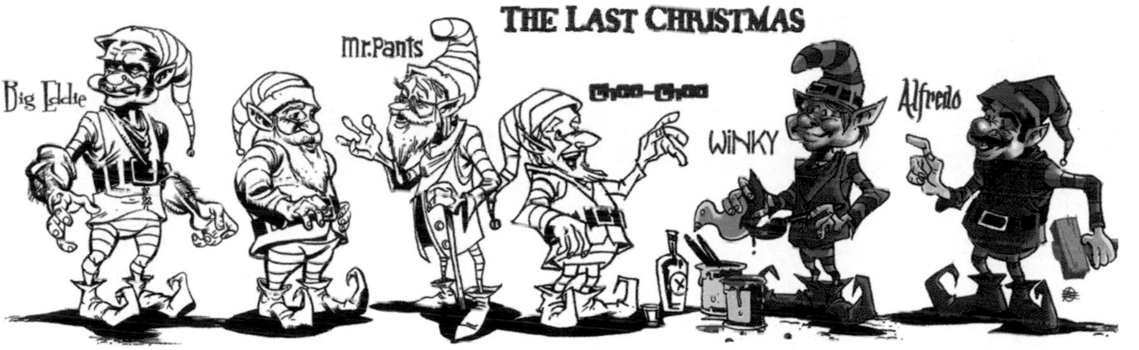
THE LAST CHRISTMAS
Big Eddie
Mr.Pants
WiNKY
Alfredo

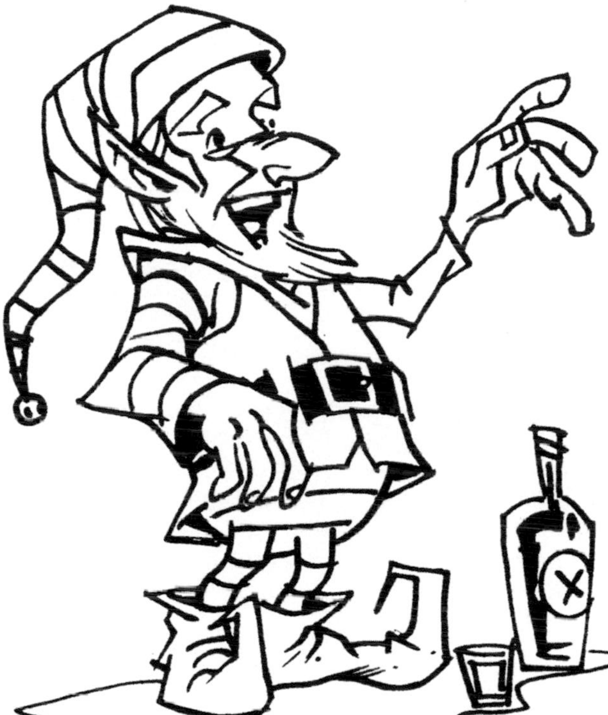

HEY, GLAD TO SEE YOU. ACTUALLY, I'M SHOCKED THAT ANYONE WHO READ THIS PILE OF SHIT MADE IT PAST THE LAST PAGE OF THE "STORY". TO BE FAIR, GERRY AND BRIAN ARE BOTH A FEW CHROMOSOMES SHORT OF MONGOLOID AND WE SHOULD ALL BE PROUD THEY WERE ABLE TO COME UP WITH A COHESIVE ENDING AT ALL.

HERE ARE SOME DESIGNS I DID OF THEIR ELVES. THEY DIDN'T INCLUDE ANYTHING ABOUT ANY AFRICAN-AMERICAN ELVES SO I GUESS THEY ARE BOTH RACIST ASSHOLES.

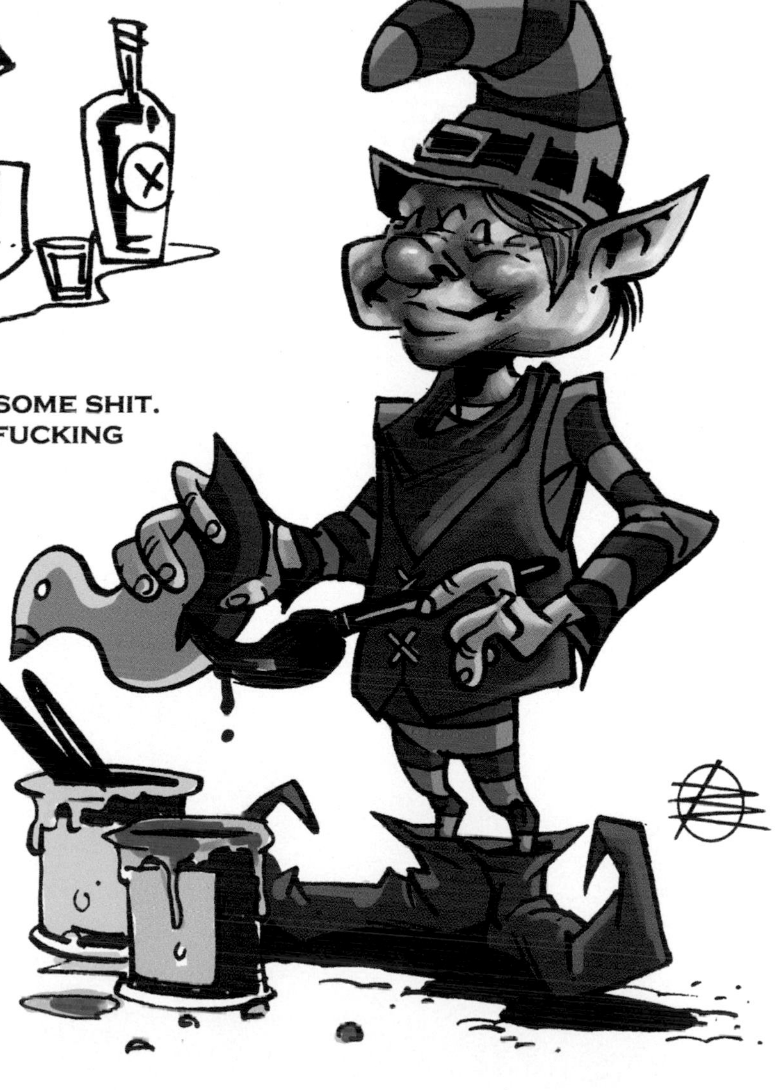

HERE IS BINKY OR BLINKY OR SOME SHIT. AS IF IT MATTERS. HE'S SOME FUCKING QUEER ELF. WHATEVER.

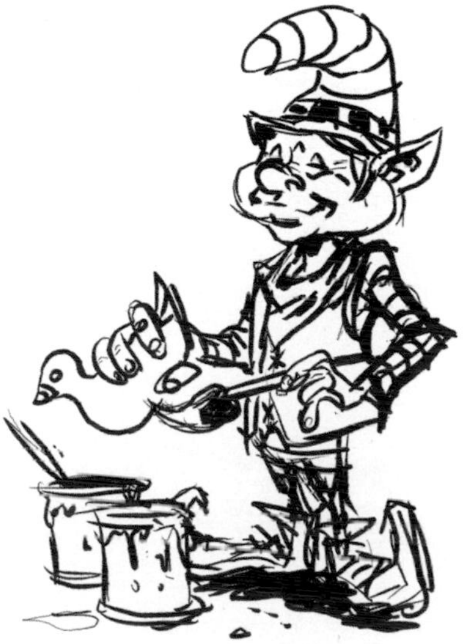

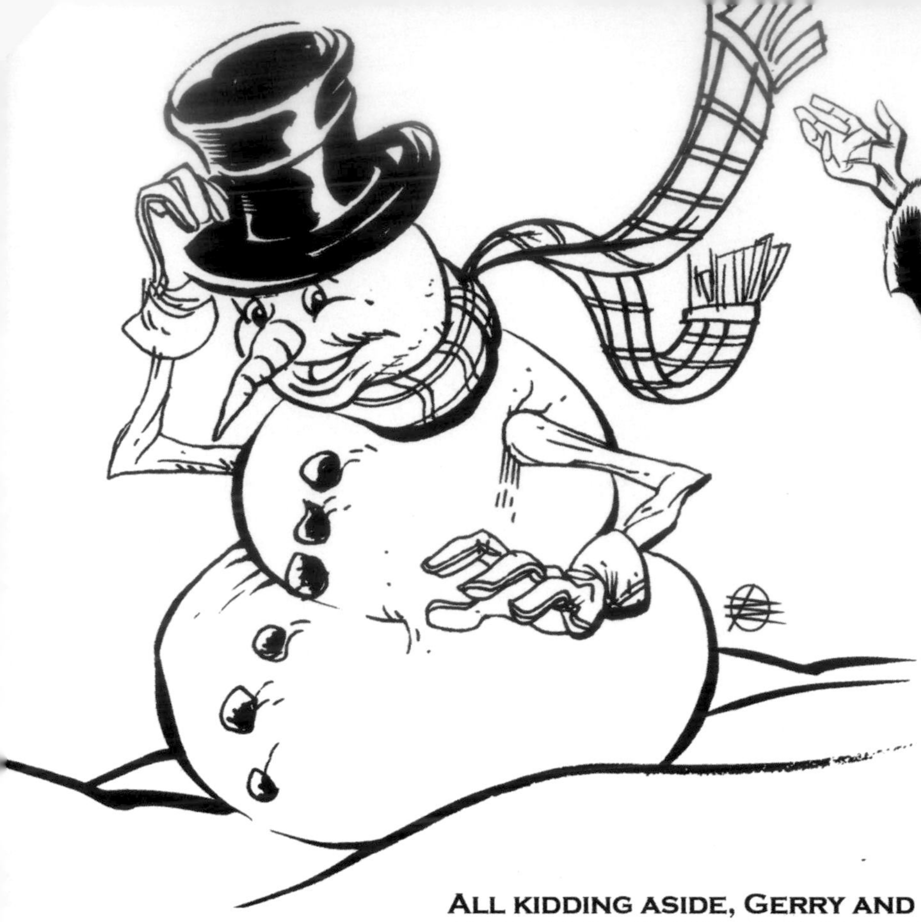

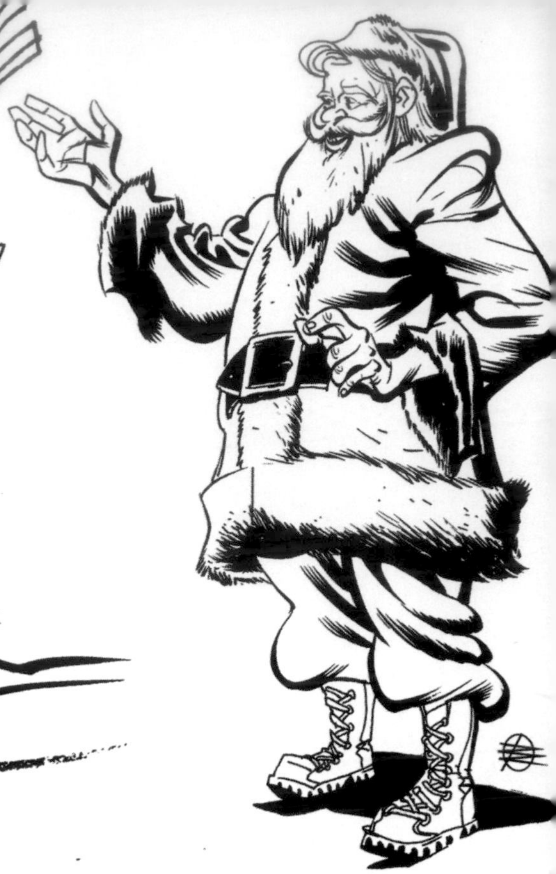

All kidding aside, Gerry and Brian are total ass-holes to work for. They made me work through Christmas and one time they pushed me down into a pool of dirty water and called me "Hardhat" and "Jive Turkey" I had fun drawing their comic but after what they put me through I'd sound like a real douche if I admitted to it.

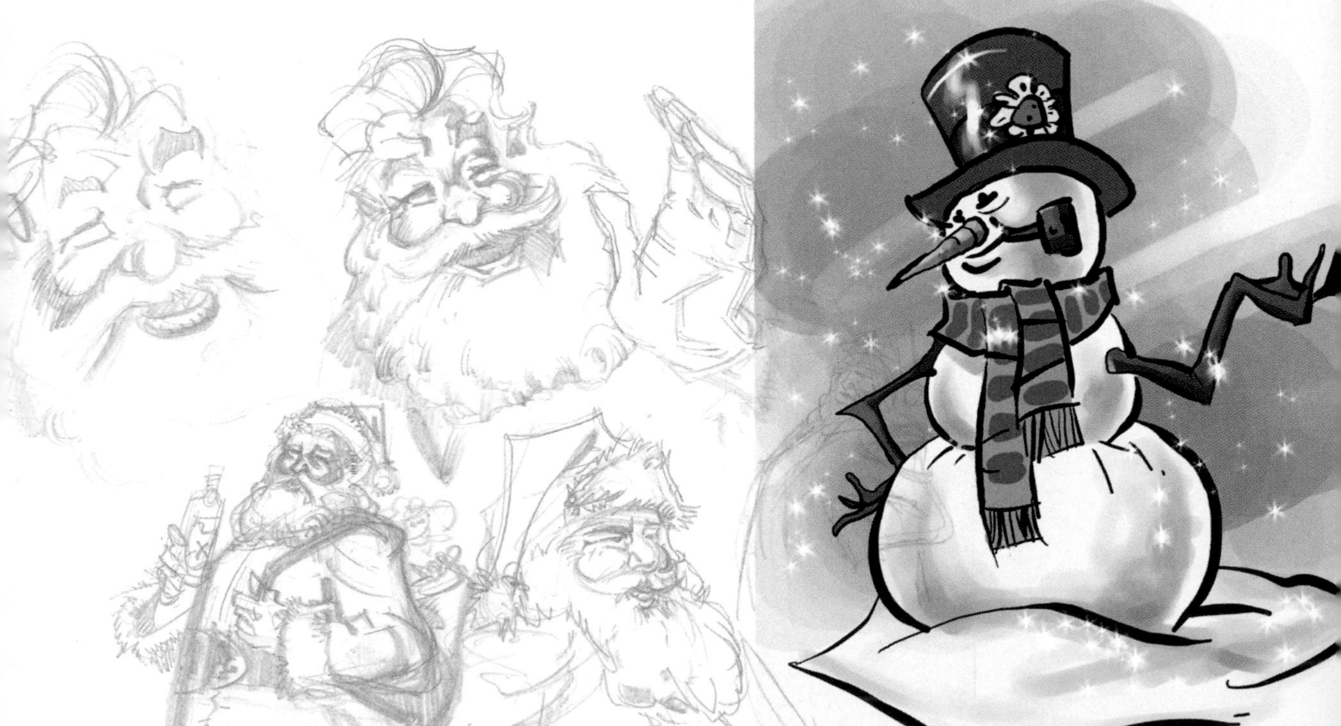

I kid, we all had a blast and hope you dug the series.

Merry Xmas, Ma-

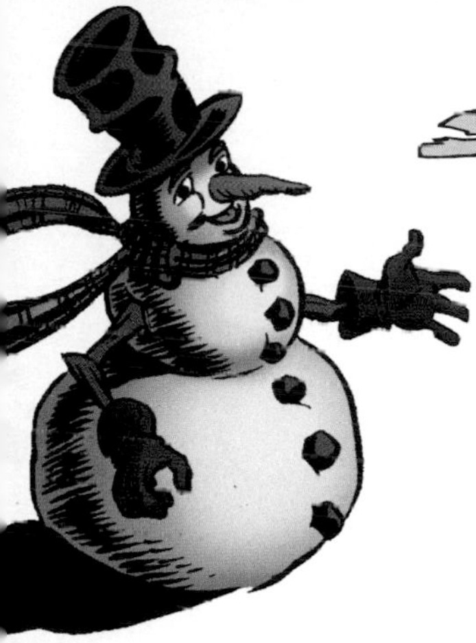

The Making of The Last Christmas

from roughs, to pencils, to inks, to print

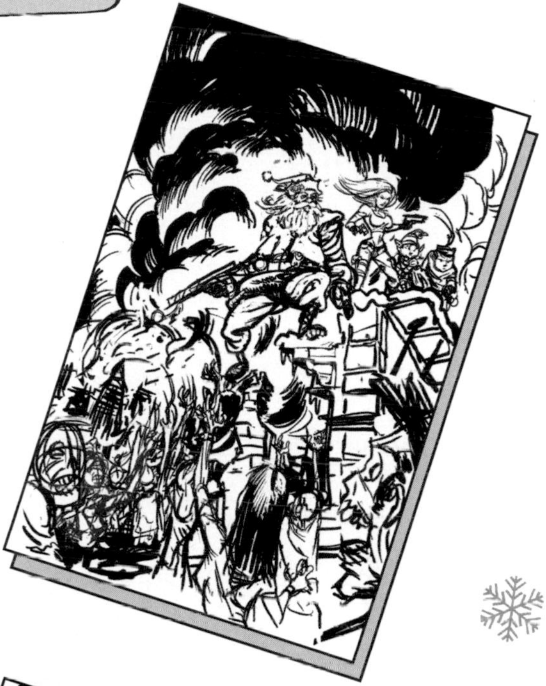

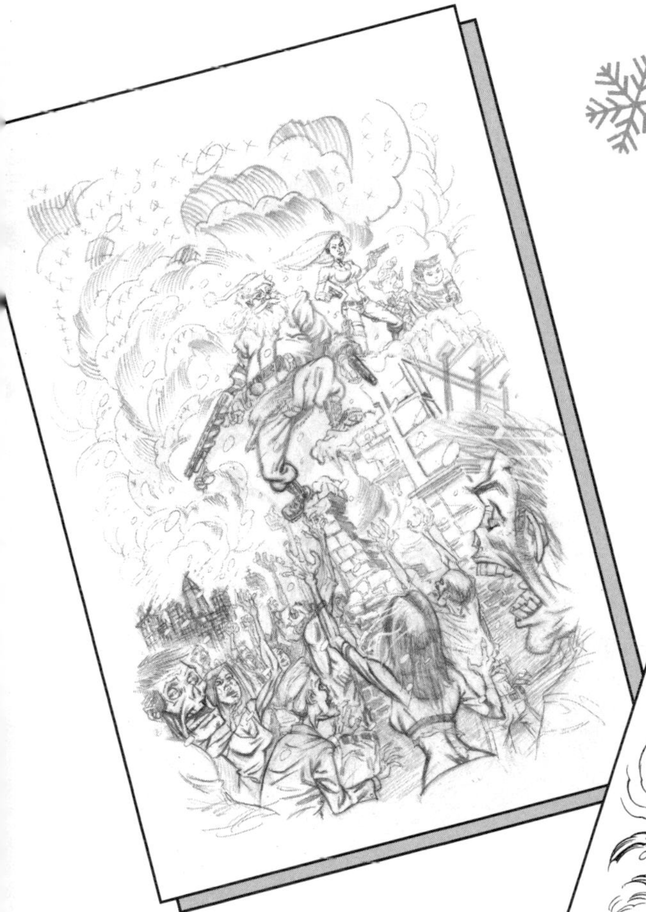

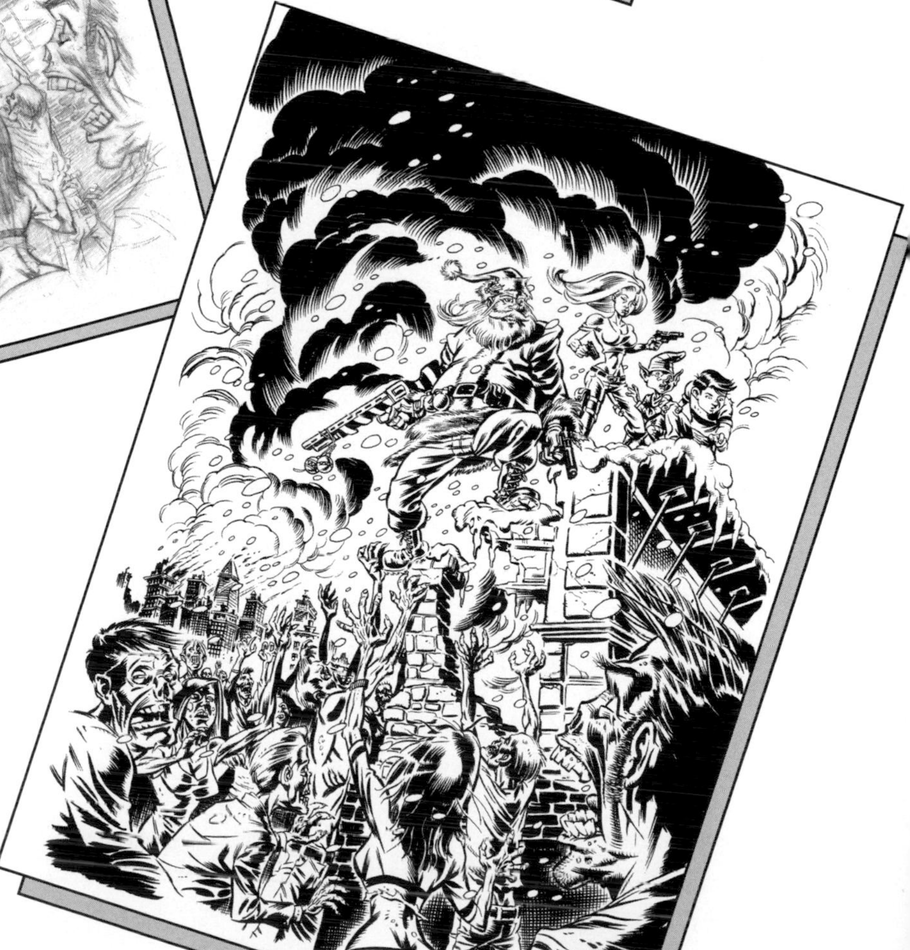

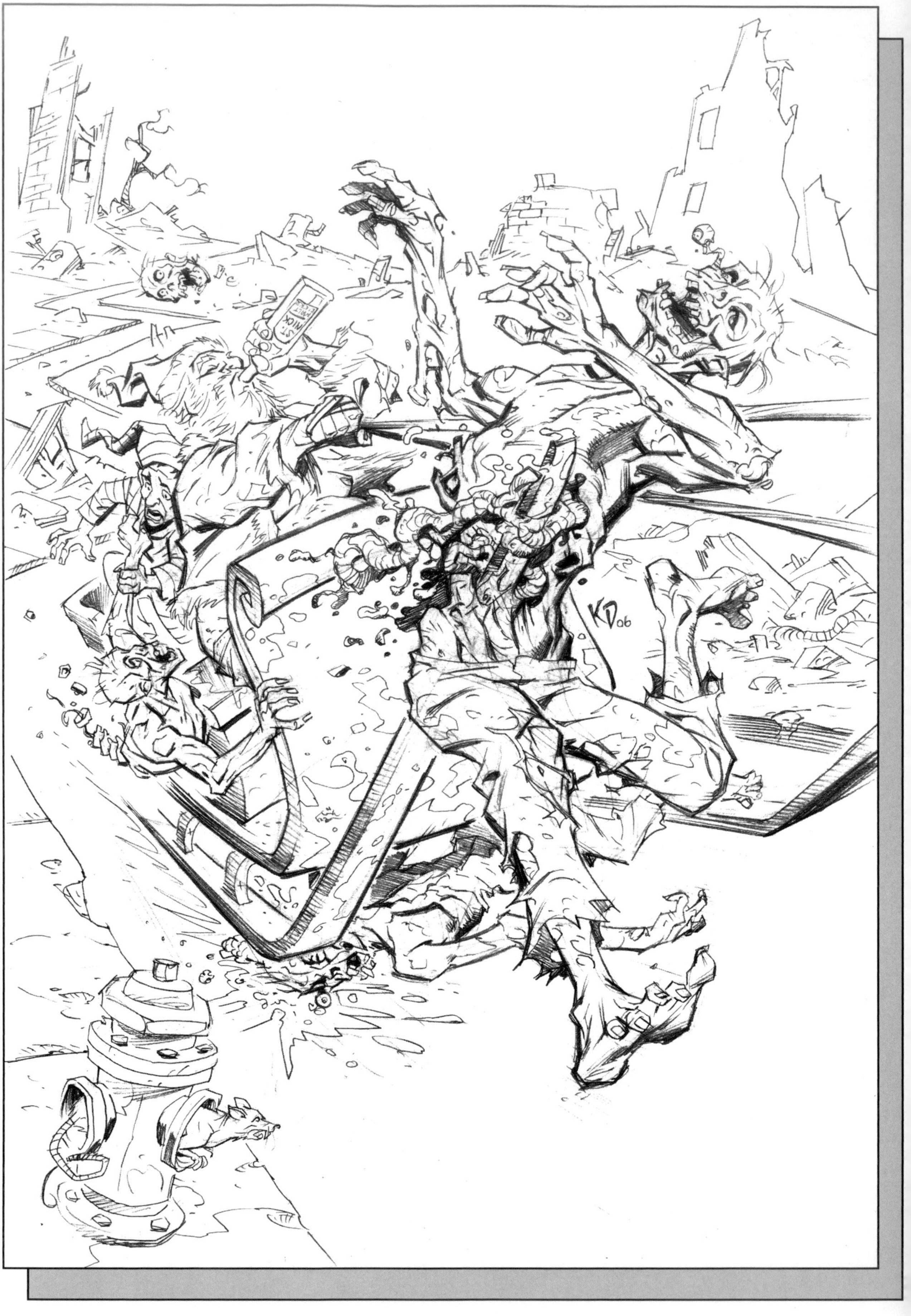
ST. NICK
MALT
KD 06

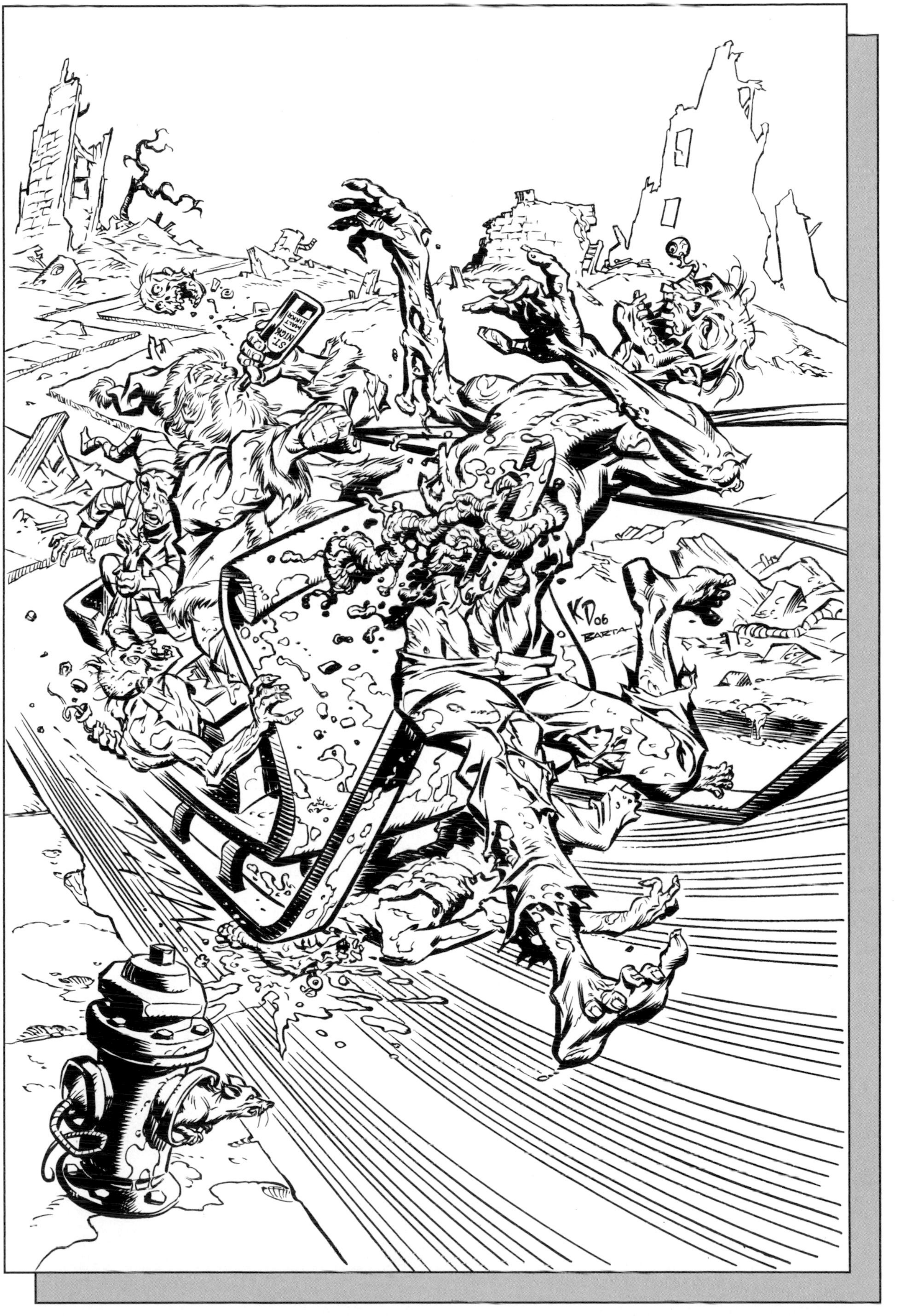
ST. NICK MALT LIKKR
KD 06
BARTA

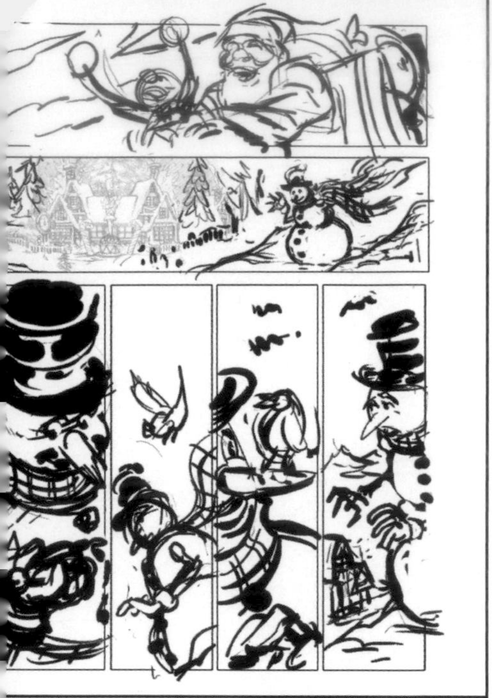

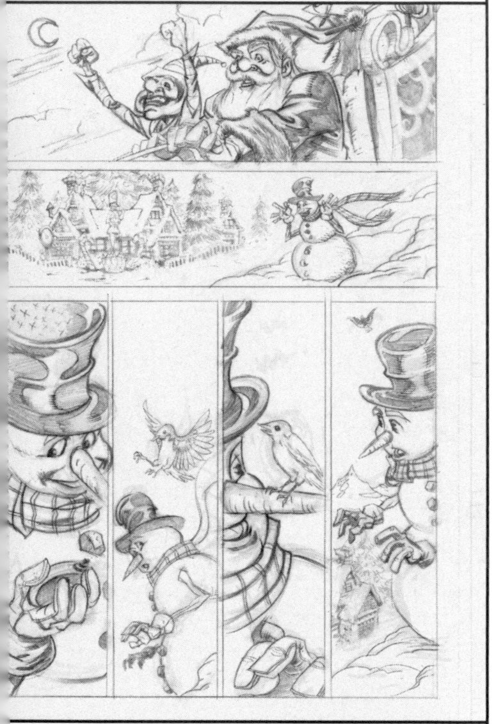

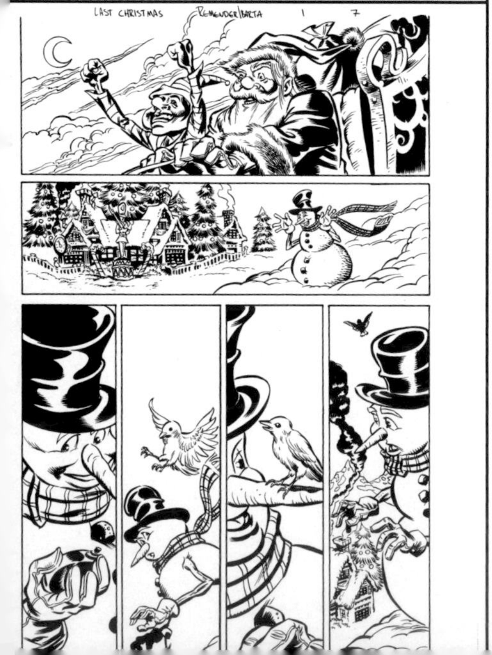
LAST CHRISTMAS
REMENDER/BARTA
1
7

PAGE 7 IS A LITTLE DIFFERENT AS THE SONG ENDS - PANELS 1 AND 2 ARE EQUAL LENGTH HORIZONTAL PANELS TAKING UP THE TOP PART OF THE PAGE, PANELS 3, 4, 5, AND 6 ARE 4 EQUAL SIZED BOXES THAT REST UNDER THE 2 LONG PANELS.

PAGE 7 PAGE 1
SANTA IS FLYING HOME, THE ELVES ARE HAPPY...A JOB WELL DONE.

SANTA
(SINGING)
This won't be the last Christmas.

PAGE 7 PANEL 2
EXT. NORTH POLE - CONTINUOUS
GARY DANCES AS THE SONG BUILDS TO A CRESCENDO AND CONCLUDES.

GARY THE SNOWMAN
(BIG FINISH WITH JAZZ
HANDS)
You would all miss us but - this
won't be the last Christmas!

PAGE 7 PANEL 3
GARY PULLS OUT HIS POCKET WATCH. GARY SPEAKS IN REGULAR WORD BALLOONS NOW - THE SONG IS OVER.

GARY THE SNOWMAN (CONT'D)
Santa should be back any moment
from another Christmas Eve toy run-

PAGE 7 PANEL 4
SUDDENLY, A BLUEBIRD FLIES IN AND LANDS ON GARY'S SHOULDER.

BLUEBIRD
(EXCITEDLY)
CHIRP! CHIRP! CHIRPCHIRPCHIRP!

GARY
What!?...slow down.

PAGE 7 PANEL 5
THE BLUEBIRD TAKES A DEEP BREATH.

BLUEBIRD
Chirp...chirp...chirp.chirp.chirp.

PAGE 7 PANEL 6
HORROR FILLS THE SNOWMAN'S FACE.

GARY THE SNOWMAN
Oh no, something terrible has
happened over at the Claus' place.

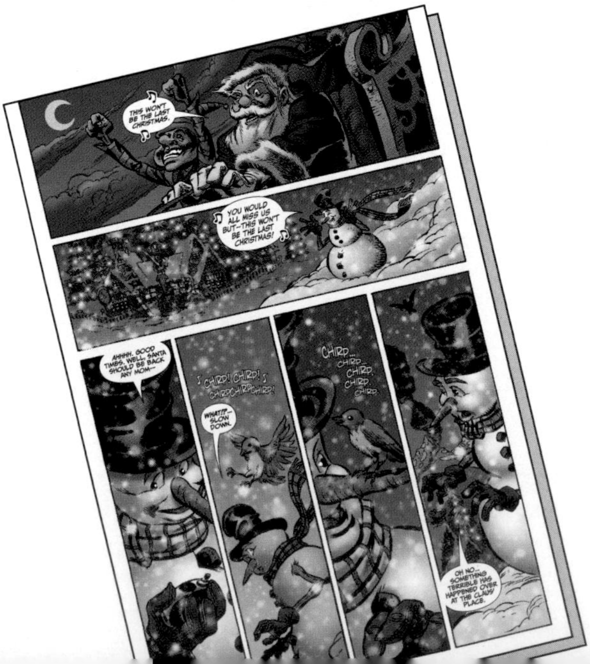
THIS WON'T BE THE LAST CHRISTMAS.
YOU WOULD ALL MISS US BUT—THIS WON'T BE THE LAST CHRISTMAS!
AHHHH. GOOD TIMES. WELL, SANTA SHOULD BE BACK ANY MOM—
CHIRP! CHIRP! CHIRPCHIRPCHIRP!
WHAT!?—SLOW DOWN.
CHIRP... CHIRP... CHIRP. CHIRP. CHIRP.
OH NO... SOMETHING TERRIBLE HAS HAPPENED OVER AT THE CLAUS' PLACE.

PAGE 8 SPLASH
SANTA'S VILLAGE: WE REVEAL THE TWINKLING WASN'T ANYTHING MAGIC OR FESTIVE...IT WAS MUZZLE FLASHES AND FIRES! THE TOP FLOOR OF SANTA'S WORKSHOP IS ENGULFED IN FLAMES. THE STRUCTURE LOOKS LIKE A LARGE CHUNK HAS BEEN BLASTED AWAY. DEAD ELVES AND TOYS LITTER THE FRONT YARD.
MARAUDERS FLEE INTO THE NIGHT, SHOOTING AS THEY GO. GARY DIVES UNDER A SPRAY OF BULLETS.

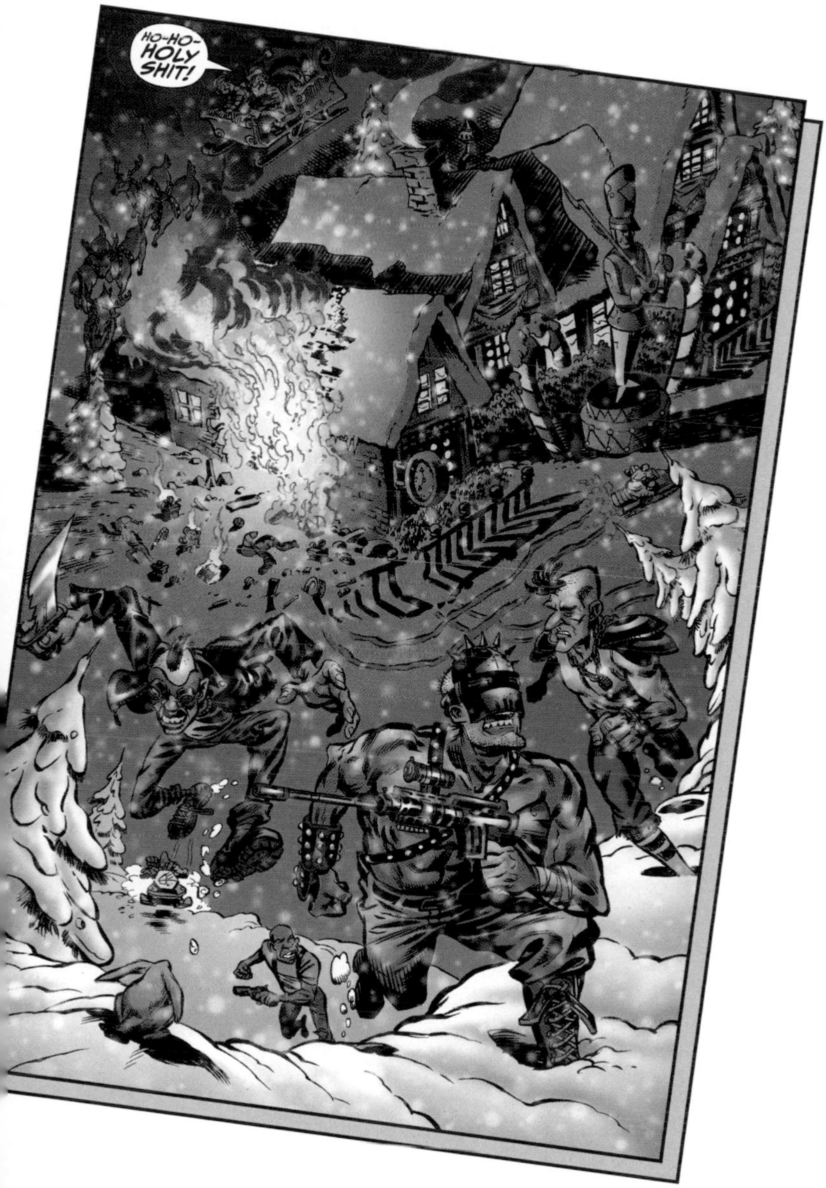
HO-HO-HOLY SHIT!

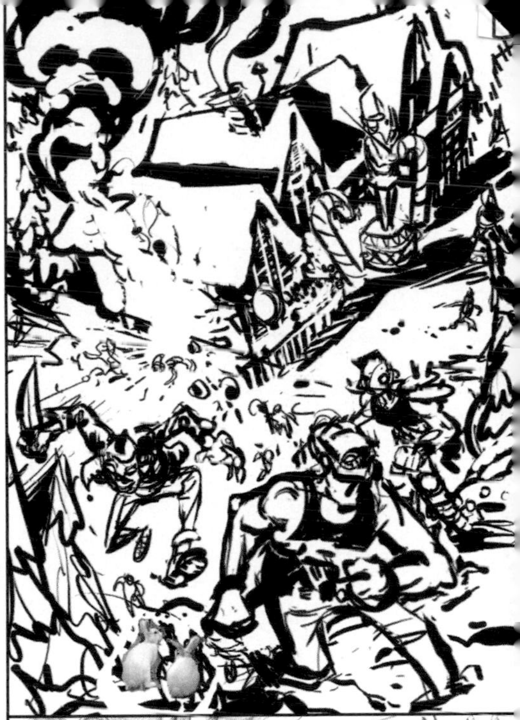

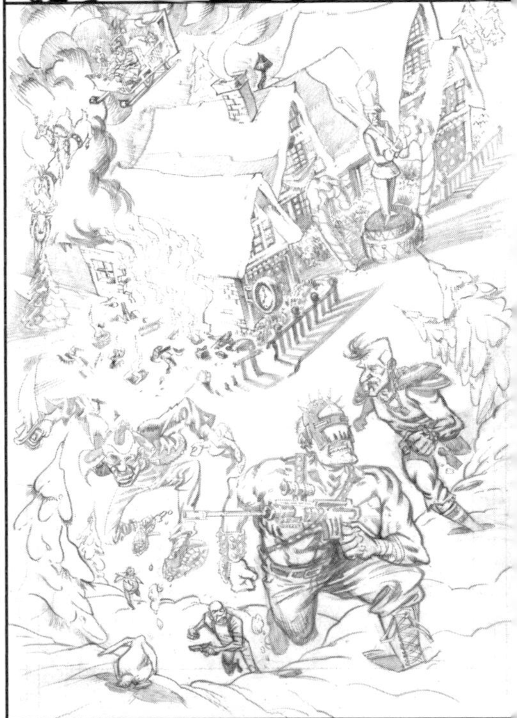

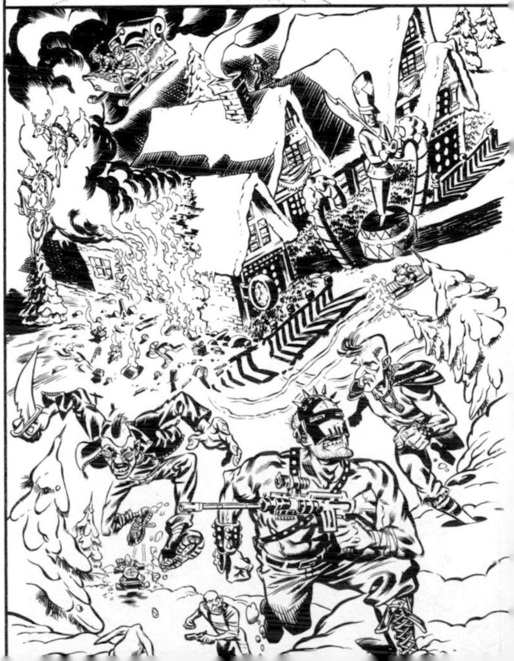

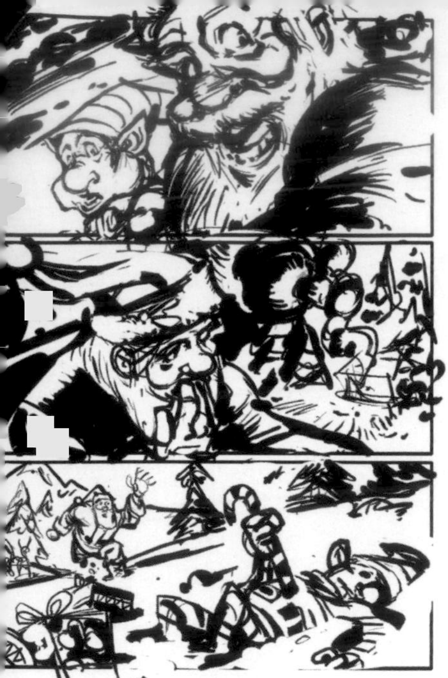

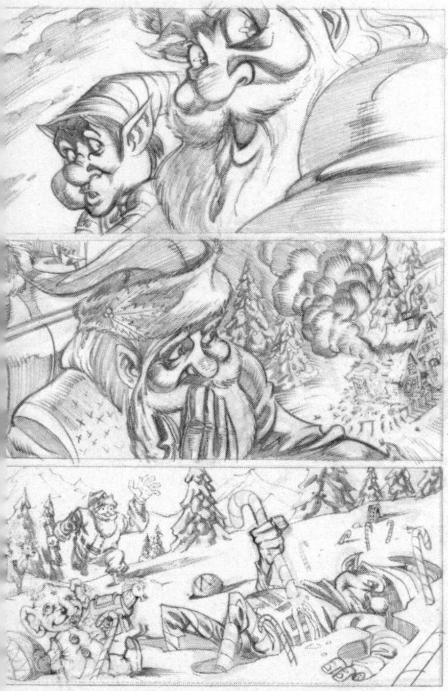

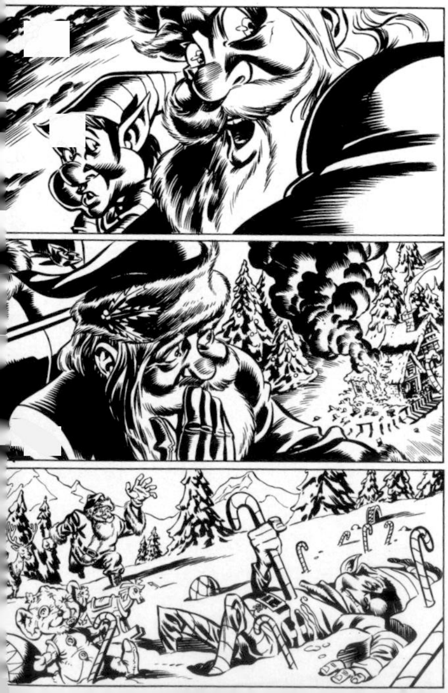

PAGE 9 IS THREE EQUAL-SIZED PANELS...

PAGE 9 PANEL 1 - TOP THIRD OF PAGE
SANTA SURVEYS THE SCENE FROM HIS SLEIGH.

SANTA
Ho Ho Hooo-ly shit!

PAGE 9 PANEL 2 SECOND THIRD OF PAGE
CLOSER ON SANTA, HORROR IN HIS EYES AS HE LOOKS DOWN. SANTA USES BOTH HANDS TO COVER HIS NAUGHTY, CURSING MOUTH.

PAGE 9 PANEL 3 LAST THIRD OF PAGE
THE SLEIGH IS LANDED AND SANTA AND RUSHES TOWARDS A TINY GREEN-CLAD CORPSE: MERV.

SANTA (CONT'D)
No! Not Merv! Not Merv!!!

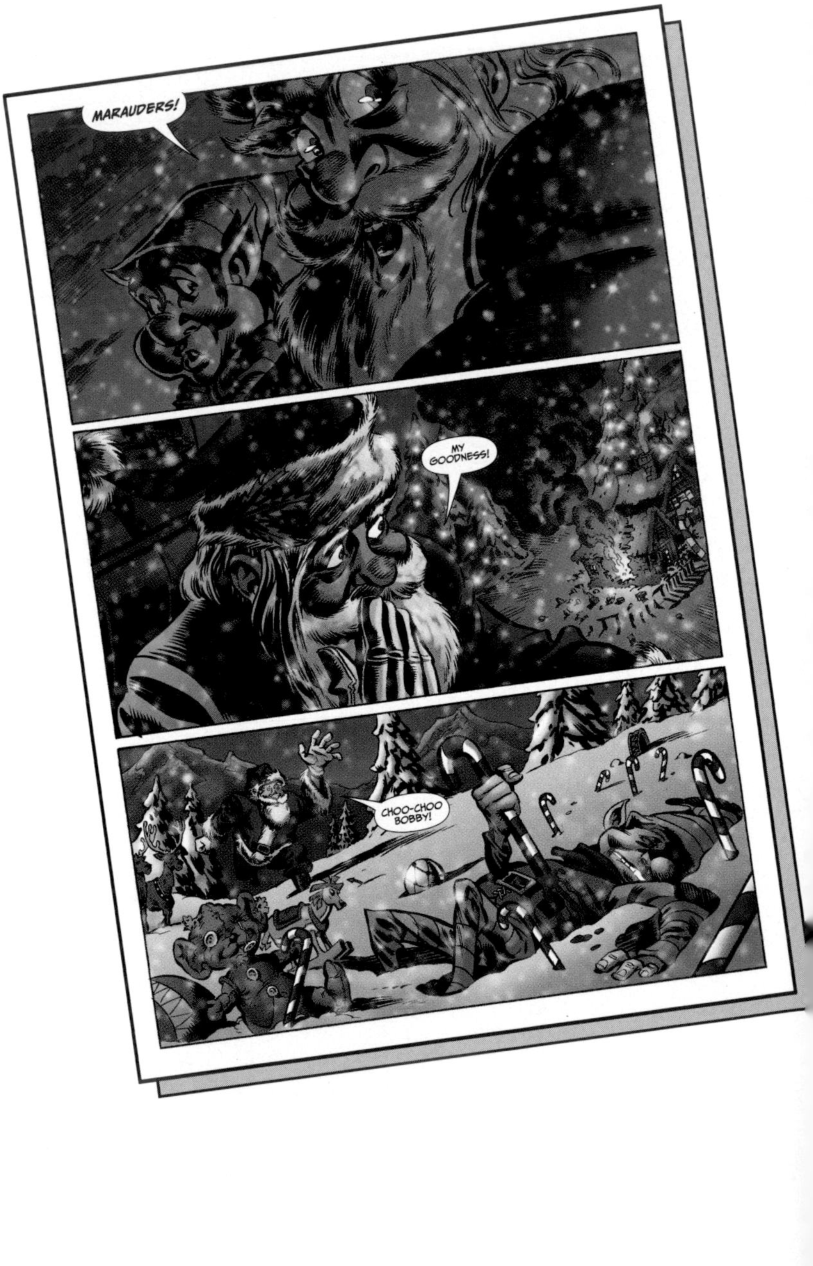
MARAUDERS!
MY GOODNESS!
CHOO-CHOO BOBBY!

PAGE 21 IS 5 PANELS

PAGE 21 PANEL 1 (THAT NIGHT)
WE'RE IN THE TOY FACTORY - WINKY, SAMUEL, BIG EDDIE ARE ALL BUNDLED UP - BLANKETS, SOUP, COCOA ETC - FROM THE FRIGID BATH THEY GOT EARLIER.

WINKY
I wish Rudolph was still here. He could cheer anyone up before he disappeared.

PAGE 21 PANEL 2

THE ELVES ALL AGREE WITH THIS. IN THE WINDOW BEHIND WINKY WE SEE SANTA DOUSE HIMSELF WITH GASOLINE.

ALFREDO
You know what I bet would cheer up Santa? Mrs. Claus!

PAGE 21 PANEL 3

THE ELVES JUST STARE AT ALFREDO...WHAT AN ASSHOLE...IN THE WINDOW SANTA LIGHTS A ZIPPO...

PAGE 21 PANEL 4

SANTA IS NOW FULLY ENGULFED IN FLAMES...

BIG EDDIE
(NOTICING THE SCENE OUTSIDE)
Can somebody get that?

PAGE 21 PANEL 5

WINKY REACHES FOR A FIRE EXTINGUISHER.

WINKY
It's my turn this time.

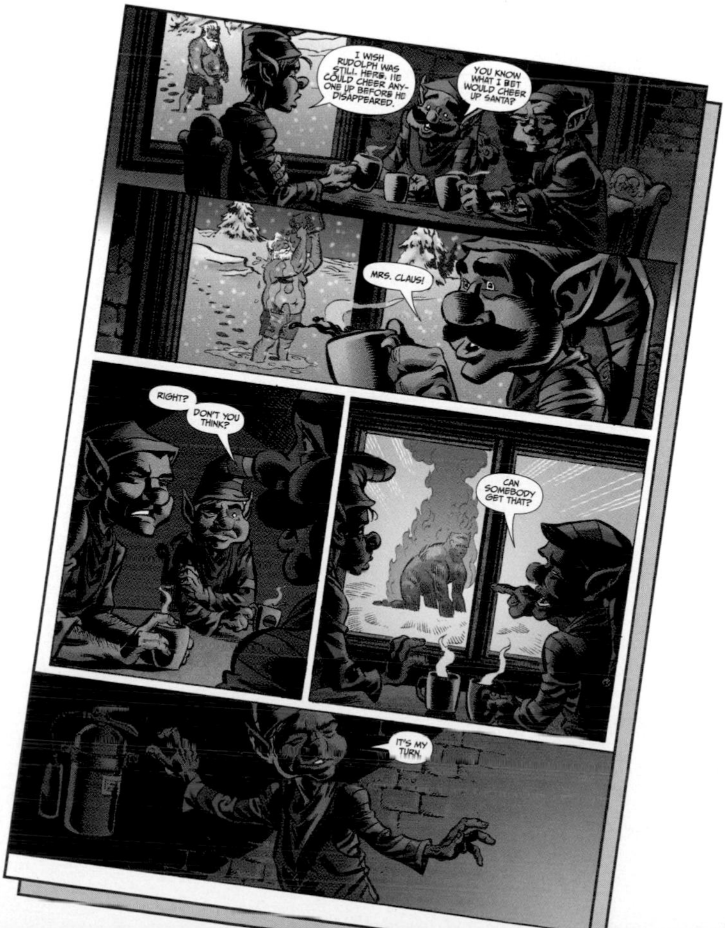
I WISH RUDOLPH WAS STILL HERE. HE COULD CHEER ANY-ONE UP BEFORE HE DISAPPEARED.
YOU KNOW WHAT I BET WOULD CHEER UP SANTA?
MRS. CLAUS!
RIGHT?
DON'T YOU THINK?
CAN SOMEBODY GET THAT?
IT'S MY TURN.

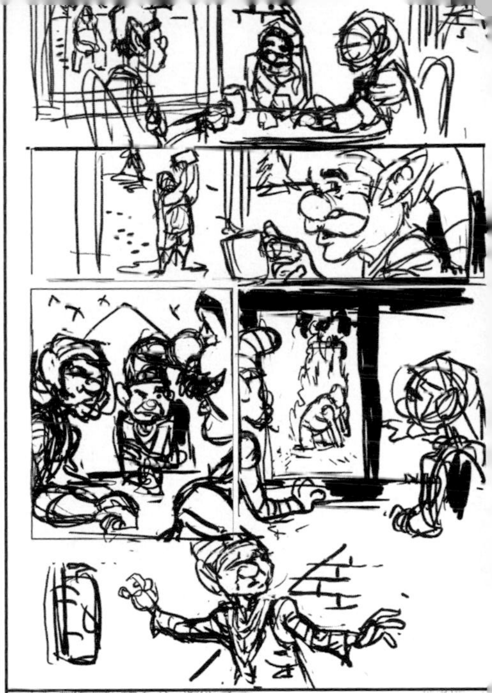

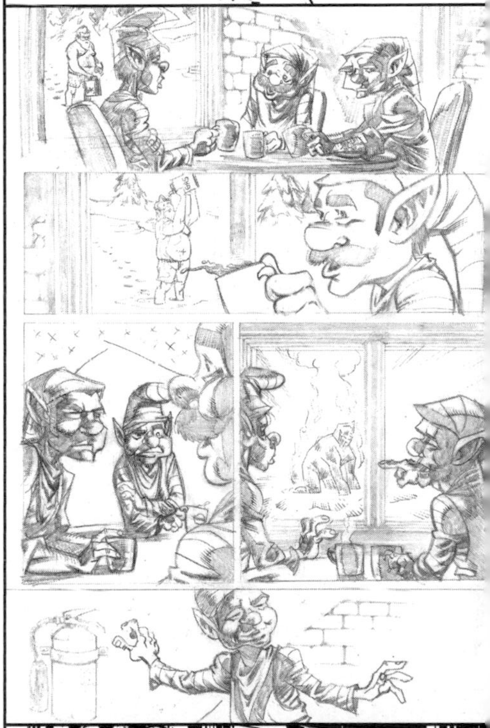

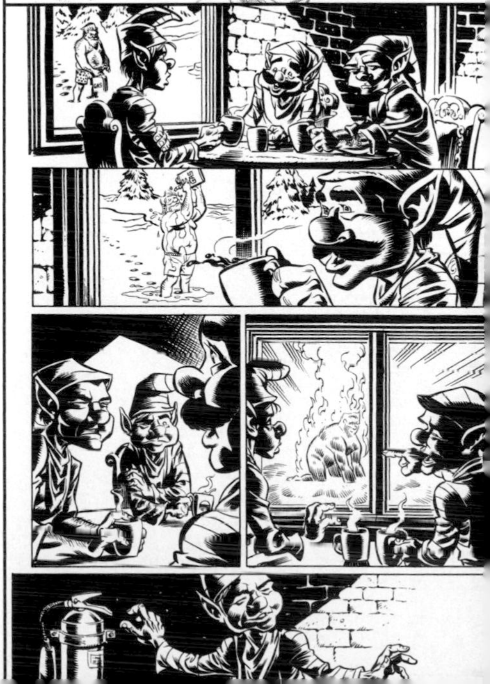

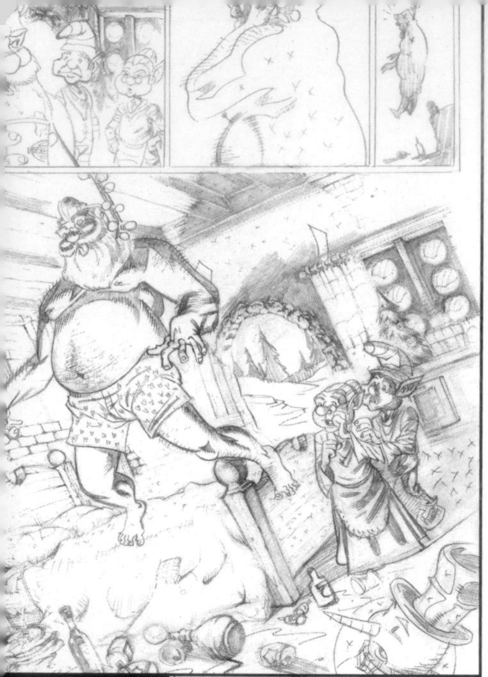

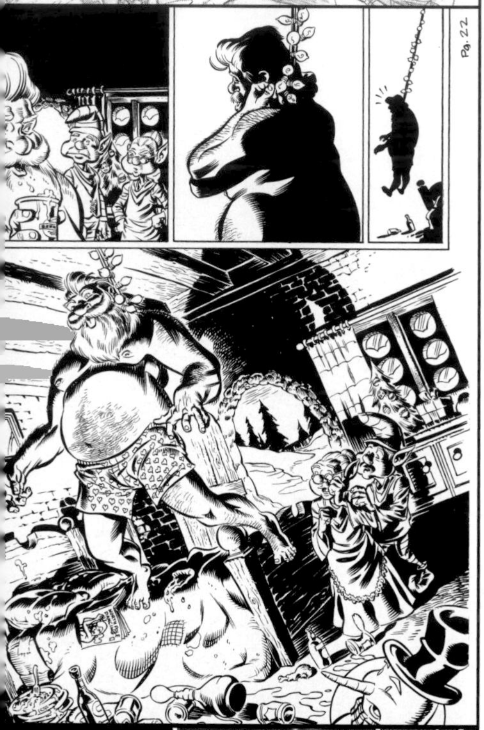

Pg. 22

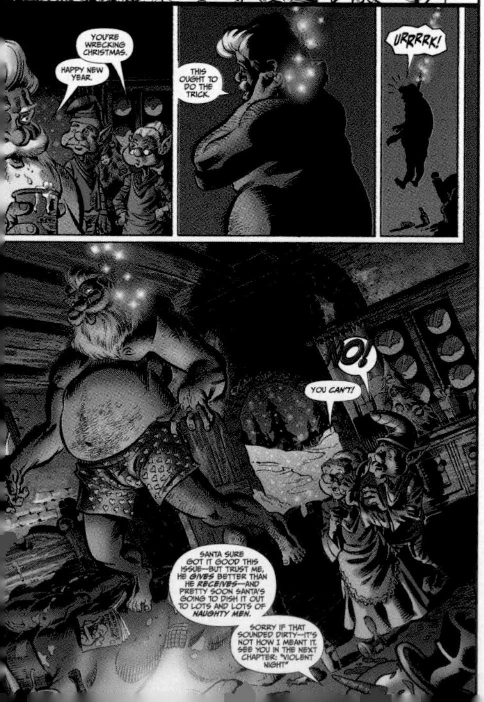

YOU'RE WRECKING CHRISTMAS.
HAPPY NEW YEAR.
THIS OUGHT TO DO THE TRICK.
URRRRK!
NO!
YOU CAN'T!
SANTA SURE GOT IT GOOD THIS ISSUE--BUT TRUST ME, HE GIVES BETTER THAN HE RECEIVES--AND PRETTY SOON SANTA'S GOING TO DISH IT OUT TO LOTS AND LOTS OF NAUGHTY MEN.
SORRY IF THAT SOUNDED DIRTY--IT'S NOT HOW I MEANT IT. SEE YOU IN THE NEXT CHAPTER: "VIOLENT NIGHT"

PAGE 22 - PANELS 1 AND 2 ARE SMALLER AT THE TOP - 3 IS A NARROW HORIZONTAL PANEL 4 - IS A MUCH BIGGER BOX BENEATH THAT - SHOULD BE MOST OF THE PAGE...AND PANEL 5 IS JUST A GUTTER BOX WITH GARY'S HEAD FOR A LITTLE NARRATION...

PAGE 22 PANEL 1

WINKY AND MRS. PANTS ARE IN SANTA'S LITTLE COTTAGE. THEY DON'T LOOK HAPPY.

MRS. PANTS
Congratulations! You just drank
your way through another Christmas.

SANTA SEEMS IMPRESSED WITH HIMSELF.

SANTA
Happy New Year.

PAGE 22 PANEL 2

SANTA (CONT'D)
All I want to do is end it.

SANTA THROWS A NOOSE AROUND HIS NECK - MADE FROM A STRAND OF CHRISTMAS LIGHTS - THE KIND WITH BIG BULBS - SO IT WILL BE EASIER TO DRAW...

PAGE 22 PANEL 3

- AND JUMPS OFF HIS BED!

PAGE 22 PANEL 4

THIS IS THE BIGGEST DRAWING ON THE PAGE - IT'S OF SANTA CHOKING OUT - THE TWO ELVES LOOK HORRIFIED... SANTA GURGLES...HIS EYES BULGE FROM HIS HEAD AND HIS FACE IS BRIGHT RED...THE LIGHTS SHOULD BE PLUGGED IN SOMEWHERE TO MAKE IT LOOK PARTICULARLY FESTIVE.

WINKY & MRS. PANTS TOGETHER
(IN HORROR)
No, you can't!

PAGE 22 GUTTER ALONG THE BOTTOM

JUST DRAW GARY'S HEAD IN THE LOWER LEFT SO HE CAN SAY THE FOLLOWING: ALSO, DOES IT WORK TO HAVE GARY'S EYES LOOKING UP AT SANTA'S BODY IN THE NOOSE? JUST A THOUGHT? IF YOU WANT TO BREAK THIS UP GARY'S STUFF INTO LITTLE PANELS FOR DIFFERENT FACIAL EXPRESSIONS - BE OUR GUEST.

GARY THE SNOWMAN
Ole' Santa sure got it good this
issue - but everyone knows Santa
gives better than he receives - and
pretty soon he's going to start
dishing it out to lots and lots of
naughty men. Sorry if that sounds
dirty - it's not how I meant it.
See you soon for our exciting
second chapter "Violent Night"

END OF ISSUE 1

PAGE 2 FULL SPLASH

BIG EDDIE BLOWS HIS HEAD CLEAN OFF

ALFREDO WHIPS A WREATH RAZOR INTO HIM ETC ETC - HAVE FUN

ALL ELVES TOGETHER
(singing)
these assholes attack!

The elves do like 18,799 points of damage to the sad, fucked up zombie - blood, guts, bits and teeth all hit the snow.

Rick - if you can fit it - maybe Gary throws up - it would be all white though - it's just snow...if not - no worries...

ISSUE CREDITS ARE IN A CUTTER UNDER THE GORE

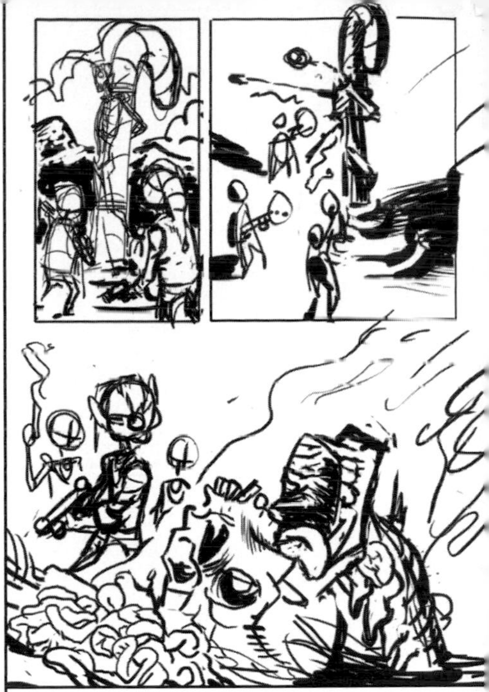

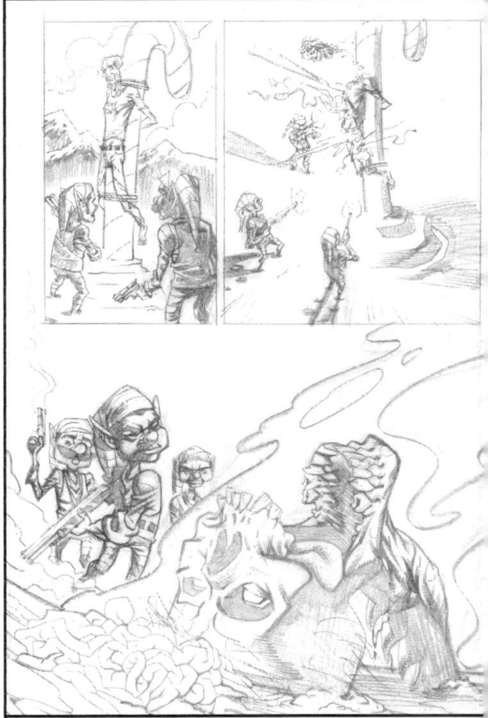

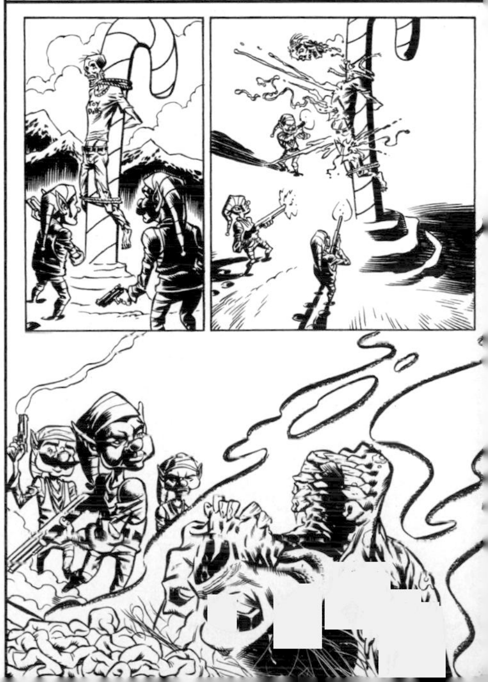

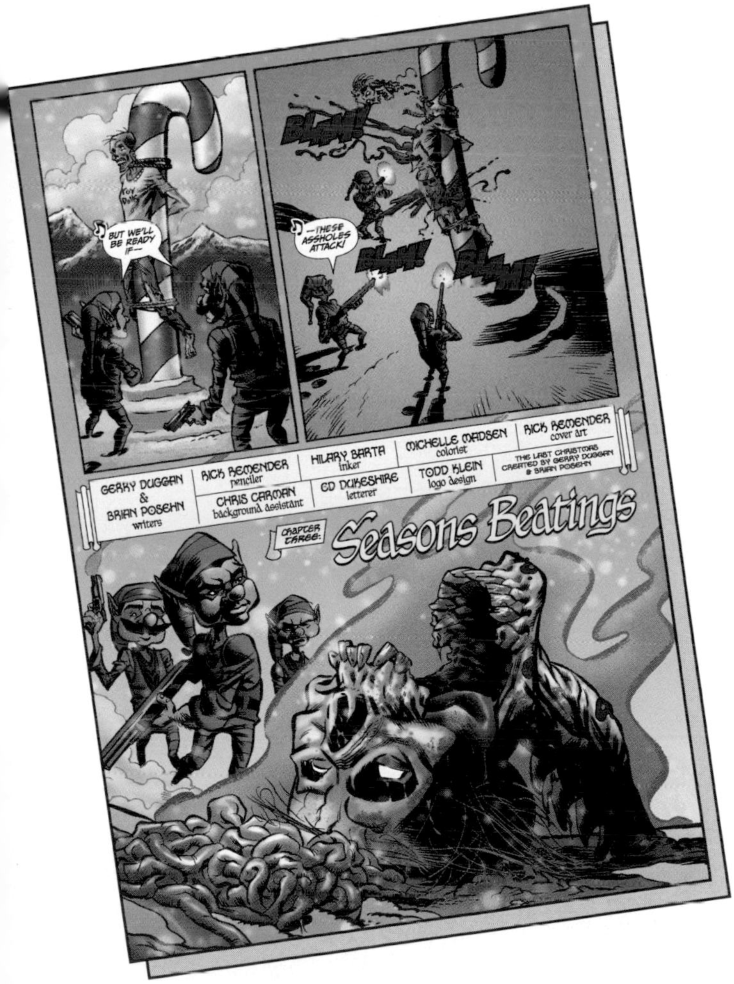
BUT WE'LL BE READY IF--
--THESE ASSHOLES ATTACK!
GERRY DUGGAN & BRIAN POSEHN writers
RICK REMENDER penciler
CHRIS CARMAN background assistant
HILARY BARTA inker
ED DUKESHIRE letterer
MICHELLE MADSEN colorist
TODD KLEIN logo design
RICK REMENDER cover art
THE LAST CHRISTMAS CREATED BY GERRY DUGGAN & BRIAN POSEHN
CHAPTER THREE:
Seasons Beatings

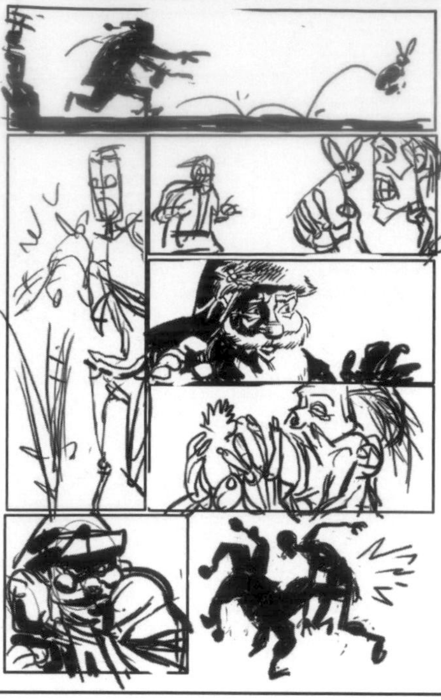

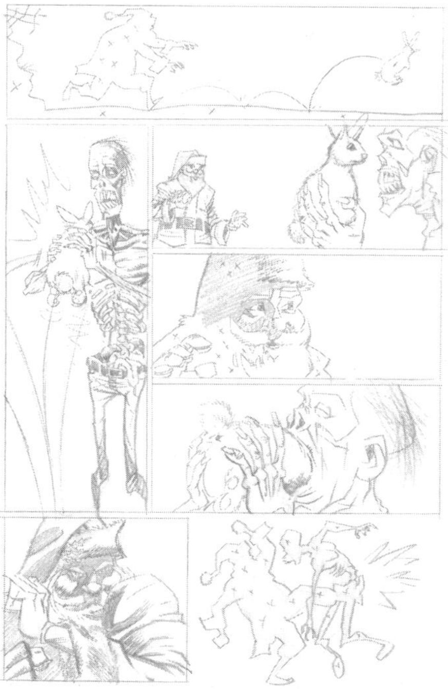

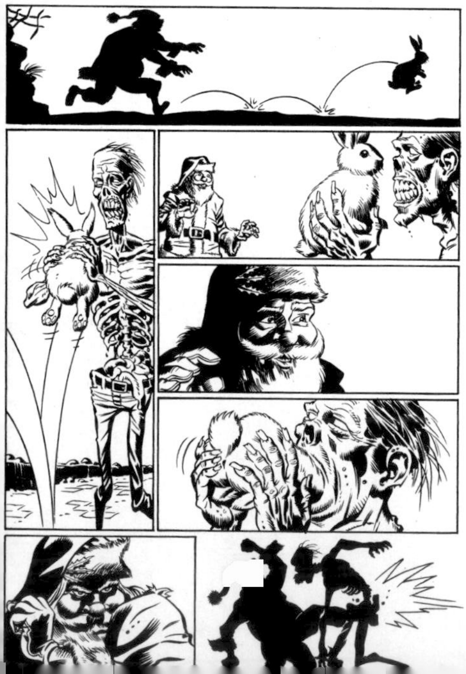

PAGE 9 PANEL 1 IS WIDE ACROSS THE TOP - 2, 3 AND 4 ARE BOXES IN THE MIDDLE AND 5 IS WIDE ACROSS THE BOTTOM

PAGE 9 PANEL 1 (WIDE ACROSS TOP)

THE RABBIT RUNS RIGHT INTO THE CLUTCHES OF A ZOMBIE.

PAGE 9 PANEL 2 (LEFT CENTER)

ANGLE ON SANTA PLEADING

SANTA (cont'd)
Please don't swallow my little bunny.

PAGE 9 PANEL 3 (DEAD CENTER)
The zombie gobbles the rabbit.

SANTA (cont'd)
(WORD BALLOON FROM OFF)
You smelly son of a bitch!

PAGE 9 PANEL 4 (RIGHT CENTER)
THE ZOMBIE SMILES - THE RABBIT HAS COMPLETELY DISAPPEARED DOWN ITS THROAT.

SANTA (cont'd)
Give me back my rabbit!

PAGE 9 PANEL 5 (WIDE ACROSS BOTTOM)

THIS PANEL IS THE EXACT MOMENT WHEN SANTA'S FOOT IS KICKED INTO THE ZOMBIE'S BALLS - CAUSING THE RABBIT'S TALE TO BECOME VISIBLE IN THE ZOMBIE'S MOUTH.

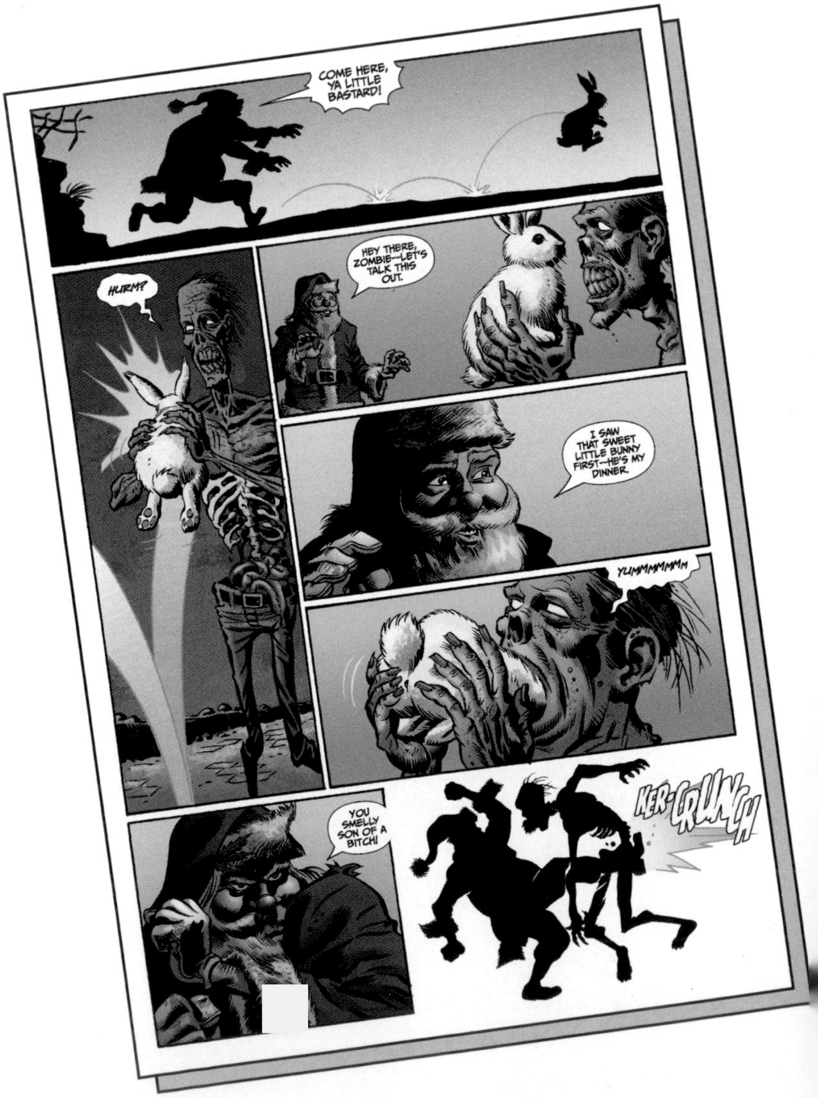
COME HERE, YA LITTLE BASTARD!
HURM?
HEY THERE, ZOMBIE--LET'S TALK THIS OUT.
I SAW THAT SWEET LITTLE BUNNY FIRST--HE'S MY DINNER.
YUMMMMMMM
YOU SMELLY SON OF A BITCH!
KER-CRUNCH

PAGE 10 - 3 BOXES ON TOP - THEN 2 EQUAL HORIZONTAL PANELS - THE LAST PANEL IS VIEWED THROUGH BINOCULARS...

PAGE 10 PANEL 1 (TOP LEFT BOX)

SANTA GRABS THE ZOMBIE FROM BEHIND - SORT OF LIKE A HEIMLICH MANEUVER - EXCEPT HE'S PULLING ON THE ZOMBIE'S EXPOSED RIBS.

PAGE 10 PANEL 2 (TOP CENTER BOX)
THE RABBIT POPS FREE OF THE ZOMBIE'S RIB CAGE

ZOMBIE
SCREAMS!

PAGE 10 PANEL 3 (TOP RIGHT BOX)

THE RABBIT HITS THE GROUND RUNNING -

PAGE 10 PANEL 4 (WIDE)

AND IS SWALLOWED WHOLE - BY A GIANT BLACK BEAR. SANTA RUNS TOWARDS THE BEAR

PAGE 10 PANEL 5 (WIDE BINOCS VIEW)

RICK PAGE 10 PANEL 5 SHOULD BE DRAWN AS THOUGH VIEWED FROM BINOCULARS FAR AWAY IN BINOCULARS:

SANTA HAS TURNED AND RUN FROM THE BEAR - THE BEAR CHASES HIM.

MARTIN
(WORD BALLOON FROM OFF)
Wow.

RICK - PAGE 11 - PANELS 1 & 2 ARE THE SAME PANEL - BUT SPLIT DOWN THE MIDDLE.

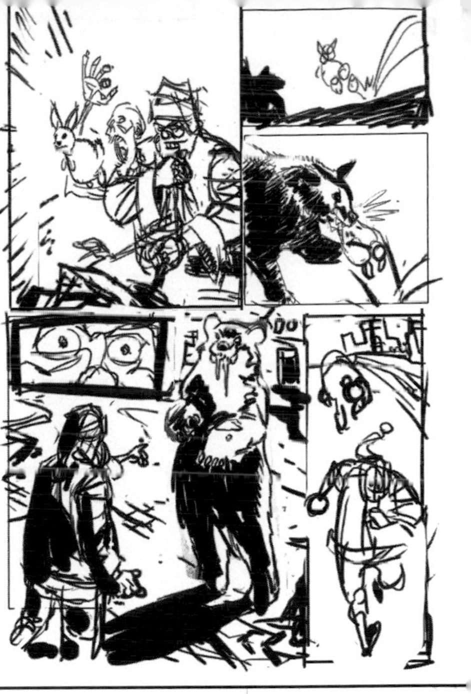

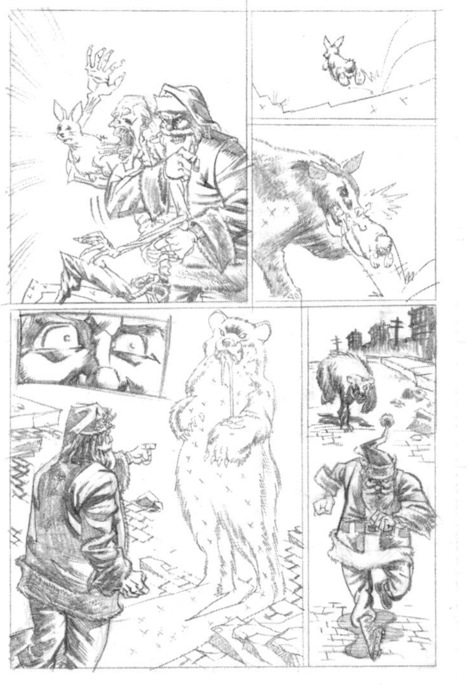

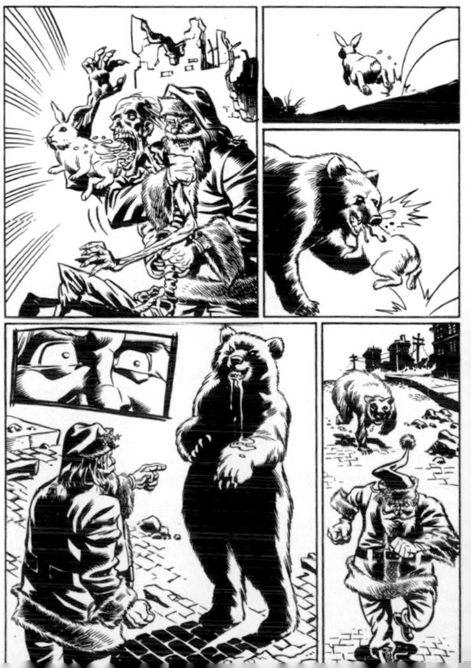

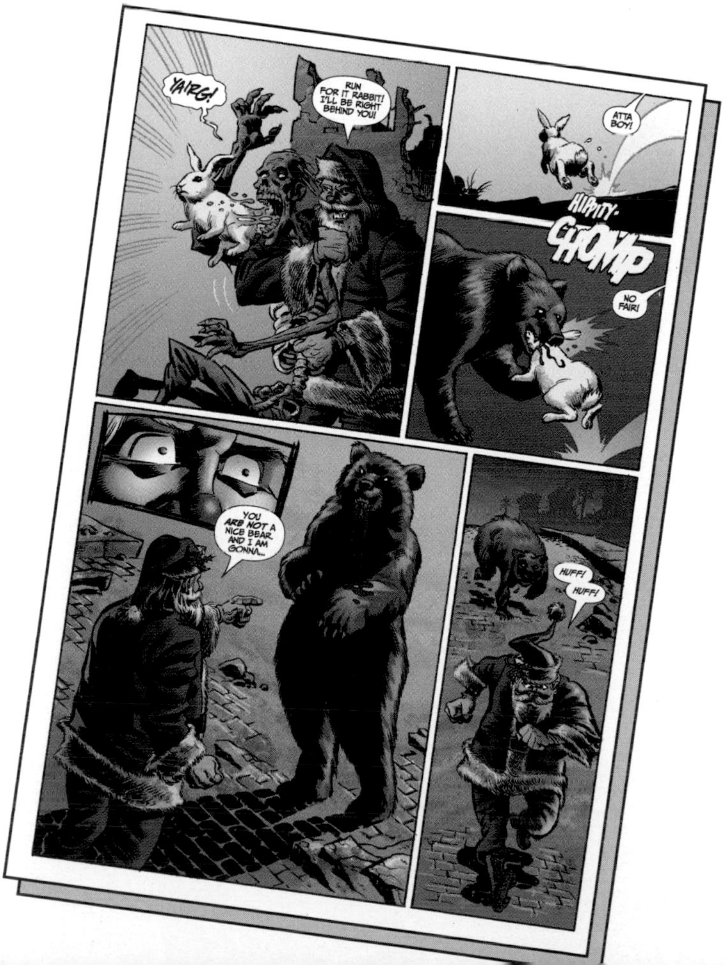
YAIRG!
RUN FOR IT RABBIT! I'LL BE RIGHT BEHIND YOU!
ATTA BOY!
HIPPITY-
CHOMP
NO FAIR!
YOU ARE NOT A NICE BEAR. AND I AM GONNA...
HUFF!
HUFF!

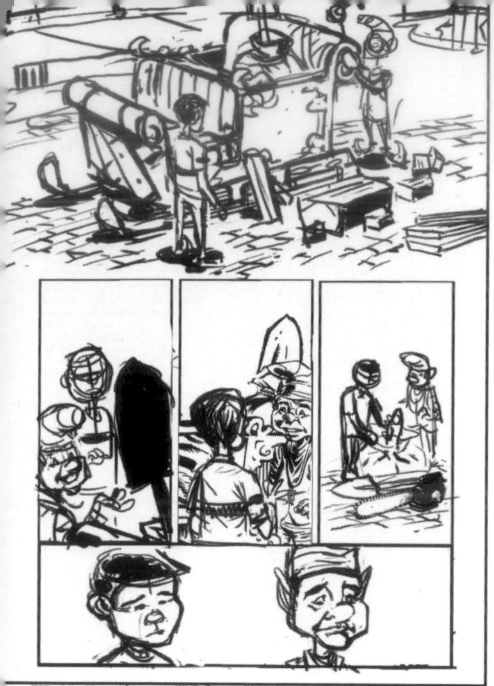

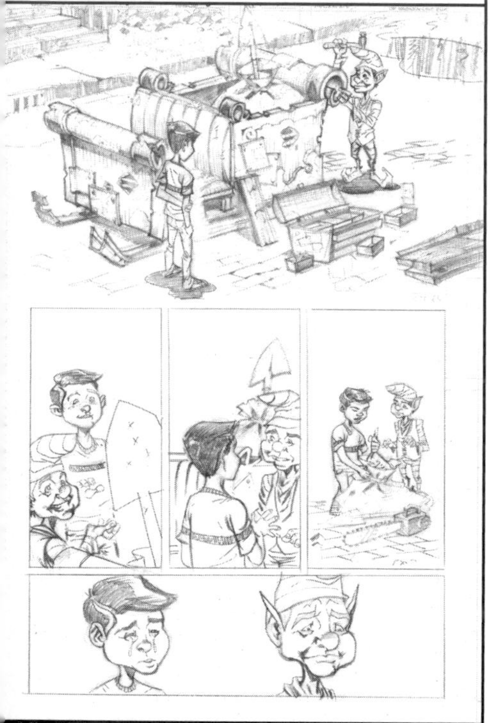

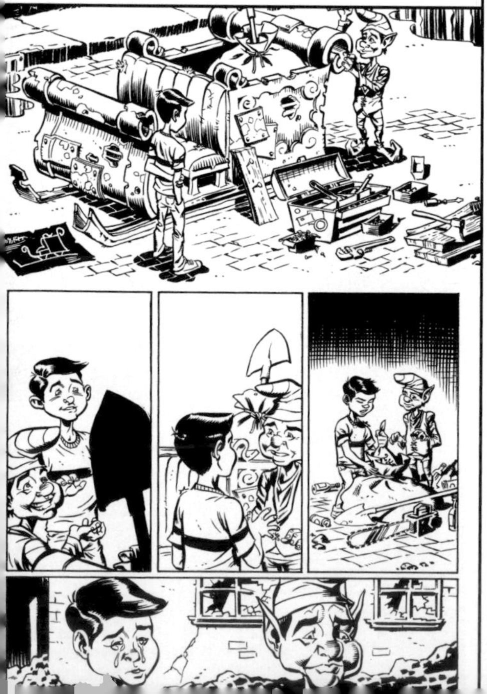

PAGE 13 IS A HORIZONTAL BAR AND THEN 4 BOXES

PAGE 13 PANEL 1 (HORIZONTAL BAR)

RICK - TO AVOID DRAWING THE SLEIGH AGAIN - HAVE THE SHOT BE LOOKING AT THE SLEIGH ON ITS SIDE - WINKY CAN BE UNDERNEATH WITH A HAMMER - LIKE THE SLEIGH WAS A CAR.

IT'S A ROUGH PATCH JOB - MAYBE A RAIN GUTTER IS THE NEW SKID.

WINKY
Thanks for helping
topatch the sleigh.

PAGE 13 PANEL 2 (box on left)

THE KID
(eyeing his present)
...yeah - no problem.

WINKY STANDS UP

WINKY
Go ahead and open it.

PAGE 13 PANEL 3 (box on right)

THE KID
Really?!

WINKY
Why not? It's addressed to you.
Besides, I'm his head elf and
I'm telling you its OK.

PAGE 13 PANEL 4 (box on left)

THE KID TEARS APART THE WRAPPING. WINKY STANDS BEHIND HIM EXCITED.

THE KID
What do you think it is?
Maybe it's a scooter!

PAGE 13 PANEL 5 (box on right)

KID'S POV: WE'RE LOOKING AT THE KID'S CRESTFALLEN FACE AS IT HOVERS NEAR THE CONTENTS OF SANTA'S DEATH BAG...

THE KID (cont'd)
I thought we were friends...

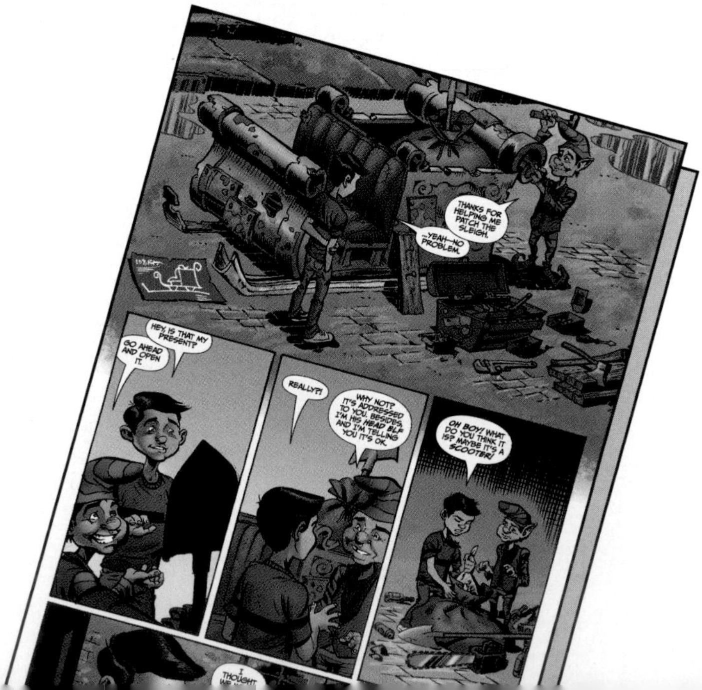
THANKS FOR HELPING ME PATCH THE SLEIGH.
...YEAH—NO PROBLEM.
HEY, IS THAT MY PRESENT?
GO AHEAD AND OPEN IT.
REALLY?!
WHY NOT? IT'S ADDRESSED TO YOU. BESIDES, I'M HIS HEAD ELF AND I'M TELLING YOU IT'S OK.
OH BOY! WHAT DO YOU THINK IT IS? MAYBE IT'S A SCOOTER!

PAGE 15 PANEL 1 (BIG PANEL)

SANTA IS DRAGS THE DEAD BEAR BY ITS HIND LEGS. (Santa's clothes are thrashed)

SANTA
Who want's some bear-b-cue?

WINKY
He opened your present

PAGE 15 PANEL 2 (WIDE)

Martin's party enters through the gates.

SANTA
(looking horrified)
There's an explanation: I thought maybe you would like to become a murderer.

PAGE 15 PANEL 3 (SMALLER BOX)

THE KID BACKS AWAY

THE KID
Stay away from me.

PAGE 15 PANEL 4 (REST OF THE PAGE)
Santa KNEELS ON ONE KNEED - AND PATS IT WITH HIS HAND - A CREEPY INVITATION.

SANTA
I know it's hard to understand but I was drinking for years when I wrapped this...I could never do it... You're a nice kid...I do have a great gift for you back at the pole...Here, sit on Santa's lap.

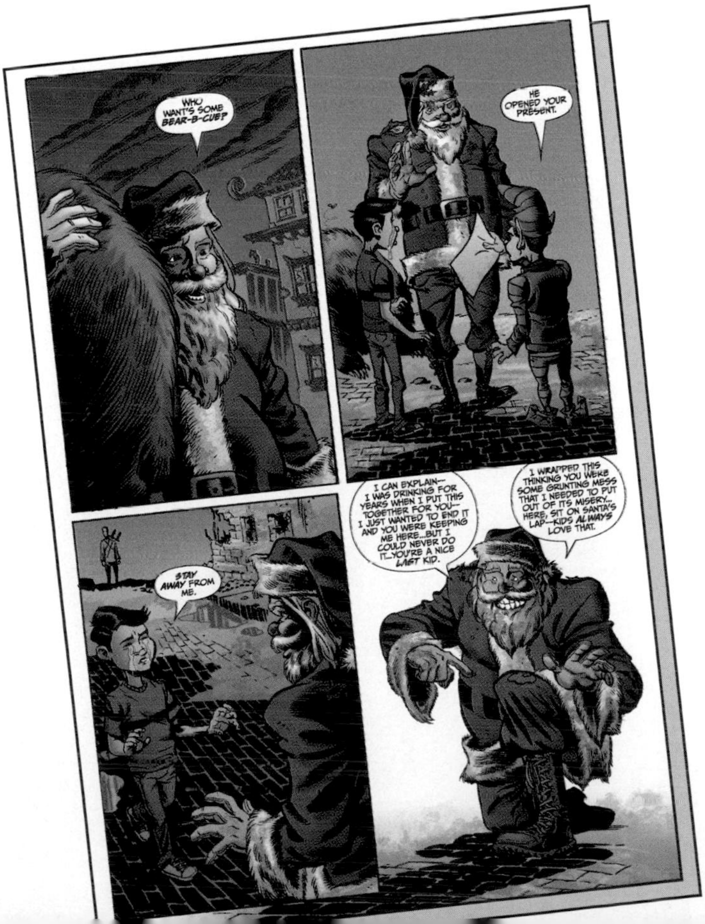
WHO WANT'S SOME BEAR-B-CUE?
HE OPENED YOUR PRESENT.
STAY AWAY FROM ME.
I CAN EXPLAIN— I WAS DRINKING FOR YEARS WHEN I PUT THIS TOGETHER FOR YOU— I JUST WANTED TO END IT AND YOU WERE KEEPING ME HERE...BUT I COULD NEVER DO IT...YOU'RE A NICE LAST KID.
I WRAPPED THIS THINKING YOU WERE SOME GRUNTING MESS THAT I NEEDED TO PUT OUT OF ITS MISERY... HERE, SIT ON SANTA'S LAP—KIDS ALWAYS LOVE THAT.

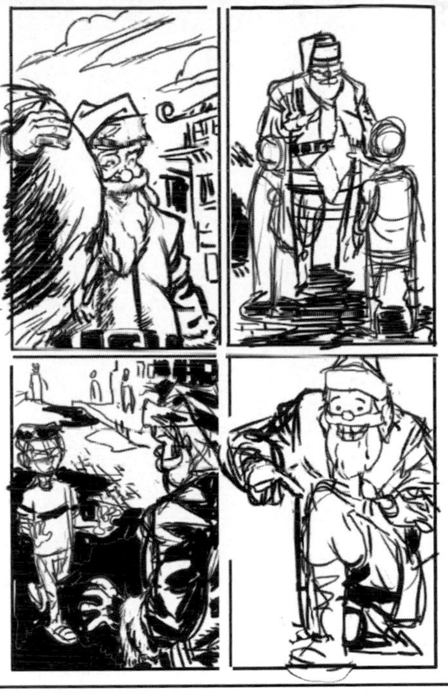

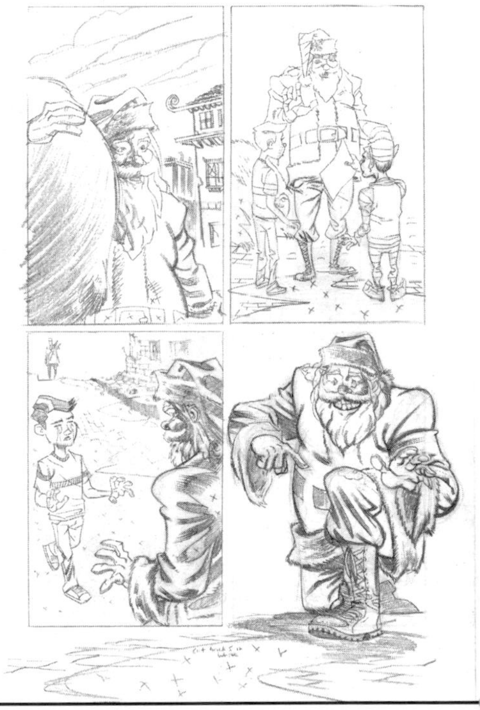

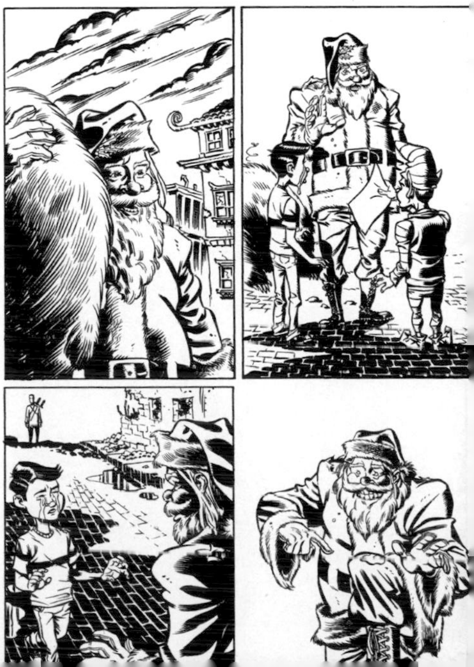

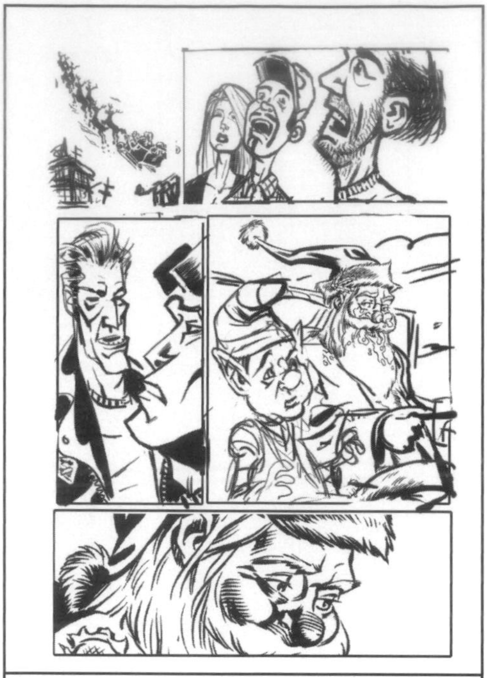

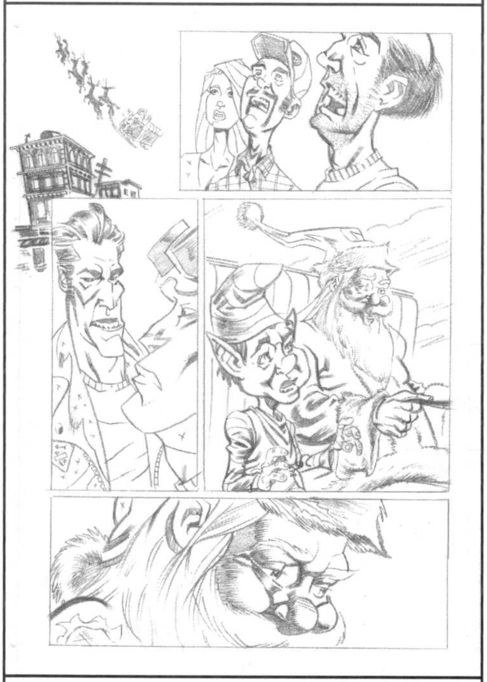

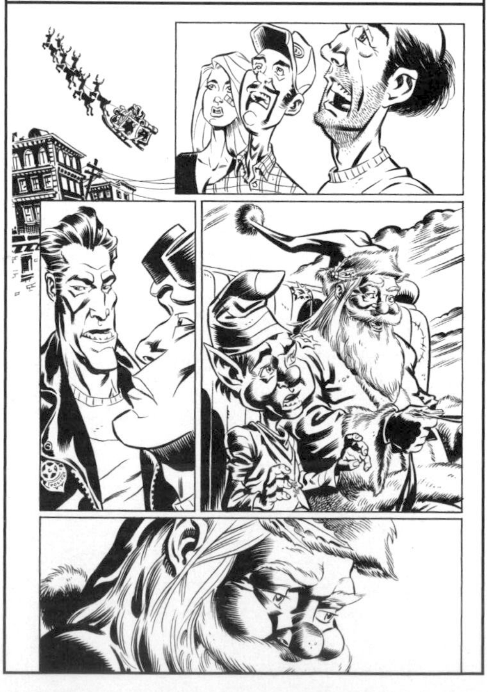

PAGE 18 IS TWO BIG, WIDE PANELS - AND THEN 2 MUCH SMALLER BOXES

PAGE 18 PANEL 1

WE DON'T SEE THE SLEIGH - JUST EVERYONE'S REACTION TO IT LEAVING - PEOPLE'S FACES ARE ALL SKYWARD.

HUMAN # 1
(in awe of the sleigh)
Wow.

HUMAN # 2
(scowling up at Santa)
I know. What an asshole.

PAGE 18 PANEL 2

Martin and HENCHMAN # 1 watch the sleigh disappear from another angle.

MARTIN
Go let our friend know that the plan just got moved up. Tell him to call in the reserves.

PAGE 18 PANEL 3

WINKY AND SANTA IN THE SLEIGH DRAWN HEAD-ON FROM THE POV - OF THE SLEIGH'S DASHBOARD - SO YOU DON'T HAVE TO DRAW IT AGAIN.

WINKY
You could bring it back. You're still Santa Claus!

SANTA
Not anymore, Winky...I'm just a boozy old sad sack.

PAGE 18 PANEL 4

TIGHT ON SANTA, SAD - RUINED

SANTA (cont'd)
Jolly always came so easy to me, but this new world...
(second balloon)
I just miss her so damn much.

IT'S GETTING DARK NOW...

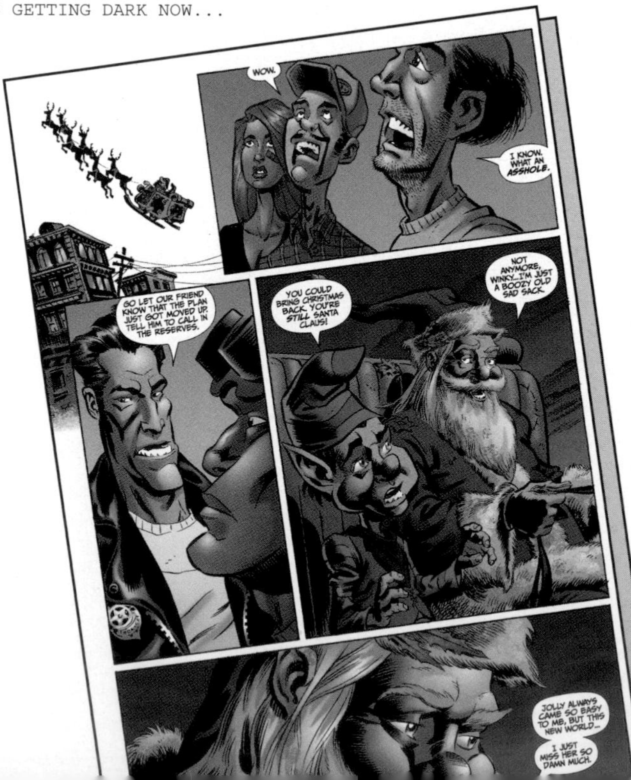
WOW.
I KNOW. WHAT AN ASSHOLE.
GO LET OUR FRIEND KNOW THAT THE PLAN JUST GOT MOVED UP. TELL HIM TO CALL IN THE RESERVES.
YOU COULD BRING CHRISTMAS BACK. YOU'RE STILL SANTA CLAUS!
NOT ANYMORE, WINKY...I'M JUST A BOOZY OLD SAD SACK.
JOLLY ALWAYS CAME SO EASY TO ME, BUT THIS NEW WORLD...
I JUST MISS HER SO DAMN MUCH.

LAST CHRISTMAS CAKE
BY
AN UNKNOWN FAN

THE GANG

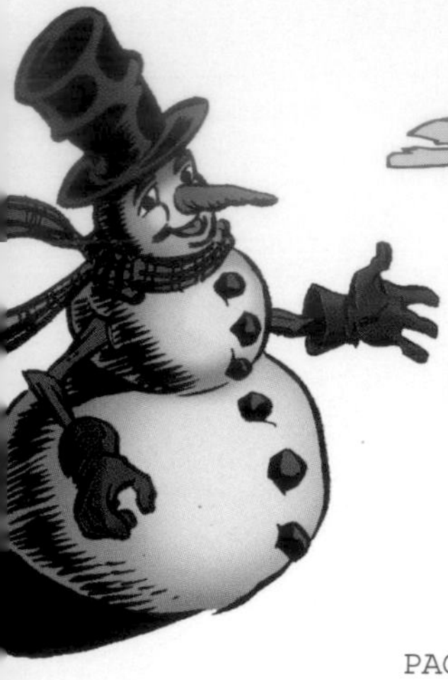

The Making of The Last Christmas

Issue 5 Final Lettering

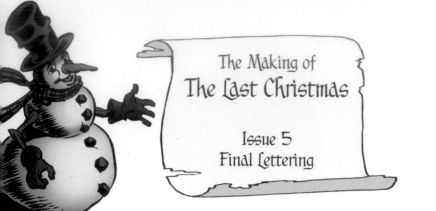

PAGE 1 PANEL 1

BIG EDDIE
(driver)
There's the Kid!

WINKY
(scowling up at Santa)
I know. What an asshole.

PAGE 1 PANEL 2

CHICKEN
Bokcluckbok.

PAGE 1 PANEL 3.

BIG EDDIE
(leaping)
I'll handle this! Stay on the Kid!

WINKY
And Karen!

PAGE 1 PANEL 4

SFX: BLAM

ELF
Whoa!

PAGE 2 PANEL 1

MARTIN
I'm going to finish you off and then kill the Fat Man. You wanna watch, Karen?

PAGE 2 PANEL 2

KAREN
(bigger font size)
No!

MARTIN
Damn it!

PAGE 2 PANEL 3

THE GUN SPINS INTO THE AIR -

PAGE 2 PANEL 4

KAREN
Oh shit!
Ed, explodes this one out for me -

THE KID
Karen!

KAREN
Sorry, Kid!

PAGE 3 PANEL 1

WINKY CATCHES HER OVER THE SHOULDER ON HIS BIKE -

WINKY
I've got you!

KAREN
You better!

PAGE 3 PANEL 2

> **KAREN** (cont'd)
> Nice catch!

> **WINKY**
> Nice...nevermind.

PAGE 3 PANEL 3

SFX: SNAP!

PAGE 3 PANEL 4 (THE FUN SHOT)

> **BIG EDDIE**

Eat my balls!

PAGE 3 PANEL 5 (INSERT)

> **BIG EDDIE** (cont'd)
> Yuck, that sounded -

SFX: BOOM!

PAGE 4 PANEL 1 (WIDE BAR ON TOP)

> **BIG EDDIE** (cont'd)
> Oh crap!

PAGE 4 PANEL 2 (WIDE BOX ON LEFT AND MIDDLE)

SFX: SCREECH

> **BIG EDDIE** (cont'd)
> Yes!

PAGE 4 PANEL 3 (SMALL INSERT BOX)

> **BIG EDDIE** (cont'd)
> (ed go a little big on
> this one)
> Wheee!

THE LINE CATCHES AROUND A CABLE -

SFX: CHIK

PAGE 4 PANEL 4 (BIG PANEL - HE CAN BREAK THE EDGES TOO)

SFX: WOOSH

PAGE 5 PANEL 1 (WIDE PANEL)

SFX: JINGLE JINGLE JINGLE (ED YOU CAN COPY FROM ISSUE 4)

PAGE 5 PANEL 2

SFX: ZIPTHUNK ZIPTHUNK

Ed - can we have the 'zip' part sort of clean and the
'thunk' kind of dirty? Thanks.

PAGE 5 PANEL 3

AN ELF OPENS THE BIG GUN ON THE BACK OF THE SLEIGH UP -
RICK, HIL, AND MICHELLE: THE GUN CAN CAUSE SOME WICKED
LIGHTING EFFECTS IF YOU WANT/fits - PICTURE THAT GUN
BURNING BRIGHTLY AS IT FIRES... ED - THE SFX COMES FROM
THE WHIRRING OF THE GUN

> **BEARDED ELF**
> Oh yeah!

SFX: WHIRRRR

> **SANTA**
> Watch my back fellas - I've got a
> job to finish.

PAGE 5 PANEL 4

Santa vaults out of the sleigh - dropping heroically with a big gun.

SANTA (cont'd)
I'm coming, Kid!

PAGE 6 PANEL 1

PAGE 6 PANEL 2

SFX: THUDSCRUNCH! (big time car-getting-totalled sound - ED, TRY A DIFFERENT LOOK FOR THE 2 SOUNDS - THANKS)

SANTA (cont'd)
Oof!

PAGE 6 PANEL 3 (BOX IN LOWER LEFT)

SANTA (cont'd)
(big and explodey)
Ya!

PAGE 6 PANEL 4 (BOX IN LOWER RIGHT)

SANTA (cont'd)
Ha Ha!

PAGE 6 PANEL 5

SANTA (cont'd)
Oh!

THE KID
SANTA!

PAGE 7 PANEL 1

CAPTION BOX
The kid's scared I'm not going to pull this off. He's not the only one.

PAGE 7 PANEL 2

SFX: WINK! (Ed - really small next to Santa's winking eye) ED, WE WANTED A "WINK" SMALL, NEXT TO SANTA'S WINKING EYE.

CAPTION BOX (cont'd)
But I give him the look - the one that lets kids know they're going to get what they want.

ZOMBIE
RAGRAW

PAGE 7 PANEL 3 (BOX IN UPPER RIGHT)

CAPTION BOX
The look that it's all going to be all right.

PAGE 7 PANEL 4 (BIG SPLASHY)

CAPTION BOX (cont'd)
But not for everybody.

SFX: BRAAP BRAAP BRAAP CLICK (GUN GOES EMPTY)

SANTA
God Damn you all - everyone!

PAGE 8 PANEL 1

SFX: CHOK (santa's fist hitting)

PAGE 8 PANEL 2

SFX: CRAK (GUN STOCK CONNECTING)

SANTA THROWS THE GUN LIKE A JAVELIN -

PAGE 8 PANEL 3

ZOMBIE
Zarr!

SANTA
Henh!

RIGHT THROUGH A ZOMBIE'S HEAD -

PAGE 8 PANEL 4

SANTA - TURNS AND LOOKS AWAY FROM UP - BACK UP THE ROAD
- A MARAUDER CAR IS ZOOMING TOWARDS HIM

PAGE 9 PANEL 1

SANTA (cont'd)
(ED - DD-style FONT?)
Here comes Santa Claus!

PAGE 9 PANEL 2 (TOP HORIZONTAL PANEL)

Ed - can each word get a little bigger here?

SANTA (cont'd)
Right down Santa Claus Lane!

DRIVER
(ed - make the gaaaagh
look all fucked-up)
Oh gaaamph!

PAGE 9 PANEL 3

SANTA
See you in hell my friend!

SFX: THUMP THUMP

PAGE 9 PANEL 4

SANTA'S THOUGHT BALLOON
I never did learn how to operate
one of these.

PAGE 10 PANEL 1 (HORIZONTAL BAR ACROSS TOP)

SANTA'S THOUGHT BALLOON (cont'd)
How hard could this driving stuff
be?

PAGE 10 PANEL 2

SANTA
(from within car)
Oopsie!

PAGE 10 PANEL 3

SANTA (cont'd)
This thing sucks at flying.

PAGE 10 PANEL 4

SFX: WABOOM!

PAGE 11 PANEL 1

PAGE 11 PANEL 2

MARTIN
I'll kill him.

PAGE 11 PANEL 3

MARTIN (cont'd)
We're hoofing it. Let's go.

PAGE 11 PANEL 4

SANTA
Unh.
(second balloon - smaller
type)
Cough...Kid...

PAGE 11 PANEL 5

MARTIN
If he comes out of there - make him
regret it!

PAGE 11 PANEL 6

MARAUDER
You should have stayed dead.
You're risking your neck for that
Kid - he don't care about you.

PAGE 12 PANEL 1

PAGE 12 PANEL 2

SOUND EFFECT: "BLAM"

SANTA
(Ed - wavy and injured)
Gah!

PAGE 12 PANEL 3

CAPTION BOX
In an instant - it all comes back.

PAGE 12 PANEL 4

CAPTION BOX (cont'd)
I've always known who's been bad or
good - I just didn't want to
remember.

PAGE 12 PANEL 5

CAPTION BOX (cont'd)
And I know just what to do.

PAGE 13 PANEL 1 (BOX IN UPPER RIGHT)

JUST SANTA'S FUCKED UP FACE: IT LOOKS LIKE HARTIGAN FROM
SIN CITY NOW - COVERED IN BLOOD ED: FUCK UP SANTA'S FONT
HERE - HE'S HURT....

SANTA
(coughs)
(now a second balloon)
You're wrong: the Kid's not done
with me - and you're out of
bullets.

PAGE 13 PANEL 2

MARAUDER
Screw you.

PAGE 13 PANEL 3

SFX: BOINK (OFF THE GUN HITTING THE GUT)

MARAUDER (cont'd)
YA!

SANTA
No, screw you.

(SECOND BALLOON)
SANTA(cont'd)
Remember when I said you were out
of bullets?

PAGE 13 PANEL 4

NOTHING HERE

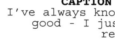

PAGE 13 PANEL 5

ED - BUMP THE FONT 1 SIZE ON "FIBBING" PLEASE - THANKS

          SANTA (cont'd)
        I was fibbing.

PAGE 14 PANEL 1

SFX: BLAM!

          SANTA (cont'd)
          Sit down.

          MARAUDER
    (ed - all wavcy and painfilled
         please)
        Aiiiiiiiigh!

     SANTA'S THOUGHT BALLOON
   I remember everything now. Without
   the booze - it all comes rushing
   back. I remember who has been bad
         or good.

PAGE 14 PANEL 2

          SANTA
    Put the boy down now!

PAGE 14 PANEL 3

          MARTIN
      Stay back!

PAGE 14 PANEL 4

CLAUS LEAPS UP INTO THE AIR -

          SANTA
   You're not such a good shot when
  you're running like a scared little
        princess!

          MARTIN
    I mean it! Keep back or -

PAGE 15 PANEL 1

          SANTA
   Or NOTHING. You're done hurting
         people.

SFX: WHUMP

          MARTIN
        Oof!

PAGE 15 PANEL 2

SANTA GRABS MARTIN'S NECK - IN A CHOKE HOLD

          SANTA
   I KNOW. I know it was you.

          MARTIN
   I didn't mean to kill her.

          SANTA
   You can't lie to me! You're
        guilty!

PAGE 15 PANEL 3

          MARTIN
   Guilty? Heh. There are no more
  laws. You've seen the world. It's
   gone. There's nothing left.

SANTA
                        (furious)
There will always be right and
wrong! You made a shitty world
             shittier.
          (second balloon)
There's always been a black hole in
the middle of your soul. Even as
kid - on your best Christmas - all
you could ever earn from me were
         shitty sweaters.

PAGE 15 PANEL 4

                        MARTIN
                That's right!

SFX: SHIKK

PAGE 15 PANEL 5

                    MARTIN (cont'd)
And I fucking hated those dumb
                 sweaters.

                        SANTA
              I know you did.

PAGE 16 PANEL 1

SFX: SPLOCH

                    SANTA (cont'd)
Here's a present from jolly old St.
                 Kick!

PAGE 16 PANEL 2

MARTIN PUKES

SFX: HURCK (PUKE)

                  SANTA (CONT'D) (cont'd)
            This is for my gumdrop!

PAGE 16 PANEL 3

                  SANTA (CONT'D) (cont'd)
           This is your last Christmas!

SFX: CRACK

PAGE 16 PANEL 4

                    SANTA (cont'd)
             You're no angel -

PAGE 16 PANEL 5

                    SANTA (cont'd)
But you'll still look good on top
               of my tree.

                        MARTIN
                 Yaaaaiiiii

PAGE 16 PANEL 6

Hey Michelle - let's see some blood from the top of the
tree.

SFX: SPOINK

                    MARTIN (cont'd)
                 Aaaiiii*

PAGE 17 PANEL 1 (wide panel across top)

1) SANTA IS DOWN ON ONE KNEE - REMOVING THE KID'S GAG.

2) It begins to snow.

SANTA
Sorry you had to see that, Kid.

THE KID
Are you kidding? That was fucking
awesome!

SANTA
Watch the F-Bombs.

PAGE 17 PANEL 2 (LARGEST PANEL ON PAGE - WIDE AT BOTTOM)
Ed, give the elves the song note in their lyric please.

THE ELVES
(music notes)
CHRISTMAS TREE, O CHRISTMAS TREE

THE ELVES
(still singing so music
notes)
Sorry is this tasteless?

Ed, big huge honking font on Santa's next line:

SANTA
Merry Christmas everyone!

BACK IN CHINATOWN:

PAGE 18 PANEL 1

KAREN
Will you miss me, Winky?

WINKY
Sure! I'm not sure which part I'll miss
the most - I mean, you know I like
all your parts. Uh...

SANTA
Walk away, little buddy.

PAGE 18 PANEL 2

THE KID
Thanks for the bike, Santa.

SANTA
Good things come to those who wait
and I'm sorry that I made you wait
so long.

PAGE 18 PANEL 3

SANTA (cont'd)
Thank you for saving
Christmas...and for saving me. You
found it in your heart to forgive
me - and I'll always be grateful -
as long as I live - there will
always be Christmas.

PAGE 18 PANEL 4

SANTA (cont'd)
I promise - you'll be seeing me a
lot more often. I'll never again
turn my back on the good people.

THE KID
Whatever, Santa. Stay off the
booze, and don't kill any kids.
Room for this bubble coming in from off on right side:

WINKY
(from off panel)
Take my picture!

PAGE 18 PANEL 5

RICK - THIS IS ABU GHRAIB PHOTO 1 OF 2

WINKY (cont'd)
Woo!

PAGE 19 PANEL 1

RICK - THIS IS ABU GHRAIB PHOTO 2 OF 2
Ed - both elves laugh - and the dog barks.

PAGE 19 PANEL 2

SANTA
Hey, hey! Cut the shit - we're
supposed to be the good guys.

THE ELF
We're sorry, Santa!
PAGE 19 PANEL 3 (BOX IN MIDDLE RIGHT)

GARY THE SNOWMAN
(TO READER)
Heh. Sorry about that zombie
nudity. One of those fellas didn't
need a black bar - but I ain't
telling which one. Anyways, Santa
kept his promise to the kid - he
brought Christmas back - with a
vengeance!

PAGE 19 PANEL 4 (BOX IN LOWER LEFT)

CLOSE UP OF SANTA IN THE SLEIGH -

SANTA
(Ed - bump up the font
size here - thanks)
Ho Ho Ho! Merry Christmas to all -
and to all a Good Night!

PAGE 19 PANEL 5

KAREN AND THE KID WAVE GOODBYE TO SANTA

SANTA (cont'd)
(BALLOON OFF FROM ABOVE)
And sorry I was such a dick!

PAGE 20 PANEL 1

GARY THE SNOWMAN
Well, that's the tale of "The Last
Christmas" which wasn't the last
Christmas after all. We've been
getting tons more mail from kids as
Santa's legend begins to grow
again. Now, I know what you're
thinking: "Santa forgot something,
right?"

GARY THE SNOWMAN (cont'd)
(SECOND BALLOON)
Wrong.

Ed along the bottom of the page - can you put something
together that reads:
Merry Christmas (all the way across)

From your pals Gerry, Brian, Rick, Hil, Michelle, Chris,
Ed, Geof, KD, Tony, and everybody at Image Comics.

Rick and Michelle - very specific look for the epilogue
- a Leone spaghetti western - very hot pages - maybe
even some wavy heat lines?

PAGE 21 PANEL 1

CAPTION BOX
A few months later...

Ed - the Judge is out of breath here...

THE JUDGE
Huff. Huff.

PAGE 21 PANEL 2

                         THE JUDGE (cont'd)

PAGE 21 PANEL 3

                         THE JUDGE (cont'd)
                             Pant. Pant.

PAGE 21 PANEL 4

Ed - can you bump down the font size of the Judge here?

                         THE JUDGE (cont'd)
                          (croaking)
                              No...

PAGE 22 PANEL 1

                         THE JUDGE (cont'd)
                 Not in the face! Not my face!

PAGE 22 PANEL 2

AND THEN A GLOVED FIST PUNCHES HIM IN THE MOUTH -
KNOCKING
OUT TEETH.

SFX ON PUNCH: POW

                         THE JUDGE (cont'd)
                       (spitting tooth)
                           Ptui

PAGE 22 PANEL 3

                              SANTA
          Tell all the mutants and marauders:
           Santa Claus is coming to town...

EPILOGUE PAGE 3 SPLASH

Ed - big and punchy here:

                         SANTA(cont'd)
         ...and hell's coming with me!